A Shield in Space?

A Shield in Space?

Technology, Politics, and the Strategic Defense Initiative

How the Reagan Administration Set Out to Make
Nuclear Weapons "Impotent and Obsolete"
and Succumbed to the Fallacy of the Last Move

Sanford Lakoff and Herbert F. York

UNIVERSITY OF CALIFORNIA PRESS
Berkeley · *Los Angeles* · *London*

California Studies on Global Conflict and Cooperation, 1

University of California Press
Berkeley and Los Angeles, California

University of California Press, Ltd.
London, England

Library of Congress Cataloging-in-Publication Data

Lakoff, Sanford A.
    A shield in space? : technology, politics, and the strategic
defense initiative : how the Reagan Administration set out to make
nuclear weapons "impotent and obsolete" and succumbed to the fallacy
of the last move / Sanford Lakoff and Herbert F. York.
        p.   cm.—(California studies on global conflict and
cooperation ; 1)
    Bibliography: p.
    Includes index.
    ISBN 0-520-06650-2 (alk. paper)
    1. Strategic Defense Initiative.   2. Nuclear arms control.
I. York, Herbert F. (Herbert Frank)   II. Title.   III. Series.
UG743.L33   1989
358'.1754—dc20   89-4888
                                                                          CIP

Printed in the United States of America
1   2   3   4   5   6   7   8   9

Contents

Preface

The subject of this book is the research project begun in 1983 and officially known as the Strategic Defense Initiative (SDI) or, more popularly, as "Star Wars." We have attempted as comprehensive a review of the project and its implications as the record of the past five years allows. We have also tried to be objective, but we have not hesitated to advance our own judgments when they seemed called for and to draw conclusions in the final chapter.

Our general findings can be stated simply: SDI is a classic example of misplaced faith in the promise of technological salvation. The project was initiated on the basis of political rather than scientific judgment in a deliberate effort to bypass the ordinary process by which innovations in military technology are proposed, reviewed, and adopted when they are considered feasible and appropriate. A popular but technically uninformed president made the decision without consulting his own cabinet or the two agencies of government with primary responsibilities for military and foreign policy, the Defense and State departments, in the hope of promoting advanced technologies that would remove the need to rely indefinitely on nuclear deterrence. So far the project has demonstrated, as informed observers knew from the start, only that comprehensive defenses will not become available in the foreseeable future. Further, even if they eventually do prove feasible, they will probably not be sufficiently impervious to countermeasures to inspire confidence that defenses alone can deter a massive nuclear attack. To suppose that there can be a last move in a technological arms race is to succumb to a patent fallacy.

In view of these realities, to allow the mere hope for a shield in space to influence defense planning or to prevent the negotiation of radical reductions in offensive arsenals would be an act of the gravest folly. In our view, the only realistic path toward secure and lasting peace is the one that begins with the achievement of greater strategic stability between the superpowers and leads to more elaborate forms of international integration and cooperation. We hope that those who read this book will become convinced, if they are not already, that to place so much faith in prospective military technology is to surrender to a dangerous illusion.

Our collaboration in this enterprise has been made possible by a generous grant from the Carnegie Corporation of New York. We are grateful to the president of the corporation, David Hamburg, and to his board for recognizing the importance of topics such as this, and to Frederic (Fritz) Mosher for shepherding us through the grant process and the completion of the work. The grant was supplemented by assistance from the University of California Institute on Global Conflict and Cooperation (IGCC), headquartered on our campus, and we are pleased that this book is being published as the first of what we hope will become a series published by the University of California Press in cooperation with IGCC. We are grateful to William J. McClung of the University Press for his encouragement, to Marilyn Schwartz for her editorial supervision, and to Kristen Stoever for her superb copyediting.

The Carnegie grant and IGCC support have also led to other publications written or edited by ourselves and several collaborators: Gerald M. Steinberg, who was a visiting research fellow during the project; Randy Willoughby, who worked with us while completing his doctoral dissertation; and G. Allen Greb, associate director of IGCC. The resulting publications are listed in the bibliography and have been drawn upon freely in the following chapters. We thank our colleagues for their invaluable work and counsel.

In the course of the research, we were also stimulated by the contributions to our understanding of SDI made by many visitors and associates. Some presented lectures to the faculty seminar on international security at the University of California, San Diego. Others took part in special SDI workshops or a conference on SDI and NATO sponsored jointly with the Friedrich Ebert Foundation, ably represented by Peter Schulze. Still others called our attention to valuable materials or commented on various drafts of particular chapters. We list them all with warmest appreciation:

Gordon Adams, Harold Agnew, Worth Bagley, Jack N. Barkenbus, Joel Bengston, Hans Bethe, Maj. Gen. David Bradburn (USAF, ret.), Harvey Brooks, Rep. George E. Brown, Jr., Harold Brown, Robert W. Buchheim, Gregory H. Canavan, Albert Carnesale, John Cartwright, M.P., William Colglazier, Ernst-Otto Czempiel, Robert S. Cooper, Steve Cohen, Jonathan Dean, Richard DeLauer, James Digby, Sidney Drell, Freeman Dyson, Ralph Earle II, David Elliott, James C. Fletcher, President Gerald R. Ford, Lawrence Freedman, Edward Frieman, Richard Garwin, Peter Goudinoff, Thomas Graham, Jr., Patrick W. Hamlett, François Heisbourg, John P. Holdren, Cecil I. Hudson, Jr., Lothar Ibrugger (member of the Bundestag), Michael D. Intriligator, Bhupendra Jasani, Frank Jenkins, Gerald W. Johnson, John A. Jungerman, F. Stephen Larrabee, Richard Ned Lebow, Pierre Lellouche, Franklin A. Long, Frank E. Manuel, Steven Maaranen, James J. Martin, Michael M. May, Robert S. McNamara, Seymour Melman, Giancarlo Monterisi, Harold Mueller, Michael Moodie, Benoit Morel, David L. Parnas, Stanford S. Penner, Richard Perle, Theodore Postol, George Rathjens, Edward L. Rowny, Elie Shneour, Alan B. Sherr, James Skelly, Alan Sweedler, Walter Slocombe, Dennis Smallwood, John Steinbruner, Jeremy Stone, Trevor Taylor, Edward Teller, Sheila Tobias, Maj. Gen. John C. Toomay (USAF, ret.), Brigitte Traupe (member of the Bundestag), Achim von Heinitz, Dean Wilkening, John Wilkinson, M.P., Roy D. Woodruff, David S. Yost, and Lord Solly Zuckerman.

Any mistakes or doubtful judgments that may remain in this book, despite their efforts to enlighten us, are solely our responsibility.

We also thank the staff members and students at UCSD who pitched in to help: Arlene Winer, Sue Greer, and Helen Hawkins of the IGCC staff; David Bernstein, Brian Bouchard, Brian Burgoon, David Geddes, and Brett Henry, our student researchers; and Anita Schiller, who unfailingly located uncatalogued materials for us in the Central Library. Above all, we are grateful to Kelly Charter Escobedo for patiently and promptly turning countless illegible drafts into neatly printed chapters.

Our debt to a host of scholars, journalists, government officials, and polemicists on all sides is recorded most fully in the notes and bibliography, but we would be remiss in not making special mention of certain sources that we have all but plundered: the three studies (one by Ashton Carter) issued by the congressional Office of Technology Assessment; the evaluation of directed-energy technologies by a committee of the

American Physical Society; explorations of the economics of SDI by the Council on Economic Priorities, the Federation of American Scientists (FAS), and Barry M. Blechman and Victor A. Utgoff; Raymond L. Garthoff's account of the Anti-Ballistic Missile (ABM) Treaty negotiations; three Senate staff reports on the progress of SDI; a report on the origins of SDI by Frank Greve in the *San Jose Mercury News;* the chronicle of events and comments provided in the *Arms Control Reporter;* survey data from the Roper Center for Public Opinion Research at the University of Connecticut; and the work of John E. Pike, specialist on space policy at the FAS.

One of us (York) has long been acquainted with the technical and policy issues involved in the development of strategic defenses, having served as first chief scientist of the (Defense) Advanced Projects Agency and then as the first director of defense research and engineering during the Eisenhower and Kennedy administrations. He also took an active part in the debate over deployment of anti-ballistic missiles in the 1960s. His coauthor became intrigued with prospects for space weapons when they became a controversial issue at a conference he attended in 1981 in Aspen, Colorado, which was convened by the American Institute of Aeronautics and Astronautics to consider the future of space exploration. Our subsequent discussions led us in 1982 to formulate a project to study warfare in space. The announcement of the SDI in 1983 made that the focus of our study. Finally, we should perhaps also thank the first director and the staff of the Strategic Defense Initiative Organization (SDIO), without whose diligent and sometimes remarkably candid efforts to explain and defend the project we should have had a harder time finding information with which to criticize it.

La Jolla, California

Acronyms
and Abbreviations

AAA	Anti-aircraft artillery
ABM	Anti-ballistic missile
ACDA	Arms Control and Disarmament Agency
ADI	Air defense initiative
AGARD	NATO Advisory Group for Aerospace Research and Development
ALCM	Air-launched cruise missile
ALPS	Accidental launch protection system
AOS	Airborne optical system
APS	American Physical Society
ASAT	Anti-satellite weapon
ATB	Advanced technology bomber, also known as B-2 and Stealth bomber
ATBM	Anti-tactical ballistic missile
AWACS	Airborne Warning and Control System
BAMBI	Ballistic missile boost intercept
BM/C^3	Battle management/command, control, and communication
BMD	Ballistic missile defense

BMEWS	Ballistic Missile Early Warning System
BSTS	Boost Surveillance and Tracking System
C^3I	Command, control, communication, and intelligence
CEP	Council on Economic Priorities
CIA	Central Intelligence Agency
COCOM	Coordinating Committee for Multilateral Export Controls
CONUS	Continental United States
DARPA	U.S. Defense Advanced Research Projects Agency
DDRE	Director of defense research and engineering
DEW	Directed-energy weapon
DEW Line	Distant Early-Warning Line
DIVAD	Division air defense
DOD	U.S. Department of Defense
DOE	U.S. Department of Energy
DOT	Designated Optical Tracker
DSP	Defense Support Program
EHF	Extremely High Frequency
ERIS	Exoatmospheric Reentry Vehicle Interceptor System
ESPRIT	European Strategic Program of Research in Information Technology
EUREKA	European Research and Coordinating Agency
FALCON	Fission-activated light concept
FAS	Federation of American Scientists
FEL	Free-electron laser
FFRDC	Federally funded research and development center
FOBS	Fractional Orbital Bombardment System
FOC	Full operating capability

GAC	General Advisory Committee to the Atomic Energy Commission
GBMD	Global Ballistic Missile Defense (plan proposed by High Frontier organization)
GEO	Geosynchronous earth orbit
HEDI	High Endoatmospheric Defense Interceptor
HF/DF Laser	Hydrogen-flouride/deuterium flouride laser
HIBEX	High-Acceleration Boost Experiment
HIBREL	High Brightness Relay
HOE	Homing Overlay Experiment
ICBM	Intercontinental ballistic missile
INF	Intermediate nuclear forces
IOC	Initial operating capability
IRBM	Intermediate-range ballistic missile
JCS	Joint Chiefs of Staff
KEW	Kinetic-energy weapon
KKV	Kinetic kill vehicle
LEDI	Low Endoatmospheric Defense Interceptor
LEO	Low earth orbit
LODE	Large Optical Demonstration Experiment
LPAR	Large phased-array radar
LWIR	Long Wave Length Infrared
MAD	Mutual Assured Destruction
MAS	Mutual Assured Survival
MHV	Miniature Homing Vehicle
MIRACL	Mid-Infrared Advanced Chemical Laser
MIRV	Multiple independently targetable reentry vehicle
MRBM	Medium-range ballistic missile
NADGE	NATO air defense ground environment

NATO	North Atlantic Treaty Organization
NORAD	North American Aerospace Defense Command
NPB	Neutral particle beam
NSC	National Security Council
NSDM	National Security Decision Memorandum
NTM	National technical means (nonintrusive systems for verifying compliance with arms-control treaties)
OSTP	Office of Science and Technology Policy
OTA	Office of Technology Assessment, U.S. Congress
PBV	Post-boost vehicle
PSAC	President's Science Advisory Committee
PVO	Protivovozdushnaya Oborona Strany (Soviet National Air Defense Forces)
RACE	Research in Advanced Communication in Europe
RDT&E	Research, development, testing, and evaluation
RF linac	Radio frequency linear accelerator
RFP	Request for proposals (used in government contracting)
RV	Reentry vehicle
SAGE	Semi-automatic ground environment
SAINT	Satellite interceptor
SALT	Strategic Arms Limitation Talks
SAM	Surface-to-air missile
SAMOS	Satellite and Missile Observation System
SATKA	Surveillance, acquisition, tracking, and kill assessment
SBAMS	Space-based anti-missile systems
SBI	Space-based interceptor (also referred to as space-based kinetic kill vehicle)
SBKKV	Space-based kinetic kill vehicle (see SBI)

SCC   Standing Consultative Commission (U.S.–Soviet)

SEWS   Satellite Early Warning System

SLBM   Submarine-launched ballistic missile

SP-100   Space power-100 kw

SPADATS   Space Detection and Tracking Systems

SRAM   Short-range attack missile

SSTS   Space Surveillance and Tracking System

START   Strategic Arms Reduction Talks

TBM   Tactical ballistic missile

TIR   Terminal imaging radar

UCS   Union of Concerned Scientists

USAF   U.S. Air Force

USDR&E   Undersecretary of Defense, Research and
                Engineering

VHSIC   Very High Speed Integrated Circuitry

CHAPTER I

Why SDI?

Since the onset of the cold war, and particularly after both superpowers began to amass large arsenals of nuclear weapons, military planners in both the East and the West have encouraged efforts to develop defenses against nuclear attack. Both sides have made effective use of "passive" defenses, such as the hardening and dispersal of weapons systems likely to be prime targets of a preemptive strike and the provision of shelters for command authorities and for vital communications centers. Some countries, including the Soviet Union, have made significant investments in civil defense as well, even though it is generally acknowledged that, at best, population shelters and evacuation plans can provide only marginal protection in the event of a massive attack on civilian targets. Both sides have also tried, with far less success, to develop "active" defenses—that is, measures for intercepting attacking bombers and nuclear warheads that might be borne by ballistic or cruise missiles launched from air, sea, or land (at long or short range) and for finding and destroying submarines before they can fire their missiles.

Even though these measures have been undertaken at considerable expense and with great technical sophistication, all efforts against this varied and daunting challenge have so far been largely in vain. Every advance in active defense has been offset by compensatory improvements in offensive forces. Partly in response to Soviet deployment of anti-ballistic missiles (ABMs) in the 1960s, the United States developed and introduced multiple independently targetable reentry vehicles (MIRVs). The Soviets followed suit. As a result, the number of warheads that can be carried on the missiles fired from a given number of launchers was greatly multiplied and the overall cost per warhead lowered, while progress in guidance improved accuracy. As air defenses were improved, penetration aids were adopted to overcome them. Bombers were hardened to withstand the effects of nuclear explosions. The United States' B-2 bomber, also known as the Stealth, or advanced technology bomber (ATB), now nearing deployment, will be less visible to radar than conventional aircraft owing to design changes that will give it a smaller radar cross section, to the substitution of composites for aircraft metals, and to the use of nonreflective coatings. A "stealthed" fighter aircraft, the F-19, is also being developed to penetrate enemy airspace and to shoot down airborne early-warning aircraft that detect incoming bombers. Electronic countermeasures now aboard aircraft enable pilots to "spoof" enemy radar. Air-launched cruise missiles (ALCMs) and "smart," "stand-off" short-range attack missiles (SRAMs) enable pilots to release their payloads without having to penetrate enemy defenses. Attacking aircraft can also jettison decoys, which lure surface-to-air missiles (SAMs) away from the attackers. Submarines are now harder to detect and locate, and the new Trident II D-5 missiles are expected to provide virtually the same "prompt, hard-target-kill capacity" as the latest U.S. version of the intercontinental ballistic missile (ICBM), called the MX, or "Peacekeeper," missile. As a result, efforts to design effective and economical defenses against the threat of nuclear attack became exercises in futility. Defenses could be overwhelmed and evaded even when they were technically feasible, and the only sure result of deploying them was to invite the addition of ever more capable and complex offensive weapons.

The apparent futility of building effective defenses against missiles was in effect acknowledged by both superpowers in 1972 when they signed the ABM Treaty. The treaty limited the two countries to no more than one hundred ground-based ABM launchers—each with a single warhead and specified radar detectors and trackers—to be deployed either around a missile field or the national capitals. This severe restriction of ballistic missile defense (BMD) appealed to leaders on both sides. In the first place, they were compelled to recognize that the technology for an effective defense simply was not available. As former secretary of defense Robert S. McNamara said, in a remarkable address in 1967 that helped to pave the way for the treaty, "While we have substantially improved our technology in the field, it is important to understand that none of the systems at present or foreseeable state-of-the-art would provide an impenetrable shield over the United States."[1] In addition, the United States and the Soviet Union both recognized that limiting defenses would reduce the incentive to add or strengthen offensive forces. The terms of the treaty, however, did not prohibit improvement of existing ABM systems or research that might lead to different defensive systems based on "other physical principles" (such as lasers) that were not part of ABM systems in use when the treaty was signed. Such research continued in both countries, but there was no substantial pressure on the part of weapons researchers on either side for a reconsideration of the technical premise on which the ABM Treaty was based.

It therefore came as a considerable surprise, even to the technical communities, when in a television address on March 23, 1983, President Ronald Reagan announced that the United States was embarking on a major new effort, subsequently called "the Strategic Defense Initiative." The initiative would be designed to determine whether effective defenses could be built against nuclear attack. Shortly afterward, Reagan expressed the hope that the research would enable the United States to replace the strategy of nuclear deterrence with a protective shield that promised "assured survival" rather than "assured destruction." The president repeatedly made it clear that he had in mind the protection of people, not merely of missile launchers or other military targets, and insisted that the aim was not to achieve military superiority by adding a partial defense to a strong offense but, rather, to make nuclear weapons "impotent and obsolete." He invited the Soviet Union to cooperate with the United States in achieving this transition to defense, offering to share the fruits of the research effort so that both countries could join in protecting the world from the threat of nuclear war.

How did this dramatic change come about? What were the motives behind the president's decision? Was it all but inevitable given the relentless advance of technology? Or was SDI more the product of other considerations—political, strategic, moral, economic?

SDI, the evidence suggests, was far from inevitable. Unlike virtually all other comparable weapons-innovation projects since World War II, this one reflected nothing so much as the mind-set of a single person— the president who enunciated it on the recommendation of a handful of like-minded political supporters. The decision was adopted without benefit of prior review by specialists in defense technology and strategy. It was not considered by the president's formal cabinet, by leaders of Congress, or by U.S. allies. The policy attracted initial support because Reagan succeeded in making a direct appeal to U.S. public opinion. He sensed correctly that the initiative would strike a responsive chord among a majority of voters, especially because it promised to remove the threat of nuclear attack by relying not on the imperfect strategy of retaliatory deterrence nor on persuading the Soviets to accept meaningful arms control, but solely on faith in the national capacity for technological innovation. The peculiar circumstances surrounding the birth of SDI, however, may also contain the seeds of its undoing. As the president's popularity declined and as his term neared an end, SDI became more and more vulnerable to attack from all the forces he had tried to bypass. Because it is so closely identified with the Reagan presidency, rather than with the coalitional consensus that sustains other major military programs, SDI is unlikely to survive Reagan's term in office for very long—at least in the form of the high-visibility, high-priority program he tried to fashion.

THE NOVELTY OF SDI

In examining the grounds for the decision to embark on SDI, the history of weapons innovation offers some preliminary guidance. But this history provides no exact parallel, and none of the usual explanations adequately applies to the case of SDI. In previous weapons innovations, certain factors have been either essential or at least implicated. Two have been especially prominent: (1) fear of being put at a disadvantage if an adversary develops a new weapon first and (2) the assurance of technical specialists that the proposed innovation is likely to prove feasible. President Franklin D. Roosevelt's order to create the Manhattan Project had both of these elements behind it. Refugee nuclear physicists had persuaded Roosevelt and his advisors that Nazi Germany was certain to be developing a weapon that might affect the outcome of the war.[2] Similarly, President Harry S. Truman approved a crash program to develop the hydrogen, or thermonuclear, bomb out of fear that the Soviets might develop it first and use it to blackmail the West. Although Truman chose to disregard the advice of a key committee of experts, he acted on the advice of officials who favored the project and received strong encouragement from other prominent scientists; even those who opposed the project thought it had an even chance of succeeding within five years.[3]

Weapons innovation involves other factors, too. Rivalry among the armed services, in addition to other manifestations of "bureaucratic politics"—salesmanship on the part of defense contractors, the interest of well-placed members of Congress in obtaining procurement contracts for their districts, the findings of strategists and other technical experts, and the general interest of the Defense Department in promoting modernization—have all figured in decisions to develop and deploy new weapons.[4] There is also some reason to suppose that innovation occurs because of an "action–reaction phenomenon," in McNamara's phrase,[5] except that the United States has usually been the initiator rather than the reactor. The United States tends to take the initiative not because it is any more aggressive than the U.S.S.R. or is less concerned about the dangers posed by nuclear weapons. The reason is, rather, that "we are richer and more powerful, that our science and technology are more dynamic, that we generate more ideas of all kinds."[6] This American penchant for innovation, however, has never been completely autonomous; it has been directed and channeled by a combination of technical and policy judgments.

On all these counts, SDI is different. The SDI decision was not reached on conventional grounds or in the conventional way. There was no reason to suppose that the Soviets were on the verge of achieving breakthroughs that had so far eluded U.S. researchers or that these breakthroughs would be sufficient to allow for a "breakout" from the ABM Treaty that would yield some tangible military advantage. Although Soviet scientists had done important research on various types of lasers and had continued to mount a major effort to exploit space for military purposes, including the development of a co-orbital anti-satellite (ASAT) weapon, they were not on the verge of developing radically new, more effective ballistic missile defenses. In 1977 *Aviation Week & Space Technology* carried sensational reports, based on information from a recently retired director of air force intelligence, Maj. Gen. George J. Keegan, that the U.S.S.R. was close to achieving an operational particle-beam weapon for BMD. These claims were reviewed by an air force–CIA intelligence panel and a panel of the Air Force Scientific Advisory Board, which rejected them as greatly exaggerated. But more credible reports began to appear, confirming Soviet research on beam weapons. So, after 1977, the DOD reviewed its assessment of Soviet progress at least once a year.[7] A review conducted by the Defense Advanced Research Projects Agency (DARPA), a year before the president made his surprise announcement on SDI, concluded that there were no technical grounds for supposing that a more advanced BMD system could be developed—one, in any event, that could not be successfully countered and would not be more expensive to deploy than the offense needed to defeat it.[8] There is little if any evidence that military contractors were actively promoting a new venture in defense, even though some have suggested in retrospect that contractors might well look to SDI to pick up the slack left as major offensive weapons reached maturity. The very few advisors whose opinions the president solicited were almost all predisposed in favor of SDI, although they certainly could not be said to represent a consensus within the technical community.[9] Officials in the Reagan administration later sought to make a virtue of this neglect of expert opinion by citing instances in which eminent scientific authorities had proved unduly pessimistic.

More than any previous major decision on weapons innovation, SDI was very much a presidential decision. As experienced observers were quick to note, it was a "top–down" decision rather than one reached, as most have been, after prolonged gestation in the defense establishment and review by expert committees. From the Truman administration onward, decisions of this sort have generally risen through the upper layers of a bureaucratic and advisory network until, if deemed viable, they are given the National Security Council's imprimatur: an NSC directive. The first such directive was NSC 68 in 1950, which was the policy basis for a major increase in defense spending to meet a perceived Soviet threat. Later, President Dwight D. Eisenhower decided to approve the development of continental air defenses and to accelerate development of intercontinental ballistic missiles (ICBMs) only after elaborate inquiries had been conducted by committees of experts drawn from within and outside of the government.[10]

SDI is an anomaly. It was a decision reached by the president without prior review by the defense establishment, in the knowledge that such a review would have been unfavorable, on the advice of an informal "kitchen cabinet" composed of political supporters, and after the president himself had begun to favor the project. It was not until *after* the March 23 speech and the issuance two days later of National Security Decision Directive 85 ("Eliminating the Threat from Ballistic Missiles") that the president issued National Security *Study* Directive 6-83 ("Defense Against Ballistic Missiles"). The study directive authorized the creation of the Defensive Technologies Study (chaired by James C. Fletcher) and the Future Security Strategy Study (chaired by Fred S. Hoffman) and charged them with examining the feasibility and potential impact of proposals already approved. Although many assumed the president must have been given the idea for SDI by his advisors, Reagan himself scoffed at the suggestion: "It kind of amuses me that everybody

is so sure I must have heard about it, that I never thought of it myself.
The truth is I did." [11]

THE POLITICAL BACKGROUND

Although the decision to establish SDI did not come altogether out of
the blue, the events that led to it were almost exclusively political and
personal. The 1980 Republican platform had endorsed a hawkish con
gressional resolution that called for "peace through strength." It included among other strategic goals the need to pursue "more modern
ABM technologies" and to create "a strategic and civil defense which
would protect the American people against nuclear war at least as well
as the Soviet population is protected." [12] In 1940, as a Hollywood actor,
Reagan starred in a film entitled *Murder in the Air,* about a secret mir-
acle weapon, an "inertia projector," that could bring down aircraft by
destroying their electrical systems. In the movie, after the weapon's promoters announce that it "will make America invincible in war and
therefore be the greatest force for peace ever invented," Communist
spies attempt to steal the plans, but a U.S. secret agent pursues them and
uses the device to destroy their airplane in midflight. The role of the secret agent was played by Reagan. [13] Almost four decades later, as a candidate for the U.S. presidency in 1979, he became aware of the country's
complete vulnerability to attack during a campaign visit on July 31 to
the North American Aerospace Defense Command (NORAD) headquarters at Cheyenne Mountain, Colorado. After observing NORAD
radars tracking thousands of objects in space, he asked the commander
of the facility, Gen. James Hill, what NORAD could do to stop a Soviet
missile once it had been identified as having been fired at a U.S. city.
According to Martin Anderson, an aide who accompanied Reagan on
the visit, the general replied that NORAD could only alert the officials
of the city: "That's all we can do. We can't stop it." On the flight back to
Los Angeles, Reagan, still disturbed by what he had learned, shook his
head and said, "We have spent all that money and have all that equipment, and there is nothing we can do to prevent a nuclear missile from
hitting us." What options would a president of the United States have,
he wondered, in the event of a nuclear attack? "The only options he
would have," the future president reflected, "would be to press the button or do nothing. They're both bad. We should have some way of defending ourselves against nuclear missiles." [14]

Later in the campaign, Reagan reviewed what he had learned on his visit in an interview with a reporter:

> We can track the missiles if they were fired, we can track them all the way from firing to know their time of arrival and their targets, and we couldn't do anything to stop the missiles. . . . They actually are tracking several thousand objects in space, meaning satellites of ours and everyone else's, even down to the point that they are tracking a glove lost by an astronaut that is still circling the earth up there. I think the thing that struck me was the irony that here, with this great technology of ours, we can do all of this yet we cannot stop any of the weapons that are coming at us. I don't think there's been a time in history when there wasn't a defense against some kind of thrust, even back in the old-fashioned days when we had coast artillery that would stop invading ships if they came.

He went on to discuss Soviet efforts in civil defense and added, significantly:

> I don't know whether we should be doing the same things of that kind but I do think that it is time to turn the expertise that we have in that field—I'm not one—but to turn it loose on what do we need in the line of defense against their weaponry and defend our population, because we can't be sitting here—this could become the vulnerable point for us in the case of an ultimatum.[15]

Impressed by the candidate's "powerful reaction" to the NORAD visit, Anderson drafted a policy memorandum on defense in early August 1979, which suggested that Reagan propose the development of a "protective missile system":

> *Develop a Protective Missile System.* During the early 1970s there was a great debate about whether or not this country should build an anti-ballistic missile system. The ABM lost, and is now prohibited by SALT agreements. But perhaps it is now time to seriously reconsider the concept.
>
> To begin with, such a system concentrates on defense, on making sure that enemy missiles never strike U.S. soil. And that idea is probably fundamentally far more appealing to the American people than the questionable satisfaction of knowing that those who initiated an attack against us were also blown away. Moreover, the installation of an effective protective missile system would also prevent even an accidental missile from landing. Of course, there is the question of reliability, especially with the development of multiple entry warheads, but there have apparently been striking advances in missile technology during the past decade or so that would make such a system technically possible.
>
> If it could be done, it would be a major step toward redressing the military balance of power, and it would be a purely defensive step.
>
> Taken in conjunction with a reasonable buildup in our conventional

forces, and an acceleration in development of cruise missiles, laser beam technology, and conventional nuclear missiles like the MX, the development of an effective protective missile system might go a long way toward establishing the kind of national security that will be necessary in the 1980s.

The question of technical feasibility and cost are critical, but we should be able to get a good evaluation of the concept from the group of national defense experts we have working with us.

Although Reagan "embraced the principle of a missile defense wholeheartedly," Anderson recounts that Michael K. Deaver, a senior campaign advisor, vetoed the proposal that it be made a campaign pledge. Deaver liked the idea in principle, but not the timing of the proposed statement, afraid it would be used by demagogic opponents to make Reagan look like too much of a "hawk" for proposing such a radical change in strategic doctrine.[16]

Although Deaver's advice prevailed and Reagan did not make public his belief in the need for a strategic defense program during the campaign, other evidence suggests that he was already strongly in favor of such a program. Another of his campaign advisors was a retired army officer, Lt. Gen. Daniel O. Graham. Although not a technologist, Graham had been head of the Defense Intelligence Agency and was already an outspoken champion of the military need to "seize the high ground of space" before the Soviets did. Graham, along with other military men and space enthusiasts ("space cadets" to their critics), was strongly convinced that just as warfare had earlier spread from land to sea and then to the air, so it was also bound to expand into outer space. An air force "Space Master Plan," setting objectives for the end of the century, would later call for a "space combat" capacity aimed at protecting air force assets and denying the enemy free access to space.[17] For Graham, as for many air force officers, the question was not whether the United States and the Soviet Union were competing for military control of space, but which side would win. He has recalled that Reagan, during the 1980 presidential race, often objected to the concept of Mutual Assured Destruction (MAD), referring to it as a "Mexican standoff." "He said it was like two men with nuclear pistols pointed at each other's heads, and if one man's finger flinches, you're going to get your brains blown out."[18] Reagan, who is known for his tendency to repeat favorite images of this sort, drew a similar analogy in explaining SDI to reporters shortly after he announced it.[19]

After the election, Graham set about building support for a space defense among the president's staunchest supporters. Early in 1981 he published an article in *Strategic Review* calling for the deployment of space-based defenses that would use "off the shelf" technology.[20] Later that year he founded High Frontier, an organization committed to the view that the United States should aim to achieve military superiority over the U.S.S.R. by making a technological "end run" on the Soviets. Space would be the key arena in which this technological edge would be exploited, at first using kinetic-kill technology—systems designed to shoot projectiles, or "smart rocks," at missiles, destroying them on impact—and later, as they became available, more advanced systems incorporating beam weapons. By taking this bold approach, the advocates of High Frontier contended, the United States would not have to be content with restoring a balance in offensive systems, but could achieve superiority by adding defenses to offenses. The cost of deploying the proposed system was estimated to be "on the order of $24 billion" in constant 1982 dollars. The ultimate aim would be to replace "assured destruction" with "assured survival."[21] Among the contributors to High Frontier were four members of the president's California kitchen cabinet: brewer Joseph Coors, retired industrialist Karl R. Bendetsen, investor and longtime Reagan friend William A. Wilson, and Jaquelin Hume, like Wilson an elderly businessman.

At the urging of Reagan appointees, High Frontier's proposal of a three-layer global ballistic missile defense (GBMD) consisting of terminal, midcourse, and boost-phase systems was examined by specialists at the Defense Advanced Research Projects Agency (DARPA), a Defense Department organization in charge of research in the general area of future technologies. DARPA found that the proposed system would be ineffective against the present Soviet missile force, vulnerable to countermeasures, and considerably more expensive than High Frontier claimed. In testimony before Congress, DARPA Director Robert S. Cooper reported on the agency's findings, noting that its researchers had worked with representatives of High Frontier:

> We do not share their optimism in being able to develop and field such a capability within their timeframe and cost projections. We have conducted several inhouse analyses and have experienced some difficulties in ratifying the existence of "off-the-shelf components or technologies" to provide the required surveillance, command and control, and actually perform the intercepts within the orbital and physical conditions described. Our understanding of the system's implications and costs would lead us to project expenditures on the order of $200 to $300 billion in acquisition costs alone for the proposed system.[22]

On the recommendation of the General Accounting Office (GAO),[23] however, the DOD in 1982 set new priorities for the research on strategic defenses and put the relevant activities under the guidance of DARPA.[24]

Also promoting strategic defenses was a "laser lobby" in Congress headed by Sen. Malcolm A. Wallop (R., Wyo.) and his legislative assistant, Angelo Codevilla. In 1979 both men drafted and sent to Reagan an article that called for immediate deployment of space-based defenses featuring chemical lasers. Reagan returned the draft with comments and annotations.[25] At Wallop's urging, the Republican-controlled Senate voted in 1982 to provide additional funding for laser defenses by a margin of 91 to 3. In the House there was some enthusiasm for the X-ray laser, as *Science* magazine reported in a story in its issue of June 4, 1982, entitled "Laser Wars on Capitol Hill." Another Republican senator, Pete Domenici of New Mexico, published an article in the conservative *Strategic Review* that called for a new program to develop space-based defenses.[26] But there were countervailing pressures. In 1982 both houses voted to deny $350 million requested by the Defense Department for research on ABM systems, and a joint resolution was introduced in the House of Representatives, signed by ninety members, calling on Reagan to negotiate a ban on all space weapons; a similar resolution was introduced in the Senate.

THE ROLE OF EDWARD TELLER

Although the specialists at DARPA were clearly unimpressed by the case for a high-priority program in strategic defense, the cause received influential support from the nuclear physicist Edward Teller. A former director of Lawrence Livermore National Laboratory, and at the time a kind of physicist-in-residence there, Teller had been encouraging a group of protégés—many of them brought to the laboratory under a fellowship program of the Hertz Foundation, in which Teller has long played a key role[27]—to investigate a "third-generation" nuclear device (incorporating fission and fusion weapons but focusing the energy of their explosions in a powerful beam of X-rays) that might have military applications. In 1967 Teller had met Reagan, when he was governor of California, and had given him a tour of Livermore Laboratory.[28]

Two Teller protégés, Lowell J. Wood, Jr., and George A. Keyworth II, also played key roles in promoting SDI. Wood, a physicist, was the leader of the "Excalibur" project team investigating the X-ray laser at

Lawrence Livermore. Later, he would often appear with Teller in congressional hearings and otherwise played an active role in lobbying for SDI in general and the X-ray laser in particular. Keyworth, then head of the physics division at the Los Alamos National Laboratory, became a strong advocate of his mentor's views in general, even though he did not share Teller's enthusiasm for the X-ray laser. On the recommendation of Teller and other leading Republicans, and after other candidates were also considered, Keyworth was appointed special assistant to the president for science and technology and director of the White House Office of Science and Technology Policy (OSTP) as of May 1981. (The fact that the post remained vacant for so many weeks into the president's term was taken by many as evidence of the indifference and even suspicion with which the president and his immediate advisors regarded the scientific community. This attitude may have been a legacy from the Nixon administration, when the President's Science Advisory Committee was dissolved after certain of its members were criticized for disloyalty to the administration and for being "advocates" rather than advisors.)

Teller had long been in favor of passive defenses in the form of civil defense, including the dispersion of population and industry, in order to limit damage from a nuclear attack. Now he pressed Keyworth to promote the development of active defenses, including research on third-generation nuclear weapons. With Keyworth's encouragement and Teller's active participation, the four members of the kitchen cabinet—Coors, Bendetsen, Wilson, and Hume—reportedly decided to act separately from High Frontier by forming an ad hoc subcommittee. They conferred at the offices of the conservative Heritage Foundation in Washington, D.C., and used their considerable influence to arrange a White House meeting with Reagan in January 1982 in which Teller took part. At that meeting they presented a report urging the president to establish a strategic defense program modeled after the Manhattan Project. On September 14, 1982, Teller met separately with the president and key advisors. Although he had been invited for a different purpose—Keyworth wanted his help in persuading the president to increase support for basic research—Teller used the opportunity (much to his protégé's annoyance) to lobby for more support for the X-ray laser project. He is reported to have warned the president that the Soviets were making significant progress in developing the new laser and to have advised him that a major breakthrough in the same effort had been achieved in the Excalibur project at Livermore.[29] Teller has said subsequently that "because the Soviets are doing it, by now it is a question of life and death," and that the achievement of the X-ray laser "would end the MAD era and commence a period of assured survival on terms favorable to the Western alliance." [30]

Teller's promotion of the Livermore project did not stem from a belief that the United States should deploy defenses only when the X-ray laser had been perfected. Nor did he propose that the United States adopt a space-based defensive system, either using kinetic weapons on satellites (like the High Frontier project) or relying on battle stations armed with laser weapons. Indeed, Teller specifically rejected the idea of satellite-based interceptors and declined to endorse the High Frontier proposals because they made use of this very basing mode. "We are not talking about battle stations in space," he told the House Armed Services Committee. "They are much too vulnerable. We should merely try to have our eyes in space and to maintain them." [31] Teller's support of strategic defense was general rather than specific, and he had long opposed any political actions—including treaties—that might hamper the development or deployment of defensive systems. In a book published in 1962, Teller was already campaigning for active defenses. "A retaliatory force," he wrote, "is important. A truly effective defense system would be even more desirable. It would be wonderful if we could shoot down approaching missiles before they could destroy a target in the United States." If the Soviets were to develop reliable defenses knowing that U.S. defenses were insufficient, "Soviet conquest of the world would be inevitable." [32] He opposed the 1963 Limited Test Ban Treaty because it prevented development of nuclear-tipped ABMs, and the ABM Treaty because it prevented the United States from deploying more than one hundred ground-based interceptors. Teller continued to believe that such interceptors would be worth having, especially in view of advances in their design. And he believed this even though the interceptors could not promise complete protection and even though, in the long run, the X-ray laser would provide a much more effective defense (if it could be popped up from submarines on warning of an attack) by intercepting missiles in their boost phase without the vulnerability of space-based satellites.

In his meetings with the president, Teller evidently emphasized the long-term prospects offered by the X-ray laser, though he very likely also reiterated his long-held belief that some defense is better than none at all. Later, Teller was to react strongly against the conclusions of the Fletcher committee. He objected on the grounds that the Fletcher report called for deferring deployment until research into all possible alternatives had been completed and because the report anticipated the deployment of a layered defense requiring some space-based systems. "The spirit is willing," Teller punned, "but the Fletch is weak." [33]

BYPASSING THE "ESTABLISHMENT"

Teller's technical judgment was given practical application as a result of meetings involving the kitchen cabinet, Graham, and a small group of White House officials, none of whom had major responsibility for foreign or defense policy. On September 14, 1981, Bendetsen, Graham, and Teller met in Meese's office with White House Counselor Edwin Meese III; Keyworth; Anderson; and Meese's assistant, Edwin W. Thomas. The outside advisors agreed to prepare a report for the president recommending that U.S. policy be redesigned to emphasize both defense and offense. There was "general agreement," according to Anderson, "that a major part of a missile defense would probably be based in space." A second, smaller meeting took place in the White House on October 12, at which the group considered adopting the High Frontier designation for the project of "Global Ballistic Missile Defense." [34]

On January 8, 1982, a meeting was arranged for the members of the kitchen cabinet to present their report. In addition to the president, present in the Roosevelt Room—adjacent to the Oval Office—were Bendetsen, Hume, Coors, Teller, Meese, Keyworth, Anderson, and William Clark, then a member of the White House staff. The meeting was supposed to last only fifteen minutes but went on for almost an hour. [35] During the discussion, the question arose of whether an ABM system should be designed to rely on beam weapons. Some also asked if the system should be expected to provide an "area defense" to protect people or a "point defense," which would protect only missile silos and other military targets. Bendetsen reportedly suggested that if one type of defense could be achieved, so could the other. The real need, he said, was to get on with the job. The president agreed. No one raised the question of whether the proposed defenses would be compatible with the obligations imposed by the ABM Treaty. The right way to proceed, the participants agreed, was for the president to issue a directive initiating a program on the scale of the Manhattan Project. For something that elaborate, Reagan observed, he would need a recommendation from the DOD. Bendetsen, who had been under secretary of the army from 1946 to 1952, observed that if that were the case, Reagan would have to talk the department into it. [36]

The others at the White House meeting recognized the force of Bendetsen's point. They knew that if the president were to try to win approval through the usual channels, he would run into so much opposition that the proposal might never reach his TelePrompTer. Within the defense establishment, the opposition was likely to be keen, especially among those who had already examined the High Frontier proposal and concluded it was premature at best. Leaders of the various services were apt to fear that large appropriations for strategic defense might jeopardize modernization of offensive weaponry. Those most knowledgeable about advanced technologies and the costs of development would be either skeptical or strongly opposed.

On the very day the president made his "Star Wars" speech, the director of DOD's Directed Energy Program told a Senate committee that although beam weapons "offer promise of making major contributions" to strategic defense, the "relative immaturity" of the technologies made it hard to know whether weapons employing them would be feasible or cost-effective. For the time being, he indicated, "our goals in this area are rather modest." The research would be unlikely to affect force structure until "the 1990s or beyond."[37] Richard DeLauer, under secretary of defense and in effect the highest-ranking technologist in the Pentagon, said later in the year that a deployable space-based defense was at least two decades away and would require "staggering" costs. To develop it, he added, eight technical problems would need to be solved, each of which was as challenging as the Manhattan Project or the Apollo Project.[38] And even if it could be developed, DeLauer was skeptical of its utility in the face of countermeasures: "There's no way an enemy can't overwhelm your defense if he wants to badly enough."[39]

The proposal would hardly have been any more welcome elsewhere in the executive branch or among most members of Congress. The State Department, if consulted, would certainly have warned that Western Europe would react adversely and that Soviet objections might undo the ABM Treaty. Arms-control specialists in the department and at the Arms Control and Disarmament Agency might have cautioned that the proposal would complicate arms-reduction negotiations with the Soviets. And, had the proposal leaked to Congress, those already skeptical toward the schemes of High Frontier and the laser lobby might well have mounted a campaign to head it off.

The president did not order further study of the kitchen cabinet's recommendation or take action on it for some months. The issue of developing defenses came up again in the meeting with Teller in September and was also discussed in a meeting with the Joint Chiefs of Staff (JCS) in December 1982. Apparently, it was only after this meeting with the JCS that the president decided to move ahead with the proposal.

The job of shaping the decision was assigned by Clark, who had succeeded Richard V. Allen as assistant to the president for national security affairs, to a small circle of NSC staff members headed by his deputy, Robert C. McFarlane. The basic strategy adopted, according to McFarlane, "was to skirt Congress, the bureaucracy, and the media." Secretary of State George P. Shultz was not consulted but, instead, was handed an advance copy of the speech, two days before it was televised, marked "eyes only"—an injunction that prevented him from sharing it with arms control advisor Paul H. Nitze, who learned about the project the day the speech was given. Secretary of Defense Caspar W. Weinberger was also not consulted. DeLauer learned of the decision nine hours before the speech. Fred C. Iklé, under secretary of defense for policy, was notified at the same time and pleaded for an opportunity to inform at least the leaders of the other NATO countries.[40] The process whereby the policy was formulated resembles the one later employed in the Iran-contra affair, in which the president also relied primarily on the staff of the National Security Council rather than on members of his formal cabinet and the relevant executive agencies.

Keyworth, who had been privy to the earlier discussions with Teller, was consulted only after the president had decided to act. He was informed of the decision five days before the date of the speech, when the NSC staff realized that the president could not announce a major high-technology initiative in a nationally televised address without having informed his science advisor. Keyworth has said that the president asked him to determine whether the objective was attainable, and that he spent several days telephoning experts before he was able to give the president the assurance he wanted. He has admitted that his first reaction was to ask for time to consider the issue: "My God, let's think about this some more. Let's think about the implications for the allies. Let's think about what the Soviets are going to think. Let's think about what's technically feasible. Let's think about what the scientists are going to say. Let's think about the command-and-control problems."[41]

Keyworth's initial concerns were reinforced when he consulted a specialist on directed-energy weapons. But in the end he overcame his doubts, largely out of loyalty to the president. In 1981 he had commissioned an independent review of prospects for space-based defense by a physicist, Victor H. Reis, whom he had appointed assistant director of

OSTP. Reis, who had worked at the MIT Lincoln Laboratory and had participated in Defense Science Board panels on strategic defense, reported that it would be much easier to counter such a defense than to build it. When Keyworth was given a draft of the president's "Star Wars" speech by McFarlane, he showed it to Reis, whose reaction was to say, "Jay, this is Laetrile" (referring to a quack cure for cancer). Keyworth admitted that he, too, had doubts about the idea but thought that SDI might be a boon to scientific research. Reis suggested that he should either resign or urge the president to submit the proposal for independent review. Keyworth knew the Joint Chiefs also favored such a review, hoping the panel would resemble the one headed by the physicist Charles Townes to consider the MX. Keyworth rejected the advice because he had confidence in Reagan's political leadership and because he viewed SDI as a research program, not necessarily as a commitment to deploy any particular system. Above all, he decided to endorse the proposal because he thought it was a political decision and that his role as science advisor was merely to make sure that the president was aware of the views of the technical community. He was also influenced, however, by findings that suggested a defense employing ground-based lasers might be developed that would require only that mirrors be deployed in space. Once he had decided to go along with the proposal, he helped McFarlane draft the speech.[42]

Several members of the White House Science Council were invited to attend the broadcast of the speech, but they, too, were taken by surprise. A year before, a panel of experts drawn from the council had been asked by Keyworth to study the potential impact of new technologies. They reported that none of them, including the X-ray laser, was likely to have a revolutionary impact in the near term. Many of the members of the council were nevertheless sympathetic to the president's proposal. Only one, John Bardeen, twice Nobel laureate and professor of physics at the University of Illinois, dissented strongly, resigning from the council in April because "such a questionable and far-reaching proposal was being made without review by the scientific community." Bardeen's complaint emphasized the lack of advance review by technical specialists:

> Reagan's speech was prepared without prior study of the feasibility of the concept by technical experts and apparently without consultation with those in the Pentagon concerned with missile defense or with his own former science advisor, George "Jay" Keyworth [II]. I was a member of the White House Science Council at the time. Although we met only a few days before the speech was given, and had a panel looking into some of the technology,

we were not consulted. We met on a Friday and left for home. Keyworth must have heard about the planned speech shortly thereafter, because telegrams were sent to some of the council members involved to return to Washington on Saturday. With the speech scheduled for the following Wednesday, there was no time to make more than minor changes. The multi-layer systems on which current SDI research is based were outlined in a report by the Fletcher Commission, formed after the speech was given.[43]

The lack of consultation was quite deliberate. The president's reasoning, which was reinforced by McFarlane, was that he needed to make a decision that would change attitudes toward defense both within the government and outside it. "The idea," as one of the participants put it, "was to make a decision and then make it happen." That way, no one had to consider whether a defensive system might work or whether (assuming it could be made to work) there would be military benefits. Nor was any thought given to the Soviets' reaction. As a White House source insisted: "None of the things you assume would be considered were considered at all. People just don't believe that the president could make such a momentous decision so impulsively. They think we must have thought through what it could do to the treaties and how it might work as a bargaining chip in Geneva, and so on, but I can't find it." Another participant said the policy initiative had been given little more consideration than "you would give the jacks before you bounce the ball." Still another gave a post hoc appraisal that implied admiration more for the way the decision had been reached than for the decision itself: "It was a fabulous study of top–down leadership," recalling that no one the president had informed thought the decision "screwy."[44]

Some who were not informed until it was all but too late to intervene were shocked. Richard N. Perle, assistant secretary of defense for international security policy, reportedly acting with Weinberger's approval, tried to delay the speech, putting in a transatlantic call in which he urged Keyworth to "fall on your sword" to stop Reagan from making the announcement, or, if that failed, to threaten to leak the plan to the press. DeLauer is said to have exploded in disbelief upon hearing of the proposal and to have told Keyworth: "That's nonsense. That can't be so." At a White House meeting, Shultz berated Keyworth for reassuring the president about his vision of a perfect defense. "You're a lunatic," he is reported to have told Keyworth.[45]

Anderson, who took part in the decision as assistant to the president for policy development (though his job was ostensibly to deal with economic and other domestic matters), has admitted that the "normal way to proceed" would have been to ask the Defense Department to study the problem and to make recommendations. "That option was never suggested," Anderson has written, "because we all knew it wouldn't work." Anderson's view was that the "bruising battle" twelve years before over ABM had made the DOD "gun shy of any serious talk of missile defense," and in any case, as an entrenched bureaucracy, it was expected to resist radical new ideas. So, instead of "going by the book," he, Meese, Keyworth, and Allen (the president's first special assistant for national security affairs) formed an informal alliance "committed to providing a missile defense shield for the country." [46]

That the president encountered no criticism is not surprising, given the disposition of those he did consult. Most of the top civilians in the administration with foreign policy responsibility shared his view that the ABM Treaty had been a mistake in that it (1) had discouraged the United States from proceeding with research on defenses while not inhibiting the Soviets and (2) had not led to the promised reductions in offensive arms. In addition to General Graham and Teller and such politicians as Senator Wallop and Rep. Newt Gingrich (R., Ga.), conservative strategists such as Colin S. Gray and William Van Cleave had condemned the treaty and were urging a renewal of defense research.

Nevertheless, there were objections to details of the president's proposal, and there was confusion among the drafters as to how the initiative should be couched. As a result, the speech was shaped to take some account of friendly criticisms and concerns. Should the president be circumspect or forthright? Should he approach the subject by saying something like "It might be a good idea to think about . . ." or: "As of tonight, I have directed . . ."? Perle succeeded in narrowing the focus of the speech to protection against ballistic-missile attack, cautioning that to include defense against bombers and cruise missiles would dramatically increase cost estimates for the United States and even more for Western Europe. Both Perle and Shultz found the initial draft of the speech unnecessarily provocative, anticipating the Soviets would object that by coupling a defense with a potent offense, the United States would be able to launch a first strike against the U.S.S.R. and then to absorb what retaliation could be mustered by the remaining Soviet missile force. The president attempted to allay that objection. ("If paired with offensive systems, [defensive systems] can be viewed as fostering an aggressive policy, and no one wants that.") Perle also pointed out that U.S. allies might conclude that the United States intended to protect itself but not them, and that a U.S. defense against ICBMs would enhance the likelihood that the United States would become "decoupled" from the defense of Europe. The drafters therefore added the clause, "recognizing the need for closer consultation with our allies," and the assurance that the United States sought a defense that would also protect them.[47]

The context in which the proposal was made is also noteworthy. The reference to strategic defense was added to a speech originally designed to rescue the president's defense-budget request from Congress's efforts to pare it. The call for research on strategic defense may well have been designed to capture public interest and to improve the political climate for the passage of the president's request for a 10 percent increase in the defense budget. But the reference was neither a hastily added afterthought nor something tacked on for publicity value. It was a major new initiative intended to move strategic doctrine and defense technology in a new direction.

In the speech, the president took care to cite one important source of support for his ideas—the Joint Chiefs of Staff. Twice the president referred to the JCS, claiming that he had arrived at his decision only "after careful consultation" with his advisors, including the JCS. In fact, the question of whether to develop strategic defenses surfaced first at a regular meeting between the president and the chiefs in December 1982, possibly by coincidence, because the chiefs were searching for something new and different to discuss with the president. The meetings were going well, but the chiefs had, in effect, run out of new things to raise with him. They did not want to tell him, one participant recalled, just that "readiness was up. . . . We wanted to bring the president something new, different and exciting." At a preliminary meeting, Adm. James D. Watkins, chief of naval operations, suggested that they discuss new technologies and the possibility that they might provide a defense against ICBM attack. He did not have in mind urging the president to launch a major program to develop such weapons. His idea was rather that the United States might pursue such weapons research gradually, after consultation with its NATO allies. The chiefs agreed to put the matter on the agenda.[48]

At a subsequent meeting on February 11, 1983, the issue of strategic defense was raised again. This time it was broached during a discussion of the JCS's politically embarrassing opposition, during congressional testimony, to the administration's "dense pack" basing proposal for the MX. The chiefs may have been eager to find an issue on which they could reestablish rapport with the president. If so, strategic defense was just such an issue. Admiral Watkins, a Roman Catholic, had become especially sensitive to the moral questions surrounding a policy of nuclear deterrence owing to his involvement in the church's discussion of the ethics of defense policy. The Catholic bishops had invited discussion of a draft pastoral letter, criticizing retaliatory deterrence as immoral. The letter contended that "collateral damage," even from a "counterforce" strike (against military targets only), would inevitably take the lives of millions of innocent civilians and that a limited nuclear attack would be likely to escalate to an all-out exchange. "Wouldn't it be better," Watkins asked, "to save lives rather than to avenge them?"—a question the president thought striking and borrowed for his speech. (Others in the administration, including national security advisor Clark and his deputy and successor, McFarlane, may also have been influenced by the discussion provoked by the draft of the bishops' letter.)

Just how enthusiastic the chiefs were about a new initiative in strategic defense, especially one designed to provide a population defense, and not merely a "point defense" to protect deterrent forces, is in dispute. Administration officials claim that the chiefs were polled on the feasibility of comprehensive defenses and concurred with the president, and that the president made his final determination to launch the program based on their advice. According to Anderson, the chiefs "recommended" to the president at the February meeting that "the United States abandon its complete dependence on the old doctrine of mutual assured destruction and move ahead with the research and development of a missile defense system," thereby confirming "the validity of an idea that Reagan had been thinking about for almost four years."[49] The reporter Frank Greve, however, was told that the ideas expressed by the chiefs were "vague and philosophical." Gen. John W. Vessey, Jr., the chairman of the JCS, and Gen. E. C. Meyer, the army chief of staff, both of whom were at the meeting, could not recall being polled. General Vessey afterward recalled that it was well recognized that strategic defense was no panacea and that the chiefs were aiming merely to tell the president that the concept deserved further study.[50] In a congressional hearing five years later, McFarlane, who had been present at the February 1983 meeting, confirmed that the president had asked the chiefs if they were endorsing an effort "to determine . . . whether defense could make a bigger contribution to our military strategy against nuclear conflict." According to McFarlane, each of the chiefs indicated his agreement. But in a dramatic colloquy with Rep. Les Aspin (D., Wis.), chairman of the House Armed Services Committee, McFarlane revealed that the chiefs had not understood their endorsement to apply to population defenses but only to the protection of military assets, and that the president had afterward knowingly altered the proposal to give it that much broader goal:

THE CHAIRMAN: But at that point, you and they were talking about defending missiles, not the Astrodome protection of the population. Is that what you are saying?

MR. MCFARLANE: The military was talking about that, I was talking about that, and also frankly about just stressing the Soviet system.

THE CHAIRMAN: Complicating their lives.

MR. MCFARLANE: That is right.

THE CHAIRMAN: How did that get transformed into an Astrodome protecting population by the time the president made his speech about a month later?

MR. MCFARLANE: Basically, the president wanted to change it, Mr. Chairman. . . . He made the point to me, and I think it was proper, he said, "You must deal and have dealt with the traditional threat that we have faced, and you deal in military terms with the military problem and military risks, and to a certain extent political risks." He said, "My job is to lead and to try to evaluate what may be feasible technologically, but to be responsive to human beings, and my responsibility requires that I try to physically protect them and to move away from a strategy of threatening to kill people." [51]

It is apparent from the president's own account that he used the Joint Chiefs' expression of interest in strategic defense to make it seem that his proposal had originated in his meeting with them. His own recollection, as he vividly recounted it in a magazine interview, was rather different from Vessey's but close to McFarlane's: "I brought up the question that nuclear weapons were the first weapons in the history of man that had not led to the creation of a defense system to protect against them. I asked if it was worthwhile looking into this. Is it possible to come up with a defense? They were all agreed it was. And right there the program was given birth." [52] From that point on, the chiefs were not involved in the actual shaping of the decision or of the program it would recommend. McFarlane assigned three NSC staff members, all senior air force officers, to think about what should be done, to propose various options, and to consider the implications for planned military systems and the possible international ramifications. Then came the actual drafting and redrafting of the speech.

THE IMPORT OF THE MARCH 23 SPEECH

Most of the president's speech of March 23 was devoted to urging support of his defense-budget request, but he introduced his remarks by saying that he would announce "a decision which offers new hope for our children in the twenty-first century." He began by noting that until this point, the United States had managed to thwart the danger of a Soviet attack by threatening deadly retaliation. This approach, he admitted, had worked for more than three decades. It would continue to work only if the United States countered the Soviet effort for over the past twenty years to accumulate "enormous military might." He showed photographs of an extensive Soviet intelligence system in Cuba and Soviet military hardware in Central America, including Grenada. Finally, he broached his surprise announcement, making sure to refer to his discussions with the JCS: "In recent months, however, my advisors, including in particular the Joint Chiefs of Staff, have underscored the necessity to break out of a future that relies solely on offensive retaliation for our security."[53] This initial reference to the United States' need to develop defenses begins, interestingly enough, in a recognition of a potential U.S. vulnerability in the offensive competition with the U.S.S.R.—a consideration that in many ways underlines and colors the character of the initiative.

It is plausible to assume from this reference to reliance on offensive deterrence that the interest in strategic defense arose not only because of its inherent attractions but also because of fear that the United States was losing ground in the offensive competition with the Soviets. The president and his military advisors were evidently convinced that while the Soviets were deploying more offensive weapons and were likely to continue doing so, the United States could not keep up—because of political and economic objections to the president's "strategic modernization" program. The administration's proposed deployment of two hundred mobile MX launchers had been stymied by resistance to the "dense pack" basing proposal. In conjunction with this intended deployment, the proposed FY1984 defense budget included a request for substantially more support for the development of new ABM technology to protect the MX missiles. Objections to this request included protests from inhabitants of the western (and strongly Republican) states, where the missiles would be based. They were concerned, among other things, with the impact the deployment might have on land and water resources. Congressional approval was obtained for the deployment of only fifty

MX missiles (which the administration decided to call "Peacekeepers"), to be housed in existing silos. Such a deployment hardly offset the Soviet advantage in the throw-weight of its heavy land-based missiles—a sore point for administration strategists—nor could it close the theoretical "window of vulnerability": in theory, the ground-based leg of the U.S. triad could still be threatened with destruction in a surprise attack. According to McFarlane's later congressional testimony, these political reverses to plans for strategic modernization prompted the Joint Chiefs' and his own interest in strategic defenses:

MR. MCFARLANE: Starting in the fall of 1983, after the loss of two proposals for MX basing, and then in December, 1982, the loss again of[,] I think[,] Dense Pack, Admiral [John] Poindexter came in one day and said[:] "It looks to me like we are going to have trouble staying in the[—]maintaining an equivalent balance with the Russians based on offense alone." And he said[, "]I raise this because Admiral Watkins, at the time the Chief of Naval Operations, had come over to him [Poindexter] and said, 'We in the Navy have been looking at recent technological breakthroughs both in the speed of computations as well as [in] traditional interceptor technologies[—]propellants, things like that[—] and we think that there has been so significant a family of changes that you ought to urge the President to make more of an investment in this.'["].[54]

There were ominous signs that the administration's other efforts to make up for perceived Soviet advantages were also in trouble, even as the Soviets were taking new steps that would widen the gap even further. A resolution calling for a freeze on nuclear weapons at current levels (which meant, in the administration view, that the Soviets would retain their advantages) had been passed in referenda in eight states, and there was growing support for the freeze in Congress. Several influential senators, Charles Percy (R., Ill.), William Cohen (R., Me.), and Sam Nunn (D., Ga.), were supporting, as an alternative to the freeze, a "guaranteed mutual build-down," which the administration also disliked. Congressional resistance to the development of ASATs was growing, even though defense officials considered them vital in view of the Soviet development and deployment of satellites that would provide "real time" targeting information, greatly improving the U.S.S.R.'s offensive threat. This prospect was considered especially serious by naval officers responsible for the defense of the surface fleet. Although they remained confident that the U.S. Navy's ability to maneuver would be sufficient to protect against a small number of targeting satellites, they thought that a large deployment of such Soviet satellites would require attack by ASATs if the U.S. fleet were to be protected in time of war.

For their part, the Soviets had shown no compunctions about testing a co-orbital ASAT, judged to be useful but not very threatening because of its low orbit as well as its unreliability and relatively lengthy attack time-line. Because of these tests, the U.S.S.R. could be said to possess an operational ASAT, despite its rhetorical attacks on the United States for "militarizing space" and its offer to ban all space weapons—an offer interpreted by the administration as an effort to preserve the Soviet advantage by halting the U.S. program, which promised to produce a better ASAT. The Soviets were also beginning to test and deploy new mobile missiles, which the administration's defense analysts feared would be harder to target than fixed launchers, especially because they could be hidden in the vast reaches of the Soviet Union or in tunnels. The U.S. Midgetman program—the favorite of some Democratic members of Congress, notably Sen. Albert Gore (D., Tenn.), and a number of senior defense analysts, who preferred it to the MX—was nevertheless mired in controversy. Although the Scowcroft Commission endorsed Midgetman, critics in the administration feared its approval would end prospects for congressional agreement to further MX deployment and, moreover, that its single-warhead configuration would further disadvantage the United States. They also worried that the cost of Midgetman and the difficulty of finding an acceptable basing mode for it would make this option at least as unpopular as the MX.

The administration's efforts to improve NATO's force structure were also meeting with objections in Europe, where unexpectedly intense protests erupted with the deployment of longer intermediate-range missiles. Requested during the Carter administration by European governments with the prompting of U.S. defense officials, these missiles were partly a response to Soviet deployments of the SS-20s against targets in Western Europe. Faced with a revival of the unilateral-disarmament campaign, leaders of the allied governments sought to distance themselves from the president's militant anticommunism and his calls for Western rearmament. It must have seemed to the president, and presumably to the Joint Chiefs as well, that the Soviets were able to do as they pleased with the development and deployment of nuclear weapons, while the United States could not even stay abreast of Soviet efforts because of political opposition at home and abroad. Equally important, the Soviets had long taken strategic defense of their leadership, the general population, and their retaliatory strategic forces quite seriously.

The traditional alternative to building more and more weapons to keep up with the Soviets was to pursue arms-control measures. But the president, like other conservatives, had come to believe that arms control was a hopeless cause. He had denounced the SALT II Treaty as "fatally flawed" and in general spoke of arms-control agreements as successful Soviet efforts to tie America's hands while the U.S.S.R. took advantage of every treaty loophole and did not stint from cheating when the loopholes were not adequate to their purposes. He had appointed representatives to the arms-control talks in Geneva on whom he could count to resist pressures to negotiate treaties that would allow the Soviets to retain advantages they had presumably won in previous rounds. Edward L. Rowny, a retired army general and the chief negotiator for the Strategic Arms Reduction Talks (START), resigned in protest as soon as the SALT II Treaty was initialed in Geneva by U.S. and Soviet representatives and opposed its ratification. Nitze, chief negotiator in the intermediate nuclear forces (INF) talks, was one of the leaders of the Committee on the Present Danger, which spearheaded the campaign against ratification of the SALT II Treaty, although he was viewed with suspicion by some in the administration because he was a Democrat and had helped to negotiate SALT I. The president showed no sign of disappointment when the Soviets walked out of the negotiations in 1983 after the United States and its European allies rejected a Soviet demand for halting deployment of Tomahawk and Pershing II missiles for the duration of the talks. On the advice of the Joint Chiefs, he was adhering to the SALT II limits for the time being, so long as the Soviets also complied. The chiefs agreed with the CIA that the Soviet Union could add more warheads to its heavy missiles than the United States could add to its Minuteman missiles if the treaty limits were abrogated.[55]

The president's dim view of arms control was shared by some specialists. The trouble with arms control, Helmut Sonnenfeldt has observed, is that "what is negotiable is not significant, and what is significant is not negotiable."[56] Thomas C. Schelling wrote that arms control "has gone off the tracks." The insistence on formal agreements, he contended, may actually prevent arms reductions. Reciprocal restraints are more likely to come as a result of tacit behavioral signals than from formal negotiations.[57] Others have taken a position even closer to the view of the president and other conservatives by arguing that the Soviets are more likely to respect the power of the Western alliance than they are efforts to conciliate them by cutting back military forces, and that the Soviets cannot be trusted to adhere to arms-control agreements.

In his 1983 speech, however, the president went beyond such standard questioning of the utility of arms control to challenge the very premise of the doctrine of deterrence by threat of retaliation. Even successful arms-control measures would not remove the threat of nuclear war. The security of the United States and its allies would continue to rest on the threat of retaliation, and the whole of Western civilization would still have to live with the fear of nuclear devastation. The president therefore raised Admiral Watkins's rhetorical question: "Wouldn't it be better to save lives rather than avenge them?" Although it might have strengthened his case to do so, he did not mention the draft pastoral letter of the Catholic bishops, possibly because, like other conservatives,[58] he found their position defeatist and even leftist. It is plausible to suppose, however, that the bishops' disapproval of retaliatory deterrence had not escaped his notice, and that in calling for a change in strategy he hoped to capitalize on their unhappiness with the status quo. The bishops had urged that the world move toward total nuclear disarmament. The president offered the same goal, but he proposed to get there by a different route, one that would not require frustrating, difficult, and possibly unsuccessful negotiations, but would instead take advantage of Western scientific and technological superiority. The belief that the United States could somehow defend itself was not altogether new, but never before had it been presented so simply, optimistically, and starkly. As to the freeze campaign, Reagan reiterated the administration line:

> A freeze now would make us less, not more, secure and would raise, not reduce, the risks of war. It would be largely unverifiable and would seriously undercut our negotiations on arms reduction. It would reward the Soviets for their massive military buildup while preventing us from modernizing our aging and increasingly vulnerable forces. With their present margin of superiority, why should they agree to arms reductions knowing that we were prohibited from catching up?[59]

While the speech was being drafted, the president made clear that he wanted defenses that would protect people, not just military targets. According to Keyworth, the president told the drafting group: "If there's one thing I do not mean by this, gentlemen, it is some kind of a string of terminal defenses around this country." It was Reagan himself who added the phrase about making nuclear weapons "impotent and obsolete," insisting on its retention when some of his advisors urged that the phrase be toned down.[60]

Reagan presented the alternative to nuclear deterrence in terms at least as appealing as those used by the champions of arms control and disarmament. "What if free peoples could live secure in the knowledge," he asked tantalizingly, "that their security did not rest upon the threat of instant retaliation to deter a Soviet attack, but on the knowledge that we could intercept and destroy strategic ballistic missiles before they reached our own soil?" (The president deliberately did not call for a defense against the "air-breathing threat" posed by bombers and cruise missiles. To listeners who did not appreciate the omission, it might well have seemed that the president was promising total safety from nuclear attack. He said nothing then or later to dispel such an illusion.)

Reagan did not claim that his goal could be achieved rapidly, but he argued that it was worth pursuing as a matter of the highest national priority. Building such a defense, he pointed out, was a formidable challenge that might not be met before the end of the century. But he stressed that the goal of rendering strategic nuclear weapons "impotent and obsolete"—a phrase that was to be often repeated, but one that proved more ambiguous than the president and his speechwriters may have realized—was both worthwhile and possible. In a pointed reference to weapons researchers, he called on those in the scientific and engineering communities to bend their efforts to developing a defense against the very weapons they had created.[61]

The president tried to fend off an objection he had been warned about when the draft of the speech was circulated. His defense was somewhat perfunctory, however, and did not prevent the criticism from being forcefully advanced. Reagan acknowledged that by deploying a defense along with a strong offense, a nation might be thought to be seeking military superiority. Such an advantage could then be exploited either for purposes of attacking an adversary or for what Schelling calls "compellence," i.e., making political capital out of a perceived military superiority and using it to force concessions. "If paired with offensive systems," the president noted in the speech, defensive systems "can be viewed as fostering an aggressive policy, and no one wants that." "We seek," he pledged, "neither military superiority nor political advantage."[62] This assurance did not prevent Soviet Premier Yuri Andropov from promptly denouncing the new initiative as a transparent effort to "disarm the Soviet Union" by achieving "a first-nuclear-strike capability," combining offenses and defenses in order to render Soviet forces unable to deal a retaliatory strike.[63] The Soviet argument was cited sympathetically by prominent domestic critics of the president's initiative, who also warned that defenses could be used to absorb a "ragged" retaliatory strike.[64]

In making the speech, however, Reagan was apparently preoccupied not with such subtleties and complications but with a simple, heartfelt concern for a strategic defense against nuclear attack. He expressed this concern with particular force a few days after the speech: "To look down to an endless future with both of us sitting here with these horrible missiles aimed at each other and the only thing preventing a holocaust is just so long as no one pulls the trigger—this is unthinkable."[65] Presidents before him had expressed the same horror at the thought that they might have no alternative but to defend the nation—an action that would carry the distinct risk of a nuclear holocaust. The difference was that Reagan's predecessors had reluctantly concluded that there was no feasible alternative but to accept this awesome responsibility. Reagan eagerly embraced the hope that one might be found and embarked on a major program based on little more than that hope. Even more important, he was determined to pursue this objective regardless of its effects on accepted strategic doctrines or on the arms-control process.

Although Reagan hoped without benefit of evidence, and deliberately sought reassurance from a very limited set of very loyal technical advisors (rather than canvassing the far larger constituency of skeptics), his decision was informed though without real understanding of the complexities involved—by technical progress in a number of relevant areas, including the third-generation nuclear weapons touted by Teller and his protégés. The program was labeled "Star Wars" in the media, after the popular film of that title, because it was assumed that Reagan envisioned the kind of space-based defense advocated by the High Frontier group. The program was also thought to involve the orbiting of laser weapons, even though the speech itself made no specific reference to space-based systems or to any particular defensive system.

Indeed, the president and his supporters at first reacted with annoyance to the "Star Wars" label and even tried to prevent the media from using it because administration critics were employing it in an effort to make the program seem like a hopeless and dangerous adolescent fantasy. As the phrase stuck, however, and the critics failed to arouse great public opposition by using it, the objection was dropped. In fact, the idea of a space-based shield proved to be appealing.[66] Perhaps it seemed as though an "astrodome" would keep nuclear explosions well away from the earth, encouraging some to conclude that even if a war came to pass, it would be fought in space. Many people may also have been ready to believe that in view of advances in space technology, the character of warfare might well be altered more or less as the president was suggesting. When the Fletcher panel reported in favor of a layered system that would emphasize deployments in space, and the president endorsed the report, any point in objecting to the "Star Wars" designation was lost.

The president's speech curiously omitted any reference to Soviet efforts in strategic defense, which left him open to the charge that he was destabilizing the superpower relationship by giving the United States an advantage in an area foreclosed by the ABM Treaty. A subsequent government publication[67] made up for this omission by emphasizing that the Soviet Union had already made considerably greater investments than the United States in defensive systems, including more than ten thousand SAM sites to defend against the U.S. bomber force (which carries more than half the megatonnage in the U.S. arsenal). The report pointed out that the Soviets were hard at work on an undeclared SDI of their own, designed to improve their existing ABM system around Moscow, perhaps to upgrade SAMs so that they might serve for BMD, to develop mobile radars, and to do research on BMD involving "new physical principles," especially beam weapons. Weinberger, in particular, stressed the need for SDI in order to prevent the Soviets from achieving a space-based defense first.[68]

The president's silence on the issue is open to interpretation. The drafters of the speech must have known about Soviet efforts, even though the Pentagon did not have much time to study the speech and react to it. They were probably reluctant, however, to make an issue of Soviet investments in defensive systems because the considerable expenditures had already been met by very effective U.S. offensive countermeasures, rendering Soviet efforts both futile and very costly. Conceivably, the president may have wanted to stress the novelty and benign nature of his proposal. (He had not long before characterized the U.S.S.R. as an "evil empire." Could such an empire have taken an initiative designed to rid the world of the nuclear scourge?)

THE STRATEGIC RATIONALE FOR THE SDI

Even before the president made his decision, advocates of strategic defense were arguing that it made military sense. Once the decision was

made, they developed its strategic rationale. Prominent among them
was Colin S. Gray, who had been a persistent critic of reliance on offensive force. Although he had earlier been skeptical of the prospects for
strategic defense,[69] Gray now argued strongly in favor of a defense transition, to be achieved in stages. The nation that achieved the first stage
earliest would have at least a temporary advantage:

> Notwithstanding the varied technological grounds upon which the 'High
> Frontier' vision of American superiority in space may be dismissed as im-
> practicable for the near future, it is important to appreciate the scale of the
> strategic revolution in question. The first country to deploy robust directed-
> energy weapons in space, in conjunction with conventional BMD, air-defense
> capabilities, civil defense, and a strong offensive counterforce capability,
> would almost certainly achieve a large measure of strategic superiority, how-
> ever fleeting.

Arguing that Britain and those who depended on its resistance to
Hitler's Germany had been fortunate that radar had not been banned in
the 1930s, Gray contended that proposals for defense technology should
not be sacrificed to poorly conceived and inequitable arms-control proposals. If the adversary developed no adequate countermeasures or an
equally effective defense, that advantage would persist. The more likely
prospect in such an event was that both superpowers would introduce
defensive weapons in order to balance the previous emphasis on offense.
Gradually, Gray argued, defense would come to dominate offense until,
eventually, the threat from strategic offensive weapons would become so
minimal as to justify the president's hope that they would become "impotent and obsolete."[70]

Those who adopted Gray's view, however, were not quite ready to
argue that a shield in space would be impregnable, or that there was no
point in deploying defenses unless they could protect civilian populations. Although the popular impression left by the "Stars Wars" speech
was just that, more sophisticated strategists argued that a "robust" strategic defense—one that would intercept all but a fraction of the attacking warheads—would effectively eliminate the threat of nuclear attack
by making it too risky for an enemy to contemplate. In the total absence
of defenses, an attacker could reasonably calculate that a large-scale
counterforce attack could significantly degrade retaliatory capacities
and that a countervalue attack (i.e., one directed against civil targets)
could cause "unacceptable damage." Faced with a robust defense, an
aggressor would be especially unlikely to launch a counterforce attack
because there could be no assurance that enough warheads would pene-

trate to their targets. Deterring a countervalue attack by relying even on robust defenses would be more difficult because the few surviving warheads could still do fearful damage. But in this case, too, the attacker could not be sure which targets would be destroyed.

Against the argument that an opponent would respond to the deployment of defensive weapons by greatly increasing the offensive threat, strategists in favor of SDI reply that defensive systems will with time become less expensive than offensive ones. Adding offenses to offset defenses will therefore become uneconomical. Why this should necessarily be so, especially in view of the complexities of space-based defenses, is not always made clear. Presumably, proponents of strategic defense anticipate a "learning curve" effect that will eventually reduce costs of defenses, whereas the need to reconfigure and equip offensive forces with penetration aids will continually increase the cost of offense.

Another problem opened up by the president's speech was its implicit recognition that the defensive shield would be ineffective against nuclear attacks not delivered by ballistic missiles. Proponents of strategic defenses acknowledge that the shield envisioned by the president would have to be complemented by an equally effective air defense but claim that some of the technologies developed for BMD (such as sensors) could also be used for air defense.[71] Air-breathing weapons, moreover, are less destabilizing because they cannot be used as effectively in a first strike. Because bombers take more time than ICBMs to reach their targets, retaliatory forces can be launched before they are attacked. Even so, the president's vision of population defense would require air defense. This concern with air defense became more acute after "pre-summit" in October 1986 in Reykjavík, where Reagan and Soviet leader Mikhail Gorbachev came close to agreeing to halve the number of strategic warheads over a five-year period. As a result, by the end of 1986 a spate of new studies and plans was devoted to the possibility of an "ADI," or air defense initiative.

As to the effects on Western strategy, SDI supporters argue that strategic defenses would make NATO's strategy of "flexible response" more rather than less credible. If the United States did not have to fear nuclear retaliation against its own territory, they contend, it would be more likely to live up to its commitment to respond militarily to a Soviet attack on Western Europe, even if that response should require the first use of nuclear weapons.[72] Because the defensive shield would be designed to protect Western Europe as well, though not from all forms of nuclear attack, it should also enhance the credibility of NATO's resolve, in the view of SDI supporters.

Supporters of the defense transition are more ambivalent about SDI's likely effect on Soviet strategic doctrine and deployments. They argue that the Soviets would be compelled to revise their stated view that nuclear weapons would inevitably be used in a superpower conflict in favor of a recognition that such weapons might not have the desired military effect. Faced with defenses much more effective than its own, the Soviet Union would have to calculate that in any hostilities initiated with conventional forces, it could no longer count on its nuclear weapons to deter a devastating Western response. If the defenses of both East and West were equally strong, then the military balance would rely on conventional forces, where the Soviets could conceivably (and in the view of some of the strategists already do) have advantages. But any Soviet effort to improve, or take advantage of, its conventional posture could be offset by the combined economic and technological resources of the West.

SDI supporters also see a different outcome. They contend that the introduction of defensive weapons could well lead, as Reagan apparently hopes, to U.S.-Soviet cooperation, though not necessarily through the sharing of technology. Most concede that sharing is unlikely because to understand a defensive technology is to learn how to defeat it and because of the superpower competition in high technology for weapons and civil economic advantages. At some stage, they argue, the Soviets will consider it in their interest to exchange monitoring data with the United States, perhaps to make use of the same surveillance satellites and in general to cooperate in order to defend against third parties (especially if the superpowers' offensive weapons are reduced without guarantees against other countries maintaining their own stocks of nuclear weapons).

In sum, then, according to the supporters of the defense transition, the United States' commitment to design and deploy defenses would not endanger the security of the West. First, defense would initially supplement offense, and second, SDI would eventually compel all powers to stress nonnuclear defenses. As a consequence, the condition known as Mutual Assured Destruction (MAD) would inevitably yield to one of Mutual Assured Survival (MAS). The Soviets would find, no less than the United States, that innovation in offense can produce only a temporary change in the military balance. But SDI aims to achieve a qualitative change in warfare, ruling out further reliance on nuclear weapons. Offensive deterrence by conventional weapons would still be necessary, however, to forestall the threat of conventional war. Even if deterrence by conventional weapons could not be completely effective, especially where the superpowers confront each other through proxies, the damage from such encounters could be contained. Most importantly, they could not escalate to the level of nuclear warfare, with its attendant catastrophic dimensions.

THE ECONOMIC RATIONALE

The strategic rationale for research into and eventual deployment of strategic defenses was buttressed by an economic one. Although it did not emerge in the president's speech—which omitted any mention of the economic consequences of the initiative—it had already been stressed by High Frontier. Once the Fletcher panel put a price tag on the research program, however, and critics began to estimate the cost of the program (some in the range of a trillion dollars), the administration began to address the economic issue. Upon receipt of the Fletcher report, DeLauer recommended, and Weinberger endorsed, a research phase that would cost $26 billion over five years, beginning with FY1985. Critics attacked this budgetary request on several grounds. They argued that it would distort research priorities in defense by competing with programs concerned with the modernization of nuclear and conventional forces; that it would contribute further to the "militarization of research" at universities, a process already under way because of the emphasis of the Reagan budgets on military R&D; and that it would be wasteful, because too many technical questions would have to be resolved before an operational system would merit testing. Critics also cautioned that the program would divert scarce talent and industrial resources from a civilian economy that was suffering from "deindustrialization" and had become uncompetitive. The real motivation for such a rapid escalation in expenditures, some argued, was to create a constituency of contractors that would provide the program with enough momentum to make it difficult if not impossible for some future administration to scale back or curtail.[73]

Administration officials responded to these criticisms with several key points: SDI is based on research that has been under way for some time. Expenditure totals should therefore be regarded as increments. In other areas, research was no longer critical because new military technologies were in a development or deployment phase. The research budget for the SDI would amount to no more than a comparatively small fraction of total military research, and would make it possible, early in the 1990s, to decide whether to proceed with the development and deployment of a defensive system. Before then, it was purely speculative to try to determine the costs of deployment. These costs, too, would in any case be spread over many years and would therefore represent a manageable fraction of the defense budget.

In addition, advocates and administration officials also emphasized the potential importance of the SDI as a source of spillover benefits for civilian high-technology industry.[74] Advances in computers, optical sensors, materials, and other aspects of SDI research, they suggested, would stimulate a resurgence of U.S. industry in much the same way as defense research had done in the 1950s and 1960s, and with greater indirect benefits than the more specialized mission-oriented research of the space program of the 1960s and 1970s. An office of Innovative Science and Technology was created within the SDIO to assure opportunities for broad-gauged research at universities; other efforts were made to assure that smaller, highly innovative companies would receive significant shares of the funding. Critics even wondered whether the SDI was in reality a covert way for a conservative administration to achieve a form of reindustrialization. The French government suspected that whatever the U.S. government's intention, massive support to U.S. industry would leave Europe in the lurch. President François Mitterrand therefore proposed the EUREKA project, a mainly civilian-oriented alternative to SDI.

THE POLITICAL RATIONALE

Although the strategic, technological rationale appears to provide most of SDI's raison d'être, with the economic rationale only a subsidiary theme, the political rationale is probably its underlying source. This rationale has both ideological and pragmatic aspects.

The Reagan administration's commitment to SDI reflected its conservative ideology, which emphasizes the goal of advancing the cause of democratic capitalism against Soviet communism and imperialism. This goal is thought to require "a strong military" in virtually every conceivable respect. The ideology is unabashedly nationalistic and skeptical of the value of arms control, détente, and international organizations. Continued nuclear testing is supported on the ground that so long as the United States remains committed to nuclear weapons, the military must be assured the weapons are effective and researchers must be free to improve them. The ABM Treaty is disliked because it inhibits the United States from developing defensive weapons, making military strength a matter of developing offensive capabilities alone.

From this perspective, military R&D of all kinds is vital. Military strength can best be assured not only by providing the armed services with the hardware they need and with the ability to attract and keep the personnel to operate it but also by encouraging the weapons laboratories to advance the state of the art. There is no room in this position for President Eisenhower's strictures against the "military-industrial complex"[75] or for the liberal and radical view that argues for economic conversion of military industry to civilian pursuits. A cardinal tenet of the conservative view in general, which applies especially to SDI, is the belief that the United States' great strength is its free-enterprise economy, especially the high-technology sector. By freeing industry from the burden of high taxes, conservatives expect to stimulate enterprise. By providing government subsidies for military R&D, they aim to direct that industrial strength to the maintenance of national security. By maintaining stringent security classifications and restrictions on exports of technology to the Soviet bloc, they aim to protect the military advantages conferred by the West's superiority over the Soviet Union in industry and most areas of science and engineering.

The fundamental beliefs informing this general policy are that the United States is locked in a deadly competition with the Soviet Union and that superiority in military technology is a critical factor. The Soviets, conservatives believe, are determined to achieve military superiority even at continued cost to the civilian sector of the economy. Unlike liberals, who tend to interpret increased Soviet military expenditures mainly as an effort to attain and maintain strategic parity with the West, conservatives hold that the U.S.S.R.'s aim is not parity but superiority—a superiority it would seek to exploit for political gain and, if possible, to achieve a military victory over the West.[76] From this point of view, détente generally serves the interest of the Soviets far more than that of the United States. Détente lets them conduct subversive proxy efforts to destabilize the West through "wars of national liberation" in the developing countries and through "low-intensity warfare," including terrorism. Wherever they can, conservatives contend, the Soviets seek to block resolution of conflicts in the developing countries, hoping to pick up the pieces or to force the West to protect its interests by committing resources to these conflicts. Within its own spheres of influence, in Western Europe or Asia, the Soviet Union remains committed to the "Brezhnev doctrine," i.e., it aims to consolidate its hold and to extend it if possible. A U.S. commitment to military improvements helps to put the U.S.S.R. on the defensive, forcing it to match Western expenditures, thereby straining its resources. Such strains are apt to inhibit the Soviets from attempting to acquire new dependencies and foment difficulties for the West, especially insofar as they find that they need access to Western technology in order to keep pace, both in military and in civil terms.[77]

In this international perspective, SDI can be regarded as merely another facet of the "Reagan doctrine"—that is, of a plan to take the offensive in the competition with the Soviets and to counter their efforts to intimidate the West.[78] The Soviets fear SDI, according to this reasoning, because they know the West can make it work and that it will degrade their efforts to achieve offensive superiority. To cope with it, they will be compelled to increase expenditures on countermeasures and defenses of their own which could put an unbearable strain on their economy. SDI, moreover, can be seen as a pragmatic response to the Soviet effort to seize the high ground of space and to develop advanced weapons. It is an effort both to steal a march on the Soviets and to make sure they do not do the same to the West.

This political rationale greatly appeals to hard-core conservatives and to a broader public attuned to the same sentiments. Adherence to the SDI has thus become a litmus test of personal loyalty not only to the president but also to his legacy. Aspirants to the Reagan mantle, like Jack Kemp and Dan Quayle, have pledged to maintain SDI as a token of their commitment to the conservative agenda, along with tax reduction and militant anticommunism. The president's acute sense for U.S. public opinion also led him to see SDI's broader appeal. To those concerned about the prospect of nuclear attack but opposed to political accommodation with the U.S.S.R., it provided hope for protection. This hope, moreover, entailed the development of nonnuclear systems in the main and therefore was not vulnerable to the usual objection that increasing U.S. military strength would only escalate the arms race. SDI thus responded to a widespread longing for a mitigation of the nuclear threat without requiring any progress in arms control or trust in the Soviets. Instead, it required only traditional American beliefs: self-confidence in the U.S. economy and in the country's capacities for technological achievement.

Although liberals claimed it would unleash a new, no-holds-barred phase of the arms race, most Americans reacted favorably to the project, even though they also favored arms-control agreements. SDI carried a particular appeal for young people because of their absorption in the romance of science-fiction-style space adventure. Even though critics warned that SDI would unleash a new, unrestrained chapter in the arms race, everywhere—even in Europe, where leaders openly expressed skepticism about its feasibility—SDI generated public enthusiasm precisely because it seemed to respond to a deep fear (ironically, one that had been reinforced by disarmament campaigns) by offering a hope that did not seem unduly provocative or warlike. A nonnuclear shield seemed a good deal less threatening than a Damoclean sword composed of fifty thousand nuclear weapons. By promising to share the technology with the Soviets and emphasizing his intention to achieve a defense for all humankind and not U.S. military advantage, Reagan couched SDI in terms that gave it a very broad appeal. In the case of SDI, as Garry Wills has observed, "others have the arguments, but Reagan has the audience."[79]

ADJUSTING THE FOCUS

Despite its widespread appeal, SDI was soon enveloped in controversy. What, exactly, were its goals? Was it designed to provide a total, i.e., "leakproof," defense against all nuclear weapons, or a "robust" defense against missile-borne weapons? What of other nuclear threats? Was it, rather, a way to get support for a program to protect only missile silos, with perhaps some minimal population coverage as a side benefit? Was it really designed to produce better ASAT systems? Or was it supposed to produce a relatively light nuclear defense that would serve as an "insurance policy" once radical reductions had been achieved in strategic offensive weapons and a "thick defense" was therefore no longer needed? Or was it just a bargaining chip to be traded for Soviet concessions in arms-control negotiations?

Although the president and administration officials continued to argue that his plan contained no contradictions or inconsistencies, others interpreted the project rather differently—including some who were engaged in it and others who have argued that, regardless of the president's declared intentions, SDI would actually work out differently.

Reagan himself clearly wanted to develop a form of defense that would protect people and not just missile silos. He also wanted it to be comprehensive, although in his speech he referred only to defense against strategic missiles. Apparently, Reagan wanted to avoid the criticism that such a total defense would be even more unaffordable than one against missiles alone. He had also been advised that BMD was the harder technical problem to solve. If a defense could be achieved against ICBMs, it would be comparatively easy to design a defense against bombers, cruise missiles, and low-trajectory SLBMs. The president's vision was of a world virtually free of nuclear weapons, but not in the sense that a space shield could guarantee that no nuclear weapons would remain in the possession of any state or that no such weapons could possibly be used against the United States. (Critics have pointed out that bombs could be smuggled into the United States or other countries and detonated by remote control, or delivered by and then detonated in ships docking at ports or in civil aircraft.) The aim was to provide an effective defense against massive nuclear attack and thus to eliminate nuclear weapons from the strategic calculations of states. By nullifying nuclear weapons as the key element in superpower conflict and, with it, the threat of nuclear holocaust facing all of humanity, the president could embrace the ends of those who clamored for disarmament without embracing their means—either mutual agreement by the superpowers (which had so far proved futile) or the unilateral abandonment of nuclear weapons, which would leave the West at the mercy of its adversary.

At the same time, the U.S. military would be strengthened vis-à-vis Soviet superiority in offensive weapons, one of the main strategic motivations for SDI. By adding defenses to offenses, the United States could blunt the effect of any Soviet military buildup, which would otherwise upset the military balance. Thus, in the short term SDI might well serve to deter a Soviet buildup. In the longer term, if the Soviets persisted, it could negate such a buildup, especially inasmuch as U.S. retaliatory forces could be defended more readily than populations.

Those SDI supporters skeptical of the ultimate prospects for population defense could endorse the president's vision but still keep their own eyes fixed on the near-term goal of strengthening U.S. security by adding defenses to offenses. Thus, the Hoffman report, commissioned by the DOD, urged that "intermediate deployments" be made to prevent erosion in the military balance and to provide protection for military targets in Europe, where Soviet short- and intermediate-range nuclear threats combined with conventional preponderance to pose an even more serious military imbalance.[80] Such a near-term deployment would run afoul of the ABM Treaty, unless it were restricted to defenses against tactical missiles and involved no transfer of ABM technology—a difficult objective inasmuch as the technology for ABMs and ATBMs is so similar as to make the systems nearly indistinguishable apart from location. The authors of the Hoffman report, and those who shared their general view, implied or asserted that the ABM Treaty was not sacrosanct and should therefore not be permitted to stand in the way of a deployment that would actually serve the purpose of the accepted view of deterrence (i.e., by protecting the capacity to retaliate) and that, in addition, would reduce the threat of nuclear attack, a reduction not achieved by the ABM Treaty.[81]

Advocates of the defense transition sought to integrate both the president's long-term vision and the military's short-term interest in deploying defenses. In this view, near-term deployments should represent "downpayments" on a fuller system, producing experience and reinforcing deterrence, while leading toward greater and greater reliance on defensive systems. In the Nitze version, this would be a period of transition in which offensive weapons on both sides might be reduced as defenses were deployed.[82]

As critics and skeptics pressed the complaint that no leakproof defense was on the horizon, even conceptually (let alone one that could meet the formidable operational requirements of such a layered defense), the president's vision was modified. A defense need not be leakproof to be effective, it was argued; even an imperfect shield would strengthen deterrence by reducing the incentive to risk a preemptive strike. More advanced technologies might make the shield virtually impenetrable, assuring "deterrence by denial" rather than "deterrence by uncertainty."

Other confusions developed over the degree to which the administration was committed to relatively rapid deployment. Although the program was originally touted solely as a research effort, designed to make it possible to decide after six years or so whether a defensive system might be feasible, and only then to enter a phase of development and deployment, it soon became evident that many of SDI's more ardent supporters regarded it as a commitment to deployment. Those in Congress in particular argued that it would be impolitic to spend the requested $26 billion unless there were a commitment to deploy defenses later on. Moreover, some members were persuaded by the High Frontier argument that effective systems could be deployed immediately, using "off the shelf" technology.

Still others, including the skeptics, viewed it as a potential bargaining chip in arms-control negotiations, although the Soviets were clearly using the issue to paint the United States as opposed to arms control and to divide the Western alliance. Concern over SDI played some role— perhaps the leading role—in persuading the Soviets to return to the arms-control negotiations. Because there was great uncertainty about whether a defensive shield that met the Nitze criteria[83] (survivability, military effectiveness, and cost-effectiveness at the margin) could ever be achieved, reluctant supporters thought the United States should be prepared to stretch out and otherwise constrain the research program in the interests of an arms-reduction agreement.

Two supporters of a defense transition, Alvin M. Weinberg and Jack N. Barkenbus, argued that defense was the key to arms reductions.[84] They proposed a "defense-protected build-down" in which units of offense would be traded away for units of defense. In this way, nuclear arsenals could be gradually reduced without affecting the strategic balance and without diminishing security. Although they found it hard to conceive of a complete elimination of nuclear weapons (agreeing with those who argued that minimal stockpiles would always be necessary for deterrence, inasmuch as affordable defenses would never be perfect), they contended that the process of an exchange-based build-down would promote a more cooperative relationship between the superpowers, which would greatly reduce tensions and diminish the prospect of conflict.

In a variation of this approach, Freeman Dyson proposed that the superpowers move from a climate of confrontation to one of "live and let live," to be achieved through the virtual elimination of nuclear weapons. To protect against cheating or third-party attacks, a relatively light, ground-based defense would be installed by both sides.[85] (This is, in fact, similar to the rationale McNamara presented in his 1967 speech, when he justified President Johnson's decision to begin ABM deployment. McNamara's proposal was commonly called a "Chinese defense," because it could address only a relatively minor attack such as one China might then have mounted.) To attempt a more elaborate defense would probably prove impossible, Dyson argued, because every defense is eventually vulnerable if offenses are not constrained. But if offenses could be reduced, even a relatively light defense might be adequate. This idea emerged in the president's reference, after the Reykjavík pre-summit, to the notion that a strategic defense might serve as "long-run insurance" to accompany radical reductions of nuclear weapons.[86] Such an insurance policy might resemble Dyson's proposal.

Controversy also broke out over the ways in which the SDI would or would not conform to the ABM Treaty. Although the president and his advisors paid little if any attention to the treaty in deciding to initiate the program, the Fletcher report made it obvious that testing and deployment in space in particular would come into conflict with the requirements of the treaty. The administration's position was that SDI was still a research program and that the United States' adherence to the treaty was an issue that could be faced later, when the actual testing of space-based systems might be necessary and decisions about deployment had to be made. Some supporters of the SDI, who had never favored the treaty in the first place, were quite prepared to see it abrogated. Indeed, in some cases, support for SDI seemed to be stimulated by a desire to abrogate the treaty. Conversely, critics of the administration's venture argued that SDI would erode the treaty and thereby open the floodgates to an offensive arms race. The president's reelection in 1984, coupled with the widespread acknowledgement that some degree of research should be conducted on strategic defense, if only as a hedge against a possible Soviet breakout, enabled him to win congressional support for SDI, though not at the budgetary levels recommended by the Fletcher Committee. Still, the question of conformity to the treaty remained in doubt, especially in view of the president's sometimes casual statements that SDI would have to involve testing as well as research. Critics argued that the experiments contemplated by the SDIO violated the terms of the treaty.[87]

The issue of SDI's conformance with the treaty arose in U.S.-Soviet discussions concerning the resumption of stalled arms-control talks. The U.S.S.R. insisted that there could be no agreement on arms reduction unless the United States abandoned its intention (the Soviets preferred to call it a "dream") of militarizing space. The Soviets referred to the contemplated weapons not as strategic defense but as "space-strike weapons" and "space-based anti-missile systems" (SBAMS). The U.S. side insisted that SDI was a research program and not negotiable in exchange for offensive reductions.

To complicate matters, debate within the Reagan administration cast doubt on its willingness to adhere to the terms of the treaty as enunciated by U.S. negotiators. Early in 1985 the Heritage Foundation circulated a paper arguing that the ABM Treaty had been improperly construed as restricting SDI testing. In September Perle—on record as critical of the ABM Treaty and skeptical of the possibilities for progress in arms control—asked a young Defense Department lawyer, Philip Kunsberg, to examine the text of the treaty to determine whether it did in fact prohibit development and testing of newer ABM technologies. Kunsberg reviewed the text of the treaty and a few days later replied that in his view it did not ban such work. Perle asked him to go over the record of the negotiations, still classified, to determine whether the record supported his interpretation. He did so and reported that there was no indication the negotiators had intended to rule out testing and development of futuristic technologies. Perle took this news to Shultz, who ordered the State Department's legal counsel, Judge Abraham D. Sofaer, to do a study of his own. Sofaer examined both the treaty and the negotiating record and concluded that the Pentagon lawyer's conclusions were correct.

Before this reinterpretation was made known, the president created a special National Security Planning Group to formulate policy on arms control, headed by McFarlane. McFarlane was apprised of the new interpretation and declared it to be administration policy. On October 6 he said: "Research involving new physical concepts, as well as testing, as well as development, indeed are approved and authorized by the treaty. Only deployment is foreclosed."[88]

When a reporter asked Gerard C. Smith, the chief U.S. negotiator of the treaty, what he thought about McFarlane's interpretation, the response was blunt: "He's got it all screwed up."[89] In a letter to the *New York Times*, Smith declared that there had been no intention on the part of the U.S. delegation that any type of technology for space-based ABM systems could be developed or tested under the treaty and that this has been the official understanding of the U.S. government as well as of the Soviet Union.[90]

At this point, the controversy became too intense to be ignored by the president. Many in Congress were furious, claiming that the administration was twisting the terms of the treaty to suit its purposes and in effect abrogating it. Shultz was shortly to address the North Atlantic Assembly and then to meet with NATO leaders. He had good reason to expect that they would express sharp disagreement with the new interpretation, especially because the president had assured British Prime Minister Margaret Thatcher that the United States intended SDI to be only a research program to be carried out in conformity with treaty obligations. As a result, a meeting was called, at which the president presided, to resolve the conflict over interpretation. The result was a statement supporting the new interpretation as a matter of principle but promising to abide by the old interpretation in planning SDI experiments. As Shultz explained to a meeting of the North Atlantic Assembly, "It is our view, based on a careful analysis of the treaty text and the negotiating record, that a broader interpretation of our authority is fully justified. This is, however, a moot point; our SDI research program has been structured and, as the President has reaffirmed on Friday, will continue to be conducted in accordance with a restrictive interpretation of the treaty's obligations."[91]

Even before this retreat from adoption of the "broader interpretation," the DOD had set up a committee to review the experiments planned for the SDI. It concluded that none of them would violate the terms of the treaty—by which was presumably meant the older, "restrictive" interpretation. All fifteen of the major experiments, the committee reported, would be in conformity with the treaty, because they would be performed "under roof" or be configured so they could not be components of an ABM system (but only subcomponents or adjuncts), or they would not be tested in an ABM mode and would not be capable of performing the functions of ABM components or systems.[92]

As arms-control negotiations proceeded in Geneva, the Soviets seemed to back away from their earlier position to the effect that all research on space-based weapons would violate the treaty. Instead, they distinguished between research in laboratory settings and testing in space. The stage seemed set for an agreement to reaffirm the provisions of the treaty, but at the Iceland meeting in October 1986, disagreement over the terms of these restrictions was said to have been the stumbling block to a comprehensive arms-control agreement.

THE SDI IN PERSPECTIVE

As the impasse at Reykjavík demonstrated, both the intention behind the SDI and its implications are open to considerable confusion and disagreement. Reagan saw it as an effort to develop a strategic alternative to reliance on the deterrent effect of a nuclear attack and as an effort to maintain U.S. military strength in the face of a continuing Soviet buildup. He also argued that the achievement of a comprehensive strategic defense would benefit humanity by providing protection against the damage a nuclear war would inflict should the present form of deterrence fail. Others see the project quite differently. To a legion of skeptics inside and outside the Pentagon, there is little prospect that its stated goals can be achieved in the foreseeable future. Technologically sophisticated critics see the SDI—especially that aspect of it oriented toward boost-phase and midcourse interception—as being based on nothing more substantial than wishful thinking. (But even some critics concede that defenses may be advisable as a means of shoring up deterrence by retaliation—especially hard-point defenses capable of protecting retaliatory capacities from preemptive attack.) Enthusiasts see the project as a way to gain superiority over the Soviets by exploiting the United States' qualitative advantages in high technology in order to seize the high ground of space, to prevent the Soviets from gaining a military advantage there, to put them on the defensive, and perhaps to compel them to give up other efforts to maintain superiority in strategic and conventional forces. Others see SDI as a possible opportunity for both superpowers to recognize the need to achieve agreements on reducing arms and controlling the testing and deployment of destabilizing weapons.

It is in this last interpretation that the best hope lies for converting SDI into a much less controversial undertaking. Even some well-informed critics acknowledge that if a comprehensive defense were really feasible, it would be desirable. Although the world has survived for forty years with the threat of a nuclear catastrophe—some would say because of it—there can be no assurance that this form of deterrence will work indefinitely. As specialists in strategy often note, the current arrangement cannot prevent an accidental launch of a nuclear weapon— an incident that could trigger a war and do considerable damage even if the launch were recognized as unintentional. More probable is the danger that a conventional war, perhaps initially involving only proxies or allies of the two superpowers, might "go nuclear," as conventional forces are introduced with "dual capable" (conventional and nuclear) weapons and either side decides to risk using nuclear weapons on a "limited" or tactical basis. A mutually deterring defensive shield might well be preferable, even though it would remove the offensive threat that NATO now uses to deter Soviet conventional advantages; any extra burden that may be required to assure a conventional balance would be small compared to the catastrophic threat lurking in the potential failure of offensive deterrence.

The desirability of defense is justification for some level of research expenditure to investigate the prospects. Even some of the severest critics of the SDI concede that research is justified in case it should lead to effective technologies and as a hedge against Soviet breakout.[93] What they object to is the projected scale of the research, which would not only be wasteful but could also lead the Soviets to refuse to abide by existing arms-control agreements or to enter into new ones. The most direct response to a promising defensive program is to build offenses and countermeasures capable of dealing with it—an effort that could be incompatible with the ABM Treaty and, indeed, with the entire effort to achieve arms control.

A commonly expressed Soviet view is that SDI is being undertaken not merely to provide the West with a strategic defense but to give the United States a decisive edge by adding "space strike" weapons. Such weapons, in their view, could be used for offensive purposes as well: to destroy Soviet reconnaissance and communications satellites (especially those that the Soviets are developing to provide real-time targeting); to enable the United States to launch a first strike against the U.S.S.R., secure in the knowledge that it could absorb a second, supposedly "ragged," strike; or to exploit its military advantage for political gain.[94] The Soviet view can claim some substantiation from official U.S. sources. The day the president made his "Star Wars" speech, DOD officials testifying before the Senate Armed Services Committee pointed out that directed-energy weapons could have offensive uses. Such weapons could "deny the use of space for collecting and distributing crisis management and targeting information while protecting our space assets that warn against a surprise attack," and they could be used to "neutralize or disrupt enemy targets" as well as to aid U.S. retaliatory strikes.[95]

The Soviets, like some domestic critics, also see SDI as a calculated effort to force them into a competition with the U.S. economy. Such an effort would confront them with the handicap of their relative backwardness in technology and production, imposing expenditure burdens that would make it impossible to meet growing demands for an improved standard of consumption as well as improved performance in the civilian sectors of the economy. It is also possible, however, that the Soviet leadership is deliberately exaggerating the threat it sees in SDI. The technological challenge of SDI serves a useful domestic purpose in making Gorbachev's economic reforms seem critical to national security. By claiming that the United States aims to "militarize space," the Soviets can divert attention from their own considerable efforts to exploit space for military purposes in the hope of inciting opposition to the United States in Europe and elsewhere. The Soviets may also be preparing the ground for a negotiating strategy whereby they would offer to accommodate SDI by accepting a broader definition of the ABM Treaty provisions on research in exchange for U.S. acceptance of Soviet activities now considered violations of existing treaties or perhaps for even more valuable concessions.

Because the SDI has been made to figure so prominently in the equation of U.S.-Soviet relations, it has a political import far in excess of its realistic prospects. Reagan and his supporters have come to see it as an ideological touchstone for long-term adherence to the conservative goal of defending the United States and its allies from what they see as an unremitting, long-term march toward world domination by the U.S.S.R. SDI has become more than just a hope for a technological answer to nuclear weapons. It is now a symbol of the U.S. willingness to use resources and know-how to ensure the survival of the West. For the Soviet Union, it is yet another example of the United States' refusal to accept parity and to acknowledge that it must respect the right of the Socialist bloc not only to maintain itself but also to extend its fraternal assistance to other nations struggling to shake off the yoke of imperialism. For the U.S.S.R., SDI is both a practical threat to strategic parity and a symbolic threat to the belief that socialism, not capitalism, is the wave of the future. Soviet achievements in space have come to symbolize a renewal of belief in the Marxist prophecy that only under socialism would the means of production be unfettered to reach their highest possible level. If the United States succeeds in exploiting space more successfully than the Soviet Union, that confidence would be as threatened as the appeal of communism now is by comparisons of industrial productivity and consumer choice. Politics, then, and not just the dream of building the perfect defense by using the latest advances in technology, explains why SDI was declared and why the Soviets perceive it as such a threat. Military researchers in both countries had long been engaged in a competition to develop defenses, but without success. SDI was a signal that the competition was to be reopened, but this time in greater earnest on the part of the United States, and in a direction that might well entail a qualitatively new phase in the militarization of outer space.

The unusually political character of its initiation, however, could prove to be SDI's undoing, at least in the short run. In the post-Reagan era, SDI will become more vulnerable to attacks that began to be mounted during Reagan's last months in the White House. The armed services will view large increases for SDI as competitive with other priorities. Members of Congress seeking ways to control the federal budget will find SDI a prime target. Skepticism rife in the defense community over the technical prospects may be expressed more openly. And, ironically, the Reagan administration's own achievements in arms control, even if limited to the signing of the treaty banning intermediate-range weapons, will leave SDI as a major obstacle in the way of broader progress toward arms reduction and better relations between East and West.

The Elusive Quest
for Strategic Defenses

Lessons of Recent History

SDI is but the latest move in a U.S.-Soviet competition to design defenses against nuclear attack and to make military use of space. In a
number of respects, however, this stage could turn out to be much different from earlier efforts. Concepts long considered only remote candidates for defensive systems are now being reviewed for development
and deployment and, if deployed, would entail fundamental changes in
military force structure and strategic doctrine. Short of deployment,
even the effort to develop such systems has serious implications for political relations between East and West and within NATO; prospects for
international collaboration in space exploration are also threatened. In
view of the difficulties posed by SDI, it is especially noteworthy that the
earlier phases of the competition to devise strategic defenses have been
costly and largely futile.

As these earlier experiences show, technological success in the development of defenses is likely to be only partial and short-lived. The active
defenses developed so far are themselves vulnerable to attack, and any
gain they have promised to confer has simply provoked offsetting offensive improvements by the other side. The Soviets have made by far the
largest investment in strategic defenses, both active and passive. Although these investments may provide some marginal benefits in improved population defense, they cannot possibly prevent a degree of
damage to civil and military assets from a massive attack that would be
considered devastating by any standard. Further, the near-catastrophe
at Chernobyl in 1986 can only have brought home to Soviet military

planners the devastation that can be created by just tens or hundreds, let alone thousands, of nuclear warheads.

It is highly doubtful that SDI, and whatever the Soviets are doing independently and in response, will make any appreciable difference. Unlike previous weapons innovations, however, SDI will probably involve the basing of offensive and defensive weapons in space—a move the superpowers have thus far avoided. And space-based weapons would certainly complicate, and might possibly rule out, any prospect of achieving deep reductions in offensive strategic weapons by negotiation. The militarization of space, which has been under way from the start of space exploration, would reach a new stage in which space will be used not only for the support of terrestrial military operations but as a new dimension of military conflict in its own right.

The efforts to build defenses have hardly been commensurate with the costs—or so experience has taught us. Defense expenditures, although difficult to compare in straightforward dollar-ruble terms, may be analyzed in terms of level of effort. This can be expressed, for the sake of convenience, in U.S. dollar terms. Soviet military procurement costs are calculated this way by both the CIA and the Defense Intelligence Agency, which "estimate production runs and then estimate the level of spending from what it would cost in dollars to produce a similar weapon in the West."[1] In the following comparisons, 1986 dollar equivalents will be used.

Like the U.S.S.R., the United States has long made significant investments in developing strategic weapons, but it has not supported the effort at a consistent level of spending. From modest beginnings in the early 1950s, U.S. expenditure on strategic defense (then almost entirely air defense) rose rapidly to $8 billion annually by 1957 but declined sharply thereafter. In 1965 U.S. spending on research and development (R&D) and procurement rose again, reaching $6 billion a year ($1 billion for air defense, $5 billion for missile defense) by 1971. After the ABM Treaty was signed in 1972, spending declined. With the announcement of SDI, spending once again increased, reaching almost $4 billion in 1987. The U.S. pattern has thus been erratic, reflecting decisions in various administrations to react to Soviet developments and perceived opportunities (Figures 1 and 2).

In contrast, the Soviets have shown a persistent interest in strategic defense, and their investments in both research and deployment have reflected this. In fact, Soviet expenditures on strategic defenses are roughly comparable to expenditures on offensive systems. Of their five military

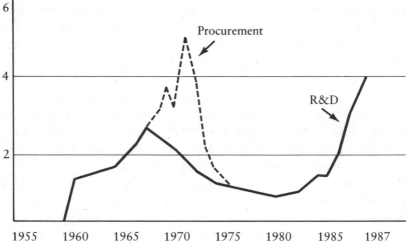

Fig. 1. U.S. Missile Defense: R&D and Procurement
(in $1986 billions)

SOURCE: From data presented in John E. Pike, *The SDI Budget and Program* (Washington, D.C.: Federation of American Scientists, February 1985).

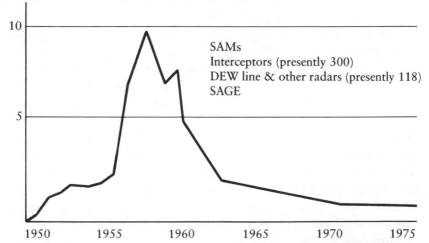

Fig. 2. U.S. Air Defense: R&D and Procurement
(in $1986 billions)

SOURCE: Based on data presented in R. L. Maust, G. W. Goodman, Jr., and C. E. McLain, *History of Strategic Defense* (Arlington, Va.: Systems Planning Corporation, September 1981).

commands, the Soviets devote the third ranking one—the Protivovoz-dushnaya Oborona Strany (PVO Strany, or national air defense forces)—exclusively to air and ballistic missile defense. The PVO Strany contains 635,000 military personnel, almost as large a complement as the entire U.S. Air Force. A comparable air-defense system (including the cost of developing new systems) would cost the United States about $24 billion annually. Given that the Soviets have maintained such an extensive air and missile defense for at least the past ten years, it is reasonable to assume that they have been spending roughly the same proportion of their gross national product (GNP) on these defenses over that ten-year period. Meanwhile, the United States has spent only token amounts of the defense budget on air defense (Figure 2) and little on BMD after the installation at Grand Forks, North Dakota, was decommissioned in 1975. On air defense alone, the U.S.S.R. appears to have spent five times more a year than the United States on all forms of strategic defense for at least the past ten years.

In addition to building and maintaining an elaborate nationwide air defense, the U.S.S.R. also maintains an ABM system designed to protect Moscow and also pursues research on other potential BMD technologies. It initiated a program to develop an ABM system in the late 1950s, shortly after the United States began developing an ICBM. In the 1960s systems believed to have an ABM capability were erected at Leningrad (Griffon), and Moscow (Galosh) (Figure 3). A system was also built at Tallinn, Estonia, but U.S. analysts had differing assessments of its purpose. CIA analysts, supported by their counterparts in the U.S. Navy and the State Department, maintained that the installation was for air defense alone. Analysts employed by the army, the air force, and the Defense Intelligence Agency contended that it was the beginning of an effort to upgrade air defenses against ballistic missiles. Although CIA Director John McCone endorsed his agency's interpretation and the second interpretation was duly recorded in the national intelligence estimate,[2] the system at Tallinn was not considered to have BMD capabilities at the time the ABM Treaty was negotiated in 1972. After the treaty was signed, the Moscow installation was the only one to remain intact; it was recently improved with the installation of new silo-based missiles and better radar. The Soviets have also pursued an active research program aimed at investigating directed-energy and other beam weapons. Such an effort in the United States would have cost some $500 billion.

Actual U.S. expenditures over the same period—since the end of World War II—have been considerably lower, perhaps on the order of

Fig. 3. Estimated Soviet Missile Defense Expenditures (in $ 1986 billions)

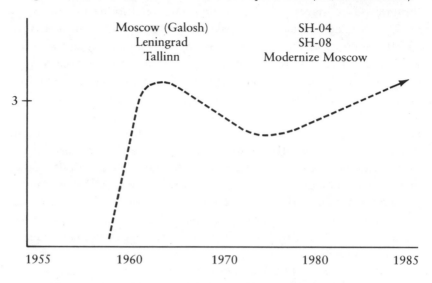

Fig. 4. Cost of Soviet Air Defense and U.S. Offensive Response
(in $1986 billions)

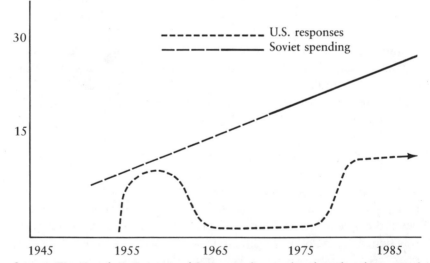

SOURCE (Figs. 3 and 4): Estimates of Soviet spending are based on data from several editions of *The Military Balance,* published by the International Institute for Strategic Studies (IISS); estimates of Soviet procurements presented in the FY1985 report of the undersecretary of defense for research and engineering (USDR&E); and in R. M. Gates and L. K. Gershwin, "Soviet Strategic Force Developments," testimony before a Joint Session of the Subcommittee on Strategic and Theater Nuclear Forces of the Senate Armed Services Committee and the Defense Subcommittee of the Senate Appropriations Committee, June 26, 1985. Estimates for the U.S. response are based on various reports to the Congress by the secretary of defense and USDR&E, particularly for FY1981 and FY1986.

$100 to $120 billion. This calculation does not account for improvements in offensive forces, many of which would probably have been made in any case. But certain key technologies—notably the MIRVed missile, the B-1 and Stealth bombers, and the various standoff missiles (such as the ALCM)—were developed primarily in order to assure a continued capability to penetrate Soviet defenses. These offensive innovations have cost roughly $100 billion (Figure 4).

As a consequence, the U.S.S.R. is not significantly better defended against a massive nuclear attack than it would have been had it not invested the equivalent of $500 billion on defenses. Similarly, the United States has not built any adequate defenses for its own territory—although, by spending about $200 billion, it has at least managed to keep abreast of Soviet efforts. The Soviets have thus been prevented from gaining any military advantage, even though they have made larger investments. The U.S. force structure has been modernized and reconfigured, and the total megatonnage in the U.S. arsenal has been reduced in order to assure penetration of Soviet air defenses. U.S. military authorities are thus confident that they can overcome Soviet defenses, even though the U.S.S.R. has outspent the United States by a ratio of five to one, accounting only for expenditures for defense on the one side and offensive modernization on the other (see Figure 4). As former secretary of defense Robert S. McNamara has noted, U.S. experts generally agree that "the billions of dollars the Soviets have spent on air defense in the past two decades have been largely wasted." He also has pointed out that a CIA analyst testified in 1985 that, "against a combined attack of penetrating bombers and cruise missiles, Soviet air defenses during the next ten years probably would not be capable of inflicting sufficient losses to prevent large-scale damage to the U.S.S.R."[3] At best, the Soviet ABM defenses provide limited protection to the area surrounding Moscow; otherwise, most of the Soviet Union is unprotected.

Moreover, until SDI, Soviet persistence in deploying and upgrading defenses kept the competition alive and also promoted U.S. interest in anti-satellite systems. Had the U.S.S.R. desisted, the United States would have spent even less on defenses and strategic modernization. Initially reluctant to develop ASATs, the United States preferred to keep its own increasingly important space satellites invulnerable rather than to encourage the Soviet Union to develop a capacity to interfere with them. But each time the Soviets tested an ASAT, impetus was added to corresponding U.S. programs. Recently, the two sides seem to have reversed positions. During the Reagan administration the United States attempted to develop strategic defenses and ASATs. Under Gorbachev, the Soviets appear interested in preventing further BMD deployments and in obtaining an agreement to ban the development of ASATs, although they, too, continue to invest heavily in defensive research. So far, the futility of earlier phases in this competition has not inhibited either superpower from pursuing the elusive goal of defending against a nuclear attack. A review of the lessons of this futile competition is thus especially relevant to any discussion of SDI.

THE UNITED STATES' DEFENSIVE EFFORT FROM THE 1950s TO 1975

The United States' first effort to deploy strategic defenses came in response to a quick series of unwelcome technical surprises. The Soviets detonated their first A-bomb in 1949, followed in 1955 with the explosion of the first full-size H-bomb. A year later the first long-range Soviet bombers appeared—the so-called Bears and Bisons. The United States responded with efforts to construct a continental air-defense system; shelter and evacuation options were also evaluated. By the late 1950s the United States was putting in place extensive deployments of surface-to-air missiles (SAMs) and interceptor aircraft, all backed up by several lines of warning radars. The U.S. Air Force (with fighter interceptors and ground-based radars), the U.S. Navy (with picket ships), and the U.S. Army (with anti-aircraft guns and missiles) were to coordinate their efforts with the help of the Canadian armed forces. To provide the necessary command, control, communications, and intelligence (C^3I) for these systems, the United States planned to install a complex system called SAGE, an acronym for "semi-automatic ground environment." The essential core of SAGE was to consist of a few—perhaps six—complexes housing large, powerful computers. Data from the various sensors would be analyzed by these computers and used to direct the interceptors—aircraft and SAMs. In 1957 the bilateral U.S.-Canadian North American Air (now Aerospace) Defense Command (NORAD) was created to pull all the pieces together.

By 1960 U.S. defense analysts had conceded that the task of defending the country against nuclear attack was impossible: the Soviets had successfully developed a first-generation ICBM, many hundreds of which, it was estimated, would soon be deployed. Eventually, perhaps, thousands would be deployed. With only a handful of highly vulnerable SAGE centers responsible for the defense of North America, it seemed likely that they would be among the first targets for a missile attack. Soviet aircraft would then essentially have unobstructed access to targets in the continental United States. The problem appeared so insoluble that U.S. policymakers in effect abandoned air defense at the very inception of the missile era. At its peak, in 1957, U.S. spending on air defenses reached more than $8 billion (again in 1986 dollars). It had dropped to a small fraction of that amount by 1962, and it has fallen further since. The United States now has no SAMs defending either civil or military targets. Only about three hundred interceptor aircraft are deployed, most of which are operated by the Air National Guard. Early warning of air attacks from the north continues to be provided by the Distant Early Warning (DEW) Line designed in the early 1950s, as well as by an old Alaskan radar network and the Pinetree Line—a chain of twenty-four long-range surveillance and height-finder radars stretched across southern Canada—but there are significant gaps in the coverage. Improved radar systems have been under development, but no new deployments are being made except for the replacement of older, mechanically steered radars by electronically steered phased-array radars (PARs) in Alaska, England, and Greenland. E-3A AWACs aircraft have been assigned to NORAD, but all dedicated SAMs have been phased out and no new interceptor aircraft have been assigned to NORAD.[4]

   Early in the Eisenhower administration, and long before *Sputnik* first orbited in 1957, many of the highest defense authorities became firmly convinced that the Soviets were engaged in a major effort to develop very long range ballistic missiles, including some capable of intercontinental flight. The U.S. response was to initiate two distinct programs; the first was to match and surpass the expected Soviet achievements, and the other was to find ways to directly counter the Soviet threat. In accord with the first objective, the United States initiated five "highest priority" programs on long-range missiles by 1955: Atlas, Titan, Thor, Jupiter, and Polaris. The second program involved a number of projects, too, including the army's Nike-Zeus; the air force's Ballistic Missile Early Warning System (BMEWS) and satellite early-warning systems. A little later, some other projects commenced under the aegis of the Advanced Research Projects Agency (ARPA), now called the Defense Advanced Projects Research Agency (DARPA).

   Nike-Zeus was a ground-based terminal missile defense system consisting of a large, powerful rocket armed with a megaton-class nuclear warhead, along with radars and computers capable of detecting and tracking the incoming warhead and steering the interceptor rocket to its target high in the atmosphere. The very large kill-radius of a nuclear weapon was believed necessary to make up for the imprecision of the early systems. At Bell Laboratories, however, where the transistor was invented in 1948, the new technology had been used to create a much improved high-speed data-processing system for tracking incoming warheads and guiding interception. Overall, the Nike-Zeus system was regarded as a logical successor to the earlier Nike-Ajax and Nike-Hercules anti-aircraft missiles, also developed by the same army agencies. By 1958 the program had advanced far enough for the army to propose near-term deployment of the Zeus ABM system. But the proposal was formally rejected in 1959 as technologically premature. It had already become evident, even in 1959, that decoys and other countermeasures would pose insurmountable challenges to the Nike-Zeus as it was then configured.

These difficulties were thoroughly exposed in a series of reviews, outside and inside government, in the executive and in Congress, over a two-year period.[5] A 1957 study by the Rand Corporation (a defense research organization which then had close ties to the air force) pointed out a number of problems with Nike-Zeus. For instance, the ABM radar might not be able to identify an incoming warhead if the warhead were accompanied by other objects—decoys, sections of the booster rocket, or "chaff" (small metal strips designed during World War II to confuse radar). The radar might be subject to blackout owing to natural phenomena such as the aurora borealis, or to deliberate interference by electronic jamming and nuclear detonations in the vicinity of the attack. An internal DOD study came to similar conclusions. It noted that penetration aids, including not only decoys but also multiple warheads with small radar cross sections, were a distinct practical threat to Nike-Zeus. The Rand study also estimated that the estimated kill-probability of a single Nike-Zeus interceptor would be so low that ten to twenty ABMs would have to be fired at each incoming warhead to achieve an acceptable rate of interception. One ABM battery, even if it comprised fifty to one hundred individual missiles, would therefore be able to defend only a small area, obtaining a high rate of reliability against only a few incoming missiles. An enormous number of ABM batteries would therefore be needed to provide a population defense. And even such a thick defensive array could not prevent detonations just beyond the range of the ABMs—then about twenty miles—which would still cause great damage.[6] As for the idea of using Nike-Zeus to defend ballistic missiles rather than civilians, the study argued that hardening, dispersal, and increased deployment, for example, could each yield similar results at a lower cost—a foreshadowing of the criticism voiced a decade later about limited ABM deployment. Added to these technical considerations was the policy adopted by the Eisenhower administration of relying on the threat of "massive retaliation" with nuclear weapons. The technical and policy drawbacks were too numerous: the administration was not eager to embark on an expensive program to deploy Nike-Zeus.

The army did not relent: Three of its senior generals, Chief of Staff Maxwell Taylor, R&D Director James Gavin, and the chief of the Redstone Arsenal, H. N. Toftoy, presented a proposal for Nike-Zeus deployment that would have cost $6 to $7 billion to be operational in 1961. A paper prepared for the Joint Chiefs of Staff echoed the criticisms in the Rand study. It concluded that the system was not sufficiently advanced to warrant such a level of expenditure and criticized its "Maginot line" thinking. Secretary of Defense Neil McElroy concurred: "There is a great deal we need to know," he observed, "before there can be any such program."[7]

Undaunted, the army continued to argue for deployment of Nike-Zeus. McElroy instituted a further review, appointing a special panel to advise him on an army proposal for a large-scale deployment to cost between $10 and $20 billion, well above the earlier estimate. The panel produced a split recommendation with two of the three members calling for a much smaller program, and the third (York) opposing any deployment as premature. When the Joint Chiefs of Staff and the President's Science Advisory Committee (PSAC) also recommended against deployment, Eisenhower rejected the proposal but authorized continuing R&D at the same high level as before—about $500 million per year—with special emphasis on efforts to cope with potential countermeasures.

Disappointed but still determined, the army took its case to Congress, where new hearings were held in 1959. The Army spokesmen tried a new tack with Congress, arguing that decisions to deploy other systems (such as the air force's Atlas and the navy's Polaris) had been made while they still faced the same uncertainties as Nike-Zeus. Although the chairman of the House Armed Services Committee, Carl Vinson, was sympathetic to the army's proposal for a crash program to deploy Nike-Zeus, the committee finally concluded, after hearing from other witnesses, that the system was vulnerable to countermeasures; a competing air force system, called "Wizard," was considered more promising. McElroy himself testified that according to the best scientific opinion, the system was not far enough along to warrant deployment. This view, he stressed, was a technical assessment, not one based on budgetary considerations. As a result, enthusiasm in Congress waned, and the project remained in an R&D mode.[8]

At about the same time that the Nike-Zeus program was initiated, two large-scale development programs for providing early-warning of missile attack were also undertaken. One was the Ballistic Missile Early Warning System (BMEWS), consisting of huge radars capable of detecting ballistic missile warheads or "reentry vehicles" (RVs) at distances on the order of a thousand miles. Three such systems were eventually deployed as far forward as possible: central Alaska; Thule, Greenland; and Fylingdales Moors, England. They are still in place, although efforts are under way to modernize them.

A satellite-based system named Midas was the other early-warning system undertaken as part of the United States' first response to Soviet ICBMs. Consisting of an infrared detector system mounted on a satellite in high orbit, it was capable of detecting rocket plumes produced by ballistic missiles during the launch phase. The original project was part of a large satellite-applications package contracted by the air force to the Lockheed Corporation in 1956, more than a year before *Sputnik I*. The project encountered a number of technical difficulties in the early phases of its development, but these were eventually overcome and the system has for years formed an essential part of U.S. early-warning capability. In recent times, it has been known as the DSP (for Defense Support Program) or SEWS (for Satellite Early Warning System).

In early 1958 ARPA initiated Project Defender, a collection of research and development projects relevant to ballistic missile defense but more advanced or speculative than those then in the Zeus program. A number of ideas first explored under this rubric eventually were widely applied in air and missile defenses as well as in other military and civil uses. The electronically steerable phased-array radars are an especially notable example.

In addition to these high-priority programs, all of which were solidly based in the technology of the time, more fanciful ideas were studied. Ballistic Missile Boost Intercept (BAMBI) and Space Detection and Tracking Systems (SPADATS) were two such programs. Both involved space-based anti-missile systems consisting of many small interceptors. In the case of BAMBI, the interceptors were all to be independently orbiting satellites; in that of SPADATS, they were to be mounted in clusters on a larger "battle station." Each of the small interceptors was to be rocket-powered and guided to its target by an infrared homing system. Each was designed to destroy an attacking missile during boost phase by colliding with it at an extremely high differential velocity. These early ideas were remarkably similar in overall design and purpose to those promoted in the early 1980s by the High Frontier group. During the late 1950s, however, these projects did not advance beyond the study-only phase and were eventually dropped from serious consideration. Beam weapons—both particle beams and lasers—for missile interception during the late, or terminal, phases of flight, were also being considered in the defense science community. They were extensively studied by ARPA and, under ARPA sponsorship, by the Jasons—a summer study-group of scientists active in DOD-supported defense research. As in the case of the space-based kinetic-energy kill systems, these programs never went beyond the study-only phase.

Development of the Nike-Zeus system continued throughout the early 1960s. There were improvements in rocket propulsion, warhead characteristics, and radar design; in addition, means were proposed for coping with at least the simpler kinds of decoys. By increasing the time between target acquisition and ABM launch, the defenders could take advantage of "atmospheric sorting," whereby lighter decoys would be slowed by friction in the upper atmosphere, enabling relatively easy discrimination of targets from decoys. Even so, the defense authorities continued to conclude that deployment remained technologically premature in view of the serious problems posed by more sophisticated counter-measures and "saturation" (attacks too large for the defense to counter). Other developments also clouded the picture. Although two 1958 nuclear-test explosions in the upper atmosphere near Johnston Island in the Pacific raised hopes among advocates (preliminary data indicated that radiation effects might destroy incoming RVs), subsequent analysis showed that RVs could still get through. The same tests also showed that high-altitude nuclear explosions created background noise that would affect radar reception. Although Nike-Zeus was designed to operate below the range at which these effects would be felt, offensive employment of atmospheric nuclear detonations might prevent defenders from extending the range of radar tracking.

Despite all the doubts, however, Secretary of Defense McNamara ordered the priority development of a BMD system designated "Nike X." This was to include a large, hardened, electronically steered radar and the high-performance Sprint interceptor armed with a small war-head and a tracking radar. The system was to be capable of tracking and discriminating among thousands of targets. Once again, studies showed that the objectives appeared unrealistic in view of the opportunities available to the offense; the cost, especially of a new large radar installa-tion, was also prohibitively high. The technologists therefore proposed construction of long-range PARs to serve many installations, coupled with an on-site missile defense radar. As in the Eisenhower years, deter-rence policy worked against defensive deployment. McNamara's com-mitment to deterrence by assured destruction, like the Eisenhower-Dulles adherence to massive retaliation, was inconsistent with Soviet deployment of ABMs. The Soviet Union was sure to follow suit if the United States deployed defenses first. For both technical and policy rea-sons, options other than territorial defense began to receive more se-rious consideration.[9]

The political climate surrounding ABM deployment changed in 1967. Lyndon Johnson was still seriously thinking of running for reelection in 1968, and he had become sensitive to the renewed political pressures in favor of deployment. Johnson feared that he would be faced with charges of an "ABM gap," analogous to the "missile gap" charge he and John F. Kennedy had hurled at the Republicans in 1960. At the Glassboro, New Jersey, summit in 1967, McNamara tried to defuse the issue by persuad-ing Soviet Premier Alexei Kosygin that both sides would be better off if they could mutually agree to refrain from developing and deploying ABMs. McNamara has recounted the exchange vividly:

> I said: "Mr. Prime Minister, you must understand that the proper U.S. response to your Soviet ABM system is an expansion of our offensive force. If we had the right number of offensive weapons to maintain a deterrent before you put your defenses in, then to maintain the same degree of deterrence, in the face of your defense, we must strengthen our offense. Deployment of a Soviet ABM system will lead to an escalation of the arms race. That's not good for either one of us."
>
> Kosygin was furious. The blood rushed to his face, he pounded on the table, and he said: "Defense is moral; offense is immoral!" That was essen-tially the end of the discussion. The Soviet Union was by no means ready at that time to discuss an agreement banning defensive systems.[10]

After that meeting U.S. policymakers from the president down agreed that the United States had to expand its offensive forces to offset pro-jected Soviet defensive deployments, which at the time seemed likely to be widespread. A decision was thus taken to proceed with development of MIRVs. The decision on deployment was deferred until further efforts had been made to persuade the Soviets to desist in their deployment of an ABM system. If such persuasion succeeded, the United States was prepared to scrap the MIRV program. First, it would no longer be justified, and second, the Soviets were bound to develop their own MIRVs; there was no need to increase the number of warheads on both sides.

But Johnson had also decided that the United States must deploy ABMs of its own. McNamara reluctantly set about implementing the decision. In an extraordinary speech in San Francisco in 1967, he first presented the arguments against a large-scale, thick defense of the nation as a whole against a determined Soviet missile attack, but then ended with a rationalization for proceeding with a "thin" deployment that would be capable of coping with attacks by a smaller power (i.e., China) or with an accidental Soviet launch of a single missile. The system would use components developed in the Nike X program: the short-range Sprint and the long-range Spartan interceptors, and both PARs and missile-site radars. Even while announcing plans for this light "Chinese-oriented ABM deployment," McNamara warned against efforts to expand it to a full-fledged deployment for defense against Soviet attack. The danger, he noted, was psychological as well as physical:

> There is a kind of mad momentum intrinsic to the development of all new nuclear weaponry. If a weapon system works—and works well—there is strong pressure from many directions to procure and deploy the weapon out of all proportion to the prudent level required.
>
> The danger in deploying this relatively light and reliable Chinese-oriented ABM system is going to be that pressures will develop to expand it into a heavy Soviet-oriented ABM system.
>
> We must resist that temptation firmly—not because we can for a moment afford to relax our vigilance against a possible Soviet first strike—but precisely because our greatest deterrent against such a strike is not a massive, costly, but highly penetrable ABM shield, but rather a fully credible offensive assured destruction capability.
>
> The so-called heavy ABM shield—at the present state of technology—would be no adequate shield at all against a Soviet attack, but rather a strong inducement for the Soviets to vastly increase their own offensive forces. That, as I have pointed out, would make it necessary for us to respond in turn—and so the arms race would rush hopelessly on to no sensible purpose on either side.[11]

As part of the process for carrying out the Johnson administration's plan, the U.S. Army began to hold public hearings in a number of cities, including Seattle, Chicago, and Boston, in preparation for deployments nearby. These plans and hearings produced a reaction that surprised the army leadership and other national authorities. Peace activists and critics of ABM deployment successfully organized campaigns against "bombs in the backyard" and forcefully brought their opposition to the attention of their legislative representatives. Some of the scientists who in the 1980s were to campaign against SDI cut their political teeth on the issue of ABM deployment. Their efforts succeeded in dramatizing the issue and provoking concern, especially in the communities where the facilities were to be located. Ad hoc coalitions of citizens for and against ABM deployment pressed their cases in public.[12]

Before the issue could be resolved, Richard Nixon became president and decided to continue with the "thin" deployment authorized by Johnson as the Sentinel system. Political opposition remained strong, however, because of local issues, continuing doubts about technical feasibility, and more general strategic concerns, including the role ABM deployment played in the overall arms race. Largely in response to this opposition, Nixon and his advisors decided to change the program objectives from defending the country as a whole against a minor missile attack to defending only U.S. retaliatory forces, particularly ICBMs, against a major missile attack. The equipment for doing so remained basically the same but the location and purpose became radically different; the project was renamed "Safeguard." The new objectives were to defend land-based retaliatory forces against a Soviet threat while preserving a "growth option" to provide an area defense against a smaller "nth country" threat. Twelve Safeguard sites were planned, but construction was initiated at only two, Malmstrom, Montana, and Grand Forks, North Dakota.

Rather than placating the opposition, this apparently opportunistic behavior on the part of the administration only encouraged it. Extensive congressional hearings on Safeguard were held in 1969 and 1970, and expert members of the defense establishment, as well as representatives of public-interest groups, testified against deployment (York among them). A number of important Republican senators—Cooper (Kentucky), Brooke (Massachusetts), and Case (New Jersey)—assumed leading roles in opposing the administration's plan. When it came to a final vote to deploy the first units of ABMs, the Senate tied 50 to 50; the vote of Vice-President Spiro T. Agnew broke the tie. The proponents of the ABM had won the battle, but ABM opponents were about to win the war: with such a razor-thin margin of support, so controversial a program simply could not proceed further along the lines its promoters had intended.

While the ABM deployment program was going through this rocky period, consideration was being given to the proposal of a treaty banning or limiting ABMs as part of an overall scheme to limit strategic weapons. The idea of limiting defensive systems arose in defense circles early in the Johnson administration and was broached to the Soviets at the Glassboro summit in 1967. The Soviet rejection of the proposal was followed by the dispatch of Soviet troops to stifle political change in Czechoslovakia in 1968, preventing further high-level exploration of the issue at the time. But Nixon revived the idea in 1969, at least partly because of the widespread opposition to ABM deployment that had developed independently of any consideration of a bilateral treaty.

The revival of interest in a treaty banning ABMs provoked a heated debate. Those who favored a ban on the weapons made several contentions: ABMs, as then conceived, would not work; they would be destabilizing; and they would cost too much. Those in favor of ABMs argued that they would work well enough to make them worthwhile; that they would, on the contrary, be stabilizing, especially in a crisis (by removing any temptation to launch a surprise attack); and that the United States must not put "the budget ahead of survival."

Perhaps the most important argument about technical feasibility involved the problem of countermeasures. Many specialists agreed that the effort to build defenses would involve an endless contest in which the offense would always be one jump ahead. In addition, no defense system could even be tested as a whole and in a realistic manner. This was a decisive fact for many experts. Individual components of the system could be tested against U.S. offensive devices on a one-on-one basis, but such procedures could never provide the information necessary for judging the utility of an ABM system against a massive surprise attack. In addition, other crucial questions, such as the ability of ABM radars to cope with the blinding effects even of defensive explosions, were never satisfactorily resolved. Those who favored proceeding with ABM acknowledged the seriousness of at least some of these problems but argued that the only way to resolve them was to mount a major program in the field, including at least enough deployment to provide some "real world" experience.

The arguments regarding destabilization took two quite different forms. The first one, focusing on the stability of the arms race, was the simplest. If one side builds a defense, it was said, the other will respond by expanding its offense, given that saturation and exhaustion of the defenses are the ultimate offensive countermeasures. This argument was supported by the fact that the United States was even then considering the deployment of MIRVed warheads as the best answer to the initial Soviet ABM deployment. Proponents of ABM countered that the Soviets could not readily respond by expanding their force, so long as ABM could be made cheaply enough, or, more technically, "cost-effective at the margin." The second argument involved the behavior of leadership in crises. Opponents of ABM deployment placed special emphasis on the easy and confident calculability of the existing situation, in which any attacker could be assured that he was engaging in a suicidal act. They argued that the deployment of ABMs would introduce the kind of uncertainties—and perhaps also a false confidence—that could lead to rash acts. Those favoring ABM emphasized that "active defenses" could help to assure the survival of military authorities and retaliatory forces and would thus reinforce deterrence. No clear consensus emerged on the strategic issues. Both sides could cite many acknowledged experts on strategy who supported their position.

The technical issues produced no such ambiguity: a clear majority of experts concluded that ABM as then conceived would not work in any useful sense of the word. In the end, doubts about the technical merits of the system carried the day. A formal limitation on ABM deployment was initiated.

The Soviets were eventually persuaded that a ban on ABMs could provide a good place to begin negotiations on controlling strategic weapons as a whole. Discussions to that end were started in late 1969, the first year of the Nixon administration, and came to fruition in 1972. The resulting treaty limited ABM deployment to two sites in each country, each site in turn being limited to one hundred ABM missiles. It was further agreed that only one such site could be near the national capital, with the other located solely for protecting retaliatory forces, more than 1300 km from the national capital. (This agreement was later modified to permit a hundred launchers, each carrying a single warhead, at one site only, at either location, in each country.)

The upshot of all these twists and turns for the United States was the brief deployment of ABMs at a Minuteman missile base at Grand Forks, North Dakota. The Grand Forks system was declared to have achieved "initial operational capability" (IOC) in March 1975 but was terminated by Congress later that year. Since then, the United States has not deployed ABMs anywhere, but the Defense Department continues to support R&D designed to explore the possibilities further.

Until the birth of SDI, U.S. research was mainly focused on the improvement of "site defense" for protecting Minuteman missiles or other high-value targets more effectively and at lower cost. ARPA and the Army Ballistic Missile Advanced Technology Program also studied a broad range of technologies relevant to BMD. In several areas, these efforts led directly to programs now being further developed under SDI. These included

> the High-Acceleration Boost Experiment (HIBEX) program that developed the basis for a more advanced interceptor now being considered, the Designating Optical Tracker (DOT) program that provided the basis for much of exo-atmospheric Long Wave Length Infrared (LWIR) sensing and discrimination knowledge, the Homing Overlay Experiment (HOE) that is developing the non-nuclear-kill-intercept technology, various directed-energy studies that evaluated particle-beam and high-energy laser BMD system concepts, and numerous other missile, discrimination, radar, optics, and data-processing technology programs related to U.S. BMD concepts.

By 1983, when President Reagan announced SDI, these programs had produced an "on the shelf" site-defense technology; its radars and interceptors were small enough to be deployed in a mobile-basing mode along with the new MX launchers and were capable of intercepting incoming warheads even at very low altitudes.[13] If any of the mobile-basing schemes proposed for MX had been adopted under Carter or in the early years of the Reagan administration, deployment of a site defense (as allowed by the ABM Treaty) would most probably have been considered. Whether it would have been deployed, in view of the protection already afforded by the mobility of the MX, is more doubtful.

Spending on the ABM program followed a course that might be expected, given such a turbulent situation. Starting from scratch in 1956, the Zeus R&D program reached a spending rate (in 1986 dollars) of almost $2 billion in 1960. In 1965 R&D spending topped out at $3 billion, but total spending continued to climb on up to about $5 billion in 1970, with procurement of equipment for the Grand Forks deployment then taking the lion's share. From then on, spending dropped sharply, falling back to only about $1 billion per year in the period following the termination of the deployment in 1975.

THE SOVIET EFFORT
IN DEFENSIVE SYSTEMS

Western understanding of Soviet intentions is often beset by uncertainties, and the case of strategic defense is no exception. Are the Soviets pursuing some long-term goal of achieving an effective defense in order to break out of the ABM Treaty? Or are they simply pursuing allowable defensive efforts to limit damage from a nuclear attack and doing research so as not to be put at a disadvantage if the United States should achieve some technological breakthroughs? Are they content to have SAMs functioning as anti-aircraft weapons, or are they secretly attempting to render them effective against ICBMs as well? Are they using the loopholes of the treaty that allow development of anti-tactical weapons and ASATs as efforts to develop technologies that will permit broader ballistic missile defense than is foreseen in the treaty? All that can be established beyond dispute is that for forty years the Soviets have pursued a large and comprehensive program in passive and active defenses, the total size of which has grown steadily, despite the ABM Treaty, and which has been supported by formidable and broadly based research efforts. So far as can be ascertained, however, the Soviet Union has not exceeded the bounds on testing and development set by the ABM Treaty. And there is good reason to believe that because it decided to agree to a limitation on ABMs, the Soviet civil and military leadership has adopted a strategy of retaliatory deterrence essentially the same as that previously adopted by the United States.

The Soviet program for BMD research was originally established by Joseph Stalin in the immediate aftermath of World War II. Stalin is thought to have been influenced by several considerations: the damage inflicted on the Soviet Union by the Luftwaffe, Britain's vulnerability to the German V-1 and V-2 weapons, and the knowledge that Soviet technologists, with the help of captured German rocket scientists and engineers, were working on the development of ICBMs.[14] At the Twenty-second Congress of the Communist party of the Soviet Union, in October 1961, Defense Minister Rodion Malinovsky announced that "the problem of destroying enemy missiles in flight has been successfully resolved," and in July 1962 Premier Nikita Khrushchev boasted that Soviet missile forces were so accurate that they could "hit a fly in space."[15]

Although these claims were wildly inflated, the Soviets have invested heavily not only in research on strategic defense but also on actual deployments—mainly, however, for defense against bomber attack rather than ballistic missiles. The Soviets apparently believe that although air defense can be "damage-limiting," a territorial defense against ICBMs is neither feasible nor affordable.

The Soviets maintain the world's most extensive missile early-warning system. It includes a satellite network for launch detection, over-the-horizon radars, and a series of large phased-array (capable of being electronically steered) radars (LPARs) on the periphery of the country (and inland, at Krasnoyarsk, in apparent violation of Article V1-b of the ABM Treaty, which requires that each party locate such radars only "along the periphery of its national territory and oriented outward"). The satellite system is capable of providing about thirty minutes warning of any U.S. ICBM launch and of determining the general area of its origin. The two over-the-horizon radars could provide the same time warning, but with less precision and certainty than that provided by the satellite network. In addition, the Soviets maintain eleven large "Henhouse" detection and tracking radars at six locations on the periphery. These can distinguish the size of an attack, confirm the warning from satellites and over-the-horizon radars, and provide target tracking in support of deployed ABMs. The Soviets are currently constructing six new LPARs, including the controversial Krasnoyarsk installation in central Siberia. According to the DOD, these systems "duplicate or supplement" the coverage of the "Henhouse" network, "but with greatly enhanced capability." [16]

An ABM system has been deployed around Moscow, as allowed under the ABM Treaty, and has been undergoing improvements since 1980. The original single-layer system included sixty-four reloadable aboveground launchers at four complexes, collectively called the Galosh system. Each complex was served by six mechanically steered "Try Add" guidance and engagement radars and all were assisted by the "Doghouse" and "Cathouse" target-tracking radars south of Moscow, which are believed to provide battle management for the defense of Moscow. The system is now being enlarged to accommodate one hundred launchers, the maximum allowable under the ABM Treaty. When completed, it will provide two layers of defense, one composed of silo-based, long-range, modernized Galosh interceptors (designated by the United States as SH-04 or ABM X-3) designed to engage targets outside the atmosphere; the other using silo-based, high-acceleration Gazelle interceptors (or SH-08) to engage targets within the atmosphere. Thus, the Soviet system will resemble the United States' combination of Spartan and Sprint missiles. It will also have associated engagement and guidance radars and a new large radar at Pushkino designed to control ABM engagements. The silo-based Gazelle launchers may be reloadable, and the system may have become fully operational in 1987. [17] Because of the range of the Galosh, the system provides some degree of regional protection. The "footprint" of the missiles extends over several thousand square miles of Soviet territory, an area that includes three hundred ICBMs. [18]

The new LPARs could supplement older radars by providing early-warning and pointing data for the new Moscow ABM system. All the new LPARS will become operational in the late 1980s and will make up a comprehensive network. The CIA estimates that this system will provide the Soviets with "a much-improved capability for ballistic missile early-warning, attack assessment, and targeting" and will provide battle-management support for a widespread ABM system.[19] In August 1986 two additional LPARs were discovered to be under construction in the western U.S.S.R. The United States has complained that the radar under construction at Krasnoyarsk is in violation of the ABM Treaty. This facility may or may not be intended to serve for eventual countrywide battle management in an ABM system. The Krasnoyarsk radar is said by the DOD to close a gap in a combined radar early-warning and tracking network: "Together, this radar and the five others like it form an arc of coverage from the Kola Peninsula in the northwest, around Siberia, to the Caucasus in the southwest." Its orientation, the DOD contends, "indicates it is for ballistic missile detection and tracking"—not space-object tracking as claimed by the Soviets.[20] Indeed, in view of the radar's capacities and orientation, it is most unlikely that it was intended for space tracking. Conceivably, the installation is intended to fill the gap in the early-warning system that could not easily be filled by the construction of peripheral radars, perhaps owing to soil conditions and the remoteness of the sites. Or, as Michael MccGwire has speculated, the radar might have been placed at Krasnoyarsk to detect an attack from Trident submarines stationed in the Bering Sea or the Gulf of Alaska—a threat not anticipated when the Soviets agreed to the limitation on placement of LPARS in the ABM Treaty—and to place the installation within a defensible perimeter in the event of an invasion through Xinjiang in northwest China.[21]

Soviet air defense is said by the Pentagon to have "excellent" capabilities against aircraft flying at medium and high altitudes, but only "marginal" capabilities against low-flying aircraft. These facilities are undergoing a major overhaul, which will result in the fielding of an integrated system more capable at low altitudes. This system will include the use of the Il-76 Mainstay airborne warning and control system (AWACS), similar to that developed by the United States, in addition to more than one hundred MiG 31/Foxhound interceptors equipped with look-down shoot-down radar and multiple-target engagement capability air-to-air missiles.[22]

The Soviets have put a very substantial effort into the development of ground-based air defenses and fighter interceptors: thirteen different surface-to-air missiles (SAMs) have been developed, each designed to counter a particular type of threat. These SAMs include the latest deployed system, the SA-10, and another under development, the SA-X-12, which may have a capability against tactical ballistic missiles such as the U.S. Lance and Pershing I and II as well as aircraft.[23] Currently, the Soviets deploy more than 9,000 SAM launchers at 2,100 sites for strategic defense, in addition to 4,600 launchers for tactical SAMs. More than 1,200 fighter interceptors are dedicated to strategic defense, and an additional 2,800 other interceptors are also available. A quarter of the interceptors are MiG-25/Foxbat A/E high-speed interceptors for high-altitude defense. The rest consist of older aircraft (one-third of the force) and two new fighter interceptors, the Su-27 Flanker and the MiG-29 Fulcrum, both of which are designed to be highly maneuverable in air-to-air combat and are equipped with two new air-to-air missiles, one long range, the other short range.[24]

To locate and target incoming attacks, the Soviet Union has deployed more than 10,000 radars of various types at about 1,200 sites, providing virtually complete coverage at medium-to-high altitudes over the country and, in some areas, beyond its borders for hundreds of kilometers. The over-the-horizon radars provide warning of the approach of aircraft flying at high altitude. Coverage of low-flying aircraft is concentrated in the western regions and in high-priority areas elsewhere. Since 1983 two new types of air-surveillance radars have begun to be deployed. These assist in providing early warning of cruise missile and bomber attacks and in enhancing air defense electronic warfare capabilities.[25] The new Soviet "Pawn Shop" missile guidance radar and "Flat Twin" tracking radar are modular and could be assembled, once mass-produced, at a number of sites within a matter of months. The Reagan administration has complained that these radars are a "potential violation" of the treaty because they fall in the category of mobile ABM systems and components that are specifically banned.[26] The usual interpretation of the treaty does not preclude systems of this type.

Of the five SAM systems now operational (designated by the United States as SA-1, -2, -3, -5, -10) and SA-X-12, only the SA-10 seems capable of defending against targets with radar cross sections as small as that of a standard ("nonstealthy") cruise missile. Sixty sites are now operational, and work is under way on at least another thirty. More than half these sites are near Moscow, suggesting that the Soviets have put a high priority on terminal defense of wartime command-and-control systems, as well as of military and key industrial complexes. A mobile version of the SA-10 is being developed to support theater forces, but it could also enhance the survivability of SAMs used in the Soviet Union for strategic defense.[27]

The SAMs and interceptor aircraft are further enhanced by anti-aircraft artillery (AAA), more than 11,500 pieces of which are deployed with units at all levels of readiness and in all regions. At battalion and company levels and with nondivisional units, as many as 25,000 shoulder-fired SAMs are stocked. More than 8,100 SAMs and AAA pieces—the largest concentration—are found opposite NATO; more than 4,200 are near the Sino-Soviet border and in other eastern areas of the U.S.S.R.[28]

The Soviets have also pursued a variety of measures of passive defense, aiming to protect missiles as well as the party and government leadership, major economic assets, and the general population. Extensive planning has been done for the transition of the economy to a wartime posture. A program has been under way for thirty years to harden command posts and establish survivable communications for military commanders and civilian managers. Commanders and managers at all levels are provided hardened alternate command posts well away from urban centers. This system, comprising 1,500 hardened facilities with special communications, is patterned after similar capabilities provided the armed forces. More than 175,000 key personnel are thought to be provided such protection, in addition to the many deep bunkers and blast shelters in Soviet cities. Vital materials have been stockpiled, many in hardened underground structures. Blast shelters have been built for workforces, and contingency plans have been drawn up for the relocation of factories and equipment.[29] ICBM silos, launch facilities, and command-and-control centers have been sufficiently hardened to resist destruction by some U.S. weapons. Means of communication have been made more elaborate, so as to provide redundancy, and have also been hardened to resist the effects of nuclear attack. New, mobile ICBMs, including the road-mobile SS-25 and the rail-mobile SS-24, have also been developed. These new missiles will complicate the attacker's targeting task, especially because these missiles can be hidden in tunnels or in special hardened and camouflaged sites. The Soviets have also developed long-range nuclear-armed submarines comparable to the U.S. Poseidon, which also help to assure the survival of its retaliatory forces in the event of a preemptive attack.

In addition, three Soviet SAMs—the SA-5, SA-10, and SA-X-12—may already have some ABM capability. The SA-5 has been tested in conjunction with ballistic missile flights but is considered to have, at most, a marginal BMD capability. The SA-10 and SA-X-12, according to the DOD, may have some ability to intercept certain types of U.S. ballistic missiles.[30] But all these missiles are likely to be effective only against older-generation SLBM warheads rather than against newer ICBM warheads; the former are generally slower and offer larger radar cross sections. The SA-X-12 might be able to engage U.S. tactical missiles, such as the Lance and Pershing I and II; it has reportedly been tested successfully against a Soviet intermediate-range Scaleboard missile. The SA-X-12 is mobile and could be stored and concealed.

The Soviet high-energy laser research program dates from the 1960s and is said to be much larger than that of the United States. The Defense Department estimated in 1979 that Soviet spending on high-energy lasers was five times that of the United States. The U.S.S.R. has built more than a half-dozen major R&D facilities and test ranges and employs more than ten thousand scientists and engineers in laser development, notably at Sary Shagan. These specialists, who are quite capable, have worked on chemical, gas-dynamic, and electric-discharge lasers; they are pursuing necessary support technologies for laser weapons, such as efficient power sources; and they have the ability to produce high-quality optical components. According to the DOD, the Soviets have already deployed ground-based lasers that could be used to interfere with U.S. satellites and are presently likely to have lasers capable of serving as ASATs.[31]

Soviet laser research is thought to be aimed at developing three types of air-defense weapons: for defense of high-value strategic targets in the U.S.S.R., for point defense of ships at sea, and for air defense of theater forces. The DOD claims that the laser intended for strategic defense is already in the prototype stage and could be deployed and operational by the late 1980s, most likely in conjunction with SAMs in a point-defense role. Also under development is an airborne laser that could have such missions as anti-satellite operations, protection of airborne assets, and cruise-missile defense. Soviet researchers are also working on space-based kinetic-energy weapons, ground- and space-based lasers, and particle-beam and radio-frequency weapons. They are reported to believe that such systems hold promise for BMD and for improved conventional defense.[32]

Some reports indicate that Soviet ground-based lasers are already available for military use. The ground-based lasers at Sary Shagan are reported to have potential ASAT capabilities against low-flying U.S. satellites. A U.S. press report has claimed that Soviet ground-based micro-waves at a facility in a mountainous area at Dushanbe, in the Tadzhik Republic (where a laser facility is reported to have been built), disabled U.S. photoreconnaissance satellites in low polar orbit on more than one occasion in 1986. The U.S. Air Force Space Command has denied such attacks, but a French commercial satellite photography service has circulated photos of a well-developed facility at the Dushanbe site.[33] The German newspaper *Bild Zeitung* quoted top-secret U.S. and NATO reports of Soviet lasers disabling optics and electronics on U.S. satellites. Others speculate that the Soviets already have the technological capability to conduct electronic warfare against space systems. In view of the Soviets' recent reported work on microwave weapons that generate single pulses with peak powers exceeding one gigawatt and repetitive pulses of more than 100 megawatts, it is also speculated that the Soviets could test a ground-based microwave weapon by the 1990s capable of damaging satellites. (Jamming reconnaissance satellites almost certainly would violate ABM Treaty prohibitions on interfering with "national technical means" of verification. The United States is working on improving the resistance to jamming of satellites by incorporating laser crosslinks, improving satellite autonomy, and developing extremely high frequency [EHF] spread-spectrum and laser heterodyne communications systems.) Senior DOD intelligence officials say the Soviets now possess a "limited operational capability" to blind some U.S. satellites. Others contend that Soviet ground-based DEWs could damage some types of penetration aids and thus indirectly serve as BMD weapons.

Nevertheless, the present Soviet missile-defense capability, even if it were made the basis of a countrywide defense, could not prevent enormous damage from a U.S. nuclear attack, or even from an attack by an adversary with a smaller arsenal. Coupled with Soviet offensive capabilities, however, it can be said to increase uncertainty in the minds of a potential attacker. Soviet offensive forces alone account for considerable uncertainty; the defensive systems add to it. (This is, of course, one of the rationales offered by SDI proponents for building a U.S. defense.) Defense also helps to enhance the prospect that Warsaw Pact forces would prevail in a conventional conflict in Europe. U.S. countermeasures—especially air-breathing systems equipped with "stealth" technology—could defeat the Soviet defenses, but as defenses cause higher rates of attrition, they compel dedication of more weapons, thus tending to nullify the strategic doctrine of "flexible response." Targeting flexibility is bound to be somewhat constrained by the addition of defensive systems, and damage expectations become less predictable.[34]

WHY THE DIFFERENT APPROACHES?

Why have the superpowers pursued such contrasting strategic defense policies? One reason is that the Soviets have to take account of the United States' heavy-bomber threat, whereas until recently the corresponding threat from the U.S.S.R. was much less fearsome. The Soviets have therefore had a greater incentive to develop and deploy air defenses; compared to missile defenses, they are technologically more promising. But these considerations alone cannot account for the broad, persistent, and costly Soviet effort to develop passive and active defenses. Sayre Stevens, a former CIA intelligence analyst, has suggested that the approaches of the two sides reflect differing views of what is strategically valuable.[35] The U.S. authorities have been reluctant to deploy defenses that they knew would have only marginal utility. Their Soviet counterparts seem to operate on the assumption that any degradation of an attack has some value. Their conviction in this regard may well be fed by memories of World War II, when the armed forces and the populace suffered gravely because of the total absence of air defenses. (If so, they may be taking too little account of the differences between nuclear and conventional weapons, and between World War II and contemporary delivery systems.) The Moscow ABM defense cannot protect against a massive U.S. attack, but it might protect the capital against an accidental launch, and it might also offer some protection against a "decapitating" attack (one aimed at the national-command authority) or a light attack. The Soviets apparently also count on making continual improvements. By constantly upgrading air defenses and ABMs and providing a more and more effective integrated system for detecting and tracking an attack, they may be hoping to lay the foundations for a much more effective system.

Another factor that may help to account for Soviet behavior is strategic doctrine. Michael MccGwire has argued that until the late 1960s Soviet military planners operated on the belief that if war with the West came, even in the form of conflict in Europe or some other theater, the war would become nuclear and would entail nuclear attacks on Soviet territory.[36] This belief was reinforced by the U.S. doctrine of massive retaliation espoused by the Eisenhower administration and the subsequent NATO doctrine of "flexible response." Accordingly, the Soviets sought to achieve a capacity to fight and win a nuclear war in order to deter a Western attack. Their most critical concern was to minimize the damage a nuclear attack might cause. For this purpose, the Soviets sought both offensive and defensive means. They set out to build an ICBM force capable of launching an effective preemptive strike against U.S. missiles and submarine and bomber bases. To complement the offense, they also set out to pursue both active and passive defenses. Thus, the relatively high priority accorded to strategic defense was a function of the overall conviction that any war with the West would necessarily entail nuclear destruction on Soviet territory. As Stevens points out, "the Soviet approach to the reduction of damage is to use not only the counterforce capability of offensive weapon systems, but [also] air defenses, civil and passive defenses, and ballistic missile defenses. The role of these strategic elements would be to limit the damage to the Soviet Union after a preemptive strike."[37] The Soviets, in other words, were under no illusion that defenses could be made superior to offenses; they believed, however, that defenses would have some value against a degraded U.S. retaliatory strike.

In 1967 and 1968, according to MccGwire's analysis, this general strategic assumption began to undergo a profound change. The Soviet authorities seem to have become persuaded that the "correlation of forces" had changed sufficiently owing to a combination of factors—military, political, and economic. As a result, the thinking went, it was no longer inevitable that conflict with the West would necessarily result in a nuclear attack on Soviet territory. They also took account of the change in Western strategic doctrine from massive retaliation to flexible response. A conflict, they reasoned, might be confined to a particular theater, such as central Europe. It was presumably on the basis of this change in Soviet strategic thinking, as well as out of a recognition that the West might exploit its technological superiority, that the Soviets decided it would be in their interest to negotiate limits on defensive and offensive weapons. They were probably also becoming more doubtful about the utility of their defenses, in view of the West's countermeasures. Moreover, both the political and military authorities may have been concerned with shifting defense budget allocations away from strategic forces in favor of building up capabilities for force projection in the Third World.[38]

U.S. policy has not precluded the use of nuclear weapons in a preemptive attack or a first strike. But, except for a brief flurry of interest in building shelters and dispersing industry and population, the prevailing view has been that there can be no effective civil defense against a massive nuclear attack. The United States' effort has been to maximize the survivability of a credible retaliatory force by adopting techniques of passive defense—redundancy, silo-hardening, mobility, and dispersion.

The change of doctrine, reflected in Soviet behavior since the late 1960s, may suggest at least a degree of convergence of interests between the superpowers. In itself, this convergence might seem to promote the possibility of agreement on the limitation of defensive systems. Unfortunately, it has been undercut by another competition—the competition by both sides in the militarization of space.

THE MILITARIZATION OF SPACE

Since the launching of the first earth satellites, both superpowers have made determined efforts to make military use of space, despite statements on both sides expressing the hope that space could remain a sanctuary for peaceful activities. In 1958 Eisenhower wrote two letters to Premier Nikolay Bulganin proposing cessation of all military activities in space, including the testing of long-range missiles, conditioned on the establishment of an international system of observation or verification. The Soviet leader rejected the overtures, interpreting them as an effort by the United States to thwart an activity in which, thanks to the success of *Sputnik*, the Soviets had demonstrated an advantage. Eisenhower may not have foreseen all the military possibilities opened by the development of rocket boosters, but he was even more concerned about the burden on the U.S. taxpayer of the effort to contain the expansiveness of the Soviet Union. To keep a lid on the defense budget, he was interested in constraining the arms race wherever possible. For their part, the successful launching of *Sputnik I* may have led the Soviets to see space as a venue in which they could quickly and economically compensate for the advantages the United States enjoyed in other areas of military technology, including its stockpile of nuclear weapons.

Even under Eisenhower, however, the United States began to exploit space for military purposes, to an extent over the years hardly less determined than that of the U.S.S.R. Together, both states have put more than two thousand military payloads into orbit since the early 1960s—two-thirds of the total number of satellites launched into space.[39] The U.S. military budget for space in FY1984 was $10.5 billion, half the total budget for all space activities. The Soviet budget is probably at least as large, taking account of the difficulty of comparing costs in the two systems.

As a result, both countries have become increasingly dependent on space satellites for military purposes. But thus far, these purposes have been in the nature of support for terrestrial activities: intelligence gathering, communication, electronic intelligence, the monitoring of military testing, and ocean reconnaissance for tracking surface shipping. Increasingly, space is also being used for navigation, for early warning of nuclear attack, for detection of nuclear explosions, for the collection of meteorological data (useful for directing photographic satellites away from cloud cover, as well as for military operations), and for obtaining geodetic data (useful for improving missile accuracy) and information about shifting magnetic fields.

So far, neither side has deployed weapons in space, but both sides have tested ASAT weapons. It is with respect to ASATs that the militarization of space threatens to become uncontrollable. The overlap of ASAT and BMD systems only compounds the problem.

THE UNITED STATES'
DEVELOPMENT OF ASATS

Early in the race to exploit outer space, the United States took the initiative in developing ASATs. In the 1950s both the navy and the air force prepared the ground by deploying radar systems for space surveillance. In 1964 the United States became the first nation to test ASATs, relatively primitive devices using Nike-Zeus ABMs and air force Thor IRBMs. Two ground-based special-purpose ASAT systems were deployed in the Pacific in the 1960s, one of which remained operational until 1975. When the expected threat—a Soviet orbital bombardment system—did not materialize, this particular deployment was abandoned. Even under Eisenhower, U.S. studies concluded that the earth was "the best weapons carrier"; the Soviets apparently came to the same conclusion. They began to test an ASAT in 1968, stopped three years later, then resumed testing in 1976, which triggered renewed U.S. interest. President Carter attempted to negotiate a treaty designed to stop further ASAT developments. Talks were held in 1978, but the Soviets were not particularly interested. Early in the 1980s the Soviets offered to negotiate a ban on the testing of space weapons, but by then the Reagan administration was becoming committed to the development of a U.S. ASAT.

The launching of *Sputnik* in 1957 galvanized the U.S. space program, bringing projects to fruition. Reconnaissance satellites had been under study from early in the 1950s and had already benefited from the adoption of the recommendation of the Strategic Missile Evaluation Committee chaired by John von Neumann in the spring of 1954, which urged that the United States give "highest priority" to the development of ICBMs. Given that a rocket capable of sending a warhead an intercontinental distance can also, in general, launch a satellite of approximately the same weight, this decision meant that a sufficient launch capacity would also be available for satellites. The official, unclassified U.S. space program, however, gave initial priority to a scientific satellite, developed in 1955 under Project Vanguard. After *Sputnik*, however, political pressure led the Eisenhower administration to establish ARPA and then to transfer responsibility for military satellites to the services and the CIA, whose Project Corona reportedly resulted in the launching of satellites that took film and ejected the cannisters for air recovery.

Even before *Sputnik*, however, the air force had initiated a highly classified program of its own, called the Satellite and Missile Observation System (SAMOS), and also cooperated with the CIA's Corona program, which reportedly used air force Project Discoverer satellites. The downing of U-2 pilot Gary Powers in 1960 stimulated further increases in funding for Project SAMOS.

In general, *Sputnik* and the U-2 incident stimulated a new commitment to the use of space for military purposes. According to widely published reports, an organization called the National Reconnaissance Office was created in 1960. Air Force officers in particular urged that military activities in space be given high priority. Thus Gen. Bernard Schriever called on the United States to achieve "space superiority," and others argued that air and space were becoming indivisible fields of military operation. The air force made a special claim to the "space mission," though both the army and the navy put their own cases forward for control of satellites.

In the Eisenhower administration, the case for observational satellites was considered compelling. Eisenhower himself believed that because the Soviet Union was a closed society, certainly in comparison with the United States, reconnaissance satellites were crucial. Despite Soviet success with *Sputnik*, it was not clear at the outset that the Soviets would agree to satellite overflights. For this reason, such overflights were cloaked in secrecy. Because the United States was even more dependent than the Soviets on satellite reconnaissance, Eisenhower was reluctant to approve the development of ASATs, inasmuch as this would give the Soviets an incentive to follow suit. He did permit exploratory development of the Satellite interceptor (SAINT) system because it was presumably designed for the interception (and inspection) of satellites rather than for their destruction.

It was well recognized, however, that U.S. satellites could not be easily protected by physical means. The United States therefore sought a politico-legal solution to their vulnerability by proposing international agreements to sanction or legitimate overflights by reconnaissance satellites. It proposed that space be used for peaceful activities, on the tacit understanding that reconnaissance satellites could be included because they were not weapons. At first the Soviets refused to agree to the proposals, but their view changed as they acquired their own reconnaissance satellites. As early as May 1960, Khrushchev expressed the view at an international meeting with other heads of state that photographic reconnaissance by satellites was permissible, even though overflights by aircraft were violations of sovereignty. At the same time, however, Soviet officials continued to object to satellite reconnaissance. In 1962 the U.S.S.R. opened a diplomatic offensive at the United Nations aimed at prohibiting such activities through the adoption of a declaration of principles holding that "the use of artificial satellites for the collection of intelligence information in the territory of foreign states is incompatible with the objectives of mankind in its conquest of outer space." [40]

The Soviets changed their tune once their own Kosmos reconnaissance program began regular intelligence gathering and as progress was also made in the test-ban negotiations. They recognized that satellite reconnaissance could provide a way around the need for on-site inspection. By September 1963, the Soviets had ceased opposing the United States' call for legitimating satellite reconnaissance.

Meanwhile, the U.S. had not restricted its efforts only to reconnaissance satellites. Both the army and the navy developed ideas for ASATs. The army considered converting the Nike-Zeus into an anti-ballistic missile, and the navy worked on modifying the Polaris missile to serve the same purpose. The air force had the most ambitious program: in response to Soviet civil space activities, it proposed in September 1961 that the United States adopt a ten-year plan for satellite interception, space-based ballistic missile defense, a fast-reaction space bomber that could reenter the atmosphere, and a manned capability in space. The Kennedy administration rejected the proposal for a manned space facility but agreed that ASATs deserved closer consideration. This decision was certainly reinforced by Khrushchev's threat to place bombs on orbiting Soviet satellites.

In the early 1960s McNamara took a highly secret decision to allow the army to develop a modified Nike-Zeus under the code name Mudflap, later designated Program 505.[41] This system became operational on August 1, 1963. Earlier that year the air force was instructed to prepare an additional ASAT, using the Thor missile (alias Project 437). This was tested in February 1964. Nike-Zeus had the advantage of using a solid propellant, but the Thor could reach higher altitudes. Both were designed to use nuclear warheads, a disability inasmuch as their use would have threatened U.S. satellites in the vicinity and their testing would have violated the Limited Test Ban Treaty. Project 437 nevertheless remained in place on Johnston Island until 1975.

In 1963 the United States proposed, and the Soviets agreed, that the United Nations should issue a declaratory ban on weapons of mass destruction in outer space. The Soviet Union had already experimented with satellites designed to carry large nuclear weapons, which the United States called a Fractional Orbital Bombardment System (FOBS). But it evidently determined, as the United States had independently, that terrestrial systems were preferable for such purposes. In 1967 both nations signed a treaty banning weapons of mass destruction from placement in space. Neither the declaratory statement nor the treaty banned the development of ASATs. The United States proceeded with ASAT development as a hedge against surprise and possible Soviet abrogation of the treaty, and also in order to have the ability to attack satellites in time of war.

U.S. concerns were aroused in 1966 and 1967 by Soviet launches from Tyuratam, Kazakhstan. Apparently, the payload portion was commanded down to earth before one complete orbit. McNamara interpreted the launches as an attempt to develop FOBS satellites designed to serve as weapons carriers that would approach the United States from the south, its most vulnerable flank. To counter this threat, the United States utilized over-the-horizon radar, with increased coverage of the southern United States, and commenced development of a new ABM—the Nike X.

As early as 1958 ARPA sponsored a series of experiments called Project Argus, designed to assess certain of the effects of nuclear explosions in space. The Fishbowl series above Johnston Island in 1962 included one large nuclear explosion with a yield of 1.4 megatons; several satellites were damaged.

The navy in 1961 also proposed a direct-ascent ASAT in its modified

Polaris. The air force's SAINT had been designed as a co-orbital device, which must go through several space orbits before it achieves the same orbit as its target. So as not to give the Soviets an excuse to shoot down U.S. reconnaissance satellites, SAINT was designated an "inspection" system rather than as an interceptor. In January and February 1958, Eisenhower sent two letters to Bulganin, referred to earlier, proposing a cessation of all military activities in space, including the testing of long-range missiles. The proposal was conditioned on the creation of an international system for observing and verifying compliance. The U.S.S.R. rejected the proposal, calling it an attempt to hinder Soviet progress. In May 1962, as part of Project HiHo, the Navy test-launched a rocket from a Phantom F4D fighter bomber with a secondary objective of launching ASATs. In 1970 research began on the Miniature Homing Vehicle (MHV), the basis of the United States' current ASAT. The MHV is an air-launched heat-seeking missile that homes in on a target satellite and destroys it by force of impact. The United States has been developing this weapon since 1977, using an F-15 aircraft modified to serve as a launch platform. It is currently estimated that this ASAT could be ready for deployment in 1990 at a cost of $4 billion.[42] Other efforts were pursued to improve space tracking and detection, which also served to improve prospects for an effective ASAT. And in the mid-1970s attention was directed to the need for an improved satellite survivability.

THE SOVIET MILITARY SPACE PROGRAM

In 1968 the Soviets began testing a satellite interceptor, or "killer satellite." By 1970 there was little doubt among Western observers that the U.S.S.R. had succeeded in developing an ASAT. The Soviet system uses a large liquid-fueled booster to launch a satellite that must move through more than one orbit until it can be maneuvered close enough to its target to be exploded. Destruction is achieved by the impact of shrapnel from the explosion. The testing stopped in 1972, resumed in 1976, and later was interrupted again when the Soviets declared an official moratorium on ASAT testing, done in conjunction with a proposal to extend the ban on space weapons to include ASATs. In 1977, however, Secretary of Defense Harold Brown asserted that the Soviets now had an operational ASAT—though it was effective only against satellites in low orbit. Given that most of the United States' critical early-warning and communication satellites are in high orbits, this first-generation system would be of limited utility. In addition, the Soviet ASAT is co-orbital, meaning that it cannot be used very effectively in a surprise attack: the time needed to put the Soviet killer satellite into operation would give the United States ample warning that the Soviets were at least contemplating such an attack.

By the time Jimmy Carter took office, unilateral Soviet development of ASATs had come to be perceived as politically, if not militarily, unacceptable. On the advice of Brown, Carter concluded that the United States should undertake a three-pronged response. First, the United States should institute the development of a general-purpose ASAT of its own. (This is the origin of the current F-15-based system.) Second, the United States should intensify efforts to make its own satellites safe from, or at least resistant to, attack by Soviet ASATs. And third, the United States should attempt to negotiate a treaty regime with the Soviets designed to eliminate, or at least inhibit, the further development and deployment of ASAT systems.

In accordance with the third objective, bilateral negotiations were conducted with the Soviets in 1978 and 1979. Despite doubts in certain defense quarters, Carter pushed for the broadest possible limitation. At first, the Soviets indicated that they doubted the desirability of a total ban on ASATs and sought to limit the negotiation to something more like the "rules-of-the-road" arrangements that prevail at sea. Before these negotiations could get very far, other events such as difficulties with SALT discussions and, ultimately, the invasion of Afghanistan brought about the termination of these formal efforts to control further development of ASATS. On April 3, 1980, the Soviets resumed ASAT testing. By then, however, the two sides were close enough to an agreement to arouse expectations that if Carter had been reelected an agreement would probably have been concluded.[43]

In August 1981 the Soviets offered to discuss a draft space-weapons treaty to be submitted to the U.N. General Assembly. This time it was the United States that showed no interest. Indeed, in June 1982 the air force announced the creation of its Space Command, headquartered at the NORAD complex at Cheyenne Mountain. In the summer of 1983, in a meeting with the U.S. senators, Premier Yuri Andropov offered to amend the Soviet proposal so as to ban the placement of anti-satellite weapons in outer space, along with the testing of any new ASAT. He also offered to eliminate existing systems. The proposal also included a provision that the Soviets knew the United States would not accept: it prohibited the testing of any manned-space vehicle for military purposes, to which the United States was committed using the space shuttle. But the Soviet proposal impressed the legislators, and they supported the amendment offered by Sen. Paul Tsongas (D., Mass.) to the FY1984 DOD Authorization Act. The amendment prohibited the use of the funds for testing the ASAT against targets in space until the president certified that the United States was negotiating the matter in good faith with the Soviet Union.[44]

Prospects for such a treaty are still unclear. Some of its U.S. advocates concede that it is now impractical to prevent the development of ASATs effective against satellites in lower orbits, but they argue that a prohibition of their deployment in significant numbers, and of the testing and development of ASATs capable of destroying satellites in higher orbits, would still be possible and would be in the interests of both powers. Prohibition of the more advanced ASATs could be especially important because most of the critical satellites are in these higher orbits. In addition, the two powers might agree to "rules of the road" similar to the agreements now operative at sea.

CIVIL SPACE COOPERATION

Although continued emphasis on the military uses of space has not yet altogether precluded international cooperation in space exploration, it has already engendered a climate of suspicion and concern for national supremacy that belies the professions of political leaders that space should be an arena for peaceful exploration in the interest of all humanity. The *Apollo-Soyuz* docking was the first, and so far the only, instance of official U.S.-Soviet activity in space. Scientific data have been exchanged, however, and the Soviets have lately been more open about their civil activities and plans, an attitude that has evoked appreciation and interest among Western space scientists, who admire the ambitious character of the Soviet program. The disarray and uncertainty that have characterized the U.S. government space policy present a sharp contrast. The Soviet Vega mission to Venus in 1984 involved considerable international cooperation, including one U.S. experiment. Otherwise, cooperation at higher levels has been hostage to general political relations. In 1982 the Reagan administration allowed an agreement on space collaboration with the U.S.S.R. to lapse, in protest against the imposition of martial law in Poland. In 1987, after the leaders of both countries concluded a summit meeting and were eager to make some symbolic gesture of amity, a new agreement was signed. The U.S. team that negotiated the agreement included DOD representatives, who made sure that technology transfer would not be included. As a result, the agreement calls for little more than the exchange of data and the coordination of mission schedules, but "carefully avoids proposing that researchers from one side fly instruments and other hardware on the other's spacecraft."[45] Leading Soviet space researchers have proposed that the two countries collaborate, in ways that would respect DOD sensitivities, on an unmanned mission to Mars scheduled for the early 1990s. NASA has so far declined to commit the United States to such a collaboration, although there is reported to be considerable interest in it.

Along with the ABM Treaty, such collaboration could well be another casualty of a decision to deploy space weapons. Although space has from the first not been treated as a sanctuary in the strictest sense, the willingness on the part of both superpowers to refrain so far from orbiting all but military support systems has preserved a basis for civil cooperation. If space is further militarized, especially by the use of camouflaged weapons, decoys, and declared "keep out" zones, such collaboration is likely to become increasingly difficult. Information on the location of satellites and on conditions in outer space is likely to be treated as a matter of national security, along with virtually all aspects of space technology.

Despite the overwhelming evidence that past efforts to achieve strategic defenses have been largely an exercise in futility, and despite the real possibility that the future militarization of space will preclude both arms reductions and civil cooperation, the elusive quest for strategic defenses continues. Do prospective technologies promise better results, or will they only repeat the folly? We examine these prospects in the next chapter.

CHAPTER 3

Measure for Measure

The Technological Prospect

The revival of interest in strategic defense is more a political act of faith in prospective technologies than an effort to exploit what is already known. As we have seen, the decision to create SDI was made, not to take advantage of progress already achieved, but to force relevant technologies to maturity instead of waiting to see whether research already being conducted would succeed. Virtually all the basic ideas receiving consideration in SDI have been put forward in the past. The most significant exceptions are the X-ray laser and the free-electron laser, both of which rely on more recent inventions. Although progress along the frontiers of research has made some of these ideas more plausible than they were in 1972, when the ABM Treaty was signed, only the most ardent believers in SDI claim that the means are already available for an effective defense against a massive nuclear attack. Most technical specialists not only disagree with such claims but are also skeptical even on the question of whether such a defense will ever prove feasible.

For its political sponsors, SDI is an act of faith based on confidence in the United States' achievements and on a determination not to repeat the mistakes of experts who underestimated technological prospects in the past. Examples are not hard to find. In 1932 Albert Einstein declared emphatically: "There is not the slightest indication that [nuclear] energy will ever be obtainable." Adm. William Leahy, chief of staff under President Truman, prophesied with equal confidence: "The [atomic] bomb will never go off, and I speak as an expert in explosives." In 1924 the well-known British chemist J. B. S. Haldane made a doubly wrong forecast about prospects for atomic bombs and space travel: "We cannot make apparatus small enough to disintegrate or fuse atomic nuclei, any more than we can make it large enough to reach to the moon." Even so distinguished a physicist as Ernest Rutherford wrote in 1933: "To those who look for sources of power in atomic transmutations—such expectations are the merest moonshine." Vannevar Bush, himself a renowned inventor and chairman of the highly successful National Defense Research Committee during World War II, scoffed at the idea that a rocket could propel an atomic bomb for three thousand miles until it "would land exactly on a certain target, such as a city."[1] But the undue pessimism of eminent researchers in the past should hardly encourage politicians to ignore the views of the most qualified and experienced specialists. In a project as complex as SDI, even if the optimists prove right with respect to specific technologies, it does not follow that (1) a defensive system in which many new elements must be successfully integrated will be militarily effective, especially against an equally skilled adversary; or that (2) the vast effort to build and maintain it will be justifiable on economic grounds.

Among scientists and engineers engaged in military projects, there are at least some who see SDI as a welcome challenge to their ingenuity. Enthusiasm for such challenges is at the core of their sense of vocation,[2] as suggested by the World War II motto of the U.S. Navy engineers, the "Seabees": "The difficult we do today, the impossible tomorrow." Certain of the younger researchers suggest that older scientists cast doubt on SDI because they are being protective of their work on offensive weapons and find it hard to accept the possibility that their achievements will be made obsolete by a new generation. Lowell L. Wood, Jr., a key figure in the work on the X-ray laser, has emphasized the special challenge of SDI: "Frankly," he told a reporter, "the offensive game, in addition to its somewhat dubious intent, is awfully easy. There just isn't much challenge there. Success consists of shrinking off an inch here and a pound there or moving the center of gravity a half an inch forward. It's distinctly an engineering problem. The intriguing thing about defensive weapons is that they have a real, semifundamental challenge to them— to making them work, work effectively, robustly, and to work at very high cost-efficiency, a high cost-exchange ratio, against the offense."[3] This vocational interest of defense researchers in continually doing advanced research, however understandable and even patriotic, is one of the factors that makes the arms race hard to control.

The problem of building an effective defense, difficult as it is in its

own right, is compounded by the need to take account of what a determined and capable adversary can do to overcome it. The complexity of
individual elements of SDI has been compared to the challenges of the
Manhattan and Apollo projects. But these analogies cannot capture the
unique, adversarial nature of the technical problem: "The moon and
nucleus," as the OTA study on SDI notes, "did not hide, run away, or
shoot back,"[4] and the Apollo mission, as others have pointed out, could
have been defeated by "a platoon of hostile moonmen with axes."[5]

The adversarial nature of this technological endeavor cannot be over-
emphasized. It is hard enough to devise systems that meet unprecedented technological standards on so many different levels. The difficulties are compounded by the presence of an ingenious and equally
dedicated adversary who is determined to nullify or evade such systems.
The "red team" may work very hard to concoct potential countermeasures, and the designers may succeed in taking account of them, but will
the system actually work in battle conditions? Even mature technologies
commonly malfunction under unusual conditions. A complex multilayered defense could not be tested under realistic conditions. Although
some countermeasures can be anticipated, there would be no opportunity to make modifications or corrections in the light of actual battle
experience, as is usually the case for more conventional military technologies. Certain of the relevant technologies, moreover, will be useful
sooner for attacking satellites (i.e., either in an offensive or counterdefensive mode) than for intercepting incoming warheads. Ironically, then, an
effort to add defensive systems to offense will, in the short run, only
make space-based military assets more vulnerable. The United States currently relies on these assets more heavily than does the Soviet Union.

Nevertheless, the advent of the new technologies and the continuing
advances in the older ones present intriguing opportunities. In the simplest terms, they seem to promise a way of putting up a "shield" to ward
off an enemy's "sword." Given the difficulty of coping with a Soviet attack by other means, these technological options are bound to be attractive, all the more so because they stand, in some cases, at the forefront
of research in the physical sciences. Besides, even if advances do not
produce a space shield, they could have benefits for offensive weapons
and civil applications. The novelty and technical sophistication of much
of the endeavor intrigues investigators. And the political excitement
thus generated promotes support for laboratory budgets.

This heady mixture of technological frontiersmanship and political
glamour is the crux of the problem. It promotes an unwarranted faith in

technology and a disdain for negotiated solutions. The hope for a technical fix stands in the way of diminishing the danger of nuclear war through arms control. Even so, many informed critics agree that some level of research into defensive technologies is warranted, mostly as a hedge against a possible Soviet breakout from the ABM Treaty, but also because of the possibility, at least over the very long run, that an effective defense may one day actually become feasible.

SDI, however, is premised on the belief that the research process can be pushed into early maturity, but that belief is not widely shared. President Reagan's 1983 speech called for a radical acceleration of research already in progress in order to provide for a deployment decision by the early 1990s. As discussed in chapter 1, the task of designing a technical program that might fulfill the president's goals was assigned to the Defensive Technologies Study Committee, chaired by NASA Administrator James C. Fletcher. After that body of well over fifty defense scientists and engineers issued its classified, seven-volume report, other ad hoc technical groups were formed to develop a more detailed "architecture." The result was the design of a "layered defense" that exhibits both the potential advantages of a defensive shield and the problems of achieving it. In 1987 a committee of the American Physical Society composed of leading defense researchers and specialists issued a review of the research to date on directed-energy weapons.[6] Other studies have examined the option of an intermediate or first-phase deployment of a layered system relying only on kinetic-kill weapons for boost-phase and terminal interception. These studies have cast considerable doubt on the feasibility of an effective defense, both in interim and long-range perspective.

THE PROPOSED TECHNOLOGIES

The technologies under investigation fall into several categories: *sensors* to detect the initiation of an attack, to track the missiles and warheads through the flight path, and to direct the targeting of defensive interceptors; *destructive devices* to damage, deflect, or incapacitate missiles or warheads in the various phases of flight; *computer systems* to process the data acquired by the sensors, to make "kill assessments" from the data in order to determine which elements of the "threat cloud" have been destroyed and which remain to be dealt with, to "hand off" data from one layer of the defensive screen to the next, and to perform other "battle management" functions—including almost certainly the decision to initiate interception; *techniques for discriminating targets from decoys;* and a variety of *methods for defeating countermeasures* that might be taken by the offense.

The effort to develop sensors draws both on well-established technology and on more exotic ideas that have not yet been developed into usable devices. Conventional infrared sensors, which are now routinely used for early warning of attack and to monitor test-firings, are thought to be particularly well adapted to boost-phase interception because they can readily identify the hot plume of exhaust gases emitted during a launch. Because the sensors must be able to detect both hot and relatively cold objects (the hotter the object, the shorter the wavelength), the sensors must have a wide range of capabilities. The ability to identify and track the plume, however, does not necessarily make it possible to track and target the missile, the position of which must be calculated from the signal produced by the plume. The plumes are, in general, very much larger than the missiles, and the missiles are not usually located in any convenient "central position" or easy-to-find "hotspot" within the plume. Other sensors are being investigated, including those that use an ultraviolet probe, in order to target the missile itself. The sensing problem becomes more acute in the post-boost phase, when the rocket exhausts are much smaller, and even more difficult in the later phases of flight, when the relatively cold warheads must be tracked in space against a background of stars. For this phase, more exotic sensors, such as those that make use of laser and radar technologies (and are therefore called "ladar" sensors), have been suggested.

There are three basic types of destructive devices: (1) conventional *ground-based ABMs with nuclear warheads,* which are directed by ground-based radars to track warheads in the terminal phase of flight (the system in use when the ABM Treaty was negotiated); (2) *kinetic-energy weapons* (KEW), which are ground- or space-launched projectiles that use the energy of motion to destroy missiles by colliding with them; and (3) *directed-energy weapons* (DEW), also known collectively as beam weapons because they make use of powerful beams of electromagnetic radiation produced by lasers (infrared, visible light, or X-rays) or beams of highly accelerated particles—either charged (such as electrons, protons, and ions) or neutral atoms.

The conventional ABM could be outfitted with a kinetic warhead rather than an atomic explosive if tracking and targeting were improved to increase the probability of interception. U.S. and Soviet ABMs developed since the early 1960s have been configured in two modes. One permits high acceleration for rapid interception in the atmosphere (as in the

United States' Sprint), and the other has a relatively slower acceleration for interception above the atmosphere (as in the United States' Spartan). Development is now under way on two kinetic interceptors for endo-atmospheric and exoatmospheric interception. Nuclear and nonnuclear systems may both benefit from recent improvements, which have enabled the hardening of radar sites and utilize miniaturized, mobile radar in addition to ladar and infrared systems mounted on aircraft.

Kinetic weapons could also be deployed from a constellation of space-based battle stations. These weapons would be accelerated and directed toward their targets either by chemical rockets or by the as-yet undeveloped electromagnetic launcher, or "railgun." The rocket-propelled projectiles would be fitted with homing devices to correct for any errors in targeting; they might also be equipped with explosives that would detonate near the target, increasing the prospect of a kill. The railgun would use an intense magnetic field to impart speeds greater than 20 km per second—at least several times faster than that achieved with conventional rocket technologies, though still far slower than speeds attained with speed-of-light lasers.

Invented in the 1950s, lasers are essentially devices that produce coherent beams of electromagnetic radiation in the form of light. The radiation may be in the visible, ultraviolet, or X-ray regions of the spectrum. "Lasing" ordinarily occurs when the atoms or molecules in the lasant matter (solid or gaseous) are "excited" by energy—electrical, nuclear, chemical, or optical—pumped in from some external source. The resulting beam can be used to damage missiles and warheads either by thermal means (delivery of intense heat that would burn through the skin of the missile or warhead and alter or destroy sensitive electronic components) or by "impulse kill" (depositing energy in a powerful pulse on the surface of the target, driving a mechanical shock wave through the target). Some lasers are better adapted for one type of kill, some for the other. To hit a target from a great distance requires very accurate targeting, a strong beam, and, for most lasers, large mirrors to focus the beam so as to compensate for its diffusion over long distances.

The lasers usually discussed in connection with strategic defense are the chemical, free-electron, excimer, and X-ray lasers. The process whereby chemicals can be combined to produce the energy needed to pump a laser is well understood, but the required energy levels have yet to be achieved. Furthermore, mirrors larger than any so far produced would have to be developed. Without these mirrors, there is no way to focus the energy to produce the brightness required.

In principle, optical lasers may be based either in space or on the ground. For space basing, weight and the provision of adequate power are major problems. Distortion and absorption of the beam by the atmosphere are the main problems for ground-based lasers. "Adaptive optics" must be employed to direct the beams through the atmosphere so as to compensate for distortion. The beam would be reflected off space-based relay and "fighting" mirrors to targets in space. The free-electron laser (FEL) is a novel concept. It uses a relativistic electron beam (generated by an accelerator rather than by a conventional lasant) to produce an intense, coherent beam of electrons whose energy is then converted into an extremely high intensity beam of light. Two competing FEL designs are currently under investigation. One, the radio frequency (RF) linac (for "linear accelerator"), is being developed by Los Alamos Laboratory and Boeing. Lawrence Livermore Laboratory and TRW are working on the other, called the induction linac. Once a choice is made between the two designs, a ground-based test version is to be built at the White Sands Missile Range in New Mexico.

The excimer laser normally produces a pulse of sharp laser light, theoretically enabling impulse kill, and would require a smaller mirror than other types of lasers because of its shorter wavelength. Both the FEL and the excimer laser require further development in order to determine whether the requisite power levels can be achieved. The weight required for both, and the power required for the free-electron laser, rule out space basing for the excimer laser and the Induction linac FEL, though not necessarily for the RF linac FEL. Chemical lasers of the hydrogen flouride type, which derive their energy from the chemical reaction of these two substances, may be made light enough for deployment in space basing for the excimer laser and the induction linac FEL, though not necessarily for the RF linac FEL. Chemical lasers of the hydrogen nuclear explosion to pump the lasant, which might be in the form of rods each aimed at a missile. Such a laser would also have to be fired from space, because X-rays are absorbed by the atmosphere, but it could also be "popped up" when needed rather than placed in orbit because it could be more effective at great distances than kinetic weapons and would not need to be housed in a satellite, as chemical lasers are. Research on X-ray lasers still has far to go before application can take place, and its testing in space would violate both the Limited Test Ban Treaty and the Outer Space Treaty. The fission-activated light concept (FALCON), under study at Sandia National Laboratory, also aims to use a nuclear reactor to pump a space-based laser. But it is estimated that the platform for this system would weigh between seven and forty tons, apart from any protective armor.[7]

In order to design computers that are sufficient for the needs of a space shield, two things are required. First, suitable high-speed hardware needs to be developed. Second, and far more problematic, software programming with enough capacity, redundancy, and reliability must also be produced. This software must be able to handle the large and diverse sets of data and data-processing suitable for an unpredictable environment: some elements of the system might be rendered inoperative, and the system would have to operate efficiently without previous testing or "debugging." The degree to which the system would have to be centralized or could be disaggregated is much disputed. The further development of Very High Speed Integrated Circuitry (VHSIC) technology is essential for adequate data processing. The relatively new gallium arsenide computer chip may also improve prospects for achieving the high-speed computations needed for this purpose.

Means for discriminating targets from decoys in space are still quite uncertain, but ladar sensors have been suggested, along with various types of "interactive discrimination." One such technique would be to use beams of neutral particles. Projected at targets, these particles can help to determine mass and thereby help to distinguish between warheads and decoys. In principle, a beam of neutral particles, when directed at a target, can ascertain mass because the object releases secondary radiation (in the form of neutrons and gamma rays) in rough proportion to its mass. Problems remain, though: it has not been demonstrated that an operational system can distinguish neutrons thus generated from neutrons naturally present[8] and that it can be made small enough to be placed in space.

To achieve battle-satellite survivability against efforts to suppress space-based defenses will require hardening the proposed battle stations against attack from lasers and from the effects of nuclear explosions (including electromagnetic pulse, which has been shown in nuclear-test explosions to disrupt electrical apparatus). Battle satellites may also have to be equipped with counter-countermeasures, such as decoys, protective satellites, rocket motors for maneuvering, and the ability to shoot back. If the satellites carry radar, they would require high-capacity power sources, which in all probability would have to be small nuclear reactors, either carried aboard the satellites or tethered to them.

Adequate launch capacity is yet another essential technological consideration. Space-based elements must be launched into orbit and then serviced and maintained. The need for this launch capacity has led the SDIO to advocate a variety of new high-capacity launch systems. The National Aerospace Plane, if it should become available, is one such system and could carry much larger payloads than the space shuttle. NASA's difficulties in achieving a reliable shuttle and in maintaining regular launch schedules suggest that the development of this still more complex and demanding launching system will take time, investment, and a further extension of the existing state of the art. The proposal for the Advanced Launch System claims that the system could put payloads into low earth orbit at one-tenth the current cost of $3,000–$5,000 per pound. A Senate staff report has underlined the difficulties involved in achieving this goal: "While the U.S. launched a total of about 350,000 pounds into earth orbit during 1985, SDIO envisions SDI deployment as requiring as much as 5 *million* pounds in orbit per year. . . . The capacity of the U.S. to launch payloads into orbit would have to be expanded enormously while the cost would have to come down by at least a factor of ten." Just how realistic this goal is, as the Senate report points out, may be judged by experience with the space shuttle. In 1972 a White House press release predicted that the space shuttle would reduce launch costs from $600–$700 per pound to $100 per pound in 1972 dollars. Currently, space shuttle launches cost $5,000 per pound.[9]

A LAYERED DEFENSE:
THE SDI ARCHITECTURE

The architecture, or basic plan, drawn up by the Fletcher Committee envisions a four-layered missile-defense system (see Figure 5). Each layer would be designed to intercept as much of the attack as possible. The attack goes through four sequential phases: (1) the *boost phase,* during which the great booster rockets bring the payload up to the speed required for intercontinental ballistic flight; (2) the *post-boost phase,* during which a "bus," or post-boost vehicle (PBV), sets each of several warheads (MIRVs) onto trajectories leading to specific targets; (3) the *midcourse phase,* during which the RVs coast along inertial paths far above the earth's sensible atmosphere; and (4) the *terminal phase,* during which the RVs reenter the earth's atmosphere and ultimately explode at or near their targets. Those who believe there is promise in this scheme base their opinion on two major factors.

First, each defensive layer compounds the effectiveness of the others. As the proponents point out, if each layer intercepts 90 percent of the warheads reaching it, altogether they would intercept 99.99 percent of those launched. Thus, if ten thousand warheads were launched, nine thousand would be destroyed in Phase I, nine hundred of the

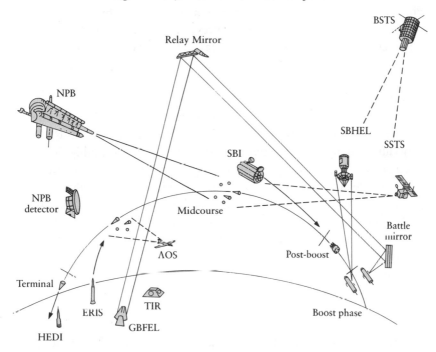

Fig. 5.   Major SDI Sensors and Weapons

SDI sensor systems
BSTS: Boost Surveillance and Tracking System (infrared sensors)
SSTS: Space Surveillance and Tracking System (infrared, visible, and possibly radar or laser rader sensors)
AOS: Airborne Optical System (infrared and laser sensors)
TIR: Terminal Imaging Radar (phased array radar)
NPB: Neutral Particle Beam (interactive discrimination to distinguish reentry vehicles (RVs) from decoys; includes separate neutron detector satellite)

SDI weapons systems
SBI: Space-Based Interceptors or Kinetic Kill Vehicles (rocket-propelled hit-to-kill projectiles)
SBHEL: Space-Based High Energy Laser (chemically pumped laser)
GBFEL: Ground-Based Free Electron Laser (with space-based relay mirrors)
NPB: Neutral Particle Beam weapon
ERIS Exoatmospheric Reentry vehicle Interceptor System (ground-based rockets)
HEDI: High Endoatmospheric Defense Interceptor (ground-based rockets)

SOURCE: U.S. Congress, Office of Technology Assessment, *SDI: Technology, Survivability, and Software*, OCA-ISC-353 (Washington, D.C.: U.S. Government Printing Office, May 1988), p. 74.

remaining thousand in Phase II, ninety of the remaining hundred in Phase III, and nine of the remaining ten in the final phase. Unlike the single-layer missile-defense systems previously considered, if the weapons systems constituting any single layer failed or were overcome by successful enemy countermeasures, the other three could, in principle, largely compensate.

Second, defensive systems have not undergone a thorough review since the early 1970s. And, of course, many of the pertinent technologies (especially lasers, infrared detectors, and computers) have evolved very substantially since that time; important new ones (notably the free-electron and X-ray lasers) have also emerged. SDI proponents claim that these new technical advances open new technological possibilities for intercepting offensive RVs during each of the four flight phases and thus lead to the very high levels of "compounding" that make a real defense against missiles truly feasible. To appreciate both the possibilities and the remaining obstacles, it is essential to examine the technical issues affecting each phase.

PHASE I: BOOST-PHASE INTERCEPT

The boost phase is the first stage of a missile's flight. It includes that part of the missile's trajectory during which the great booster engines of the rocket are under power—that is, from takeoff until the last engine is shut off, typically at an altitude of about 250 km, some three minutes after launch. SDI research has focused most attention on interception during this phase. There are three good reasons for doing so.

First, offensive missiles are in their most vulnerable, or "softest," state during the boost phase. Boosters consist mainly of fuel tanks that must be as light as possible. It is therefore far easier to puncture these tanks or otherwise damage the missiles while they are still in powered flight. Otherwise, either the bus or the RVs themselves must be destroyed during later phases. Second, typical modern strategic missiles carry many nuclear warheads—up to fourteen in one case. Successful interception in the boost phase stops them all and thus accomplishes much more than would the interception of a partially empty bus or a single RV in one of the later phases. Third, the offensive systems are especially easy to identify and track during this phase. Both the United States and the Soviet Union have long had satellites deployed in geosynchronous orbits that are capable of detecting and, in principle at least, tracking the brilliant rocket plumes so characteristic of the boost phase. Current systems can provide early warning that an attack is being launched, but they cannot provide the kind of tracking information needed for an actual intercept. SDI planners are therefore seeking to develop the Boost Surveillance and Tracking Satellite (BSTS), which would have this added capability. Essentially, the aim is to achieve a very substantial upgrading of the systems now in place in order to make them adequate for this new, more demanding purpose.

After the enemy strategic missile has been detected and tracked, it must somehow be destroyed. There are two quite different approaches to this problem. One is based on kinetic-energy kill weapons (KKW) devices, and the other on "directed-energy weapons" (DEW). Each is further subdivided into a number of specific technical possibilities.

According to SDI advocates, the most promising near-term boost-phase interceptor is one based on the use of Space based kinetic kill vehicles (SBKKVs), designated in 1987 as space-based interceptors (SBIs). As currently conceived, these vehicles would be relatively small (approximately 100 kg) missiles capable of accelerating a small but destructive payload (a projectile) up to velocities of several kilometers per second. They would be equipped with homing devices, presumably relying on infrared sensing, capable of causing the projectile to collide directly with and thus destroy the offensive missile while it is still in its boost phase. Individual SBKKVs would be mounted in groups (perhaps of ten) on a "mother" satellite—sometimes called a garage, sometimes a battle station—that would release them at the proper time. The mother satellite itself would also play a role in overall command and control and perhaps in acquiring and tracking the target as well.

Given the finite velocity of the SBKKV (perhaps 6 km per second) [10] and the short duration of the boost phase (currently some hundreds of seconds), the battle stations must be within roughly 1,000 km of their targets at the moment they are needed. This in turn means that they must be in low earth orbits and hence moving at very high speeds, comparable to those of their ICBM targets and the SBKKVs themselves. In order to be ready to intercept an attack at any arbitrary time, the battle stations must be scattered at locations above most of the earth's surface. Only a relatively small fraction of them will be in range of any particular missile launch at the moment it takes place. Thus, many more SBKKVs must be in orbit than would be needed to destroy the total inventory of enemy ICBMs. The interceptors that cannot reach their targets in time are called "absentees."

The "absentee ratio" (the ratio of the total number of interceptors to the number in position) was much debated during the first years of SDI. Some asserted one particular ratio, and others denounced the use of differing ratios as politically motivated. In fact, the actual absentee ratio is critically dependent on the detailed parameters of the systems involved, including especially the maximum speed of the SBKKVs and the duration of the boost phase of the offensive missile. There is thus no such thing as *the* absentee ratio but, rather, a very wide range of possibilities from as low as 7 : 1 for the most optimistic assumptions (implicit in the Marshall Institute report, for example) [11] up to values many times that figure.

In view of the obvious importance of the weight and the speed of the KKWs, the current R&D program focuses much attention on both parameters. Most analysts agree that the current weight (approximately 300 kg if the KKWs are outfitted with the current F-15 ASAT payload) must be reduced by ten- to thirtyfold in order for the system to become economically practicable, and that speeds closer to 10 km per second would be advantageous. No physical laws stand in the way of either goal, but the engineering problems are formidable. For instance, for the rockets now available, the final weight of a rocket warhead accelerated to 6 km per second is less than one-twentieth of its initial weight, and the final weight must include the homing system as well as its destructive component.

Other KKW systems under consideration are based on alternative means of producing very high velocity projectiles, such as electromagnetic railguns, but the acceleration and guidance systems for such projectiles are still at a highly speculative stage. For chemical rockets, the final velocity of the payload is limited by practical considerations to values a few times that of the rocket-exhaust gases, which in turn have a practical limit of 3 km per second. In the proposed electromagnetic railgun, no such limits apply, at least in theory, because the projectile is propelled to extremely high velocities by a combination of fields of electrical currents. But adequate means for controlling and steering such projectiles have not yet been invented.

SDI advocates also believe that a number of directed-energy weapons hold promise for use as boost phase interceptors in the long run. These include chemically and electrically driven optical lasers, the free-electron laser, and the new and potentially much more powerful X-ray laser. In principle, the properties of lasers are particularly well suited for such applications. These devices produce extremely intense beams of so-called coherent light or other forms of electromagnetic radiation that can be focused down into an extremely tight beam—one that spreads out very much more slowly than any other known type of light ray—as it travels for great distances. Within the atmosphere, various scattering processes can cause the beams to disperse, but in empty space beams can travel indefinitely over great distances without much diffusion.

In some cases (the chemical laser, for example) the laser would be mounted on a battle station, which would aim the laser at a particular target and cause it to operate at just the right moment. In other cases (such as the FEL, discussed below), the laser would be mounted on the ground, and the beam produced would be passed to a series of relay mirrors in space, eventually focusing it on the target. Because the velocity of light is for these purposes practically infinite, these systems are not constrained by time-of-flight considerations, as is true of the SBKKV, which must be within perhaps 1,000 km of the target in order to reach it in time.

But even a laser beam spreads out after it travels very large distances. So huge mirrors must be used to focus the laser beam down to an adequately small spot, perhaps a meter or less. The larger the source-to-target distance, the larger the mirror has to be. For typical situations (involving infrared lasers operating in space at a power level even as high as 25 mw), the mirrors would have to be 10 meters or more in diameter. For a configuration in which the lasers are mounted on the ground and their beams routed to the target by relay mirrors, the primary mirror must be even larger. Mirrors up to a few meters in diameter have been used both in space and on the ground, but the giant mirrors apparently required for the purposes of SDI are still only theoretical possibilities. A currently favored approach is to break the single huge mirror up into a large group of smaller ones, making a so-called segmented mirror. Such mirrors must be aligned with each other to an unprecedented degree of precision, however, in order to get them to act in the sort of unison required to produce tightly focused beams. In technical parlance, their output beams must all be "coherent" in order to achieve the focusing that a single large mirror produces. In principle, this is possible, but it has never been accomplished on the scale or in the circumstances required for this application.

The absentee problem also applies to DEWs. Each available laser must therefore destroy many targets sequentially and quickly. To do so, the "dwell time" on any one target, combined with the time needed to "slew," or move, to another one, must be kept very small—seconds or less. This in turn means that the power of the laser—the energy it can deliver in unit time—must be correspondingly large when used in a BMD mode.

The study produced for the American Physical Society noted that chemical-laser technology is not yet adequate for the demands of boost-phase interception: "We estimate that chemical laser output powers at acceptable beam quality must be increased by at least two orders of magnitude for HF/DF [hydrogen fluoride/deuterium fluoride] lasers for use as an effective kill weapon in the boost phase." [12]

The free-electron laser (FEL) is a very powerful device that, in its current versions, is large and heavy and requires great amounts of electric power. In the first place, it involves the construction and operation of an extremely powerful electron-beam accelerator. For typical SDI applications, the energy of the individual electrons must be at least 100,000,000 electron volts, the currents must be from 10,000 to 100,000 amperes (for a total peak power of 1 to 10 trillion watts), and the quality of the beam must be very finely controlled. The beam is passed through a magnetic "wiggler" that produces certain crosswise oscillations in the beam's motion. Under the right circumstances, this "wiggling" beam can be used to generate (or amplify) light to form an extremely powerful and highly focused laser beam. By varying either the beam energy or the spacing of the wiggler, it is possible to vary the wavelength of the light emitted. Thus, in principle, the FEL has considerably more flexibility than most other lasers, including the chemical type described above. The idea is to deploy FELs on the ground and to deliver the laser energy to the targets by means of a series (at least two) of huge relay mirrors orbiting in space. Problems include the construction, maintenance, and operation of these mirrors (including fast slewing). In addition, because the laser is ground-based, the output optics must cope with distortion caused by the atmosphere—the very distortion that causes stars to "twinkle." For the application envisioned here, such distortions, if uncorrected, would cause the beam to spread out to such a degree that it would become totally ineffective.

In brief, the distortion of FEL beams could be corrected by, first, determining the nature and cause of the instantaneous distortions by means of a "reference" beam. The laser's main beam-forming mirror would then have to be distorted so as to compensate for them. Corrections are feasible, in principle—but, again, they have never been accomplished on the scale and in the circumstances involved in SDI applications. In addition to all these other problems, ground-based lasers cannot penetrate cloud layers. Therefore, enough FELs must be deployed in many meteorologically independent locations, each with good enough average weather so that there are virtually no periods when all might be blocked by clouds. The APS report concluded that for strategic-defense applications, FELs "require validation of several physical concepts" [13] thus far only theoretically developed.

The nuclear-pumped X-ray laser is a novel concept dating from the late 1970s. The enormous energy of a nuclear-weapon explosion is used to energize the lasing medium, which creates a laser beam consisting of relatively soft X-rays. The X-rays produced by such devices are readily absorbed by air, however, and are therefore useful only when operated in outer space and fired against objects that are themselves located at extremely high altitudes, generally above 80 km. Research on these unusual devices is said to be making progress, but nearly all authorities believe they are still a very long way from any military application. The total energy that could be produced by such a system is huge and can be divided, in theory, among many independently directed beams. Precisely because the X-ray laser is potentially so powerful and destructive, it would constitute an especially rich and attractive target for any counter-defensive action that might precede a large-scale offensive strike. For that reason, its advocates usually propose that it not be placed permanently in orbit, but be employed in a "pop-up" mode instead. That is, it would be deployed on the surface or in submarines and be lofted into space only when needed. But the pop-up mode requires the system to be forward-based, very near to Soviet territory; the rockets would have to be ready to be launched on seconds' notice.

Because such constraints and requirements greatly limit the utility of such a device in a strictly defensive mode, the X-ray laser is now usually thought of as a potential counterdefensive system—that is, a weapon for destroying an enemy's space-based defenses, including its own counterpart. Thus, the nuclear-pumped X-ray laser might be used in the first phase of an attack to destroy an enemy's space-based strategic defense. Such a strike would assure successful penetration of the follow-on offensive forces. In this role, the X-ray laser would be used essentially as an ASAT, a role that is always less demanding than BMD. The APS study reserved judgment on the military utility of the X-ray laser pending further demonstration of the technical potential, concluding that these devices "require validation of many of the physical concepts before their application to strategic defense can be evaluated." [14]

Countermeasures and Counter-Countermeasures   Countermeasures designed to thwart all of the boost-phase systems described above have been proposed and were reviewed at the outset by one of the panels of the Fletcher Committee. Decoys and certain tactical ploys can be used to confuse the boost-phase acquisition and tracking system. In the case of the interceptors themselves, the easiest countermeasure to institute and the hardest for the defense to overcome is the so-called fast-burn booster. Indeed, existing U.S. ICBMs and the generation of Soviet ICBMs (in particular the SS-24 and SS-25) now being developed have much shorter burn times than the aging Soviet SS-18, against which the first-generation SBKKVs are oriented. Moreover, by pushing currently available solid-rocket technology to its limits, the offense can, at only a modest penalty in performance, cause the rocket boosters to complete the task of accelerating payloads in less than 60 seconds while still at an altitude of only about 80 km—greatly aggravating the "absentee" problem. In the view of most analysts, the number of battle stations that would then be required for SBKKVs is so high as to become impossible in practical terms. The lower altitude of booster burnout also makes the X-ray laser much less promising: X-rays can penetrate the atmosphere down to only about 80 km. And to counter the type of directed-energy weapons that can easily penetrate the atmosphere, the booster may also be spun about its long axis so as to spread out the incoming laser energy; lightweight protective coatings may also be added for further protection.

It is possible, in addition to deceiving and foiling the defenses, to attack them directly as well. All the space-based components are vulnerable to attack by similar systems deployed by the other side or by so-called space mines; they can be attacked by ground-based ASAT systems as well. As already noted, the pop-up version of the X-ray laser is one example of such a counterdefensive system.

But the story does not end there. All these countermeasures have, conceptually at least, counter-countermeasures. The deployment of more, lighter, and especially faster SBKKVs might mitigate the problems created by the fast-burn booster. Lasers with still more power might come along to defeat the boosters' defenses against earlier DEWs. And the space-based defensive assets could deploy a variety of self-defenses— including proliferation, maneuvering, decoys, and deception—to foil or confound a counterdefensive attack.[15]

The basic point is that this process is endless. In a "man-against-nature" contest, such as getting a man to the moon, once the problem is solved it stays solved. In a "man-against-man" contest, once a particular problem is solved, once we have learned to deal with a particular countermeasure, another arises to take its place—and so it goes, on and on, generally without ever coming to an end. There is no "last move." It is misleading to suggest there might be. Strategic defenses are not something that can be developed and installed at a certain time; they must be viewed as a process that, once begun, never reaches a permanent end.

The forty-year contest between the strategic arm of the U.S. Air Force and the Soviet National Air Defense Force (PVO Strany), reviewed in chapter 2, is a case in point. Throughout that long period, the Soviets have been creating and modernizing a defense in depth against an airborne attack. They have tried to build, in effect, a multilayered air-defense system analogous to that promoted by Reagan and the SDIO for defense against missiles. Over the same forty years, however, the U.S. Air Force has been constantly improving and updating its procedures and technologies for assuring bomber penetration. These have included electronic countermeasures, greater speed, the ability to fly very close to the ground, and a variety of standoff weapons, from the Hound Dog of the 1950s to the SRAM and ALCM of today. At no time during this long period has the total multilayer Soviet defense ever even approached the 90 percent kill-capability that SDI advocates project for each individual layer of the proposed missile-defense system. The U.S. Air Force remains confident of its ability to penetrate Soviet defenses.

There is at present no reason to believe that the final result of an effort to build strategic defenses will be any different in the case of SDI than in the case of the Soviet air-defense system. The problem for both offenses and defenses will be far more complex, but the results will not necessarily favor the defense. Michael M. May has hinted at the possibilities in a way that makes the use of the Star Wars label especially apt:

> If space-based weapons were to be developed and deployed . . . all space assets, whether needed for defense or offense, for warning or other purpose, would have to be operated in a hostile environment. They would have to be hardened beyond anything now contemplated, at commensurate cost, or alternatively, be mobile, defended, proliferated or hidden. Space hardware would replicate the characteristics of earthbound military hardware. We would have the space analog of tank corps, carrier battle groups and stealth bombers.[16]

PHASE II: POST-BOOST-PHASE INTERCEPT

After the boosters burn out, a post-boost vehicle, commonly called a "bus," launches each of its RVs onto trajectories leading to particular targets. This procedure takes several minutes, requiring the bus to fire small, on-board rocket engines more or less continuously as its course

is adjusted from one trajectory to the next. It is therefore possible, in
theory, to detect and track the bus by means similar to those used for
the main booster. But the engines of the post-boost vehicle produce
much less thrust and energy, so the detection systems must be much
more sensitive. Similarly, once acquired and tracked, the bus may be attacked by systems similar to those used for the boost-phase intercept.
But, again, the problem of attacking the bus is harder because it is
smaller, less visible, and generally tougher than the booster. As the bus
deploys its RVs and decoys, interception gets progressively harder, and
the third phase begins. Moreover, a bus is not an absolute requirement
if independent guidance systems were to be incorporated into each warhead. All of the defensive weapons described above as interceptors for
Phase I can be used for interception in Phase II, including some of those
SBKKVs on platforms that were out of attack range during Phase I.

PHASE III: MIDCOURSE INTERCEPT

After phases I and II are completed, the midcourse phase, lasting some
twenty minutes, begins. During this phase the individual RVs (perhaps
originally amounting to ten thousand, but perhaps greatly reduced by the
interceptions effected during the previous phases) ineluctably follow ballistic trajectories toward the targets. They still emit infrared radiation,
but at longer wavelengths and at far lower power levels than during the
previous phases. Indeed, the individual RVs are about the same size and
temperature as a human being. One may therefore understand the problem by comparing it to the task of detecting a human being just by the
heat the body radiates using a device located thousands of miles away.

As in phases II and IV, perhaps the most effective countermeasure in
Phase III is the deployment of decoys. As long as the RVs remain in
outer space, the decoys may be of very low density—in the form, for
example, of metallic balloons. There is no drag, and only the surface
characteristics of the decoys—shape, reflectivity, emissivity—need to
mimic the real thing. The decoys are usually thought of as weighing one
one-hundredth as much as the RV itself, so there could be about a hundred times as many of them.

Those who are optimistic about SDI's prospects generally believe that
detection and analysis of the emissions from the RVs and the decoys will
enable discrimination. To distinguish the RVs from the decoys, they propose the use of various means of "active" or "interactive" discrimination. One such technique involves the use of laser beams that would

transfer enough momentum to a lightweight balloon to change its velocity by an amount that could be detected by a Doppler laser radar. Another involves the use of a beam of high-energy, neutral hydrogen atoms that penetrate deeply into even the heavy RVs and interact very differently with balloons and decoys. It is also assumed that interceptors similar to those employed in the initial phases would also be used here. For both detectors and interceptors, however, the task is much harder in Phase III. As a result, less attention has been devoted to interactive discrimination, and none of the near-term deployment schemes focuses on it. An elaborate experiment, code-named "Delta 181," was conducted in February 1988, at a cost of $250 million, to collect information on how objects look in space, including potential decoys. Some important elements of this experiment failed, but large amounts of data were produced, which have yet to be fully analyzed.

PHASE IV: TERMINAL DEFENSE

Finally, the offensive RVs, hidden among a cloud of decoys, come to a point where they must reenter the atmosphere. Atmospheric drag then effectively slows down the balloon decoys, and the RVs must proceed on their own, unprotected during the last minutes of the flight—save, perhaps, for a few, much heavier, decoys.

The means proposed for intercepting the warheads that remain at this point are similar to those first proposed in the 1950s. In brief, ground-based radars, perhaps housed in movable vehicles and aided by an airborne optical system (AOS), would detect and track the incoming warheads. The radars would pass the information on to the computers, which would interpret it and then instruct interceptor rockets to lift off and proceed on a course toward the incoming RVs. When in range, the interceptor missiles would release a KKV, which would use a passive or active homing device to intercept and destroy the incoming RVs by impact or explosion nearby. This intercept system might be extended into the late midcourse regime if there were no cloud of decoys at that point. The current plan for accomplishing terminal defense includes two contemplated missile systems, the High Endoatmospheric Defense Interceptor (HEDI) and the Exoatmospheric Reentry Vehicle Interceptor System (ERIS). HEDI is designed as a high-acceleration weapon that would intercept any remaining warheads. The objective would be to destroy the warheads as high in the atmosphere as possible because they could be salvage-fused to explode on contact; an explosion at a low altitude, even if not yet on its target, would still do severe damage. ERIS would also be ground-based but with slower acceleration and longer range; it could intercept warheads in late midcourse, just before they reenter the atmosphere.

Countermeasures against this type of defense have been known for a long time. They include exhausting and saturating the defenses, using heavy decoys, countersimulation, precursor nuclear bursts, and the like. If a terminal defense were the only layer deployed, such countermeasures would probably work. But if it were deployed as the last of a four-layer system, it could probably destroy the remnants of even a large attack, depending on how the other layers had functioned, of course.

BATTLE MANAGEMENT

In any defense system, the various elements have to be alerted and generally "told what to do" before they can even begin to perform their functions. Always difficult, this problem is compounded enormously in the case of the multilayered system contemplated under SDI. A master command, control, communications, and intelligence (C^3I) system, in this case usually referred to as a battle-management system, must not only alert and instruct the first layer and initiate the entire defensive process, but it must also somehow instruct each layer in sequence, "handing off" the problem from one layer to the next as the attack progresses. In addition to the usual problems such systems face, a special problem, called "kill assessment," assumes importance here. Many of the proposed defensive systems either leave the RVs and other objects more or less intact, but nonfunctional, or break them into large fragments that may still look threatening. The overall battle-management system must somehow determine which RVs have been put out of action—that is, it must make a kill assessment and pass this assessment on to succeeding layers in order not to waste ammunition over and over again on objects that are already out of the battle. (The problem of kill assessment has been combined by SDIO with surveillance, acquisition, and tracking in a program package called SATKA.) Large quantities of data from the sensors and the battle satellites must be rapidly processed and the results assimilated and communicated to the satellites and to ground controllers.

The entire supersystem, battle management included, must perform all of its functions correctly the first time under actual battle conditions, and it must have an overall sensitivity threshold such that the entire defensive process is certain to be set in motion when the alarm is real while, in the event of a false alarm, nothing at all is done. And there will be many opportunities for false alarms, especially if both sides deploy space-based defenses. Under such circumstances there would be a great many objects in space, and plenty of launchings from enemy territory to set the alarms ringing. Even if only one side has space-based defenses, operating and replenishing them involves events that might trigger operation of the entire system in a sort of autoimmune-like reaction.

Another unique problem of battle-management derives from the extremely short response times following a launch warning. The response times for space-based defenses are very much shorter than those associated with ground-based BMD. The fifteen- to thirty-minute response time for the latter allows for at least the possibility of human intervention. The record shows that, so far, when false alarms have been sounded,[17] the human operators of the system have used the time available to determine that the alarms were indeed false, and thus avoided a catastrophic reaction. In the case of space-based defenses, response times drop to minutes or seconds or even less. Moreover, the entire system must be fully automated if it is to have any chance of responding in a timely manner. This obviously means that the false-alarm suppression mechanism must also be both purely automatic and much more finely set than it would ever need to be for ground-based terminal defenses of the classical kind.

The need for quick reaction poses the question of whether the defensive shield would have to operate automatically, without a human being "in the loop." SDIO officials have assured Congress that an "affirmative" human decision would be required before any lethal element of a space shield could be activated. Congress has mandated, in P.L. 100-180, that SDIO must not develop command-and-control systems that would make it possible "to initiate the directing of damaging or lethal fire except by affirmative human decision at an appropriate level of authority."[18] In order for an interception to be made successfully, however, the time for such "affirmative human decision" will inevitably be extremely short—on the order of minutes or even seconds. The "appropriate level of authority" is therefore likely to reside not with the commander-in-chief but with a designated subordinate, very likely a military officer directly in charge of the space shield who would have been "preprogrammed" to know what to do in a variety of contingencies.

The battle-management systems must be designed and programmed so as to avoid the difficulties and to solve these problems. It has been estimated by experts that the necessary software program would involve

ten million or more lines of code. SDI opponents point out that no such
program has ever been constructed and that experience would indicate
that even if it could be built, it would be rife with untestable and undetectable errors.[19] Proponents say the software could be assembled in
smaller pieces, which could probably be tested adequately or otherwise
made "fault-tolerant." In such a fast-moving field, there is no sure way
to predict the outcome of this issue. Clearly, however, the experts are
hardly in agreement that the battle-management problem can be solved.
One acknowledged expert, Frederick P. Brooks, has said he sees "no
reason why we could not build the kind of software system that SDI requires with the software engineering technology that we have today."[20]
Others share the view bluntly expressed by Robert Taylor, formerly the
director of computer research programs for DARPA, and currently head
of the research center at the Digital Equipment Corporation: "I think
it's pretty clear that it can't be done. The goals of the SDI put demands
on software that are just absurd in terms of the state of our knowledge."[21] After examining the problem in detail, the Office of Technology
Assessment concluded that even if the system could be designed and
built, it would be highly prone to failure: "In OTA's judgment, there
would be a significant probability (i.e., one large enough to take seriously) that the first (and presumably only) time the BMD system were
used in a real war, it would suffer a catastrophic failure"—defined in
the study as "a decline of 90 percent or more in system performance."
The OTA also found that no existing software system (such as the long-
distance telephone network or the Aegis ship-defense system) provides
an adequate model for developing, testing, producing, or maintaining
the software required for a BMD system.[22]

THE TESTING PROBLEM

One problem with building the sort of system required by SDI is that
it could not be tested in a fully realistic fashion. Individual components
could, of course, be tested against real U.S. or imaginary Soviet equipment and countermeasures, and the operation of the total supersystem,
as well as each of the various layers, could be simulated with computers.
A special project intended to do just that (called the National Test Bed)
is under construction. In it, the various components of the system will
be electronically connected to each other as they are developed, so that
the whole problem can be dealt with in an incremental fashion. On the
one hand, the ability to make such simulations and use them to predict

real world events reliably is rapidly improving. On the other hand, the complexity and unpredictability of events in a real battle are truly unprecedented. It seems very likely, therefore, that in the race between the continually growing complexity of the problem and the ability to simulate it accurately—a race which is inevitable in this sort of man-against-man contest—complexity would always be ahead.

A major human paradox is also at work here. If a comprehensive defense were deployed, many defense researchers would be eager to announce the discovery of grave flaws and weaknesses in it. These analysts are apt to be the same ones who tend to find some grave Soviet threat just around the corner (claims that the Soviets are on the verge of decisive breakthroughs in strategic defense technology are current examples). Even if a robust shield is built, and even if it could be reasonably expected to work as advertised, critics will come forward with claims that it is unreliable and that the other costly activities needed to maintain the old-fashioned kind of deterrence must still be supported. The irony is that those who will find the flaws in even a robust strategic defense are apt to be the same researchers who are now urging the United States to proceed with SDI before the Soviets do it first. They alternately encourage and denounce because they have a professional interest in all forms of military technology. They take pride in being able to find the flaws in existing systems and in figuring out how to get beyond the current state of the art. Although they will readily admit that nontechnical policy considerations must ultimately determine what is to be deployed, they tend to support political decisions favoring the development and deployment of the weapons systems with which they are, or could be, associated. They are thus the natural allies of those who are predisposed to see a never-ending Soviet threat that requires continuing improvements in the technology of warfare. A space shield, no matter how elaborate, cannot be protected from zealous defense researchers who want to breach the next frontier lest the adversary do so first.

THE APS STUDY

Shortly after SDI was announced, the leadership of the American Physical Society (APS) decided to undertake some sort of major study designed to elucidate the physics issues involved in the Fletcher Committee's report. After some hesitation on the part of this leadership, a plan eventually emerged that called for the establishment of a special ad hoc group to study and report on what was currently known about the sciences and technologies underlying the various directed-energy weapons (DEWs) then under serious consideration by the SDIO.

The study group was cochaired by two distinguished physicists, Nicolaas Bloembergen, a Nobel laureate on the faculty of Harvard, and Kumar Patel, a senior official at the AT&T Bell Laboratories. They were joined by fifteen others, all directly involved in one or more of the sciences and technologies concerned. A review committee (including York) chaired by George Pake, president of the Xerox Corporation Laboratories, was also established. Among the members of the two groups was Charles Townes, who had received a Nobel Prize for inventing the laser technology in the first place. Also included were three experienced researchers from the nuclear-weapons laboratories (two from Sandia and one from Lawrence Livermore), one from the Air Force Weapons Laboratory at Albuquerque, one from the U.S. Military Academy at West Point, one from the Jasons group (which for many years had been studying most of the advanced ideas relevant to the various schemes), and other experts from a number of first-rank academic and industrial laboratories, all engaged in work in science and technology relevant to the overall project. Perhaps most important in this context, several of the members had direct and deep experience in directing the conversion of advanced scientific ideas into large, complex engineering projects. Such experience is not common among physicists generally, but it is essential in understanding the practical problems and time scales that are always involved in the adaptation of advanced physical principles into working devices and systems.

A few of those involved in the study had publicly indicated their opposition to the Strategic Defense Initiative as it eventually took shape, but most had taken no position on the matter, and all were prepared from the beginning to make a serious and politically unbiased study of it. The anti-SDI biases that had already become evident from a poll of the members of the National Academy of Sciences, in the actions of so many academic physicists in pledging to boycott SDI, and in such public interest groups as the Union of Concerned Scientists (UCS) and the Federation of American Scientists (FAS), were carefully and deliberately avoided in setting up this particular study and review.

The APS team worked closely with the president's science advisor (then still Keyworth) and the SDIO staff in elaborating the scope of the work and the means for carrying it out. This cooperation continued throughout the entire study period. The study group was given classified briefings concerning the work then in progress, including projects at the nuclear-weapons laboratories, but the final version of the report itself was written so as to be entirely unclassified and thus available for the widest possible distribution and use. Because of these arrangements, the final report was submitted for clearance to the SDIO before being published in April 1987.

In the words of the report itself, it "concentrated on the physical basis of high intensity lasers and energetic particle beams as well as beam control and propagation. Further, the issues of target acquisition, discrimination, beam-material interactions, lethality, power sources, and survival were studied." [23] The study and the report did not review any of the several varieties of kinetic-kill weapons (KKW) then being proposed. The members of the study group and the government officials directly involved agreed that this limitation would lead to a better and more effective result. The study also did not attempt to estimate the cost of the programs that would be necessary to achieve any particular level of defense capability. And most important, as the review committee noted, the study "does not, and could not, address the global question of whether and on what scale or at what pace the United States should proceed with programs intended to create strategic defenses." [24] The decision to eschew consideration of strategic and policy issues was reached by the members of the study group themselves, their primary rationale being the simple conviction that consideration of these issues would needlessly undermine the credibility, and hence the value, of the rest of the work. All of these limitations were thoroughly discussed with the governmental parties as well, and everyone involved understood what they meant and intended.

The study group's work is summarized in one general finding and twenty-six specific conclusions about as many different elements of the total DEW program. (Several of these specific conclusions were quoted earlier in this chapter in the section on SDI architecture.) The general finding focuses on the current status of knowledge in the sciences involved, with particular attention to the most important gaps in it:

> Although substantial progress has been made in many technologies of DEW over the last two decades, the Study Group finds significant gaps in the scientific and engineering understanding of many issues associated with the development of these technologies. Successful resolution of these issues is critical for the extrapolation to performance levels that would be required in an effective ballistic missile defense system. At present, there is insufficient information to decide whether the required extrapolations can or cannot be achieved. Most crucial elements required for a DEW system need improvements of several orders of magnitude. Because the elements are inter-related,

the improvements must be achieved in a mutually consistent manner. We estimate that even in the best of circumstances, a decade or more of intensive research would be required to provide the technical knowledge needed for an informed decision about the potential effectiveness and survivability of directed energy weapon systems. In addition, the important issues of overall system integration and effectiveness depend critically upon information that, to our knowledge, does not yet exist.[25]

Unfortunately, in publicly presenting the report, the APS council allowed the strongly anti-SDI views of some of its members to be expressed as though they reflected the views of the study group. In a statement issued only one day after the report itself was made public, the council observed that "the SDI program should not be a controlling factor in U.S. security planning and the process of arms control" and argued against early deployment of any SDI components.[26] This bit of advice was a nonsequitur at best, inasmuch as the elements of the early deployment schemes then being considered most seriously were based on the use of KKWs, which had been specifically excluded from the review.

THE CONTROVERSY
OVER THE APS REPORT

Given the highly charged political atmosphere surrounding SDI, it is not surprising that the manner in which the council presented the report stimulated some very strong reactions to the report itself. Fortunately, neither the president's science advisor nor the senior officials of SDIO confused the council's statements with the report itself. Although they clearly would have preferred a more optimistic tone, they accepted the report with reasonably good grace. Shortly after the report was issued, Louis C. Marquet, deputy director of SDIO for technology, declared in a press interview: "I think, frankly, that they carried this study out in a very responsible fashion. . . . I frankly think that both of us gave each other A's. . . . There was nothing in their report which says we're completely out of our minds, that something is beyond the laws of physics."[27] A handful of the most fanatical advocates of the project had a different response. Ordinarily, the opinions of such a small group would not matter very much to the general public. But given the highly charged politics and exuberant rhetoric that have surrounded SDI from the beginning, their reaction had at least a short-lived impact. The core members of the group were Lowell Wood of the Livermore Laboratory; Gregory H. Canavan of the Los Alamos Laboratory; Angelo Codevilla, a fellow at the Hoover Institution and formerly a member of Senator Wallop's staff; and Frederick Seitz, a former president of the National Academy of Sciences and then chairman of the official SDIO advisory committee and of the unofficial Marshall Institute study group. A few congressmen well known for their strong advocacy of the president's initiative worked closely with the group.

The counterattack on the APS study was launched at a special seminar and press conference staged by some of SDI's congressional advocates. At these events Seitz said that the report was not worthy of serious consideration: "I know of no precedent, in my long association with the American Physical Society, for the issuance of so seriously flawed a document as this." It contains "numerous errors, inconsistencies and unrealistic assumptions," he said, that are, "as far as we can tell, always in one direction—such as to make the plan for defending the American people against a Soviet nuclear attack seem more difficult than it really is."[28] The thrust of this remark, to the effect that the APS report reflected the putative political biases of its authors, also permeated the remarks of the others who spoke at that seminar and press conference. Seitz also criticized the report for ignoring kinetic-energy weapons, despite the clear understanding on the part of the study group and the relevant government officials that this type of weapon had been omitted deliberately. Later, Seitz elaborated on his views by saying that the whole experience reminded him of the 1930s when the German scientists adjusted their scientific views to conform to the demands of the Nazi leadership.[29] Wood added that the executive summary of the report was written "with a political goal in mind,"[30] and that he and Canavan noted that none of the six "very senior and eminent reviewers" had worked on the technological areas at issue "for at least a quarter of a century." They added that two of the six had publicly opposed the SDI before the report came out and two others had privately expressed reservations about it.[31] Wood later changed this to "five of whom had taken public positions against SDI."

This same group also found fault with a number of technical details in the report and presented papers describing its flaws at various congressional seminars, hearings, and press conferences already cited. The APS study group considered all of the charges, conceded that the report contained some ambiguities, and issued a measured but firm reply: "On the whole, we stand by the findings of the Report, and we consider the arguments posed in these two [Wood and Canavan] papers to be without merit."[32] The details of these charges and replies are not easily summarized or paraphrased, but perhaps the flavor of the situation can be conveyed with the following examples.

One of the issues in controversy was the prospect for chemical laser weapons. Wood and Canavan charged that the study group had mis-stated the facts. In particular, they noted that the executive summary of the APS report had asserted that such lasers had been tested to date only at a power level of 200 kw, whereas in fact lasers of this type had been operated at more than a megawatt. Thus, the technology of chemical lasers did not have to be extrapolated nearly as much as the APS study had estimated in order to achieve the brightness needed for space-defense applications.

The APS group replied by first noting that its original draft had actually presented a higher value for the laser power levels already achieved experimentally, but that in its last full meeting, the group was informed by SDIO officials that for reasons of security the conclusion *must* read 200 kw. Even so, the statement in the report was not as misleading as it might at first appear because the higher power levels, while actually achieved, were produced in lasers whose output beams were substantially less well focused than those needed for the ultimate application, and the particular laser involved in the higher power experiments "cannot be scaled to significantly higher powers" in the range of those needed for the ultimate application.[33]

Wood and Canavan charged that the report's conclusion that a ground-based excimer laser would require a larger source of power—1 gigawatt (1 billion w)—was inconsistent with its own calculations, which should have led to the conclusion that only 6 mw (6 million w) were needed. The study group responded by pointing out that the critics confused the calculations for impulse kill with those for thermal kill. For an *impulse* kill, the report estimates that a 100-megajoule laser would be required: Canavan arrives at a lower requirement by assuming a smaller diameter spot on the target, based on a much shorter engagement range and a larger mirror than the study group considered workable. For a *thermal* kill, where energy efficiency is much lower, the APS found that power of 1 gigawatt (gw) would be necessary—a calculation not disputed in the Canavan study. Finally, the group noted, SDIO's own actions in relegating the excimer laser to a "back up" technology indicated disagreement with Canavan's assertion that excimer lasers "could be legitimately scaled in a single step to the levels required, from present modules."[34]

Wood and Canavan claimed that a 4 mw free-electron laser would be adequate for purposes of strategic defense, and could operate at 40 percent efficiency. Thus, only 10 mw of delivered power would be required, rather than the 1 gw the APS calculated. The study group replied that Wood and Canavan reached their conclusion by assuming that the efficiencies achieved in an experimental "ETA accelerator" at Los Alamos could be achieved in FELs configured for the more demanding requirements of boost-phase intercept. "To our knowledge," the group reflected, "no one—including the SDIO itself and the laboratories, including Los Alamos and Livermore, building the FELs—currently predicts efficiencies for such devices that are anywhere close to those obtained on ETA."[35]

Another issue raised by Wood and Canavan concerns the power supply needed for space-based satellites. The APS report noted that nuclear reactors would probably be required to provide "station keeping" or "housekeeping" power for satellites carrying surveillance and directed-energy kill mechanisms. Wood and Canavan contended that the study group had greatly exaggerated the need for electrical power by assuming that a continuous supply of between 100,000 and 700,000 watts would be needed for each of the one hundred satellites in the hypothesized architecture. Although that level of power could only be met by nuclear reactors, "the power needed for satellite housekeeping," according to Wood and Canavan, "is not hundreds of thousands of watts, not for *any* of the satellites considered in *any* of the 'baseline architecture' by the SDI program." The satellites under actual consideration, they claimed, would require only a few thousand watts, which are "routinely supplied" by solar photovoltaic cells and storage batteries. Higher levels of power would be needed, they pointed out, only if the satellites were to include radar units, "but the SDI has no plans for radars on *any* of the satellites in *any* of its baseline architectures."[36]

The study group replied that the upper limits of its estimates did in fact take account of the power requirements for satellites bearing radar units,[37] evidently on the assumption that in some proposed configurations, radar units would be mounted on at least some of the satellites. The lower limit, the study group acknowledged, was "about a factor of two higher than the estimates provided for us by SDIO officials . . . not an unreasonable disagreement on such a speculative engineering project." The SDIO's lower limit of 50,000 watts, the group noted, was itself considerably higher than the several thousand watts posited by Wood and Canavan.[38]

Did the APS estimates grossly exaggerate the power needs defined by the SDIO? Since its inception, SDIO has been cooperating with NASA and the Department of Energy in a joint project known as "SP-100" (for Space Power—100 kw). SDIO's interest in the project reflects the finding of the Fletcher Committee that "the overall success of certain concepts is highly dependent upon the ability to generate tremendous amounts of electrical power." [39] In its 1986 report to Congress, SDIO observed that SP-100 "is the cornerstone of the research and technology effort seeking long-term continuous power supplies." The project was needed both "to provide moderate continuous power levels for a variety of projected SDIO needs" and for other civil and military space missions. [40]

In order to determine the official administration view of this matter, Rep. Edward Markey (D., Mass.) asked the Department of Energy to assess the objection raised by Wood and Canavan to this part of the APS report. On behalf of the department, Under Secretary Joseph F. Salgado replied that he had to "take strong exception to Dr. Wood's claims. There may be some people who have the same view as Dr. Wood, both within and external to SDIO, but the official documents provided to us and the decisions reached in concert with the Director of SDIO indicate that higher power levels are required." In a detailed commentary attached to the letter, the department noted that it "strongly disagrees with Dr. Wood's contentions regarding SDIO's 'housekeeping' power requirements," because current SDI studies indicate requirements "from a few 10's of kWe to over 100 kWe for non-burst power duty cycles." The commentary noted that "the overall SDI architecture is still under development, and therefore the power requirements cannot be precisely defined," adding that "history would indicate that the power requirements will rise with changing mission requirements." Although some SDI staff specialists had expressed interest in lower power levels, "SP-100 technology was baselined in all of the recently sponsored SDI space power system architecture studies for providing 'housekeeping' power." [41]

Whatever the eventual outcome with respect to power requirements for a space-based system involving directed-energy weapons, the SDIO's statements and the view expressed by the Department of Energy made it obvious that Wood and Canavan, not the APS report, grossly misstated the officially adopted parameters of the SDIO with respect to projected power levels.

These exchanges are typical of the controversy between Wood and Canavan on the one hand and the majority of informed specialists on the other. The latter are more skeptical about the prospects for strategic defense. The details of the arguments put forward by Wood and Canavan are frequently accompanied by polemics and ad hominem remarks that serve only to confuse the nonexpert and make the argument as a whole hard to follow. Although polemics are not unknown in exchanges among partisans on such issues—and anti-SDI forces have used similar tactics—in this case the attack misfired and only weakened the optimists' position in the eyes of other technical specialists.

THE PROPOSAL FOR EARLY DEPLOYMENT

Very soon after Reagan launched the Strategic Defense Initiative, proposals for early deployment rose insistently in certain defense-oriented quarters. Indeed, the early deployment of the High Frontier version of the SDI was being strongly advocated by Graham and his supporters in and out of government even before the March 1983 speech. Given the fundamentally political nature of the whole affair, and especially the intrinsically political objectives of those who advocated early deployment, it is not surprising that this particular subissue evoked some especially strident controversy. Indeed, even within the defense establishment, the meaning of the term "early deployment" was itself debated. Clearly, in the minds of some of the more politically oriented advocates, the drive for early deployment was stimulated primarily by the desire to get as much of the project as possible committed during the Reagan administration in order to make it difficult—even, they hoped, impossible—for a future president to back away from it. But if the purpose of the drive for early deployment was clear to the politicians, it was not so clear to the technologists, including those who are sympathetic to the basic idea.

To the authors of the Marshall Institute report, early deployment meant abandoning what they called a "business-as-usual" approach to the initiative. Deployment of a partial "three-layer defense" system based on KKVs could, they said, begin in seven years, or in 1994, if the government used "streamlined management and procurement procedures," while under "business as usual" conditions, "deployment of the full 3-layer defense cannot commence until the late 1990s."[42]

The highly respected defense expert Robert R. Everett, who was chairman of the Defense Science Board's Strategic Defense Milestone Panel and had been president of the Mitre Corporation, saw matters differently. In a 1987 memorandum to Under Secretary of Defense Richard Godwin, he remarked—plaintively, it seemed—that "the term early deployment, which is sometimes heard, appears to mean only that a first phase would necessarily be earlier than later phases and not earlier than previously suggested. In any event, current plans and decisions deal only with continued research and development, and deployment will come later." [43]

Despite this uncertainty about what, if anything, early deployment might mean, plans for going ahead with the deployment of "phase I" of a combined ground and space multilayer defense system were continuously being elaborated. As of the fall of 1987 the Defense Acquisition Board advanced six SDI technologies to the "demonstration and validation phase," recognizing their potential roles in a first-phase deployment: [44]

1. SBKKVs—Space-based kinetic kill vehicles, now called SBIs (space-based interceptors). Their purpose would be to destroy "Soviet missiles shortly after lift-off during the boost phase."

2. ERIS—Exoatmospheric Reentry Vehicle Interceptor System. These would be ground-based rockets "to intercept nuclear warheads after they have been released by the ballistic missile, but before they enter the atmosphere." An ERIS missile would be launched toward a point in space where data from sensors indicated an RV could be intercepted.

3. BSTS—Boost Surveillance and Tracking System. This system would rely on "a space-based satellite to . . . provide the first alert of the launch of ballistic missiles and give initial tracking data to the SBIs."

4. SSTS—Space Surveillance and Tracking System. Designed "to locate and track Soviet missiles in space (i.e., the midcourse)," this system would accept data from the BSTS and later hand the data off to the terminal-defense system.

5. A Long-Wave Infrared Probe System would be based on the ground and launched into space only when notified that an attack was under way. It would provide necessary data to "the Strategic Defense Battle Management/Command Control and Communications (BM/C^3) System during late midcourse and early terminal phases."

6. A BM/C^3 System to assemble all the data provided by the other systems and to coordinate the entire defense process.

Oddly, as of summer 1987 HEDI was not on the Defense Acquisition Board's list of phase I projects. As SDIO director Lieutenant General James A. Abrahamson, Jr., put it, "We think the other layers have more advantage and contribute more to the stability equation and deterrence equation."[45] HEDI is included in most other unofficial versions of early deployment, including that described by the Marshall Institute (it is, in fact, the recommended third layer; without it there would be only a two-layer system).

In April 1988 the SDIO accepted the Everett panel's recommendation calling for the reordering of Phase I priorities to emphasize space surveillance (in the form of the BSTS and SSTS projects and communication). The panel recommended against inclusion of space-based interceptors and called instead for consideration of an initial deployment of one hundred ground-based, long-range interceptor missiles similar to the proposed ERIS missiles, but possibly larger in order to provide greater range. These missiles would be deployed at the existing Safeguard site in Grand Forks, North Dakota, and would be intended to provide site defense for a missile field, as contemplated in the ABM Treaty, and only a very thin area defense. This proposal resembles the "Accidental Launch Protection System" proposed for "debate and serious exploration" by Sen. Sam Nunn (D., Ga.) in January 1988. Notably absent from either the Everett panel recommendation or the Nunn proposal was any endorsement of the early deployment of space-based kill systems. As a result of the adoption of the Everett panel recommendations, research on neutral-particle-beam devices for midcourse discrimination and the testing of the space-based "Alpha" chemical laser will probably be delayed.[46]

On the basis of the Everett report, the Defense Acquisition Board recommended in June 1988 that the plan for Phase I deployment in the late 1990s—which the board had recommended, and Secretary Weinberger had approved, a year earlier—should be reassessed. Just prior to receiving that recommendation, the under secretary of defense for acquisition, Robert Costello, reportedly sent a memorandum to Abrahamson on May 27, 1988, outlining new, more modest objectives for SDI, indicating, as a report in *Science* magazine observed, "that the program is being brought more tightly under the control of the civilian managers of the Defense Department." Previously, as the report noted, Abrahamson "had broad authority to set the goals and structure of the program and he reported directly to the secretary of defense." In keeping with Secretary of Defense Frank C. Carlucci's decision that the planned Pentagon budget would need to be cut by $300 billion over the next five years, SDI was coming to be regarded not as a sacrosanct program but one

TABLE 1. SDIO's PHASE 1 GROUND-
AND SPACE-BASED BMD ARCHITECTURE

Component	Number	Description	Function
First phase (approximately 1995–2000):			
Battle management computers	Variable	May be carried on sensor platforms, weapon platforms, or separate platforms; ground-based units may be mobile	Coordinate track data; control defense assets; select strategy; select targets; command firing of weapons
Boost-phase surveillance and tracking satellite	Several at high altitude	Infrared sensors	Detect ballistic or ASAT missile launches by observing hot rocket plumes; pass information to tracking satellites
Space-based interceptor (SBI) carrier satellite	100s at several 100s of km altitudes	Each would carry about 10 small chemical rockets or SBIs; might carry sensors for tracking post-boost vehicles	On command, launch rockets at anti-satellite weapons (attacking BMD system), boosters, possibly PBVs
Probe	10s	Ground-launched, rocket-borne infrared sensors	Acquire RV tracks, pass on to ERIS interceptors
or			
Space surveillance and tracking system	10s	Satellite-borne infrared sensors	
or			
Space-based interceptor carrier satellites	100s	Satellite-borne infrared sensors	
Exoatmospheric interceptors (ERIS)	1000s on ground-based rockets	Rocket booster, hit-to-kill warhead with infrared seeker	Cued by satellite-borne or rocket-borne infrared sensors, home in on and collide with RVs in late midcourse

SOURCE: U.S. Congress, Office of Technology Assessment, *SDI: Technology, Survivability, and Software*, OCA-ISC-353 (Washington, D.C.: U.S. Government Printing Office, May 1988), p. 60.

that would have to be compared with other research priorities.[47] Nevertheless, SDIO planning continues to assume that deployment, in several phases, will take place as research continues (see tables 1 and 2).

Indeed, the more exuberant technological optimists continue to believe that the technology is now in hand to build a ballistic missile defense that would have significant strategic benefits. Indeed, the thrust of the High Frontier study was that this technological plateau had already been reached in 1982. The Marshall Institute report, reportedly written with the benefit of briefings by SDIO staff members, expresses no doubts whatever that a three-layer system "93 percent effective" against a "threat cloud" of ten thousand warheads and a hundred thousand decoys could be built in seven years for $121 billion and operated for between $10 billion and $15 billion per year.[48]

The Everett panel reached a very different set of conclusions. Reporting some months later than the Marshall Institute did, this panel had been asked by the under secretary of defense for acquisition to review the SDI program and to comment on the state of SDI technology, systems design, costs, organization, management, and readiness to move toward deployment. (The Everett memorandum cited above was sent on the occasion of the completion of this review.) "Much remains to be done," the panel concluded, "before a confident decision can be made to proceed." It also observed that "a number of significant technological problems remain to be solved. Cost estimates are, therefore, highly uncertain." It went on to list "the principal pieces of missing technology": (1) the technology for the survivability of the SBKKV bus, (2) targeting the rocket hard body (i.e., the booster) in the presence of the rocket plume, (3) the ability of the passive infrared detectors on the probe and the SSTS to discriminate anything but the most primitive decoys and debris, and (4) the technology for the manufacture of the very large IR focal planes (i.e., the basic component of the infrared telescopes that determine the effectiveness of the probe, SSTS, and improved BSTS)—by no means a trivial list. The panel's report goes on to note that there "is little information on how objects look in space or how rockets look in boost phase. Component and systems design are proceeding on the basis of assumptions and calculations which may or may not prove reliable."[49] It should be noted that all these cautionary remarks came from people who were, in the main, sympathetic to the project. Critics could easily suggest a number of other major missing pieces, but this list is nevertheless formidable as it stands.

Project insiders had other misgivings about early deployment, as evi-

TABLE 2. OTA's PROJECTIONS OF EVOLUTION OF
GROUND- AND SPACE-BASED BMD ARCHITECTURE
(Phases II and III)

Component	Number	Description	Function
Second phase (approximately 2000–2010), replace Phase I components and add:			
Airborne optical system (AOS)	10s in flight	Infrared sensors	Track RVs and decoys, pass information to ground battle management computers for launch of ground-based interceptors
Ground-based radars	10s on mobile platforms	X-band imaging radar	Cued by AOS, track RVs as they enter atmosphere; discriminate from decoys, pass information to ground battle managers
High endoatmospheric interceptors	1000s	Rocket with infrared seeker, nonnuclear warhead	Collide with RVs inside atmosphere, but before RV nuclear detonation could cause ground damage
Space surveillance and tracking satellite (SSTS)	50–100 at few 1000s of km	High-resolution sensors; laser range-finder and/or imaging radar for finer tracking of objects	Track launched boosters, post-boost vehicles, and ground- or space-launched ASATs; Track RVs and decoys, discriminate RVs from decoys;
		May carry battle-management computers	Command firing of weapons

Component	Numbers and altitudes	Description	Function
Space-based interceptor carrier	1000s at 100s of km altitudes	Each carries about 10 small chemical rockets or KKVs; at low altitude; lighter and faster than in phase one	On command, launch rockets at anti-satellite weapons (attacking BMD system), boosters, PBVs, and RVs
Space-based neutral particle beam (NPB)	10s to 100s at altitude similar to SSTS	Atomic-particle accelerator (perturber component of interactive discrimination; additional sensor satellites may be needed)	Fire hydrogen atoms at RVs and decoys to stimulate emission of neutrons or gamma rays as discriminator
Detector satellites	100s around particle beam altitudes	Sensors to measure neutrons or gamma rays from objects bombarded by NPB; transmitters send data to SSTS and/or battle management computers	Measure neutrons or gamma rays emitted from RVs: heavier objects emit measurable neutrons or gamma rays, permitting discrimination from decoys

Third phase (approximately 2005–2015),[a] replace Phase II components and add:

Component	Numbers and altitudes	Description	Function
Ground-based lasers, space-based mirrors	10s of ground-based lasers; 10s of relay mirrors; 10s to 100s of battle mirrors	Several laser beams from each of several ground sites bounce off relay mirrors at high altitude, directed to targets by battle mirrors at lower altitudes	Attack boosters and PBVs

SOURCE: U.S. Congress, Office of Technology Assessment, *SDI: Technology, Survivability, and Software*, OCA-ISC-353 (Washington, D.C.: U.S. Government Printing Office, May 1988), p. 61.

[a] Dates have been amended to correct a misprint in the source.

denced by a report drafted by three analysts at the Livermore Laboratory.[50] The report points out that the optimistic projections (e.g., the Marshall report, in particular) are based on calculations involving the characteristics of the Soviet SS-18, the most ponderous and vulnerable of all current Soviet missiles. Changes in the Soviet force structure, now under way, will greatly complicate the problem of interception. The report also stated that possible future modifications of Soviet forces, including some that are less extreme than those projected in the Fletcher report, make interception by SBKKVs of the type now being developed impossible. For example, the Livermore report concludes that whereas 20,000 interceptors in orbit could intercept 90 percent of the currently deployed enemy RVs during the combined boost and post-boost phases, about 100,000 interceptors would be required by the mid-1990s, given the DOD's projections. The projected threat consists of missiles and warheads whose development and deployment must have been well established even before Reagan's "Star Wars" speech. The so-called near-term responsive threat (that is, the threat designed and planned in response to the speech) is widely estimated to be such that the kind of SBKKVs the United States now knows how to make would have virtually no intercept capabilities at all.

The issues raised by the Livermore study may be further clarified by analyzing them in terms of the fraction of SBKKVs able to reach their targets after a suitable launch warning. According to the Livermore group, in the case of Soviet SS-18s intercepted by SBKKVs accelerated to 6 km per second, only 2.5 percent of the KKVs would be available for boost phase interception, 13 percent for interception before completion of the post-boost phase. (This latter figure agrees, at least roughly, with the conclusion presented in the Marshall report; i.e., that a force of 11,000 SBKKVs can handle an attack launched by 1,600 ICBMs.) For missiles like the U.S. MX and the Soviet SS-24 (a new ICBM now being deployed), these percentages fall to 1.3 percent and 9.5 percent respectively. For missiles like the current U.S. Minuteman and the Soviet SS-25 (yet another new missile) they drop to 1.6 percent and 2.3 percent respectively. In other words, fewer than one-fifth as many SBKKVs can reach an SS-25 as can reach an SS-18. For the Fletcher report's so-called fast-burn booster, these percentages are both zero.[51]

There are still further difficulties that can easily be derived from the Livermore analysis. Recall that in the case of the SS-18, 13 percent of the SBKKVs are able to reach at least the post-boost vehicles, or buses, before they finish off-loading their RVs, but only 2.5 percent can reach the boosters before burnout. This means that 80 percent of the interceptions ($[13 - 2.5]/13$) take place during the post-boost phase. Three important problems result. First, the bus is smaller, tougher, and much easier to decoy than the booster. The demands on the SBKKV are therefore much more severe than they are in the boost phase. Second, the rocket exhaust during the post-boost phase is far dimmer than in the boost phase. This means that the surveillance and tracking system, both in the BSTS and on the KKV itself, will require much greater extrapolations from "off-the-shelf" items than the optimists usually imply. Third, and probably most important, the buses are continuously discharging RVs all during the post-boost phase. Even if an SBKKV succeeds in destroying a bus, on average, more than half of its RVs will already be en route to the targets. And to make things even harder for the defense, the attacker could redesign the post-boost system so that all the RVs were released simultaneously rather than serially, thus greatly reducing the engagement time. A Senate staff report echoed these findings in even sharper terms:

> Based on our briefings, it appears that SDIO is designing its Phase I space defense against an optimistic version of the Soviet threat. They appear to take a relaxed view of the smorgasbord of response options available to the Soviets to counter SDI. Phase I is being designed to address the Soviet threat of the mid 1990's, yet it probably will not even begin to be deployed until the late 1990's and will have the bulk of its deployment life in the following decade. The far more sophisticated threat environment of that later period would appear easily capable of defeating the Phase I system. In short, Phase I likely would be obsolete the day it was deployed.[52]

These skeptical assessments are important not because they indicate there is anything especially defective in the way optimists tend to present the prospects for successful boost-phase interception, but because these complexities are typical of all elements of SDI. Without exception, the various components under development in the project all turn out to be (even ignoring countermeasures) much more difficult and much further from current capabilities than simplistic claims make them appear.

The Livermore report went on to point out—as have other proponents of strategic defense in general—that changes the Soviets are already making to take account of possible U.S. defenses present less of a danger to the United States than the current Soviet offense poses. The Soviets have had to reduce the size and lethality of their forces in order to assure penetration of potential U.S. defenses. Thus, the Livermore analysts say, "the deployed defense has resulted in significant reductions without firing a shot."[53] This effect, in fact, parallels what the Soviets have achieved with their (enormously expensive) air defenses. U.S. responses to the U.S.S.R.'s continuing improvements in its air defenses over the years have involved the substitution of penetration aids (e.g., standoff missiles, electronic countermeasures, etc.) for some of the explosive megatonnage previously carried by bombers. Thus, the Soviets have achieved a considerable reduction in the force of a potential U.S. attack "without firing a shot." SDI puts the United States in a similar position. The big question, of course, is whether the construction of extremely expensive defenses is the best way to accomplish such a reduction. Negotiated arms control may be much easier to achieve and is obviously a good deal less expensive.

Clearly, there is a very wide diversity of views, even within the defense community, about the status of the relevant R&D; about the meaning and prospects of what is already known and in hand; and about the feasibility, cost, and value of any kind of early deployment. In every instance—and even among those who favor SDI—the better-informed and more competent the group, the more cautious and hedged the claims.

A MORE MODEST PROPOSAL: ALPS

A much more limited defensive deployment was raised as a possibility meriting consideration. In a speech in January 1988 Senator Nunn proposed the "Accidental Launch Protection System" (ALPS), reminiscent of the 1967 proposal of a "thin" Sentinel system designed to defend against an attack from a small nuclear power such as China or from an accidental launch. ALPS calls on the defense planners to "seriously explore the development of a limited system for protecting against accidental and unauthorized launchers."[54] Such a system might involve the basing of one hundred ERIS launchers at Grand Forks, North Dakota, the site of the one decommissioned ABM system allowed under the ABM Treaty. An upgraded version of the old perimeter acquisition radar might be used, possibly along with AOS sensors. The ERIS missiles, as previously noted, are designed to intercept warheads in late midcourse, relying on built-in infrared sensors to home in on targets, once guided to the vicinity by data from other sensors.

Such a system might be deployed in compliance with the ABM Treaty, except for changes that could be negotiated, perhaps in the Standing Consultative Committee, to allow, for example, for mobile radars or airborne sensors. The developer of ERIS, the Lockheed Corporation, estimates that such a deployment would cost $3.55 billion, although other observers put the estimate at more than $16 billion, taking into account auxiliary systems as well as the cost of ten years of operation and support.[55]

This system might be effective against a small or accidental launch of ICBMs, but it would not be effective against shorter-range, depressed-trajectory missiles launched by a submarine, which have a much shorter flight time. Protection against shorter-range missiles would require additional deployments at several sites, in violation of the ABM Treaty. ALPS could not provide protection from bombs delivered by more conventional methods, including air attack. Furthermore, a serious problem with reliance on ERIS is that, according to U.S. intelligence data, Soviet nuclear warheads are now salvage-fused so as to detonate on impact. If one such warhead were intercepted by an ERIS missile, the resulting explosion would complicate and perhaps prevent the interception of any remaining warheads released by the same accidentally launched missile. As *Aviation Week & Space Technology* reported: "Remaining ERIS missiles would be unable to find their way to the other warheads lofted by an accidentally launched missile. They would have been rendered 'dumb and blind' by the first blast's radiation, which would paralyze the microelectronics indispensable to the system's command and control."[56]

FROM "SMART ROCKS" TO "BRILLIANT PEBBLES": ANOTHER SUPPOSED LAST MOVE

Another proposal, put by Teller and Wood to Reagan, George Bush, and other high-ranking government officials at a classified White House briefing in July 1988,[57] would change the emphasis of SDI research from "smart rocks" housed on large satellites (as proposed for Phase I) to "brilliant pebbles" (technically known as "singlets," or small, self-contained kinetic interceptors) orbited in very large numbers to intercept a missile attack.

This proposal amounts to a resurrection of the BAMBI project of the 1950s discussed in the previous chapter, updated to take advantage of the very considerable progress made since then in miniaturization and computer power. According to Wood, each of the "pebbles" would contain its own optical sensors in the form of silicon microchips ("eyes

which look out for targets"), a small but very high performance computer on the level of a CRAY-1 supercomputer ("a brain to recognize
targets"), and fuel for propulsion ("legs to execute the brain's target seeking commands"). Each device would weigh only between 1.5 to 2.5 kg,
and cost, when produced in quantity, "about $20,000 per pebble,
assembled and tested," or "perhaps $50,000 each in the early 1990s."
The cost of deploying each weapon, including launch costs, would be
around $100,000. To suppress roughly one thousand Soviet ICBMs—
"with maximum clustering of mobile launchers in the worst case imag-
inable"—would require about one hundred thousand of these brilliant
pebbles. The total cost of such a deployment would be $10 billion, or, if
actual production costs prove higher than estimates by the usual multipliers, $30–$50 billion—still, in Wood's words, "an eminently affordable strategic defense system." Furthermore, because these "Stingers-
in-the-sky" would rely only on nonsensitive technologies, the system
"could be fully shared with the Soviet Union with minimal complications for national security." [58]

A similar concept was put forward earlier by the physicist Richard L.
Garwin, who noted that for "mid-course intercept, a microminiature
homing kill vehicle, a 'hornet,' could be a very effective defensive
weapon." Garwin was careful to point out, however, that even a vast
swarm of such hornets could be rendered less effective by countermeasures. Decoys would confuse the sensors. Offensive RVs could be
enclosed in relatively large balloons, making targeting of the enclosed
warheads more difficult. As a result, "there would be little kill or kill
assessment." Space mines could be orbited to shadow and destroy the
hornets—and the mines could be even cheaper to deploy than the
hornets. [59]

Garwin is skeptical of the new proposal not only because it leaves
such potential countermeasures out of account but also because it is
being advanced with the same overblown confidence that characterized
earlier schemes: "The audacious moniker, 'Brilliant pebbles;' the argument that because there is no law of physics known to the proponent to
prevent the desired performance, then it is achievable; the breath-
takingly optimistic schedules for capabilities that would have enormous
commercial and military significance if they could be achieved—have
all been seen before from the same source." [60]

Indeed, all that can be said at present about this ingenious idea is that
it may or may not prove workable and cost-effective after research and
testing, which will surely take much longer than anticipated. Even if it

proves feasible, however, it will hardly dumbfound a determined adversary. If all else fails, even a belt of sand looped around the equator would do considerable damage over time to these pebbles, or hornets— and, of course, to every other vehicle in space. To guard against such countermeasures, the defender might be able to add shielding to his weapons, but that would make them considerably heavier and add to the cost, whereupon the adversary would devise different countermeasures, and so on, ad infinitum—so long as those who are asked to pay the costs are gulled into believing there can be a last move in a technological arms race.

WHAT MIGHT COME OF THIS RESEARCH?
FOUR POSSIBILITIES

What are the possible outcomes of the current program? We will here consider just four possibilities. In each we explore what would happen if the current R&D program clearly pointed to one of the following possible outcomes: (1) There is *great promise;* it begins to look as though Reagan's vision of a truly effective space shield may eventually be fulfilled. (2) There is *some promise;* it begins to seem possible that a somewhat effective, but not impenetrable, system can be designed that meets the "Nitze criteria" of survivability and cost-effectiveness at the margin. (3) There is *little promise;* the situation continues to look the same as it does today, that is, very dubious at best. (4) There is *no promise;* it soon becomes clear that the whole thing is a wild goose chase.

CASE I: GREAT PROMISE

Suppose that in the next few years the current R&D program shows that there is a substantial possibility of eventually building a strategic defense that would be reliable; survivable; cost-effective (even in the light of the currently foreseeable chain of responses and counterresponses); and on top of all that, leakproof, or very nearly so. If a majority of researchers and key political leaders become convinced of its ultimate feasibility, the resulting course of action is easy to imagine. The United States would, and probably should, go ahead with an accelerated effort, arguments about transition problems and costs notwithstanding. Even in this case (one seen as extremely unlikely by well-informed analysts), the political authorities would still be well advised to make no other changes in strategic policy until it becomes completely clear that this wondrous outcome could be achieved soon. This admonition applies equally to U.S. arms-control efforts, alliance arrangements, and plans for modernizing the strategic forces—assuming, of course, that these policies are all currently correct as they stand. To the extent that the remainder of U.S. strategic policies make sense now, they will continue to do so for at least the foreseeable future and should not be substantially changed on the basis of a very improbable, even if highly desirable, outcome for SDI. Even if the researchers' most optimistic expectations are fulfilled, developing and deploying a multilayered defense will take decades. In the interim, it would be most imprudent to behave as though the outcome were a foregone conclusion.

CASE 2: SOME PROMISE

Suppose it soon becomes widely apparent both inside and outside the defense establishment that the current program may eventually lead to strategic defenses that are reliable, survivable, and cost-effective, even in the face of the first round of likely countermeasures—but, alas, clearly far from perfect. That is, suppose it remains as obvious as it is today that even if a BMD system fulfills the Nitze criteria, there would still be so many pathways through it and around it that the United States and its allies would continue to be threatened with great, probably total, destruction. Most analysts believe that even this more modest outcome is very unlikely; but, conceivably, it could come to pass. Let us suppose it does.

Then, as in Case 1, the United States would, and under certain conditions probably should, go ahead with the program on an accelerating basis. The usefulness of cost-effective but imperfect defenses has been much discussed. In general, even quite imperfect defenses can make preemptive attacks more uncertain and more difficult. If, for example, active defenses are deployed to protect the retaliatory forces, the attacker must increase the size of his strike in order to bring the potential result back to the level that had existed before the deployment of defenses, and he cannot be fully confident of doing so even then. (So-called preferential defenses, to be described in the next chapter, in which only certain specific, but unidentified, units of the retaliatory forces are in fact defended, greatly exacerbate this problem.) The same consideration applies to the defender's command-and-control system. If an attacker believes he knows where the defender's vital control units are located, then, in the absence of defenses, he can at least calculate that a certain level of attack would destroy them all. In the presence of even partially effective defenses, he can no longer be sure of doing so. Given the size of today's forces, even a relatively small remnant is easily sufficient to threaten annihilation of the attacker's cities and population, and this remains so even if the attacker has the same imperfect defenses. Thus, improving the survival chances of even a modest remnant of the defender's forces reinforces deterrence.

In sum, the potential value of imperfect but robust and cost-effective defense lies in the fact that such defenses would in general reinforce deterrence. Thus, the probability of an attack would be reduced even if the defenses could not adequately blunt the attack on cities and population. There are, however, alternate means for reinforcing deterrence. Besides, simply meeting the Nitze criteria is not enough by itself to justify building active defenses. These alternative means in general are also based on increasing the survivability of the various elements of the deterrent forces, including especially the command-and-control system. For the immediate future, the most promising appear to involve better protection of national-command authorities and the further application of mobility, dispersal, and other forms of deception designed to render retaliatory forces untargetable. Active defenses, if they are to be deployed, would in general have to be cheaper than the alternatives to make them worthwhile.

But if strategic defenses were to hold promise of eventually surpassing the Nitze criteria by a substantial margin, and not merely meeting them on an equal cost basis, the United States would probably choose to go ahead with them even if there were other ways to make offensive forces more survivable. In such a case, the deployment of strategic defenses might well lead to a world in which there was progressively more emphasis on defense than on offense. Some sort of useful transition away from the current dreadful situation—in which peace is based mainly on the threat of mutual suicide—might occur. Such a transition is too far off and too speculative to foresee its details, but it might include such things as substantial arms reductions, a defense-protected build-down, and a general shift away from the current high-strung nuclear confrontation with all the extraordinary dangers inherent in it.

Such an outcome also seems to us and to most defense analysts to be very unlikely. But the possibility, however slight, that it might emerge is one of the important reasons that many of the defense experts who oppose the current SDI program, with all the rhetoric and politics that have surrounded it, endorse a substantial, continuing research program in all areas of defense technology, including its newest and most exotic forms.

CASE 3: LITTLE PROMISE

Suppose things continue as they are. Avid proponents continue to project great results and SDI activists in the defense establishment try to lock the program into the political system by making major spending commitments and promising some sort of early deployment. The opponents of the program in the wider technical community, and the doubters inside the defense establishment, both of whom form substantial majorities in their respective milieus, continue to see little promise for fulfilling even the Nitze criteria—except, possibly, for the special subcase of ground-based, hard-point terminal defenses. What then may we expect to happen?

This is, perhaps, the most likely case, at least for the near term. It is also the one most susceptible to the play of domestic and international political forces. We see two distinct possibilities if this case prevails. One will apply as long as the United States is governed by a president who has the same passions for this approach to strategic issues as Ronald Reagan. In this particular scenario, the project will continue at about the same expenditure level it reached in 1988—roughly $4 billion per year. Attempts to increase this expenditure or to commit the nation to early deployment of space-based systems will likely fail. The present organization, built largely so that the R&D program could be rapidly expanded and made to evolve quickly into an early deployment, will live on even so.

The other scenario will apply if the United States is governed by a president who hasn't Reagan's passion in the matter. In that case, the project and its supporting organization will evolve as in Case 4 below.

CASE 4: NO PROMISE

Suppose the view of the opposing majority takes hold in the post-Reagan years. The force of the president's idiosyncratic desires, in addition to the personal loyalty to Reagan of the majority of the Pentagon staff, were surely major factors supporting the SDI and the SDIO. It is therefore at least possible if not in fact probable that without Reagan in the White House the entire edifice will collapse. The package of programs called the SDI may be disaggregated and treated as they were before the March 1983 speech. Even during Reagan's tenure, the funding for strategic-defense programs as a whole did not grow very much beyond what was called for in the plans and programs in place before the speech. Total expenditures for SDI for FY1984–89 will be just over $17 billion, compared with $14 billion projected by the DOD before SDI was declared. The really big differences before and after the speech were that the U.S. and international bodies politic were flooded with grand rhetorical promises about a radically new future, and that a special office, the SDIO, reporting directly to the secretary of defense and bypassing all normal staff offices, was set up. Neither of these two changes is essential or normal to the conduct of an R&D program of the type likely under either Case 3 or Case 4. With this peculiarly dedicated president out of office, they could therefore both easily disappear. Such a denouement is what many observers expect. It is also what most SDI contractors fear and (privately) prepare for.

The technological difficulties in the path of SDI are formidable, but they are by no means the only ones. The strategic issues that surround a commitment to develop and deploy a shield in space involve still more complex uncertainties. We examine these in the next chapter.

A Defense Transition?

SDI and Strategic Stability

In evaluating the technical prospects for early deployment of a partial spacebased defense, the Defense Science Board's Strategic Milestone Panel raised the key question: Even if they should prove technically feasible, are strategic defenses desirable? [1] Plainly, this question must be answered before the United States proceeds beyond fundamental research. Would deployment meet the objectives of a sound military strategy? "Strategy" has been defined by one of its most astute modern students, Basil Liddell Hart, as "the art of distributing and applying military means to fulfill ends of policy." [2] The most fundamental end of U.S. foreign policy is to promote security and in particular to deter aggression against the United States and its allies. Therefore, the case for deploying defenses must rest on a positive assessment of their ability to serve that objective as compared with other military and diplomatic options.

All discussion of the strategic implications of a defensive system must remain speculative so long as SDI's technological prospects and the adversary's likely reactions remain uncertain. Even when the technological issues are relatively well understood, uncertainty about the adversary's responses—or what in technical jargon is called the "responsive threat"—clouds the issue. For example, the technologies needed for terminal ground-based defenses are understood well enough for deployment to be practical, but their cost-effectiveness and utility cannot be determined without taking into account the changes they provoke in the configuration of the responsive threat. Even in this instance, then, any discussion of the strategic implications of deployment is bound, as we have noted, to be speculative. Benjamin S. Lambeth, in examining the Soviet view of SDI, has described the problem well:

> Assuming that the SDI does lead to a deployed first-generation system, the Soviets will be driven to respond within the limits of their technical and budgetary resources. Any effort to anticipate this response must start with a cataloguing of options that are technically feasible, intuitively reasonable, and consistent with past Soviet practice. But that is fairly straightforward compared to the far more daunting task of predicting what they *will* do. The latter calls for a forecast in the presence of compound uncertainty regarding not only the concerns, motivations, and intentions of the *Soviet Union* but also the ultimate accomplishments of the *United States* in the SDI realm.[3]

Opinion is sharply divided among those who have ventured into this speculative realm. Those who favor SDI do not all envision a long-term transition to a nuclear-free world. Either because they agree that the prospects for a comprehensive defense are still uncertain, or because they favor continued reliance on nuclear weapons as the basis of deterrence, some SDI proponents, such as Zbigniew Brzezinski and Henry Kissinger,[4] maintain that defenses are a desirable way to protect offensive weapons because they make deterrence more credible. Other supporters of SDI, like Edward Teller, argue that defenses could provide some protection for population and military targets and that some such defense is better than none.[5] Others agree with Reagan that as defenses are deployed, stage by stage, the existing imbalance between offense and defense will be corrected. After a period of "defense dominance," the threat posed by nuclear weapons would effectively be eliminated, even though some of the weapons themselves might remain in existence.[6]

On the other side, opinion tends to be more unified. Those strongly opposed to SDI on strategic grounds argue that deployment would inevitably be destabilizing and therefore counterproductive. In their view, the current condition of mutual deterrence rests on the assurance that both sides are able to threaten the other with unacceptable destruction in the event of an attack. To the extent that defenses would diminish the credibility of the retaliatory threat, they can produce only instability.[7] Some in this camp concede that terminal deployments to defend offensive weapons could be stabilizing, because they would help to bolster confidence in the efficacy of the retaliatory threat. They are also likely to point out, however, that the same objectives can be achieved in other, less provocative, ways and that even the deployment of limited defenses by one side is bound to result in efforts to improve offensive measures as well as to match the other side's defenses. The result, in this view, can

only be an unrestricted, destabilizing arms race in which either side may
be tempted to suppose that it has achieved or can attain superiority, in
which case it can attempt to threaten the other for political gains. Another destabilizing effect of SDI is that either side might fear it is losing
its ability to retaliate, in which case it might be tempted to risk a preemptive attack. (In technical terms, the first sort of instability is called
"arms race instability," the second, "crisis instability.") If space systems
are deployed, then both sides are also likely to deploy anti-satellite systems. In a climate of hostility and suspicion, such deployments could
lead to crises that would prove unmanageable. Richard Ned Lebow has
envisioned one such scenario:

> The United States is committed to developing a space-based defense against
> ballistic missiles, something the Soviets strongly oppose. Moscow has al-
> ready dropped hints that it is prepared to interfere with the deployment of
> such a weapons system. Suppose the United States, deeply committed to the
> project, disregards Soviet warnings and at some point begins to put impor-
> tant components of a missile defense in space. To show their displeasure, the
> Soviets orbit space mines in the vicinity. The United States, in turn, sends up
> a shuttle mission to remove or disarm the threat. But the mines, having been
> salvage fused (set, that is, to go off if tampered with), explode and kill six
> astronauts.[8]

In view of such risks, the critics of SDI argue that the current prohibition of BMD is preferable to the deployment of defenses because it promotes stability and allows for efforts to reduce nuclear arsenals on both
sides. Although few of the critics hold that disarmament measures can
succeed in eliminating nuclear weapons entirely, they generally contend
that the best approach is, first, to eliminate weapons that could tempt
either side to contemplate a first strike and, second, to continue to rely
on mutual deterrence, but at sharply lower levels. With further steps to
improve confidence and communication, potential crises could be better
managed and the way would be open to a broad range of agreements
designed to curtail the arms race and to lessen the danger of war.

Supporters of SDI rebut this view by pointing out that nuclear deterrence is dangerous in view of the risks that accompany crises when the
threat of retaliation may fail. In any event, they argue, the strategy is
becoming less and less credible. Thus Colin S. Gray cites with approval
Fred C. Iklé's observation (in 1973) that it is probably unreasonable to
expect nuclear deterrence to work indefinitely.[9] As the U.S.S.R. has increased and diversified its strategic offensive arsenal, supporters argue,
neither the United States' adversaries nor its allies will consider a threat

of nuclear retaliation credible. "A unilateral Soviet deployment of . . . advanced defenses," the Reagan administration has argued, "in concert with the Soviet Union's massive offensive forces and its already impressive air and passive defense capabilities, would destroy the foundation on which deterrence has rested for twenty years."[10] SDI advocates also argue, as Secretary Weinberger did, that the strategic situation is asymmetrical because if defenses were deployed by the United States, they would be used only for that purpose, whereas the Soviets, presumably because they are inherently bellicose, could not be trusted to refrain from using defenses in conjunction with offenses for aggressive purposes.[11] In any case, SDI proponents argue, if the Soviets should wish to avoid confrontation, they will cooperate with the United States in achieving a managed transition to greater mutual reliance on defenses, as both sides simultaneously reduce offenses and introduce defenses. The United States' pursuit of strategic defenses, they claim, could encourage the Soviets to follow suit; a defensive arms race would be preferable to an offensive one. Whatever the Soviets should decide, however, it would be in the United States' interest to develop whatever defenses prove possible in order to counteract Soviet offensive improvements and move toward "a defense-dominated strategic environment in which the United States and its allies can deny to any aggressor the military utility of ballistic missile attack."[12] In the first phase, a deployment of defenses would be designed to reinforce the credibility of retaliatory deterrence ("deterrence by uncertainty"), and in the later stages it would achieve deterrence by protecting against a missile threat ("deterrence by denial"). In the best of all possible worlds, the condition of mutual assured destruction would be replaced by that of mutual assured survival or security.

Even those who advocate such a defense transition do not generally suppose it will be easy to achieve or that its principles will prove readily acceptable. Paul H. Nitze, for example, has emphasized the need to engage the Soviets in elaborating the details of the transition. Otherwise, he argues, it would be more expensive and harder to achieve, although he readily admits that making this cooperative transition "could be tricky."[13]

In its most radical form, a defense transition would entail a fundamental reversal of the strategy of nuclear deterrence developed over forty years. Such a reversal requires careful justification. If the Soviets were on the verge of achieving some defensive breakthrough, no such justification would be needed. As we have noted, however, the Soviets appear to be doing no better than the West in this effort. Although some level of research can be justified as a hedge against a possible breakout by the Soviets, a commitment to the deployment of comprehensive defenses is warranted only if they are desirable whatever the Soviets may do.

The opponents and advocates of SDI have such divergent assumptions and predictions that the issue cannot be resolved merely by appeals to logic and evidence. We cannot know enough about the future results of research or about the future of the East-West conflict to foreclose the debate or resolve it to universal satisfaction. Is there perhaps a middle course? We think so. This course would call for continued pursuit of research without premature commitment to deployment and in the context of an arms control regime designed to reassure both sides that neither can achieve some unilateral breakthrough that will confer strategic superiority.

THE MIDDLE COURSE

Even among those skeptical about SDI, there is a recognition that defenses may, in principle, be desirable. Thus, former secretary of defense Harold Brown has observed that "if technology promised the certainty of a successful defense of the American population against strategic nuclear weapons, or even a high probability of overall success, it is likely that policymakers and defense analysts would agree that the United States should seek that objective." Along with many others experienced in military technology, however, Brown strongly doubts the objective is attainable: "Technology does not offer even a reasonable prospect of a successful population defense." [14]

The existing situation is fearful to contemplate. Although the threat of retaliation has inhibited armed conflict, it has sometimes perilously teetered on failure, as in the Cuban Missile Crisis of 1962. So long as the superpowers maintain their nuclear arsenals, war could start because of an accident, a miscalculation, the escalation of a conventional war (perhaps one between client states), or because either side might become convinced that the other side was about to strike and conclude that going first is preferable somehow to mere retaliation, however awful the result of attacking first might be. Should deterrence fail, for whatever reason, the resulting war could be catastrophic and not easily brought to a halt before much of the fabric of civilization is destroyed. An effective defense, even one that is not completely leakproof, could, in principle at least, offer some protection in the event that deterrence failed.

The trouble with this reasoning is, of course, that there can be no assurance at this stage that defenses will succeed against future offensive developments or that they would actually perform as designed. We can be assured, however, that an unrestricted competition to develop such defenses would cause political leaders on both sides to wonder whether their retaliatory capabilities were still reliable and whether their adversary was planning to take advantage of some presumed weakness. The fear that both sides might achieve some fundamental breakthrough would spur both sides to intensify their own efforts, making the total militarization of space a self-fulfilling prophecy. Given the extremely short time-lines involved, space-based defenses take political authority out of the loop entirely, opening the possibility for war to result because of a technical malfunction.

In view of the difficulties involved in strategic defenses, we must answer two questions: would the world be better off if defenses replaced offenses, and would the effort itself merely to develop and deploy them be destabilizing? Provided both sides recognize the risks and take the necessary steps to minimize them, research aimed at resolving SDI's extremely complex technological questions can proceed, at least for the immediate future, without causing such instability. In order to show that a postponement of deployment is the best alternative, we will review the argument in greater detail and present the options that now seem possible.

THE CASE FOR A DEFENSE TRANSITION

The argument for a defense transition assumes that the superpowers are in effect engaged in a technological race that will eventually produce something useful. Supporters of SDI often argue that the West has no choice but to pursue strategic defenses unless it is willing to accept Soviet domination. They contend that a determined Soviet offensive modernization and enlargement program is making the U.S. retaliatory force increasingly vulnerable to a surprise attack and that an undeclared Soviet SDI is designed to enable a breakout from the present mutual restraint on the deployment of BMD. If the U.S.S.R. should achieve a significant BMD capability, and if it should be in a position to threaten an attack that would degrade the West's retaliatory capacity (with the assurance that its defenses could absorb most of a U.S. retaliatory launch), it would also be in a position to contemplate a first strike, or at least to try to extract political concessions in a crisis. If the United States developed defenses first, it would be in a similar position, although U.S. authorities insist that its superiority would not be used to threaten a first strike. In any case, supporters of SDI argue, the United States has offered to negotiate an orderly transition and even to share Star Wars technology with the Soviet Union so that neither side would be threatened and humanity could escape the peril of nuclear war.

The problem with this argument is twofold: SDI supporters greatly exaggerate the possibility of the erosion of the present situation, and they cannot demonstrate that a transition could be stable. The Soviet offensive buildup has not rendered the U.S. retaliatory force so vulnerable that the Soviets could conceivably have any incentive to launch a first strike. The Scowcroft Commission put to rest the fear that the Soviets might exploit a theoretically conceivable window of vulnerability.[15] Offensive developments in the United States, most of them initiated before the Reagan administration came into office, have kept the U.S. retaliatory force versatile and capable of surviving any first strike with more than enough residual power to inflict a fearful response. Even if the Soviets could count on destroying all or most of the U.S. land-based missile force, they would still face not only U.S. bombers, equipped with penetration aids and standoff weapons, but also a submarine-launched attack, which will soon employ missiles fully as useful as ICBMs for attacking hard targets. And, in any event, if any or all major components of U.S. strategic forces became vulnerable to preemption, the United States could always go to a launch-on-warning strategy, however undesirable that might otherwise be.

Critics have properly complained that SDI could lead in two very different directions. The original version, or "Star Wars I," would seek to realize Reagan's vision of a comprehensive defense of population and would not be primarily devoted to protecting retaliatory capacity— reasoning that such limited defenses would only perpetuate mutual assured destruction. It would almost certainly be necessary, therefore, to mount a full-scale layered defense, including space-based or pop-up systems, supplemented by an equally effective air defense capable of dealing not only with bombers and cruise missiles but also with low-trajectory ballistic missiles launched by submarines lying off the U.S. coast. Until such a system could be developed and put in place, at whatever considerable cost, the United States would still have to make substantial investments, at least at the prevailing level, in order to maintain and improve its offensive forces.

"Star Wars II" would be designed to provide a more limited defense, one that would provide at least partial protection for elements of the retaliatory force and C³ facilities, while perhaps also providing some marginal population defense. Such a defense might enhance the existing form of deterrence but it would not meet Reagan's grand objective of making nuclear weapons "impotent and obsolete."

"These two visions of Star Wars," McNamara argues, "have diametrically opposite results." [16] Star Wars I would mean the elimination, or virtual elimination, of reliance on nuclear weapons to defend the United States and its allies. Star Wars II would mean, at best, a somewhat more reliable nuclear deterrent. It would not allow any abandonment of the doctrine of assured destruction but, instead, would complicate the commitment to flexible response should the Soviets deploy a comparable system of silo defenses. It is also not clear that such deployments would preserve whatever stability can be said to exist because both sides can inflict unacceptable damage in retaliation. As we have already noted, to the extent that one side perceived its defenses as significantly better, that side would have an incentive to launch a preemptive attack in a crisis. In this sense, crisis stability would be adversely affected. Again, as argued earlier, arms-race stability would also be jeopardized because the credibility of each side's nuclear deterrent would be threatened by any development or deployment of defenses. Neither side would have any incentive to negotiate agreements calling for equivalent levels of offense or even to abide by existing treaties. Even surveillance by national technical means might no longer be accepted once the strategic objective is to raise uncertainty about the effectiveness of any offensive deployments. In any case, a full-scale militarization of space would obscure the differences among types of satellites. Moreover, in a world in which both sides deployed "Star Wars" systems, those satellites originally deployed for defensive purposes would have the added mission of destroying the other side's space-based defenses in order to clear the way for retaliation. This is the so-called counterdefensive use of space-based strategic defense systems, clearly simpler (the ASAT mission is easier to achieve than missile defense) and more dangerous (the time lines in the counterdefensive mode are even shorter than those in the missile-defense mode).

Supporters of SDI might respond to such criticism by arguing that the effort to distinguish between Star Wars I and Star Wars II is an attempt to sow confusion. What is called Star Wars II should be understood, in their view, as a first step in a larger defense transition, the ultimate goal of which is Star Wars I. In the short run, a limited defense may be advisable to guarantee the survivability of the ground-based leg of the triad as well as to protect C^3 facilities so as to assure the continued credibility of "assured retaliation" before a population defense can be deployed. Even a limited defense could provide some population defense as well as protection against a small-scale accidental launch of nuclear missiles or an attack by a lesser nuclear power or terrorists. Indeed, the collective "footprint" of the projected force of ERIS missiles would cover most of North America. Those who advocate SDI argue that such initial deployments would provide experience with defensive systems and would persuade the Soviets of the seriousness of the U.S. commitment to a defense transition. By demonstrating the economic logic of defenses, moreover, an incremental approach to deployment would help persuade the Soviets to agree to a jointly managed transition.

But supporters of SDI would surely agree with Nitze that the transition to a comprehensive defense would be tricky. Even if offenses could be constrained at their present levels, defenses would be both expensive and hard to make survivable. To the extent that defenses would be considered effective, they might enhance the credibility of deterrence. But they might also lead to reckless action, by either side, such as mounting (and even using) counterdefensive systems. Efforts to promote cooperation in other respects might also become more difficult because neither side could be confident of its ability to protect itself either directly or by threatening a devastating counterattack.

FOUR OPTIONS

In order to come to grips with the strategic implications of SDI, it is essential to consider the four major alternatives and their implications.

1.   Continued reliance on offense-dominated deterrence, with more or less the existing structure of strategic arms control agreements.

2.   Modification of the current status quo by the deployment, either unilaterally or concurrently, of active and passive defenses designed to protect retaliatory forces and C^3 facilities, including those housing national command authorities.

3.   Modification of the status quo by means of negotiated radical reductions of offensive forces, coupled with an agreement to maintain existing ABM Treaty prohibitions on development and deployment of defenses, at least until technological progress makes clear that cost-effective defenses can be deployed. At that time, negotiations would be

undertaken to alter the treaty to allow for deployment of defenses while the size of nuclear stockpiles is further reduced.

4. An unregulated competition in which both sides aim to deploy defenses while improving offenses in order to defeat the other side's defenses.

All but the fourth of these options would permit continued research on strategic defenses without greatly increasing the risk of instability. The second would provide enhanced security only if it could be achieved in conditions of offensive and defensive parity. Both sides would deploy roughly comparable defenses and accept constraints on offensive deployments of an equivalent character. This option resembles the proposal for a defense-protected build-down, to be discussed below. Although we are sympathetic with the aim of this proposal, we believe it would be difficult, if not impossible, to implement. The first option has the virtue of being familiar and of having "worked" so far—i.e., having inhibited the two sides from becoming involved in a direct military conflict—but it is also open to criticism on various scores, not the least important of which is that if it should fail, the consequences would likely be catastrophic. The last option would be the least desirable, entailing large expenditures that would probably result only in greater instability. To show why, of all the options, we think the third is clearly preferable, we proceed to examine the implications in more detail.

OPTION 1. DETERRENCE AS USUAL

For forty years deterrence of nuclear war by the threat of retaliation has been the guiding principle of U.S. strategy, despite early discussions of nuclear preventive war and later considerations of the possible first use of nuclear weapons in Europe, Korea, and Vietnam. There is evidence, reviewed in chapter 2, that although Soviet military strategists were slower to accept this principle, preferring to think of nuclear weapons as war-fighting elements, not only the Soviet political leadership but also the military elite have come around to the same view. As Michael MccGwire has observed, "the evidence now suggests that the Soviets will wait to launch their strategic forces until they have warning of a U.S. attack. In other words, they are braced for NATO and the United States to launch first in the course of a war." [17]

This form of deterrence is often said by students of strategy to be stable in the two senses of crisis stability and arms race stability, but neither is foolproof. Both benefit from such factors as diversity and re-dundancy (as in the case of the U.S. triad of land-based, sea-based, and air-based weapons), hardening, dispersal, and security of communications. Both are impaired to the extent that each side relies on weapons with rapid hard-target kill capacity, because these weapons are hypo-thetically most useful in a first strike. The degree of stability that may realistically be expected under the best of circumstances is inevitably relative and uncertain, because the forces deployed by the two sides are different in character, because the propensity to use such weapons is affected by all the factors that may influence the judgment of political leaders in a crisis, and because accidents could trigger an unintended train of consequences. By its nature, moreover, this form of deterrence implies the possibility of nuclear war. The weapons are there, ready to be used at short notice, in case deterrence fails. If it fails even once, the consequences would be catastrophic. Realistic estimates suggest that a full-scale exchange of thermonuclear warheads, given the size of the ar-senals available to both sides, could result in the deaths of hundreds of millions of people, with casualties possibly amounting to a billion or more, and in the contamination of whole continents, even if not the global "nuclear winter" that some analysts also fear.[18]

To the practical deficiencies of this form of deterrence have been added criticisms on the level of moral principle. The Roman Catholic bishops in the United States have criticized it because it violates the just war maxim, according to which an act of self-defense must not be di-rected against innocents. "Specifically," the bishops noted, "it is not morally acceptable to intend to kill the innocent as part of a strategy of deterring nuclear war." Because even counterforce strikes would kill in-nocent civilians, and since a limited nuclear strike would probably lead to a wider exchange, the bishops expressed serious reservations about the morality of current U.S. policy.[19] Fred C. Iklé has described mutual assured destruction as "assured genocide," though he does so in order to defend a policy of relying on counterforce targeting by accurate mis-siles with relatively low-yield warheads.[20]

Although the moral criticism of nuclear deterrence raises serious issues, it is open to several responses. One of these is that in the absence of international law and a supranational government capable of enforc-ing such law, states cannot be expected to observe the same moral re-strictions that individuals ordinarily respect in domestic environments in which adherence to accepted norms is enforced by collectively autho-rized sanctions. States customarily put the survival of their societies ahead of other moral obligations. If survival requires inflicting or threat-

ening to inflict incidental harm on innocents, they will do so when necessary to national security, as governments have done through history.
Such behavior may be deplorable, but moral indignation alone will not
change it.

Just war principles, moreover, were formulated and applied, however
haphazardly, during periods when a fairly sharp distinction could still
be made between war among combatants on the battlefield and the extension of warfare to civilians who had little if anything to do with the
conduct of war. In the era of total war, that distinction has been obliterated. Particularly in World War II, political and military leaders on both
the Allied and Axis sides undertook campaigns of "strategic bombing"
on the principle that a nation's ability to carry out a war depended critically on communications and transportation networks, manufacturing
capacity, access to raw materials, and even the morale of the civilian
populations. All of these became "legitimate" targets. In view of this
precedent, and of the collocation of civilian populations and such targets, as well as the large lethal range of nuclear weapons, it is hard to
imagine that a future war involving superpowers will be confined solely
to the front-line combatants. As a result, the actual conduct of warfare
will inevitably blur the distinction between belligerents and civilians.

Though the issue is debated among philosophers, there is a significant
moral difference between posing a threat to use force in self-defense and
actually using that force.[21] To be sure, if a threat is to be meaningful, it
must be credible, in the sense that it reflects a readiness to make good on
the threat. Even Leon Wieseltier, who defends this form of deterrence,
admits it is immoral inasmuch as it is "a promise of murder." As he observes: "If the deed cannot be called moral, the threat cannot be called
moral."[22] For this reason, he, like the Catholic bishops, finds a strategy
of retaliatory deterrence provisionally defensible only if it is accompanied by serious efforts to achieve nuclear disarmament. Our views,
while in general parallel to those of the Catholic bishops, have a different basis. We assume that the overarching moral imperative of our time
is the avoidance of a nuclear holocaust. Arms control and disarmament
activities that serve to support that goal are good; actions that work
against it are bad. Nuclear force postures, policy declarations, and military deployments are to be judged in the same way. In the long run, we
believe, human society must find some way to introduce a functioning
legal order among states, and thus to eliminate both war and the nuclear
threat. In the meantime, the goal must be to avoid nuclear war for as
long as it may take to work out a better arrangement.

On moral grounds, we believe there is a significant difference between threatening to retaliate and actually carrying out a retaliation. The threat and the overt act are not equally blameworthy. Most people would not criticize a property owner for posting a sign warning that his home is protected by a vicious dog, even though they might criticize him, and the law might punish him, for actually loosing the dog on a trespasser, especially if the trespasser enters the property by accident, unarmed, and without intent to commit harm. When nuclear weapons are designed to serve as instruments of deterrence, and when they are actually integrated into strategic planning in this form, rather than as war-fighting elements, we believe they can be said to serve a moral purpose—the preservation of peace. This is all the more the case when such weapons are maintained with the clear understanding that their actual use could well amount to an act of suicide. Under these circumstances, we do not agree that the threat to use nuclear weapons is no different morally from actual use. Just as the threat of lawful punishment, when used by a state authority to deter domestic crime, should not be equated morally with the commission of an act of violence in violation of the law, so the threat of retaliation in self-defense should not be considered as blameworthy as an act of aggression.

Nor should morality ignore practical considerations. On practical grounds, it can be argued plausibly that the existence of credible nuclear retaliatory capabilities, more than any other factor, has kept the two contending alliances from going to war with each other in times of crisis. Prior to the development of nuclear weapons, there was no such inhibition. Possession of less lethal means of destruction has sometimes only encouraged nations to make war, in the hope of achieving objectives that would outweigh the costs. In the nuclear era, leaders on both sides have acknowledged that a nuclear war would be an insane and futile undertaking, with no conceivable victor. Reagan has said repeatedly that a nuclear war cannot be won and should not be fought. Peace between the superpowers has indeed become, as Churchill prophesied it would, the sturdy child of terror.[23] Even in situations where they might otherwise have been tempted to make use of conventional forces, both superpowers have been inhibited by fear of escalation to nuclear conflict. In this important sense, nuclear weapons may be said to have served a moral purpose far better than previous declarations of peaceful intent or treaties like the Washington Naval Disarmament Agreement of 1922.

In practice, whatever their status in moral theory, nuclear weapons have been significant restraining influences in at least two well-known cases: the U.S. decision not to respond to the entry of China into the

Korean War by carrying the war above the Yalu River, and the Soviet decision to back down during the Cuban Missile Crisis. In the first case, President Truman decided that even though the war against China would be fought with conventional force against a nation that was not a nuclear power, it could provoke intervention by China's then ally, the Soviet Union, which was already a nuclear power, though one without an arsenal equivalent to that of the United States. Similarly, the Soviets backed down in the Cuban confrontation even though the first stages of the conflict that threatened to ensue would probably have been fought with conventional forces. The fear that any such confrontation would escalate to the nuclear level may well have been an inhibition. It is important to bear in mind, however, that the Soviets made the decision to withdraw knowing that they were not yet the equal of the United States in strategic nuclear power. In some future confrontation, having achieved the parity they subsequently set out to acquire, they would presumably feel less pressure to make concessions. Nevertheless, neither the Soviets nor the United States could have any incentive to engage even in a conventional conflict just because it could escalate to the use of nuclear weapons.

The lesson of these examples is that the advent of nuclear weapons and intercontinental ballistic missiles has compelled political leaders and generals to recognize that the Clausewitzian formula, whereby war is an extension of policy by other means, is obsolete. The behavioral restraint produced by this recognition has been more impressive than any verbal testimony. Military leaders who at first regarded nuclear weapons as simply very large conventional weapons are now sometimes among the first to decry the waste of resources in building nuclear "overkill." Many recognize that because nuclear weapons are not likely to be used in a war, it is useless to acquire more of them than are necessary for purposes of deterrence. As retired Adm. Noel Gayler (U.S. Navy, ret.), former commander-in-chief of U.S. Pacific forces, has noted: "There is no sensible use of any of our nuclear forces. Their only reasonable use is to deter our opponent from using his nuclear forces."[24] These military leaders would prefer to see resources channeled into conventional weapons more likely to be needed in an actual combat situation—combat, that is, not involving the other superpower, but third countries, and therefore less likely to escalate into nuclear war.

Deterrence relying on retaliation is significantly supported by arms control agreements. Even the agreements that now exist between the superpowers, which are by no means as thoroughgoing as advocates of arms control would like them to be, serve a useful purpose in promoting both crisis stability and arms control stability. By preventing either side from deploying territorial missile defenses, they reinforce the credibility of the retaliatory threat and minimize the importance of marginal advantages that may be gained by offensive modernization. By permitting surveillance by "national technical means" (NTMs), they promote assurance that arms limitations are being observed, as well as provide information about weapons systems the other side has under development. NTMs also contribute to crisis stability by keeping the other side informed of what its adversary is actually doing during crises, thus preventing false rumors or worst-case analyses from precipitating decisions to act preemptively.

As is also now well understood, the success of this form of deterrence depends on a country's ability to maintain retaliatory forces in a state so that enough of them are adequately invulnerable to a surprise attack. The United States has chosen to emphasize diversity in its deployments and to put special value on submarine-launched missiles, because these are considered to be the least vulnerable. The Soviets have chosen to put somewhat less emphasis on diversity and to rely mostly on land-based ICBMs, presumably because they are the most accurate systems and the easiest to control and because Soviet competence in long-range aircraft and submarines has historically been less advanced. The Soviets clearly recognize the need to maintain invulnerability, especially in the face of the increasing accuracy of U.S. land- and submarine-based missiles, and are therefore shifting toward greater reliance on mobile missiles that will be harder to locate and target. In principle, there is no reason that both countries should not be able to continue to deploy, for the indefinite future, relatively invulnerable retaliatory forces—forces, that is, which cannot be so heavily degraded by a surprise attack as to be incapable of inflicting unacceptable damage in retaliation.

Proponents of strategic defenses often dispute this contention. As we note in chapter 1, they make several arguments. The Soviets, they contend, are engaging in a massive buildup of offensive forces that will soon outstrip those of the United States, despite the existing arms-control agreements (or indeed, as they would say, thanks to those agreements, which have had a more inhibiting effect on the United States than on the Soviets). The Soviets are also investing far more money than the United States in building and deploying strategic defenses. Some claim the Soviets are building toward a breakout from the ABM Treaty; others claim they have already broken out of the treaty and are in the process of erecting a nationwide territorial defense. Once this defense is fully in place, the Soviets would be in a position to use their offensive superiority more effectively against the U.S. retaliatory force. Even as of now, the DOD estimates that the highly accurate Soviet ground-based ICBMs, notably the SS-18 launchers, could successfully destroy as much as 80 percent of the U.S. ground-based missile force.[25] Such an attack could also destroy a significant portion of the U.S. bomber force, which is not on active alert and is thus incapable of escaping attack, as well as perhaps 50 percent of the U.S. submarine force, which could be destroyed in port. If the attack also included a decapitating strike against the national command authorities, it is not clear that the United States would be in a position to organize, much less to order, a retaliatory attack, or that it would have much incentive to do so if Soviet defenses could absorb much of what was left of the U.S. retaliatory arsenal. This threat will only grow larger as the gap between U.S. and U.S.S.R. offenses widens and as and if the Soviets improve their ASW capabilities so as to be able to target and destroy the currently least vulnerable branch of the triad.

This scenario makes a great many convenient assumptions that turn out to be doubtful on closer examination. The possibility that a Soviet strike could eliminate 80 percent of the U.S. Minuteman arsenal depends wholly on theoretical calculations. The Soviets have never actually fired their missiles over the North Pole and do not therefore know with certainty how the gravitation fields of the polar region might affect ballistic trajectories. They would also have to have great confidence that all the missiles would work as expected. U.S. missile silos have been hardened to withstand all but very close hits. It is at least conceivable, moreover, that some of the U.S. missiles might be launched while under attack. Indeed, such a policy has often been advocated as a way of putting to rest concerns over the supposed window of vulnerability.[26] Another assumption is that the Soviets are making significant progress in the development of *effective* strategic defenses against air attack, an assumption we argued against in chapter 2. If the Soviet Union were to break out or even creep out of the ABM Treaty by deploying a nationwide territorial defense, the United States would have no reason to remain within the bounds of the SALT agreements. The United States could and almost certainly would respond to such a Soviet breakout by building up its offensive forces so as to saturate any Soviet defenses. If these are only ground-based defenses (which at present seems likely) modeled on the Moscow ABM, there is no reason to suppose they would be effective against a saturation attack, or that they would represent a cost-effective strategy on the part of the Soviets.

The notion that the Soviet Union is doggedly committed to an unrelenting buildup of strategic forces ignores evidence that its leaders have changed course since they began to build up their forces after the Cuban Missile Crisis and, having achieved parity with the United States, are now more interested in improving their conventional war fighting capability. It also ignores the evidence of the Soviet offers to reduce offensive forces initially by as much as 50 percent, and even more radically in the future. Even if these can be regarded as propagandistic gestures, they do not support the view that the Soviets are determined to outstrip the United States in offensive forces; at most, they may be said to reflect an effort on the part of the Soviets to maintain a status quo in which they may suppose they have an edge in some respects important to their strategic doctrine. In general, the prospects for a successful surprise attack can hardly arouse great enthusiasm in the minds of Soviet political or military leaders. As McNamara has aptly observed, "only madmen would contemplate such a gamble. Whatever else they may be, the leaders of the Soviet Union are not madmen." [27]

For the foreseeable future, then, SDI is unnecessary as a means for reinforcing deterrence if the objective is to meet any conceivable new Soviet threat. Its only value is to provide a hedge against the possibility that Soviet research efforts will produce greatly improved techniques for BMD. So long as both sides have adequate and sufficiently invulnerable nuclear retaliatory forces, neither side needs to deploy BMD simply for the sake of maintaining deterrence. This consideration was precisely the one that served as the foundation of the ABM Treaty and also provided a reasonable basis to expect reductions in offensive forces and agreements to move away from reliance on weapons with first-strike potential to those useful primarily for retaliation.

A major commitment to SDI, especially one that involves early deployment, can only serve to undermine the status quo. Even if it does not eventually succeed in producing effective comprehensive defenses, it would create a climate of apprehension in which both superpowers would be reluctant to reduce their offensive arsenals. The willingness of the United States to contemplate reductions would be read by the Soviets to mean that deployments of defenses are being planned that would negate the value of the remaining Soviet offenses. Far from necessarily standing as an earnest of an intention to achieve a defense transition, this offer on the part of the United States (to the extent that it is coupled with a strong commitment to SDI) may well suggest to the Soviets an effort to upset the prevailing equilibrium in favor of U.S. superiority. The Soviets can have little incentive to agree to major reductions in offensive forces if they expect such an outcome. They may think the likelihood of SDI succeeding is doubtful, and they may believe they can deal with any impending defensive threat by countermeasures, but all the same they would be foolish to commit themselves to reducing their offensive forces if such a commitment might remove the possibility of using superior numbers to defeat a defense—especially an "intermediate" defense that would rely heavily on terminal ABMs. Nor would they have an incentive to abide by the ABM Treaty restrictions on the deployment of ground-based systems and the testing of space-based weapons. Having called for the extension of the ban on space-based weapons of mass destruction to include all weapons, the U.S.S.R. would surely read U.S. insistence on pursuing the SDI (by testing in space and by making deployments that would patently violate the ABM Treaty) as an indication that it was no longer interested in maintaining parity with the Soviet Union but had become committed to a no-holds-barred arms race.

As things now stand, it is difficult enough for the United States and the Soviet Union to find common ground in the search for mutually acceptable measures of arms control. When missile defenses were eliminated from the equation, as seemed to have been done in 1972, at least the agenda for maintaining equilibrium was narrowed. Even this relatively narrow agenda has proved difficult to manage because of the asymmetry in deployments and the other pressures that prevent agreement. The pursuit of strategic defenses in ways that are certain to go beyond the restrictions of the ABM Treaty forces the issue of defense back onto the agenda in such a way as to crowd and complicate it. As a result, the status quo can be maintained only if the competition to develop strategic defenses can be contained within agreed boundaries; the entire issue could then be ignored.

OPTION 2.
THE CASE FOR A LIMITED DEPLOYMENT

The case for a limited deployment of defensive systems to protect retaliatory forces and C^3 centers rests on at least three considerations. The first is that improvements in offenses may make important elements of the retaliatory force more vulnerable unless they are protected by active defenses. The second is that active defenses may be needed to protect command-and-control authorities from a decapitating attack. The third argument is that limited defenses could provide some population protection against accidental or terrorist attacks. The first two are more compelling than the third.

One of the impulses behind both the High Frontier program and

Reagan's SDI was the claim that U.S. ground-emplaced missiles were vulnerable to a Soviet first strike. If so, an entire leg of the triad was at risk. As previously indicated, the same fear extended to the long-range bombers and submarines that might be caught at their bases in surprise attack. Only if a defensive layer could be added could the United States be sure of producing enough uncertainty in the mind of a potential attacker to make it desist from attempting such an attack. Such defenses, however, need not be comprehensive or space-based. Assured protection of a fraction of the land-based missile force can be achieved by preferential defense—defense concentrated on protecting a certain proportion of the assets the enemy would have to target. Preferential defenses force the adversary into an impossible guessing game and make it cost-ineffective to target everything with equal force. As a result, they virtually guarantee the survival of at least a fraction of the retaliatory force. A ground-based defense is probably more feasible now than it was in 1972, or in 1975, when the Grand Forks ABM system was deactivated, because radars can be made harder and mobile and can be supplemented with airborne detectors.[28] In addition, the nonnuclear interceptors now under testing could provide a more effective two-layer terminal defense with better homing ability than was possible in 1972. Because of these advances, even some critics of SDI support the construction of terminal defenses to protect missile silos.

But why protect these silos when the alternative exists of moving to mobile or deceptive basing? This alternative has been proposed for the MX missiles and for the smaller, single-warhead Midgetman mobile missile. Although the MX proposal proved politically unacceptable, the Midgetman is still under active consideration. Deployment of these missiles on military bases, either on trucks or railroad cars, would provide a cost-effective alternative to sole reliance on silo-based ICBMs. Barrage attacks against the bases would not be sufficient to assure the destruction of such mobile missiles. The Soviets are already moving in the same direction, which may account for the willingness they have expressed in arms-control talks to consider reducing their strength in stationary ICBMs. Strategic defenses could conceivably prove to be more cost-effective, but that has yet to be demonstrated, and their deployment could incur other costs that can be avoided by relying on mobile missiles.

The argument that terminal (or other) defenses are advisable to protect against attacks from smaller nuclear powers or terrorists or against accidental launches is weak, inasmuch as other delivery methods can readily be used by terrorists. Small countries and terrorist groups, "if they did manage to acquire a nuclear weapon," as McNamara points out, "are far more likely to deliver it by the smuggled suitcase bomb than by the long-range ballistic missile."[29] The case for intercepting accidentally launched missiles is more cogent, except that a limited deployment might not have a large enough footprint to intercept more than a small fraction of accidentally launched missiles. In addition, it is unlikely that an ABM system would be designed with a "hair trigger" sensitive enough to make it react to a single missile launch, or even a small handful of such launches.

In general, then, the case for deployment of terminal defenses to protect missile silos and national-command authorities can be appealing under certain circumstances, and does not vitiate the case for relying primarily on deterrence by retaliation. On the contrary, terminal defenses could make that strategy more credible by further reducing the chances for destroying even one leg of the triad in a first strike. The Soviets have already deployed substantial ground-based air defenses, but since the ABM Treaty does not prohibit defenses against bombers, this is entirely legitimate, even though it creates an asymmetry between the United States and the U.S.S.R. in this respect. This asymmetry could, perhaps, be partially offset by limited deployment of terminal ABM defenses.

The problem with this approach, of course, is that a deployment beyond the allowable one hundred launchers would violate the ABM Treaty as it now stands. One way to seek a remedy would therefore be to renegotiate the Treaty so as to allow for a higher level of ABM deployment, at a minimum the two hundred launchers allowed under the treaty as it was originally conceived. (In the original version, half the launchers would be deployed to protect a missile field, the rest around the national capital to protect national-command authorities. They might all be in one place in a renegotiated arrangement.) The Soviets, who are so strongly committed to defense, might not object to such a renegotiation, especially given that they have production lines available for such missiles, which are already deployed around Moscow. For supporters of SDI, initial deployment of terminal defenses could be regarded as a downpayment on a fuller system. The net immediate effect, however, would be to shore up the prevailing strategy of deterrence by retaliation, and to do so within the terms of the ABM Treaty.

In more general terms, partial deployments of BMD could pose serious complications. As an OTA study points out, certain BMD systems can be conceived as operating in a "randomly subtractive" mode. Those

deployed in space or on the ground with very large footprints all fall in
this category. These would be designed to shoot at as many enemy RVs
as possible, without attempting to distinguish among them. In that case,
BMD would not be limited to hard-point defense, and the utility of the
defense would depend upon the efficiency of the kill ratio. A defender is
likely to consider this option only if he can mount a defense in which the
kill ratio per shot or per available quantity of interceptors and RVs is
high enough to make defense cost-effective.

Even if the kill ratio were well below 100 percent, preferential defenses could assure the survival of at least some high-priority assets. A
completely reliable preferential defense of unique or uncommon targets
would be difficult, if not impossible, to achieve because the adversary
could shoot enough RVs at such targets to exhaust the defenses. A
"semi-preferential defense" is a more attractive possibility. Such a system would be based on a preexisting plan designed to protect at least a
fraction of a specified set of targets. Some of these targets might be over-
defended while others would be underdefended. A guessing game would
inevitably ensue between the defender and the attacker. The attacker
would allocate RVs to targets based on an estimate of their importance
to the defender. If the attacker chose to devote enough RVs against the
preferred targets to exhaust their defenses, it could defeat the intention.
In practice, the need to allocate multiple warheads to all targets would
make it likely that some fraction of the target set would survive. If the
U.S. strategy were to be completely preferential, the U.S.S.R.'s best tactic would be to attack all the silos with the same number of RVs. If the
defense could destroy a fraction of the attackers, it would preferentially
destroy all the RVs directed at some portion of silos and save that portion. Thus, if the Soviet Union attacked the 1,000 undefended U.S.
ICBM silos with 5,000 RVs, they could hope to destroy all of them. If
the United States had BMD capable of destroying 1,250 RVs, 250 silos
with 700 RVs could be saved from destruction. A semipreferential defense, because it concentrates defenses, could be more effective unless
the Soviets greatly increase their volley of RVs or guessed correctly which
silos were being protected preferentially.[30]

If the Soviets deploy equally effective limited preferential defenses,
fewer U.S. than Soviet RVs would survive an attack because the current
Soviet ICBM inventory of five thousand RVs is twice that of the United
States. Defensive deployments alone, even if they are equal, do not guarantee equal results.[31]

On balance, the OTA study concludes that a limited defense designed to protect missile silos and national-command authorities could be beneficial by contributing to the credibility of the retaliatory capacity, but that a higher level of defense could be destabilizing unless it promised virtually complete protection of all assets. The OTA study is pessimistic, however, that such a total defense could possibly be achieved: "Assured survival would probably be impossible to achieve if the Soviets were determined to deny it to us" [32]—and vice versa, without doubt. As we have previously noted, there can be no successful "last move" in the contest between offense and defense, except in the case in which one side simply abandons the contest.

Limited defenses designed to protect military assets would not impair crisis stability, and might enhance it by providing additional insurance that retaliatory forces could be used, if not as counterforce weapons, then as retaliatory weapons aimed at civil assets. If they are deployed on the basis of negotiated agreement, and especially if they can be deployed in tandem with reductions in offense, or at least with controlled levels of offense, they could contribute to stability. But the OTA study cautions that if the Soviet Union is able to use more warheads to attack U.S. missiles than the United States has warheads on those missiles, the net effect of symmetrical defense on both sides would be to reduce the total size of the potential U.S. retaliation. The study also cautions that a defense transition would take many years and could involve instabilities if either side perceived its defenses to be either more or less effective than the other's. Just how complex the situation would be during the transition is evident in the reasoning of the OTA analysts:

> While we would not necessarily fare worse in a nuclear exchange under these circumstances than if there were no defenses—indeed we might fare considerably better—we *might* fare worse. The Soviets *might* be able to strike first and defend completely against our retaliatory strike. In one view, the expanded uncertainty in the minds of the Soviets regarding the outcome of a nuclear exchange would aid deterrence. In another view, the possibility that the Soviets could strike first and suffer no damage, a possibility that does not exist if the offenses dominate, would undermine deterrence. [Some believe that while the United States currently has the weapons to retaliate for a first strike, the Soviets may believe that the United States lacks the will to retaliate.] The knowledge by each side that the other might be able to strike and suffer no retaliation has important implications for stability. [33]

In estimating these strategic possibilities it is important to bear in mind that effective large-scale defenses capable of successfully handling foreseeable Soviet reactions are, at best, very far off in the future—so far, in fact, that it is idle to make predictions about such major factors as the details of the technology of that time, or the U.S.-Soviet military balance, or even the general political configuration of the world as a whole. In such circumstances it is clearly impossible to make the kind of system-analytic calculation that would be necessary to determine whether or not the strategic relationship would be stable or unstable.

OPTION 3. ARMS REDUCTION AND A
MORATORIUM ON DEPLOYMENT

Before SDI was announced, the United States and the Soviet Union had embarked on a process that was supposed to lead to negotiated arms reductions. In SALT I and II the process produced accords designed to take advantage of the agreement to rule out more than a minimal deployment of BMD. SALT I did put limits and sublimits on launchers but did not prevent the enlargement of warhead inventories through MIRVing. Nor did it or SALT II prevent modernization of existing weapons and the development of certain new ones. Nevertheless, these agreements were understood by both sides to be tentative steps along the road to more restrictive agreements. Such future agreements, however, would have to satisfy the basic military needs of the two sides, as each perceived them to be. Asymmetries in force structure inevitably led to suspicions on both sides that the existing treaties left the other with advantages. The Reagan administration came into office convinced that SALT II was "fatally flawed" because, among other things, it left the Soviets with an advantage in heavy missiles capable of prompt hard-target kill. This advantage was said to have created a "window of vulnerability" by putting the entire land-based leg of the U.S. triad at risk in a preemptive attack. The Reagan administration reluctantly agreed to abide by the treaty limits informally so long as the Soviets would, too, and to discuss further arms-control agreements with the Soviets. But there was no great enthusiasm for these negotiations in the administration, and as a result a coherent policy was not adopted during Reagan's first term.[34]

In the second term, however, after the president declared SDI, the negotiations picked up steam for reasons to be examined in chapter 5. Reagan appeared to have undergone a change of heart, and U.S. policymakers may also have been eager to counter the propaganda gains that the Soviets were threatening to achieve from Gorbachev's peace offensive. The Reagan administration was hardly of one mind, however. There were those high in its councils who clearly would have preferred that there be no arms-control agreements with the Soviets. They did not expect the Soviets to abide by any such agreements, and they feared that such agreements would freeze a situation in which the Soviets were in the stronger position. The U.S. edge in technology would not be exploited, and the peace forces in Congress and elsewhere would use an agreement to clamp a lid on defense spending. The net result would be to weaken rather than strengthen U.S. defenses. The cross pressures within the administration were scarcely resolved. (A good illustration is the administration's decision to call for a ban on mobile missiles, which was in direct contradiction to the recommendation of the Scowcroft report, and which the administration may not have intended to honor in negotiations.)

The signing and ratification of the INF Treaty left the larger question of strategic offenses and defenses unresolved. If the Bush administration elects to continue to disregard the SALT II limits and to call for early deployment of space-based strategic defenses, any momentum afforded by the INF Treaty could well be lost. It is possible, however, that the INF agreement will "break the ice" and lead to further negotiations, all the more because this would be an agreement signed by a president who came into office convinced that the U.S.S.R. was "an evil empire" given to lying and cheating on all its agreements, and who seemed more interested in challenging the Soviets to a renewed arms race than in controlling it. The president's defenders have argued, however, that Reagan was concerned to get *serious* arms reduction, and that his approach of making it clear to the Soviets that he would not settle for just any agreement paid off in the case of the zero option and will eventually also pay off in the other areas. If this interpretation proves correct, an INF accord should lead to strategic arms reduction. How it can do so in the absence of an agreement to restrict SDI to what is permitted under the ABM Treaty is hardly obvious.

In domestic political terms, even the achievement of a broad framework agreement (modeled on that adopted by Ford and Leonid Brezhnev in Vladivostok in 1974) on offensive arms and SDI would have important consequences in forging a bipartisan consensus and assuring the continuation of the SDI program in some form. That program could otherwise be in serious difficulty in Congress and with the defense establishment. But the larger question that the Bush administration must resolve is how an arms-control agreement can be compatible with the desire for strategic modernization and SDI. In other words, the issue is what strategic commitment the administration intends to make—is there any coherent strategic commitment, or is there merely a ragged patchwork of ad hoc agreements and concerns?

That there could be a coherent strategy is indicated by Nitze, who has argued that the U.S.S.R. had become complacent about negotiations with the West because it enjoyed a certain strategic superiority. In his view, it now enjoys a strategic superiority in conventional forces and a geographic advantage in Europe. The U.S.S.R. has a particular advantage in prompt hard-target kill capability because of its large land-based ICBMs. In addition, "they were quite satisfied with the pre-SDI imbalance in strategic defense activities between the U.S. and the U.S.S.R. They see little advantage in moving cooperatively to a more defense-reliant regime under which their current advantages in both offense and defense would be reduced or balanced." [35] Nitze therefore argues that SDI played a significant role in compelling the Soviets to think more seriously about negotiations with the United States. They are "genuinely nervous," he suggests, about a concerted effort by the West to develop exotic technologies and apply them to defenses. They may well fear that "the marriage of Western technological genius and American space expertise can lead to U.S. dominance in the military uses of space." [36] Nitze doubts the Soviet Union seriously fears that the United States has a hidden agenda in SDI that aims to develop offensive space weapons because, he says, they know that an SDI system would be optimized for defensive purposes, whereas the strategic modernization program aims to develop new systems to attack ground targets. SDI gives the Soviets an incentive to agree to or at least to recognize the need to allay Western discontent with Soviet advantages. Having traded away their SS-20s, the Soviets now appear prepared for serious negotiations aimed at reducing conventional forces in Europe, but these moves would not affect the competition with the United States in strategic forces. Something more would be required on both sides.

Nitze argues that both sides would benefit if they could agree to the concept of a defense transition to be managed cooperatively. He admits that the Soviet negotiators have expressed little interest in the concept, but he sees this reluctance as largely tactical, because the Soviets have committed themselves to the public argument that SDI is designed to produce "space strike arms" and to militarize space, and they are reluctant to acknowledge that what is really at issue is the extent to which it may be possible to rely on a more defense-dominated strategy—one that would permit the United States to equalize what Nitze sees as the current Soviet advantage in combined offensive and defensive forces.

But Nitze admits that the Soviets may be skeptical that the United States would deliberately "introduce future strategic defenses in such a way that neither side would gain unilateral advantage."[37] To remove these suspicions, U.S. negotiators would need to engage with their Soviet counterparts in serious, detailed discussions about how such deployments might be made.

The Reagan administration balked at entering into such discussions, because the Nitze view was not shared by others influential in the administration. The discussion within the administration—originally led by Weinberger—of an early deployment of space-based defenses, ran counter to Nitze's idea of a cooperative transition. It reflected a willingness to proceed unilaterally to achieve a transition, on the theory that in the short run a deployment of defenses would reduce or eliminate the advantage the Soviets have in land-based missiles. Eventually, the thinking went, such a deployment would create so much uncertainty in the minds of the Soviets as to negate the value of such weapons and lead, either through negotiations or otherwise, to the elimination of such weapons as a concern. The Weinberger approach, in other words, seems to deny any need for Soviet cooperation in a defense transition. It seems to be based instead on the assumption that an affordable U.S. program can be pursued that would install intermediate defenses—based on relatively conventional technology—in the short run, and replace or supplement this system with more exotic technologies as they become available. In the process, the United States would at first maintain its efforts at strategic modernization, so as not to rely entirely on the space shield, but would gradually increase the role of defenses in comparison to that of offensive forces; the Soviets would simply be compelled to follow suit because they would not be able to rely on their offenses.

It is not clear whether future administrations will feel a need to choose between these two approaches, but it is clear that they are very different. Nitze's approach does not anticipate early deployment of space-based systems unless and until it can be shown that they meet the stiff criteria he set, and Nitze himself has said that as of now the systems being proposed do not meet those criteria. Weinberger, in effect, introduced new criteria—of affordability and, even more important, of demonstrating to the Soviets and to the American people that the United States intends not just to do research on strategic defenses but also to make use of that research to deploy actual systems. Such deployments, if they are even partially effective, would force the U.S.S.R. to make expenditures it would prefer to avoid to modernize its offensive forces, and to impose penalties on those forces, which would make them far less threatening to U.S. military assets and perhaps also to the U.S. population. If in the process the existing arms control agreements were scrapped, this would presumably be all to the good, in that it would remove the illusion that the security of the West can be based on such agreements rather than on the will to resist Soviet expansionism by maintaining the strongest possible defensive capabilities.

So long as the U.S. administration is of two minds on the issue, U.S. negotiators can present no coherent proposal for a defense transition to the Soviet Union. Even if they could, there is no indication that the Soviets would be willing to go along with it. They might have good reasons for rejecting any such proposal. They may calculate that they benefit from their present advantages in strategic defenses and may be unwilling to give up that advantage until the United States actually makes a commitment to deploy space-based defenses. Just as they resisted proposals to consider the zero-zero option until the West began to deploy its responses, the Soviets may elect to wait until the United States makes a decision to deploy a space-based defense. They are well aware that the proposal has strong domestic opposition and would be costly. They also have the alternative of concentrating on countermeasures to defeat the system, on the theory that countermeasures might be cheaper and more reliable than any kinetic space-based system the United States could orbit in the near future. They may well also believe that one of the best countermeasures to such a system would be not only to maintain their current missiles and warheads but also to build still more missiles, more modern than present missiles (especially those with faster-burning boosters).

At Rejkyavík, however, the Soviets gave evidence of a willingness to agree to reductions in offensive missiles, along the lines previously agreed to at Geneva, so long as the United States would agree to abide by the ABM Treaty for at least ten more years. But that extension would have included a commitment not only to refrain from deploying strategic defenses not permitted under the treaty but also to restrict research so that there would be no testing in space. If the United States is willing to wait until SDI research produces results that would meet the Nitze criteria—results that would certainly take at least ten years, in the opinion of such qualified technical observers as the APS review panel—then an agreement to reduce nuclear weapons is within reach. How significant that reduction would be is another question. A 50 percent reduction would still leave both sides with more than enough accurate offensive capability to inflict devastating damage. But if the sublimits can be negotiated to the satisfaction of the United States, then the Reagan administration's concern over the threat of the Soviet SS-18s could be considerably alleviated.

An alternative to an agreement to reduce nuclear weapons, coupled with a moratorium on development and deployment—the defense-protected build-down—has been proposed by Weinberg and Barkenbus.[38] This proposal would couple reductions in offense to deployment of defenses. Initially, these defenses would be ground-based. The reductions might either be arranged by negotiations or by tacit bargaining. Each time one side substituted a unit of defense for a unit of offense, the other side would reciprocate, until virtually all offenses were replaced by defenses.

There are a number of difficulties with this proposal.[39] One is that it does not fit the current national strategy of extended deterrence. In that strategy, there must be enough offensive weapons to make an attack possible on the enemy's military forces, perhaps even in a first-strike mode. The number of such weapons is much larger than the number needed for threatening cities in a "minimum deterrence," or purely retaliatory, mode. It is therefore not possible simply to trade off offensive weapons for the kind of defenses that would guarantee the survival of a few ICBMs. In addition, defenses cannot be tested as effectively as offenses and must meet more stringent criteria. An offensive weapon can cause great damage even if it explodes at some distance from its intended target. A defensive weapon must be able to intercept a target with a high degree of accuracy in a very short time. Whether military officers would be willing to substitute defensive for offensive weapons is questionable, in view of such inherent disadvantages to the defensive systems. Parity would be hard to assure in view of the different characteristics and effectiveness of the various components that would constitute the defensive systems. This would become even more of a problem when the components in question would be not only the conventional nuclear-tipped BMD missiles but exotic technologies, which might be either ground-based or space-based and would depend on a variety of sensors. Would a space-based sensor be considered the equivalent of a ground-based radar? Would all types of defensive missiles or laser weapons be considered interchangeable units for purposes of achieving parity? Could such deployments possibly be made subject to adequate verification? In principle, the idea of achieving a defense transition by means of a defense-protected build-down is attractive, but in practice it would be very hard to implement. As the OTA study noted: "Nobody has suggested how the problems of measuring, comparing, and monitoring disparate strategic forces—problems which have plagued past arms control negotiations—could be satisfactorily resolved in the far more difficult situation where both offensive and defensive forces must be included." [40]

That difficulty could be postponed and perhaps avoided altogether if both sides could agree to reaffirm the ABM Treaty, under its traditional interpretation, while reducing nuclear weapons by half. Such an agreement need not be thought a dead end. Many experts agree that further reductions could be envisioned that would reduce the stockpiles to a level no higher than several thousand warheads each without affecting each side's ability to continue to deter the other by the threat of retaliation. If these warheads were all on systems that would not threaten a first strike, crisis stability would be enhanced. Neither side would be inhibited from continuing research on more effective defensive systems or from modernizing offensive weapons to enable them to penetrate existing defenses or defenses that might be contemplated. But a climate of cooperation would have been established that could lead to cooperation in the deployment of defenses. Freeman Dyson has argued cogently that the effort to develop defenses will prove impossible if both sides are free to build countermeasures and offensive forces to defeat them. It is not impossible, however, as he has also noted, that if the offensive forces can be reduced significantly by mutual agreement, relatively inexpensive defenses could be introduced that would be effective enough against small stockpiles to serve as insurance against third-party attacks and enable virtual nuclear disarmament to take place. [41]

"General and complete" nuclear disarmament is probably too much to hope for. Nuclear weapons cannot be uninvented. Small stockpiles could be hidden, although sophisticated delivery systems might be harder to hide. But the inspection required to make certain that no weapons at all were secreted somewhere would be so intrusive as to be virtually intolerable to sovereign states. In a time of crisis, moreover, any state capable of producing such weapons could do so on fairly short notice if the facilities and materials had not been destroyed. And there would always be the paradox that in a world in which nuclear weapons have been reduced to very low levels, a state possessing even a small number could become a superpower by virtue of those few weapons.

The big advantage in accepting such an agreement would be, first of all, that the present system of deterrence would not be rendered uncertain, as it would be by a decision to develop and deploy a substantial defense of uncertain effectiveness. Both sides could continue to count on the efficacy of their deterrent forces and would not need to restructure those forces or reorient their production facilities immediately to take account of impending defensive systems. Such modifications to offenses could be introduced gradually. This would be of obvious advantage to the Soviets, but that advantage would translate into greater assurance for U.S. allies that the Soviet Union would not seek to compensate for inferiority vis-à-vis the United States by raising the threat to them. The political gains of accommodation could be enormous in maintaining or restoring the momentum of the process of arms control and possibly promoting the broader form of détente that eluded Nixon and Kissinger in the 1970s, but that the present Soviet regime shows signs of being interested in. Nor would such an agreement stymie SDI. On the contrary, the president or his successor could properly claim that SDI had helped to bring about the agreement, and that only its ultimate success would make possible further reductions that would lead to the substitution of defenses for nuclear weapons. This would be a potent formula to assure support of a regular, if modest, level of expenditures prior to the decision to move to development and deployment—a decision that could be affected for the better by Soviet agreement to modify the terms of the ABM Treaty to allow for specific forms of testing and deployment.

OPTION 4. UNRESTRICTED COMPETITION

The most troubling alternative to some form of agreed transition or to a postponement of any final decision about such a transition is unrestricted competition in both offensive and defensive weapons. The consequences, as McNamara points out, would be very serious:

> A unilateral shift to Star Wars would have disastrous consequences. The ABM Treaty, the most important arms control agreement of the nuclear age, would be the first casualty. Because of the resulting race in strategic defense weaponry, each side would begin to build up its offenses to ensure deterrent capability. Thus, the existing SALT agreements would be the next casualty. Future accords to restrain the offensive arms competition would be impossible until the Star Wars race was halted and reversed.[42]

In strategic terms, any decision by either side to proceed unilaterally to violate the ABM Treaty (not in some specific way—as the Soviets did in the case of the Krasnoyarsk radar—to take advantage of a loophole without affecting the general aim of the treaty, but in a way that would undermine the treaty in an essential way by producing a territorial defense or even a major defense of missile silos) would certainly be read by the other side as a commitment to achieve military superiority, either to prepare for a preemptive strike or simply to be in a position to harvest political benefits. Such an effort would be met by a concerted effort on the part of the other side to match the buildup or, possibly, to defeat the defenses. During such a competition, both sides would have reason to fear that their retaliatory deterrents could be put in jeopardy. Under the circumstances, there would be both crisis instability and arms race instability.

If both sides were to deploy space-based defenses using speed-of-light weapons, the temptation to strike first, in a counter-defensive mode, would be greater than it is in a condition of offensive mutual deterrence. Under such circumstances the stage would be set for what a Senate staff report called "a 'high noon' shoot-out in space."[43] Each side would have to recognize that the first to shoot would win, unless—as is highly unlikely—weapons and sensors can be made undetectable or invulnerable. Directed-energy weapons will very likely be even more effective against satellites, including those that would carry strategic defense sensors and weapons, than they would be against ballistic missiles. Although such a conflict would not itself involve the use of nuclear weapons, it could easily lead to their first use by the side whose defenses were under attack, if that side should become convinced that it was being put into a situation in which it must either "use them or lose them."

Those in favor of SDI nevertheless argue that whatever response the Soviet Union might make, the United States would have an advantage in military technology and could exploit this advantage to develop defenses that would be so cost-effective that the Soviets would have no choice but to recognize that their offenses had indeed become "impotent and obsolete." Meanwhile, of course, the United States would continue to rely on its offensive deterrent to forestall any Soviet preemptive attack. But this argument falters on the issue of cost. It is easy enough to postulate that the United States can develop defenses while maintaining a potent retaliatory force, but given that an effective defense would have to include a layered screen capable not only of intercepting virtually all ballistic missiles fired at the United States and its allies—whether from long-range or short-range weapons—but also as air-launched cruise missiles, bombs, and standoff weapons, such a defense is bound to be extremely costly; vast sums must meanwhile be spent on keeping offensive forces up to date. The possibility that the Soviets would shift to a policy of emphasizing conventional war, perhaps conducted by proxies, against vital U.S. interests, or that other threats would develop (like that posed by Khomeini's Iran in the Persian Gulf) would force the United States to spend possibly even more than it now spends on conventional military forces. That a defense transition would be feasible under these circumstances altogether ignores the pressures for trade-offs among military options as well as the pressure exerted during peacetime on the domestic budget. A strategy that is not affordable and is not likely to be sustained politically is one that cannot be maintained in either strategic or economic terms.

A strategy must also take into account the psychological and other effects on the structure of alliance in which the United States plays a leading role. To the extent that SDI has already aroused misgivings among U.S. allies, because it seems to endanger the process of arms control and détente, a decision to proceed beyond the present research stage into development and deployment would risk gravely exacerbating these fears, quite possibly arousing such political opposition as to bring about the collapse of the alliance. The alliance has been held together for four decades on the assumption that the nuclear shield would serve as a deterrent against Soviet aggression. The abandonment of that nuclear shield in favor of a defensive system in which the allies have no confidence, and which might trigger Soviet counterefforts against them could strengthen the current trend to regard the Soviets as less of a threat to Europe than the United States. A strategic revolution of the kind implied by the idea of a defense transition can be promoted only internally only at great peril to the alliance. This is especially the case inasmuch as West Europeans are likely to fear that if both superpowers achieve even reasonably effective strategic defense not only would the independent deterrents of France and Britain be nullified but also the way would be open for the U.S.S.R. to exploit what is perceived to be its advantage in conventional force in Europe.

The issue of strategic defense also runs into the problem posed by the possible resort to conventional force. Although both sides have maintained considerable conventional forces and both have brought these forces into play in military engagements—the United States notably in Korea and Vietnam, the Soviet Union in Czechoslovakia, Hungary, and Afghanistan—they have been inhibited in the use of conventional force in situations that could lead to direct confrontation and escalation to the use of nuclear weapons. In that sense, nuclear weapons have had an inhibiting effect on the actual or threatened use of conventional force. To the extent that that option or danger is removed, would the world be made safe once again for conventional war? The U.S. guarantee of extended deterrence for its allies would be rendered meaningless, because it rests not on its ability to help Europe to deter a Soviet attack by providing conventional support but on its "nuclear umbrella."

Even now, Western Europeans doubt whether they can rely on the U.S. nuclear guarantee. They wonder whether, despite formal commitments, a U.S. president would risk the safety of the United States by ordering a nuclear strike against the Soviet Union to defend Europe. Those who express this doubt often argue that NATO should be better prepared to check any Soviet aggression by conventional means in order to minimize the need to rely on the threat of U.S. nuclear forces. For the same reason, two European states, Great Britain and France, have felt compelled to develop independent nuclear deterrents. If these were nullified, the conventional threat would indeed become more serious.

If the conventional threat became more serious, however, the West Europeans could be expected to take the case for conventional armament more seriously. Until now, they could avoid taking the hard decision to increase spending and to devote more manpower to the defense of Europe by relying on the U.S. nuclear guarantee. If they could no longer rely on such a guarantee, they might simply have to respond by building up conventional defenses. This will become more and more difficult as the Soviets acquire more accurate conventional weapons with which to strike at NATO airbases and command facilities, but it is certainly not impossible for the West to build up its conventional forces to an extent that could deter the Soviets or to negotiate asymmetrical reductions.

Outside Europe, the U.S. nuclear shield is even more dubious. The United States may formally pledge to defend the vital interests of the West by any military means necessary, but the unwillingness to rely on nuclear weapons led to the Carter administration's creation of the Rapid Deployment Force, a move reinforced by the Reagan administration's decision to create a new command for mobile and swift intervention. Although the defense of Japan and South Korea also involves the nuclear option, here, too, conventional force deployment is seen as a vital complement to a credible defense. It is not obvious that the elimination of the nuclear umbrella would necessarily place these allies at greater risk, or that the risk could not be kept minimal by the deployment of greater conventional force.

In Europe and other theaters, significant expansion of conventional forces would entail costs, but these could be shared with allies who can now well afford to contribute more to their own defense. The costs are therefore not a significant deterrent to a shift to greater reliance on conventional forces. Nevertheless, it would remain possible that the deterrent effect of conventional forces would be far smaller than that created by nuclear weapons. There have been major wars not involving the superpowers—in the Middle East, for example—in which the sides were not inhibited from going to war because they did not fear nuclear attack. It is at least conceivable that in Europe or the Far East, either side might be prepared to enter a conventional conflict to achieve some limited objective. War, in other words, might become more "thinkable" among the superpowers than it has been since both acquired the means to deliver great numbers of nuclear weapons.

For this reason, the abandonment of the strategy of deterrence by the threat of retaliation in favor of the development of assured defense—always assuming such a defense is possible—could indeed increase the danger of conventional war. This danger is compounded, as previously noted, if the atmosphere is characterized by mutual mistrust and there are no constraints on the development of military forces of all types. The effort to develop defenses against conventional attack may succeed in allaying some of the difficulty, but there is little reason to suppose that such defenses could be good enough to forestall conventional wars altogether, under favorable circumstances.

IS THERE NO BETTER ALTERNATIVE?

If defenses against nuclear attack are not built, is there no way to escape the danger that nuclear weapons might be used in the event deterrence fails? There are ways (through arms-control measures of various sorts, including confidence-building measures) to lessen the likelihood of a failure of deterrence. It is also possible to remove by agreement weapons that are especially valuable in a first strike or those that are so vulnerable to preemption that they are usable only in a first strike, and instead to leave both sides with weapons more suitable for purposes of retaliation. But the existence of large arsenals of nuclear weapons would mean that the danger of atomic war would persist. The danger of the effects of such a war can be reduced by reducing the size and lethality of the stockpiles. If both sides come to see nuclear weapons as deterrents rather than as war-fighting weapons, they should be willing to reduce them to minimally acceptable levels by agreements, particularly if lesser powers are willing to reduce their nuclear stockpiles as well. Such agreements could seriously inhibit further proliferation of nuclear weapons and lead to more agreements patterned after Latin America's agreement to achieve further regional bans on the deployment of nuclear weapons.

So long as the weapons exist, so long as there are no effective defenses against them, and so long as war remains a "normal" way of resolving conflict, the danger would remain that they might be used. To minimize this danger further, some forms of defense—both passive and active—may be desirable and could be put in place by both sides without threatening the other or the credibility of its deterrent. As such steps are taken (quieting fear and antagonism), institutional changes might be made in the form of recognized boundaries and spheres of influence such as have already been achieved in Europe. These institutional changes could be coupled with measures to increase trade and communication, in line with recent developments. In a climate of cooperation, political changes could strengthen integration and make international agreements more enforceable.

In view of the potential for stability, it seems an act of folly to commit the United States to a unilateral pursuit of strategic defense on the ground that this will somehow lead to a cooperative defense transition, whether the other side agrees or not. The decision to rely on military force alone, and not on political bargaining and negotiation, is defensible only if it would necessarily redound to national security. And, as we have seen, such an outcome is hardly inevitable. The vigorous pursuit of an illusory perfect defense hardly promises to offset the risks and costs that would certainly be involved.

A better approach would be to maintain the present strategy of deterrence while working to reduce the size of the nuclear arsenals presently considered necessary for this purpose by both sides and, in addition, to attempt to substitute conventional weapons for nuclear ones. The arsenals can be greatly reduced without jeopardizing security. In view of improvements in accuracy, U.S. ICBMs, SLBMs, and air-borne standoff weapons can destroy Soviet targets with less redundancy. Shorter-range military missions can be accomplished by using recently developed, highly accurate short-range missiles with conventional warheads.

Neither the United States nor the Soviet Union would risk any loss of international power or prestige by agreeing to such a mutual reduction in nuclear forces. Their arsenals would remain significantly larger than those of other states, and their agreement to reduce arsenals would be a powerful incentive for them to prevent further nuclear proliferation and the buildup of nuclear arsenals by states that already belong to the nuclear club but are still dependent on the superpowers for military and economic assistance. Superpower cooperation would provide an incentive for the settlement of regional conflicts, especially those that may set the superpowers against each other.

An agreement to restrict the military use of space to present practices would have other significant strategic benefits. Both sides could be confident that the satellites they rely on for early warning and treaty verification would not be readily attacked. Although there could be no perfect certainty (ground-based lasers, for example, could be used in a surprise attack to blind satellites), unilateral measures could be taken by each side to protect satellites and to harden them against the possibility of breaches. Civil cooperation could be undertaken without compromising military objectives. Technology transfer would be less restricted under this approach. Otherwise, the rules would have to take account of potential benefits for space warfare. Another major benefit would be that both sides would not have to make hard trade-offs between space weapons and other forms of military modernization. The military services on both sides would probably welcome a decision to avoid space warfare (with the exception of those with a vested interest in making war in space). It would, in addition, relax pressure on military budgets and thus make it easier to gain support for modernization efforts in other areas.

Nor should the positive opportunities be ignored for transforming the cold war. To some extent, at least, the persistence of hostilities between the superpowers is a function of mutual mistrust and fear. To the extent that the superpowers can maintain the arms-control process and achieve greater strategic stability, the result will be worth more than many a new weapons system. Reliance on weapons systems alone does nothing to alleviate mistrust and uncertainty, however much it induces restraint on the part of potential aggressors. So long as fundamental issues regarding values and interests divide East and West and the international system remains anarchic, it would be too much to expect that cooperation in arms control will by itself change the cold war into a warm peace. But arms-control measures can contribute greatly to the prospects of détente and to cooperation in other respects by eliminating some of the grounds for suspicion. The introduction of techniques for verifying nuclear explosions and adherence to treaties by on-site inspection and monitoring will also help to diminish tensions. Although hard experience has taught us that linkage between arms control and other forms of détente is by no means automatic, extensive superpower collaboration on arms control could lead to cooperation in managing other conflicts. We therefore turn next to the implications of SDI for arms control.

CHAPTER 5

"Don't Ask the Soviets. Tell Them"

SDI and Arms Control

Whatever military and strategic impact SDI will ultimately have, it has already had important, if controversial, consequences for arms control. The most zealous advocates of the project have been largely indifferent to these consequences, believing that what matters most in the East-West confrontation is military power, not paper agreements incapable of deterring the Soviets from seeking to exploit any military advantage they can acquire. Some of the most prominent supporters of SDI, however, share the generally accepted view that although arms-control measures alone cannot remove the sources of conflict, verifiable agreements to limit arsenals and regulate development of new weapons can promote stability, ease economic burdens, and possibly lead to more far-reaching forms of cooperation.[1] Until the declaration of the SDI, there was also general agreement that the constraints on the deployment of strategic defenses against ballistic missiles and on the development of new types of defenses (agreed to by the superpowers in the 1972 ABM Treaty) were the necessary condition of progress in the limitation and reduction of offensive arms. Since the announcement, the prospect of such progress has been shrouded in the ambiguity of the Reagan administration's vision of a comprehensive defense. Further offensive reductions are likely only if that ambiguity is resolved. An admission that no space-based deployment is feasible for the foreseeable future, coupled with continued adherence to the limitations on testing prescribed by the treaty, is an essential condition for further achievements in arms control. To the extent that either or both superpowers proceed to develop and deploy comprehensive defenses (not just to conduct research on the possibilities, as a hedge against a breakout), the very premise of strategic arms reduction is called into question. This is the key problem. SALT I and SALT II proceeded on the assumption that the two sides would be equally deterred from attacking each other because of their equal vulnerability to retaliation. The premise of comprehensive defenses shifts the basis of deterrence (insofar as the defenses are reliable) from fear of retaliation to confidence in the ability to survive a nuclear attack of great magnitude. As the advocates like to say, "assured survival" would replace "assured destruction." But while both sides are busy designing and constructing such defenses, they lose all incentive to reduce offensive forces unless and until it becomes pragmatically (and not just theoretically) demonstrable that such defenses can reliably absorb an attack of any size and that additional units of defense can be deployed less expensively than additional units of offense. Until both these demanding criteria, reliability and cost-effectiveness, can be met, the obvious response to the deployment of defenses is to build offenses capable of overcoming and saturating them. Other things being equal, the larger the offensive threat, the larger (and more expensive) defenses must be and the greater the likelihood that a significant fraction of the attack will penetrate the defenses. Either side would therefore be foolish to relinquish any of its offensive punch while the other is building defenses. At most, a sensible counterstrategy would be to trade some offensive power for greater assurance of penetration. Once a commitment is made by either side to develop and deploy comprehensive defenses, therefore, the ABM Treaty would become a dead letter. It could no longer be expected to serve as a foundation for agreed reductions of offensive capacity.

This obvious consequence has been somewhat obscured by developments in the immediate aftermath of the declaration of SDI. At first, Soviet leaders warned that if the United States were to violate the terms of the treaty by testing or deploying "space strike" weapons, they would take whatever measures they considered necessary to maintain strategic parity. The Reagan administration reacted by accusing the Soviets of having themselves violated arms-control agreements but promised U.S. allies that for the time being the terms of the treaty would be respected in SDI experimentation. Arms control negotiations were suspended following a Soviet walkout prompted by the deployment of intermediate-range weapons in Western Europe, so the issue was not joined. In 1985, however, the two sides agreed to resume negotiations over intermediate-range and strategic weapons and—at Soviet insistence—also over space weapons; the Reagan administration announced a new "broad" interpretation of the treaty's testing provisions. Success in the INF negotiations in 1987, coupled with agreement on the outlines of a strategic reduction agreement, still left SDI as a major unresolved issue. It may not prove to be an insuperable barrier in the Strategic Arms Reduction Talks (START) if both sides can "agree to disagree" about it, or, better still, if they can reach an understanding on what types of testing *are* permitted under the ABM Treaty. SDI has nevertheless seriously complicated the arms control process. Although some of its supporters claim that it helped to bring the Soviets back to the bargaining table, the president himself insisted all along that SDI was not a bargaining chip. The Soviets, in any event, had other strong motivations for reopening negotiations. In retrospect, the injection of SDI into the already difficult arms control process shows that ill-considered commitments to new military technologies complicate rather than reinforce the pursuit of national security. Unless both sides keep their work on strategic defenses consistent with the ABM Treaty, or some modified version of it, arms-reduction talks could well grind to a halt.

THE ABM TREATY AND SALT:
THE LINK THAT FAILED

The centrality of the ABM Treaty to strategic arms control was well recognized when the treaty was negotiated in 1972. The premise that seemed to have gained acceptance was that both sides had an interest in restricting deployment of defenses against ballistic missiles. Such deployments, it was reasoned, would lead only to an expansion of offensive arsenals and to uncertainty on each side about the reliability of its retaliatory deterrent. The shapers of U.S. strategy had earlier become convinced that in view of these consequences, in addition to the technical difficulties of achieving a meaningful defense against ballistic missile attack, a mutual decision to forgo such defenses would be advisable.

As we discuss in chapter 2, the effort to forge a link between strategic defense and arms control first emerged in the 1960s when the United States learned of Soviet plans to deploy ground-based defenses. The Soviet defenses resembled those the United States had been working on sporadically, such as the Nike X. The seeming futility of such research efforts, coupled with fear that both sides were being drawn into a spiraling strategic arms race, led the Johnson administration (at the urging of

Secretary of Defense McNamara) to propose a treaty banning the deployment of ABM systems. (This idea was probably introduced in the Pentagon by Jack Ruina, then director of DARPA, in 1962 or 1963. Ruina and the physicist Murray Gell-Mann discussed it at the Pugwash Conference in 1964, the first time the Soviets were made aware of U.S. thinking on this subject.) McNamara's view was that offensive and defensive systems were interactive: The deployment of ABMs by one side would lead the other to develop offensive forces, rendering the defensive effort futile. Because the proliferation of offensive forces was cheaper than the development of defenses, it seemed that the advantage conferred on the offense by the advent of nuclear weapons—coupled with high-speed ICBMs and SLBMs—could not be offset by defenses. The defensive systems of the 1960s were thought to be highly vulnerable to saturation attacks, and the technical experts were far from unanimous in considering them reliable even in simpler situations. As a result, McNamara urged that the issue be raised with the Soviets. It was therefore brought up at the meeting with Premier Kosygin in Glassboro, New Jersey, in June 1967. As we note in chapter 2, Kosygin was at first outraged, arguing that offenses were "bad," and defenses were "good" because they did not harm anyone or serve any aggressive purpose. McNamara tried to persuade him that deployment of defensive systems only complicated the problem of achieving a strategic balance that both sides could afford by forcing each side to proliferate offenses in order to overcome the defenses. In effect, he argued that stability would be enhanced if both sides were to forgo defenses and accept strategic parity so as to promote mutual deterrence based on the possession by both sides of an invulnerable capability to retaliate.[2]

McNamara's argument eventually took hold, leading to the SALT I negotiations and the signing of the ABM Treaty in 1972. Although the treaty had only an interim agreement (SALT I) to limit offensive weapons, it was hoped that the signing of the treaty would lead to further agreements to reduce offensive weapons, once the fear of defenses had been eliminated. The results of agreement to limit defenses, however, were mixed. As a result of SALT I, a rough parity was achieved in strategic delivery vehicles—2,200 for the United States, 2,400 for the Soviets—but warheads began to multiply with the mounting of MIRVed warheads on the delivery vehicles. (Ironically, MIRVed warheads were promoted in the 1960s as the answer to ABM, but when ABMs were renounced, MIRVs remained.) Even though both sides proposed major reductions, offensive reductions went unrealized for several reasons—

some having to do with the political context of arms control, others with its inherent limitations.

One explanation for the lack of progress on offensive reductions is that the political climate was uncongenial. In effect, arms control came to be held hostage to other aspects of the superpower relationship. The failure of the United States to ratify the SALT II agreement resulted from its displeasure with the Soviet Union's invasion of Afghanistan and suppression of discontent in Poland; in addition, President Carter's leadership had been badly weakened by the hostage crisis in Iran. From the Soviet point of view, the failure of the United States to ratify SALT II was evidence of a stubborn refusal to accept the military parity resulting from Soviet investments and other changes in the global "correlation of forces." The collapse of the détente of the 1970s was made final by the advent to power of Ronald Reagan, who was opposed not only to SALT II, which he described as "fatally flawed," but also, it seemed, to the entire process of arms control as it had been conducted by his predecessors. Those who believed in arms control, he implied, were naïve in supposing that a hostile and expansionist "evil empire" could be trusted to enter into and observe equitable agreements.

Equally important in the failure to go beyond the ABM Treaty and the SALT II agreement was the Soviet Union's insistence on adding to and diversifying its strategic forces and the United States' modernization of those it already had. In SALT II both sides agreed to limits that did not affect expansion and modernization in areas where both were seeking to gain certain military advantages. Thus, the Soviets were not inhibited from deploying intermediate-range missiles in Europe (hardly demonstrating the spirit of détente), maintaining heavy ICBMs that threatened the land-based leg of the U.S. triad, developing new strategic bombers capable of attacking the United States, continuing to expand and improve their strategic air defenses, and designing and testing more accurate and mobile missiles to complicate U.S. targeting policies. For its part, the United States proceeded with the development and deployment of the MX—a more accurate missile than the Minuteman and regarded as a first-strike weapon by many observers. The development of the Trident submarine and the Trident II D-5 missile gave the United States a new and potent capability against Soviet silos. In addition, two new bombers—the B-1 and the ATB (Stealth, or B-2, bomber)—along with a new generation of cruise missiles capable of air- and sea-launch, strengthened the third leg of the U.S. triad. These offensive developments, like those of the Soviets, hardly indicated a real willingness on the part of military planners and their political supporters to wind down the arms race or to accept any kind of freeze on potentially destabilizing developments.

Arms-control progress has also been affected by the refusal of both the U.S.S.R. and the United States, despite the ABM Treaty, to abandon efforts to develop defenses against nuclear attack. As we note in chapter 2, the Soviet Union has mounted the most sustained and elaborate effort in strategic defense. They have also exploited the two most glaring loopholes in the ABM Treaty, which does not forbid the development either of tactical ABM (ATBM) weapons capable of intercepting short- and intermediate-range ballistic missiles or of anti-satellite (ASAT) weapons. When the Soviets tested (anti-aircraft) SA-X-12 against an RV with the characteristics of an intermediate-range weapon, they stepped into a gray area. U.S. analysts were bound to think the move might lead to a full-scale breakout from the treaty. If the Soviet ATBM could intercept intermediate-range missiles, it could also intercept submarine-launched missiles, considered by both sides as strategic weapons. If the SA-X-12 could be further upgraded to intercept ICBMs, the U.S.S.R. would quietly acquire a territorial defense while supposedly complying with the treaty. The Soviets also developed and tested a co-orbital ASAT, which poses a threat to U.S. satellites in low orbits and could lead to a new generation of ASATs capable of threatening communications satellites in high orbit. Although ASATs could not provide an ABM defense, they threaten the U.S. offensive capability by jeopardizing U.S. command, control, and communications. The Soviets, whose emphasis on land-based missiles enables them to put more reliance on ground communications, are not as threatened by the development of ASATs. The development of ASATs also strongly indicated the Soviets' readiness to exploit the loopholes in the ABM Treaty. The Soviets were also known to be working on advanced lasers that could conceivably serve as ASAT and ABM weapons.

The most egregious instance of Soviet noncompliance with the treaty was the construction of a phased-array radar near Krasnoyarsk, in central Siberia, hundreds of miles from the nearest coastal region. In order to prevent the creation of a radar network that could serve as a basis for a nationwide territorial defense, Article VI(b) of the ABM Treaty limited the emplacement of large phased-array radars (LPARs) to positions "along the periphery" of both countries and required that they be "oriented outward." The Soviets, however, pointed to Agreed Statement F, which allows for the inland location of phased-array radars "for the purposes of tracking objects in outer space," which, they claimed, was to be the function of the Krasnoyarsk facility. U.S. specialists responded that in its outward dimensions the radar is identical to the Pechora-type radar used for ABM purposes and that its location violates an explicit treaty provision. It is much more elaborate than would be needed for space tracking and is wrongly oriented for that purpose in any event. They therefore concluded that the Soviets were deliberately building an expensive facility in full knowledge that it was incompatible with the treaty regime.

During the Nixon, Ford, and Carter administrations, questionable Soviet activities were queried by the U.S. representative to the Standing Consultative Commission established under the treaty to allow for clarification of its provisions and to deal with problems of implementation of ABM limits and the limitation of offensive weapons. Robert W. Buchheim, the U.S. commissioner until 1981, has asserted that despite difficulties, "overall Soviet fulfillment of major obligations under agreements, whether ratified or in effect on a de facto basis, has been generally good."[3] The Reagan administration, however, made only limited use of this confidential forum and instead brought allegations of Soviet violations of this and other treaties to public notice. This policy mirrored a larger one of treating the post–SALT II negotiations as opportunities to tell the U.S.S.R. that the United States did not intend to be as accommodating as the Carter administration had been. Indeed, the United States' only interest in the negotiations, according to this new policy, was to secure Soviet concessions, specifically the withdrawal of SS-20s from Europe and the elimination of the threat posed by the heavy land-based ICBMs, especially the SS-18s.

The Soviets saw more to gain by withdrawing from the negotiations. They hoped to score propaganda gains and to drive a wedge between Western Europe and the United States by denouncing Reagan as a cold warrior interested only in restoring U.S. military superiority and in dictating to the Soviet Union. The Soviets argued, often effectively, that this U.S. policy represented not only a departure from the U.S. policy of pursuing peaceful coexistence but also a return to a full-fledged arms race, leading inexorably to the abandonment of the SALT II Treaty—which the United States was observing on the basis of an informal understanding with the Soviets—and of the whole effort to achieve progress in arms control.

Once NATO overrode domestic Western European objections to the deployment of longer intermediate-range weapons, the Soviets decided to resume negotiations. The announcement of SDI in 1983 may not have been intended to promote arms control, but it nevertheless gave the Soviets an excuse to return to the negotiating table. They almost certainly wanted to return for other reasons, including the end of the interregnum created by Brezhnev's extended illness and eventual death. SDI enabled the Soviets to claim that a new and ominous challenge had been added, and that they had compelled the United States to address the issue of the militarization of space. A previous Soviet proposal to extend the ban on weapons in space had been rebuffed by the Reagan administration. The revived START talks could thus cover three subjects—intermediate-range weapons in Europe, the proposed reduction of offensive strategic weapons, and the issue of weapons in space (both ABMs and ASATs). SDI was at least the catalyst for the renewal of the negotiations, even though it was later to prove a serious obstacle.

FROM DEADLOCK TO DASHED HOPES: THE IMPASSE AT REYKJAVÍK

The unexpected resumption of negotiations put domestic critics of SDI in an awkward position. Those in favor of SALT II and of arms control in general had denounced SDI as a tactic designed to undermine adherence to the ABM Treaty, at the very least. They saw in it the hand of those who had opposed the treaty in the first place. These critics argued plausibly that the president and his supporters favored SDI because it seemed to bypass the need to negotiate with the Soviets and relied instead on unilateral U.S. initiatives. It was being advanced, they also argued, to disguise the fact that the United States had deliberately refused to negotiate seriously in the Geneva talks, preferring to use the failure of the talks as a way of putting the onus on the Soviets while proceeding with the administration's modernization efforts. Instead of seeking to reassure the Soviets about the United States' peaceful intentions, the Reagan administration's approach (illustrated by the SDI) was to threaten them with (1) an expensive arms race (in the expectation that if it did not bankrupt the U.S.S.R. it would at least expose the weakness of its economy) and (2) a new military capacity that would confer military superiority by seizing the high ground of space before the Soviets could. The proponents of the ABM Treaty and of arms control in general therefore saw the entire effort as one designed to subvert negotiations in favor of space-age saber-rattling.

But when the Soviets agreed to resume negotiations in 1985, despite their denunciations of SDI, many of these proponents of the ABM Treaty and of arms control took a somewhat different line. Although still convinced of the folly of SDI, they admitted, if only grudgingly, that it had been useful in bringing the Soviets back to the bargaining table and began to view it as a valuable bargaining chip. Although the president himself denied that he would allow SDI to be traded away, those in favor of the treaty and of further arms control argued that SDI could well present a historic opportunity If, as seemed to be the case, the president had changed his tune and was now eager to achieve radical reductions of strategic weapons (having been concerned in his first term to win reelection, but in the second to win a place in history), then he might recognize that restraint on SDI was a small price to pay for achieving a breakthrough on arms control.

Gradually, the pieces of such a historic breakthrough seemed to fall into place. When Reagan and Gorbachev met at the Soviet leader's request in what was billed as a "pre-summit" at Reykjavík in 1986, this breakthrough was actually within grasp. There the Soviets agreed in principle to the zero–zero INF proposal, to the equal astonishment of those who had first proposed it and critics who had denounced the president's offer as nonnegotiable and therefore insincere. The Soviets also seemed to agree to a proposal for a 50 percent reduction in offensive warheads that was not very far from the administration's formula, especially because it would have reduced the Soviet advantage in the heavy missiles, which the administration had particularly emphasized. But the price of such concessions, as the Soviets made more or less clear in the final session at Reykjavík, was that the United States agree to restrict research on SDI to the laboratory and to forgo testing of any kind in space. They may not have intended to be quite so categorical and may have been insisting only on a reaffirmation of the traditional interpretation of the ABM Treaty. Whatever the intention, their adamantly stated view was enough to lead the president to abort the negotiations.

Postmortems of Reykjavík suggested that the Soviets were deliberately trying to entrap a gullible president ill-equipped to appreciate the nuances of arms control and to cause further difficulties in relations between the United States and its allies. Although he refused in the end to accept the Soviet proposals, Reagan aroused the ire of many U.S. and allied strategists by apparently agreeing to a Soviet proposal to eliminate all ballistic missiles (or, possibly, all nuclear weapons) over a ten-year period. Among most mainstream Western strategists, it is taken for granted that U.S. possession of nuclear weapons is a vital counterweight to Soviet conventional strength, especially in Europe. Shock over Reagan's readiness to abandon the nuclear deterrent, as well as the prospect of an INF accord, made Western European political leaders uneasy. Without nuclear weapons based on European soil and with the prospect of a reduced U.S. retaliatory force, they feared that the military balance in Europe would swing toward the Soviets unless agreements on strategic weapons were accompanied by reductions in Soviet short-range nuclear forces and in conventional forces—subjects neglected in the Reykjavík talks.

THE POLITICAL EFFORT TO SHORE UP SDI

When Reagan terminated the Reykjavík meeting without agreement, his staunch conservative supporters expressed relief, though they often couched their feelings in the form of praise for the president for having the courage to say "no" to a deal the Soviets had put forward only as a trap. But the conservatives had been unhappy to start with—that the president appeared to be edging closer to an agreement. Just before the first Reagan-Gorbachev summit earlier in 1985, Secretary of Defense Weinberger took the extraordinary step of writing a "top-unclassified" letter to the president in which he warned the president not to agree to limit or abandon SDI or to make other concessions. Even more extraordinary was the leak of the letter, evidently by forces in the White House who shared Weinberger's opposition to arms control and were convinced that Secretary of State Shultz was leading the president in the direction of détente. After Reykjavík, these forces were on the defensive, but they could at least argue that the president had come to his senses when he saw what the Soviet design really was, however much his instinctive desire for peace had tempted him to suppose that there might be something serious in the deal the Soviets were proposing.

After Reykjavík these same conservatives lost little time in deciding that the only way to prevent the president and his secretary of state from making concessions on SDI was to demand early deployment of a strategic-defensive system. This demand was couched in terms of the unexpectedly early success of SDI research—a success that informed critics saw as dubious—with the evident intention of nullifying any attempt in Congress to kill or emasculate SDI. The proponents sought to maintain momentum by showing that the initiative was not simply a research program to be pursued for decades. Still another motive in proposing "early deployment" was to force the hands of those who had been able to avoid open opposition to SDI by supporting research. A call for deployment would compel them to take a stand either for or against SDI (and the president). Finally, if successful, a move for early deployment would force abrogation of the ABM Treaty by mandating testing in space and deployment of space-based systems. The same forces conveniently argued that the Soviets had already violated the treaty, so it had already ceased to be an operative restraint on the Soviets' own undeclared SDI.

When Weinberger endorsed the proposal for early deployment, he once again exposed the disagreement within the administration over the virtues of arms control. At Reykjavík, the president had offered to refrain from deployment (though not necessarily from testing in space) for a period of ten years. The Weinberger proposal ran counter to this offer. Further underscoring the disagreement, the president's arms-control negotiator in Geneva, Max Kampelman, reiterated that the U.S. proposal at Reykjavík still stood. In his January 1987 State of the Union address, the president straddled both positions. He reaffirmed support for the SDI but reiterated his interest in achieving an arms-control agreement with the Soviets. As the two sides edged closer to a treaty, a reaffirmation of the ABM Treaty came to seem essential.

Despite the confusions, the debate over SDI at least had the virtue of illustrating the pivotal role of the ABM Treaty in arms reductions. A decision to deploy strategic defenses not permitted under the 1972 ABM Treaty would require either the treaty's abrogation or amendment; even the effort to develop such systems would at some point entail one or the other. Paradoxically, some supporters of SDI acknowledged that U.S.-Soviet cooperation is essential because no defense could possibly prove feasible unless accompanied by constraints on offensive deployments. Nevertheless, the relationship between SDI and arms control remained politically vexing. On the one hand, supporters of arms control argued passionately that to tamper with the ABM Treaty is to remove the cornerstone of the whole process; on the other, supporters of SDI contended that arms control is a means to an end and that if technology can obtain that same end—a peaceful world—then arms-control measures would have to accommodate the technology. Other supporters saw SDI as a substitute for arms control, contending either that arms control had failed or that it is essentially a Soviet device to achieve equivalent status as a great power with the United States, and nothing more. They therefore argued that the United States would do better to rely on its technical, economic, and military capacities to thwart aggressive moves by the U.S.S.R.—moves that are inevitable given the conflict between the two systems and the expansionist character of the Soviet Union. In this debate, the precise terms of the ABM Treaty assumed a new importance.

THE TERMS OF THE ABM TREATY

As amended by a 1974 Protocol, the first three articles of the treaty forbid both parties from deploying ABM systems "for a defense of the territory of its country" or for more than one region with a radius of 150 km. Both sides are allowed only one ABM site of one hundred interceptors and one hundred launchers positioned either around the national capital or at one ICBM deployment area. Strict limits are put on the number of ABM radars at the permitted site (the numbers differ, depending on whether the ABMs are protecting missiles or area). Article V limits efforts to develop, test, and deploy weapons and components except for those that are fixed and ground-based. Article VII specifically permits "modernization and replacement" of permitted ground-based systems and components.

Several of the final articles of the treaty spell out its binding character. According to Article XV, the treaty is "of unlimited duration." Article XIII provides that disputes over compliance and other relevant matters are to be referred to a Standing Consultative Commission (SCC), composed of representatives and advisors appointed by both parties. Article XIV allows for amendments in the event of new developments. Article XV allows withdrawal on six months' notice if either party determines that its "supreme interests" are no longer served.

The treaty was accompanied by an interim agreement establishing launcher limits on ICBMs and SLBMs. The expectation was that a new treaty would be worked out to limit offensive weapons comprehensively, i.e., to include bombers and/or cruise missiles that could reach the territory of the two superpowers. The guidelines for such a treaty were established in the Vladivostok accords between President Gerald Ford and the Soviet leader, Leonid Brezhnev, in 1974. The SALT II agreement was signed in 1979 by representatives of the Carter administration, but it was withdrawn from consideration in the Senate after the Soviet invasion of Afghanistan. It had also aroused considerable opposition in and of itself because of doubts about its verifiability and because it allowed the Soviets to retain certain numerical advantages and throw-weight advantages in land-based missiles considered to be the most accurate available systems.

In the course of negotiations, certain interpretations were spelled out in the form either of "agreed statements" or "common understandings" appended to the treaty along with "unilateral statements," added by the U.S. side only. Additional protocols and understandings were later reached in the SCC, but some ambiguities remained. "Some key definitions and concepts used in the treaty," several of its defenders admit, "were not clarified by agreed interpretations during or subsequent to SALT I,"[4] but even a leading critic of its ambiguities has acknowledged that "it is concise and elegant as treaties go."[5]

In essence, the treaty bans the deployment of ABM systems that would provide or prepare a base for a defense for the entire territory of one of the parties. It also limits testing and development of ABM systems and components. Even a regional defense is banned (except for a radius of 150 km, presumably for the national capital area, which is considered subregional). An ABM system is defined (in Article II) as any designed to counter strategic ballistic missiles or their elements in flight. The article describes such systems as "currently consisting of" ABM missiles, launchers, and radars. Testing is permitted (by Article IV) at "mutually agreed upon test ranges," at which no more than fifteen ABM launchers are permitted. Article V explicitly prohibits not only deployment of systems designed to be based in the air, in space, at sea, or to be mobile land-based but also the testing and development of such systems. Article VI bars the application of ABM capabilities to non-ABM systems or the testing of non-ABM systems in an "ABM mode," (These systems, not defined in the treaty, include air defense, anti-tactical ballistic missiles, strategic offensive missiles, and anti-satellite missiles.) The same article stipulates that ballistic missile early-warning radars are to be located only along the periphery of the national territory and oriented outward, so that they could not serve as the basis of a territorial defense system. Article IX prohibits the transfer to other states and deployment outside national territory of ABM systems or their components.

The agreed statements amount to negotiated clarifications of treaty language. One of the statements makes clear that the parties intend to ban launchers with multiple interceptors from being mounted on the allowable launchers. Another stipulates that transfers of technology to other states include technical descriptions and blueprints. In 1978 the SCC also developed protocols specifying criteria for "testing in an ABM mode." The criteria are classified. The one that has proved to be most controversial, Agreed Statement D, stipulates that in the event ABM systems "based on other physical principles" are "created in the future," limitations on such systems would be "subject to discussion in accordance with Article XIII and agreement in accordance with Article XIV," which covers amendments.

THE TESTING ISSUE

When the treaty was submitted to the Senate in the summer of 1972 for "advice and consent," testimony concerning its various provisions made clear, at least to those especially concerned with the issue, that development and testing of "exotic" technologies such as lasers would be permitted only in the case of ground-based systems. The journalist John Newhouse later reported in a book on the negotiations that the U.S. delegation had been under instructions not to agree to any clauses that might have precluded the development of ground-based lasers in an army project.[6] In a legal analysis prepared on May 24, just two days before the signing of the treaty, John B. Rhinelander stated unambiguously that Article II and Agreed Statement D prohibited all efforts to develop "future systems" that might be substituted for those then in use: "An ABM system is described in paragraph 1 of Article II in terms of 'current' ABM components. This does not, however, limit the generality of the term ABM systems as used in the Treaty to systems composed of 'current' ABM components, but would also include 'future systems' based on physical principles other than those used for 'current' ABM components and capable of substituting for 'current' ABM components."[7]

In Senate hearings, several Nixon administration officials, including Secretary of Defense Melvin Laird and DOD Director of Research and Engineering John Foster, testified that although development of ground-based lasers was permissible, no other development and testing of such unconventional systems would be allowed. In a written reply to a question from Sen. Barry M. Goldwater (R., Ariz.), regarding the effect of the treaty on the development of boost-phase missile defenses (presumably relying on satellite-based lasers), Secretary Laird expressed the same understanding. He noted that there is "a prohibition on the development, testing and deployment of ABM systems which are space-based" but "no restrictions on the development of lasers for fixed, land-based ABM systems" and that the prohibition of the development and testing of ABM systems other than those that would be ground-based does not apply "to basic and advanced research and exploratory development of technology which could be associated with such systems, or their components."[8] Sen. Sam Nunn (D., Ga.) was to point out in 1987 that this "formal, written executive branch response . . . clearly sets forth the traditional interpretation of the treaty with respect to exotics, permitting development, and testing only in a fixed, land-based mode. The reply makes it clear that mobile/space-based exotics are subject to the comprehensive ban on development, testing and deployment, with the understanding—as stated in Secretary Laird's reply—that the treaty only permits 'basic and advanced research and exploratory development.'"[9] Foster, under questioning from Sen. Henry M. Jackson (D., Wash.), was even more explicit in this exchange:

SENATOR JACKSON: Article V says each party undertakes not to develop and deploy ABM systems or components which are sea-based, air-based, space-based, or mobile land-based.

DR. FOSTER: Yes, sir, I understand. We do not have a program to develop a laser ABM system.

SENATOR JACKSON: If it is sea-based, air-based, space-based, or mobile land-based. If it is a fixed, land-based ABM system, it is permitted, am I not correct?

DR. FOSTER: That is right. You can develop and test up to the deployment phase of future ABM system components which are fixed and land-based.[10]

To clarify the testing issue, in response to a direct question from Senator Jackson, Foster subsequently inserted into the record of the hearings a fuller explanation:

Article V prohibits the development and testing of ABM systems or components that are sea-based, air-based, space-based, or mobile land-based. Constraints imposed by the phrase "development and testing" would be applicable only to that portion of the advanced development stage following laboratory testing, i.e., that stage which is verifiable by national means. Therefore, a prohibition on development—the Russian word is "creation"— would begin only at the stage where laboratory testing ended on ABM components, on either a prototype or bread-board model.[11]

As Senator Nunn also later pointed out, testimony from military officers presented the same understanding of the restrictions on testing. One of the officers specifically indicated that the Joint Chiefs of Staff "were aware of the limits on development and testing of laser ABM's, had agreed to them, and recognized that this was a fundamental part of the final agreements."[12]

In response to a question from Senator Jackson during testimony before the Senate Armed Services Committee on July 18, 1972, Amb. Gerard C. Smith, the chief U.S. negotiator, submitted a written clarification (based on a review of the SALT delegation's reporting cables) of the treaty's provisions restricting development and testing. According to Smith, the treaty prohibits

> that stage of development which follows laboratory development and testing. The prohibitions on development contained in the ABM Treaty would start at that part of the development process where field testing is initiated on either a prototype or breadboard model. It was understood by both sides that the prohibition on "development" applies to activities involved after a component moves from the laboratory development and testing stage to the field testing stage, wherever performed. The fact that early stages of the development process, such as laboratory testing, would pose problems for verification by national technical means is an important consideration in reaching this definition. Exchanges with the Soviet delegation made clear that this definition is also the Soviet interpretation of the term "development."[13]

As Smith noted, the understanding of the ban on mobile systems, including those based in space, had been clarified in a meeting of the Ad Hoc Working Group headed by U.S. representative Sidney Graybeal and his Soviet counterpart, Viktor Karpov, in Helsinki on September 15, 1971. A U.S. "memorandum of conversation" ("memcon"), made public in 1987, recorded that "Karpov agreed with Graybeal's interpretation that the Soviet text meant 'any type of present or future components' of ABM systems."[14]

When the treaty was ratified in the Senate by a vote of 88–2, two of the senators explained their differing votes on ratification by referring to testimony on the testing issue. Sen. James Buckley (R., N.Y.) said he had decided to vote against ratification because the treaty ruled out the development and testing of space-based laser weapons:

> The agreement goes so far as to prohibit the development, test or deployment of sea-, air- or space-based ballistic missile defense systems. This clause, in Article V of the ABM treaty, would have the effect, for example, of prohibiting the development and testing of a laser type system based in space which could at least in principle provide an extremely reliable and effective system of defenses against ballistic missiles. The technological possibility has been formally excluded by this agreement.[15]

Sen. Strom Thurmond (R., S.C.) announced that he was voting to confirm the treaty only reluctantly because he objected to the ban on the development of space-based lasers, which he thought "effectively prevents us from ever having the means to protect our population from a Soviet first strike."[16]

In the years following ratification of the treaty, this understanding became official policy (reflected, for example, in the ACDA's annual arms-control impact statement prepared in conjunction with the presentation of the defense budget to Congress). As late as 1985 the ACDA report declared that "the ABM Treaty prohibition on development, testing and deployment of space-based ABM systems, or components for such systems applies to directed energy technology . . . used for this purpose." [17]

REINTERPRETING THE TEXT:
THE RISE OF THE "LEGALLY CORRECT" INTERPRETATION

Despite such clarifications and pronouncements, the issue of what the treaty permits became problematic in 1985. Reagan's national security advisor, Robert McFarlane, revealed during a "Meet the Press" appearance on October 6 that a review of the treaty language had indicated that development and testing of systems based on "other physical principles" was actually allowable: "Research involving new physical concepts . . . as well as testing, as well as development indeed, are approved and authorized by the treaty. Only deployment is foreclosed." [18] McFarlane's announcement was the outgrowth of a legal review of the treaty initiated in the Department of Defense by Richard Perle, assistant secretary for international security policy, and Fred C. Iklé, under secretary for policy.

The question of the permissibility of developing new technologies not incorporated in ABM systems in 1972 had first been raised in 1975 by Donald G. Brennan of the Hudson Institute. Abraham S. Becker and William R. Harris, both affiliated with the Rand Corporation, raised it two years later—independently. Brennan's query stimulated a correspondence with several of the negotiators, at the end of which he pronounced himself satisfied that the text did in fact ban the development of "exotic" systems, except for those that would be ground-based and could be tested at the agreed test ranges. In a letter in 1977 to Rhinelander, Brennan made a full and gracious concession, noting that "any further insistence that the Treaty does not necessarily ban the development of (among others) space-based exotic ABM systems would have to be reckoned willful, indeed obstinate, stupidity." [19] Becker raised the issue publicly in a letter to the editor of the journal *International Security,* commenting on an article by Raymond L. Garthoff, who, as executive secretary of the U.S. delegation, had played a key role in negotiating the language dealing with testing. In terms that anticipated the line of reasoning later used in the Reagan administration, Becker contended that Agreed Statement D could plausibly be read to permit testing of new systems based on "other physical principles":

> One might ask why Agreed Interpretation [D] was necessary at all. Does not the introductory phrase of Article III—"Each Party undertakes not to deploy ABM systems or their components except that"—rule out any deployments other than those permitted by the two following paragraphs? Why then is that special provision necessary for the contingency of exotic systems? The answer seems to be that the Treaty's core limitations in Article III relate to a specific form of ABM technology. Thus there was a need to adapt the limitations of Article III to possible future systems using alternative technologies.
>
> However, this raises the more general problem that Article II, Paragraph 1 defines ABM systems for the purpose of this Treaty as consisting of ABM interceptor missiles, ABM interceptor missile launchers, and ABM radars. Presumably, Article V . . . also refers to such systems. There would, therefore, appear to be no prohibitions against developing, testing, or deploying any system . . . that does not employ the canonical ABM triad. The only bar to such an interpretation consists of one word in Article II, Paragraph 1— "currently."

In a response in the same issue, Garthoff, who had drafted Agreed Statement D, denied that text was ambiguous with respect to systems based on "other physical principles":

> Mr. Becker incorrectly interprets Article V as *not* applying to futuristic types of systems *including* components capable of substituting for ABM interceptor missiles, ABM launchers, or ABM radars. The reason for his erroneous interpretation is that he curiously assumes that "the only bar to such an interpretation consists of one word." The same could be said of each of the Ten Commandments. One word can indeed make a critical difference, and the word "currently" was deliberately inserted into a previously adopted text of Article II at the time agreement was reached on the future systems ban in order to have the very effect of closing a loophole to the ban on futures in both Articles III and V (and several others). The wording of the key introductory sentence of Article III was also agreed on at the time and for that purpose.
>
> While admittedly the result has a Rube Goldberg air to it, the interlocking effects of the final wording of Articles II and III and Agreed Interpretation [D] was [sic] intentionally devised and clearly understood—by *both* Delegations—to *ban* future "ABM systems based on other physical principles and including components capable of substituting for ABM interceptor missiles, ABM launchers, or ABM radars" unless specific limitations short of a ban were agreed on under the amendment procedures. The negotiating history fully supports the interpretation given by the Delegation, Mr. Rhinelander, and myself.[20]

In 1980 Harris advanced a view much like Becker's in discussions with Michael E. Pillsbury and David S. Sullivan, who were on the Reagan administration transition team responsible for ACDA and had hired him as a consultant to help prepare a study of purported Soviet arms-control treaty violations.[21]

The issue surfaced again when Perle asked a DOD lawyer with no previous background in arms-control matters, Philip Kunsberg, to re-examine the text of the treaty in the light of a paper credited to an anonymous administration official (identified later as Bretton Sciaroni) and published April 14, 1985, by the Heritage Foundation. Kunsberg spent less than a week reviewing the text before producing a nineteen-page report in which he concluded that the prevailing interpretation was incorrect. He is reported to have drawn on the view expressed by Harris in a paper submitted at the request of T. K. Jones of the Office of the Secretary of Defense, who knew that Harris had been promoting an interpretation that would have allowed for space testing of the beam weapons being considered under SDI.[22] Perle then asked Kunsberg to review the classified record of the negotiations, and this review became the basis of a second report in which Kunsberg found that although U.S. negotiators had proposed a total ban on ABM systems of any kind, the Soviets had rejected the proposal. Under the terms of the treaty as negotiated, he argued, both sides were free to test technologies based on other physical principles than those incorporated into the ABM components specifically mentioned in the treaty (launchers, missiles, and radars). Kunsberg even went so far as to suggest that Agreed Statement D could be read to allow for the unilateral deployment of such technologies, in the event that the parties did not agree on what to do about them after the discussions called for in the statement.[23]

Kunsberg's two reports set off a kind of chain reaction. Perle, who said he "almost fell off the chair" when he saw the second report,[24] passed on the findings to the Special Arms Control Policy Group set up by the National Security Council to review SDI-related matters. When Secretary Shultz, a member of the group, heard the news, he asked the newly appointed legal advisor to the State Department, Abraham D. Sofaer, who had been a judge on the federal district court in New York, to review the findings. Sofaer assigned the task to several staff members, and their study essentially corroborated the new interpretation. Then Sofaer looked at the issue himself and discussed it with Nitze, the one member of the ABM negotiating team in the Reagan administration, and reported to Shultz on October 3 that in his opinion the testing of technologies based on other physical principles was permissible under the treaty but that deployment would violate the language and aim of the agreement.[25] Sofaer's view was quickly adopted as that of the DOD, and the question of how the issue should be handled was discussed on October 4 by the interagency Special Arms Control Policy Group, chaired by McFarlane, and then with the president on October 11.[26] The issue assumed special urgency once McFarlane revealed the new interpretation during an appearance on NBC's "Meet the Press." Asked his opinion of McFarlane's remarks, Gerard C. Smith replied: "All that is permitted for space-based systems is research. That means in a laboratory."[27] McFarlane's response was unyielding: "It's a simple matter of reading the text. The fact of the matter is that when you are dealing with new principles—and by that we mean principles other than ground-to-air missiles—research other than pure research in the laboratory is allowed."[28]

McFarlane's comments aroused a storm of controversy. The chairman of the House Foreign Affairs Committee, Dante B. Fascell (D., Fla.), reacted angrily and promised to summon administration officials to explain the apparent decision to reinterpret the treaty. Rep. Norman D. Dicks (D., Wash.) said he and Sen. Albert Gore, Jr. (D., Tenn.), would amend the SDI authorization bill to assure that none of the funds could be spent on activities that would erode the treaty's ban on development of ABMs. Hearings were held later in October in both the House and Senate. Rhinelander testified that McFarlane's interpretation was "in effect a repudiation and abrogation of the Treaty."[29] Smith testified that the new view makes the treaty "a dead letter." The reinterpretation, he charged, was designed to evade the treaty's intention and express prohibitions: "It is one thing to have research programs as we now do for insurance against a Soviet technological breakthrough in defensive systems; it is quite another for an American president to announce a major quest to develop the technological basis for systems presently banned by international law."[30] Spurgeon Keeney, former deputy director of ACDA, said the administration's position meant that the United States was "no longer going to respect the treaty."[31] Urgent inquiries and warnings also reached the White House from allied capitals.

An attempt to deflect the criticism was made after the meeting with the president on October 11, at which Shultz was reported to have expressed strong reservations about the wisdom of adopting the new interpretation as official policy. He was scheduled to meet with representatives of the other NATO countries on October 15, after addressing the North Atlantic Assembly in San Francisco. The day before that meeting, Shultz issued a statement indicating that a compromise had been reached within the administration. The new, or "broad," interpretation, he said, was "fully justified," but the question involved a "moot point" because "our S.D.I. research program has been structured and, as the President has reaffirmed on Friday, will continue to be conducted in accordance with a restrictive interpretation of the Treaty's obligations." [32]

Despite Shultz's effort to put the controversy to rest, it continued to simmer. In response to congressional demands, Sofaer made available under strict rules of access excerpts from the negotiating record and a new classified report he had prepared. On December 1, however, Sen. Carl Levin (D., Mich.) criticized the new interpretation as unjustified by the text or the negotiating record, and Senator Nunn, the leading Democratic spokesman on defense issues, publicly warned Reagan that by reinterpreting a treaty ratified by the Senate without consultation he was courting a "constitutional confrontation of profound dimensions." [33] On May 13, 1987, Sofaer released a declassified and revised report, quoting excerpts from the negotiating record. Six days later Senator Nunn delivered a detailed rebuttal of the report on the floor of the Senate.

In his declassified report, Sofaer marshaled the arguments and evidence in favor of the broad interpretation, which by now was being referred to within the administration as the "legally correct" interpretation. The report is quite revealing in offering a glimpse at the complexities and confusions of the negotiations, even though the case Sofaer makes has been persuasively rebutted.

SOFAER'S CASE
FOR THE "BROAD" INTERPRETATION

Sofaer's analysis begins by referring to generally accepted principles for interpreting treaties. Under the usual standards of international law, he notes, the meaning of treaties depends in the first instance on the treaty language itself. When the language is ambiguous, other considerations may be taken into account, notably the parties' understandings as reflected in subsequent agreements, the practical construction of the terms in subsequent conduct, and the record of the negotiating process. Sofaer argues that the review conducted by his office had confirmed his earlier finding that "the Treaty text is ambiguous, and that the negotiating record establishes that the Soviet Union had refused to agree to prohibit the development and testing of mobile ABM devices based on OPP [other physical principles]."[34]

Sofaer's case is based on the interpretation of several provisions in the treaty text—the definition of "ABM system" in Article II(1) of the treaty; the prohibition of development, testing, and deployment of nonfixed land-based systems and components in Article V(1); and Agreed Understanding D, which deals with future systems based on "other physical principles." He contends that there are three possible interpretations of the testing issue as it is dealt with in these provisions. The "restrictive" interpretation holds that the definition in Article II refers to *all* ABM systems and components, whether they were in existence when the treaty was negotiated or are substitutes introduced later. In this view, the only new systems that can be developed (in the sense that they are brought to the stage of field testing, and not merely worked on in preliminary phases of advanced research) are those that are designed to be used in fixed, land-based systems. Agreed Statement D is only a clarification that establishes no exception for exotic technologies. The "broad" interpretation holds that the language in the text refers only to systems and components using then available technology, and that Agreed Statement D implicitly permits the development of new technologies that could substitute for existing ABM systems by referring to ABM systems and components "created in the future." Deployment of such weapons is prohibited pending consultation and agreement between the parties, and might require amendment. A third even broader interpretation adds that deployment is permissible, according to Agreed Statement D, if the parties discuss the question but cannot agree on deployment restrictions.

These are the relevant passages Sofaer cites:

Article II

1. For the purpose of this Treaty an ABM system is a system to counter strategic ballistic missiles or their elements in flight trajectory, currently consisting of:
    (a) ABM interceptor missiles, which are interceptor missiles constructed and deployed for an ABM role, or of a type tested in an ABM mode;
    (b) ABM launchers, which are launchers constructed and deployed for launching ABM interceptor missiles; and
    (c) ABM radars, which are radars constructed and deployed for an ABM role, or of a type tested in an ABM mode.

Article V

1. Each Party undertakes not to develop, test, or deploy ABM systems or components which are sea-based, air-based, space-based, or mobile land-based.

Agreed Statement D

In order to insure fulfillment of the obligation not to deploy ABM systems and their components except as provided in Article III of the Treaty, the Parties agree that in the event ABM systems based on other physical principles and including components capable of substituting for ABM interceptor missiles, ABM launchers, or ABM radars are created in the future, specific limitations on such systems and their components would be subject to discussion in accordance with Article XIII and agreement in accordance with Article XIV of the Treaty.

Sofaer dismisses the third, or "broadest," interpretation as very doubtful in view of the reference in Agreed Statement D to the obligation not to deploy ABM systems except as provided for in the treaty and in view of the fact that the treaty is of unlimited duration. If Agreed Statement D were read to permit the parties to proceed with the deployment of ABMs based on other physical principles, the essential stated aim of the treaty in barring any deployments other than those expressly allowed would be undermined. Although the statement does not explicitly ban such deployments but only calls for discussion prior to a decision to deploy, the fact that the discussion is to be held in accordance with the provision of articles XIII and XIV is significant, he points out. Because those provisions call for periodic review, clarification of ambiguities, and amendment in the light of new developments, the intention could not have been to give the parties a way of circumventing the prohibition on deployment. But Sofaer also argues that the "restrictive" interpretation, though plausible and acknowledged in some officially adopted U.S. statements, is not the most persuasive interpretation of the treaty language or a reflection of what the negotiating record reveals about the parties' understanding of the provisions.[35]

The negotiating record, as revealed selectively in his study, suggests that the U.S. delegation made a considerable effort to win Soviet agreement to language that would specifically and unambiguously ban both the testing and deployment of all possible "devices" that could be used as ABM systems or components, except for those components that might substitute for existing fixed, ground-based ABM components or systems. The record also indicates that the Soviet delegates balked at such all-embracing language, ostensibly on the ground that there was no sense in banning nonexistent weapons and that new developments could best be dealt with in the SCC, in its role of monitoring compliance. Acting on the basis of National Security Decision Memorandum (NSDM) 117 (July 2, 1971), the U.S. delegation was instructed to propose that the agreement should ban "any systems" capable of countering ballistic missiles unless allowed by the treaty—though in the same month it received another instruction to hold off, pending an internal review.

The Soviet position, by Sofaer's account, was ambiguous. For example, on September 15, 1971, Soviet delegate Viktor Karpov stated that the term "ABM systems and components" in the Soviet draft was intended to cover "future components." Sofaer argues that this does not indicate Soviet recognition that testing of systems based on other physical principles was to be covered by this understanding. More likely, he argues, it referred to new components designed to substitute for existing ones relying on conventionally applied physical principles. If the Soviet understanding had been otherwise, he contends, the U.S. delegation would not have felt a continuing need to press the Soviets for more express language covering future systems and technologies. Between that date and December the Soviets rejected definitions that would have unambiguously included unknown devices based on other physical principles. Finally, however, an agreement was struck during the period between December 1971 and February 1972. The language of Article II was changed (to include the phrase "currently consisting of") and the Agreed Statement was adopted to address future technologies. Contrary to the views of all the leading negotiators except Nitze, however, Sofaer interprets the Soviet assent to the revision and the Agreed Statement as a refusal to treat new technologies in the same restrictive way as existing ones were treated. Presumably, the Soviet delegation (perhaps in response to promptings from the military) wished the treaty language to permit testing of exotic systems. Why else would they agree that such systems might be "created," to use the language of the Agreed Statement—a term clearly meaning development and testing outside a laboratory?[36]

According to Sofaer, the record indicates that at first the decision makers in Washington and the negotiating team were divided on the issue. Some negotiators wanted a total ban on ABM systems. These included the lead negotiator, Gerard Smith. Gen. Royal Allison and Amb. J. Graham Parsons doubted that such a ban was practical because of verification difficulties. On July 20, 1971, President Nixon instructed the delegation, in NSDM 120, not to agree to prohibit deployment of future systems other than those currently in question. In a back-channel cable to National Security Advisor Henry Kissinger, Smith expressed his belief that the United States should try to obtain a ban on future devices, but Kissinger was impatient at the lack of progress over the main issues of deployment owing to controversies over "a plethora of esoteric issues." Smith was sensitive to Kissinger's wish for more rapid progress, but asked that the decision makers provide him with necessary guidance. Did they want to limit all ABM systems or only those that were then known and in use? Smith queried Kissinger on August 7, 1971: "Do we seek an ABM constraint to provide greater stability by . . . maintenance of retaliatory capability, halting a buildup of defensive systems that could threaten that capability and lessening pressures for buildup of offensive systems—or just a temporary truce in ABMs—until such time as more effective futuristic ABMs are developed and deployed?"[37]

In Washington, the Office of the Secretary of Defense wanted to prohibit only the deployment of future systems; indeed, the Joint Chiefs of Staff opposed even this policy, fearing it would be hard to obtain support for R&D if deployment were prohibited. As the JCS chairman, Adm. Elmo R. Zumwalt, Jr., wrote:

> The Joint Chiefs of Staff strongly recommend that futuristic ABM systems not be banned. If deployment of futuristic systems were to be banned but research and development permitted, as advocated by some government agencies, such an approach would make it extremely difficult to get funds for such research and development (R&D) and could lead to unilateral U.S. neglect of the field. In all likelihood, the Soviets would proceed with R&D on such systems. It seems imprudent to foreclose options on future systems that cannot now be defined or envisioned or which may be unverifiable, particularly in view of the numerical super[iority] of Soviet offensive missiles involved in the proposed interim strategic offensive agreement. Under any circumstances, R&D programs must be kept viable to avoid technological surprise.[38]

Kissinger was annoyed by this effort to clarify the status of "exotic" devices. In a meeting of principals of the NSC Verification Panel, he argued that the negotiation was becoming stalled because the U.S. delegation was raising "nuances" and "academic" issues. He urged that the issue of seeking a ban on exotics be deferred, given that it would not become a problem until at least the 1980s and could be handled by other existing provisions for review and withdrawal. In August, in response to another request for guidance from Smith, Kissinger cabled back that although the United States had made clear to the Soviets its desire for a comprehensive agreement, it was important to take advantage of Soviet willingness to work out even a partial agreement, and that Soviet reluctance to deal with all possible issues should not be a deterrent: "In matters affecting so directly their vital interests, it is understandable that the Soviet leaders have preferred to move to an initial agreement of limited scope."[39] Kissinger's statement seemed to imply that the delegation need not be concerned about such matters as the "exotics" issue, which might be dealt with at a later stage. Nevertheless, the next day, August 12, 1971, an instruction was issued to the U.S. negotiators calling for inclusion of potential new weapons in the terms of the agreement:

> The agreement should contain a provision whereby neither side shall deploy ABM systems using devices other than ABM interceptor missiles, ABM launchers, or ABM radars to perform the function of these components. (This provision along with that in the next paragraph, should not prohibit the development and testing of future ABM components in a fixed, land-based mode.) . . .
> . . . The agreement should contain a provision whereby neither party shall develop, produce, test, or deploy: (a) sea-based, air-based, space-based, or mobile land-based ABM launchers, ABM missiles, or ABM radars; (b) ABM components other than ABM interceptor missiles, ABM launchers, or ABM radars to perform the functions of these components.

But, the instruction continued, the delegation should not "invite a detailed negotiation or discussion of future ABM systems. Our objective is to reach agreement on the broad principle that the agreement should not be interpreted in such a way that either side could circumvent its provisions through future ABM systems or components."[40]

Pursuant to this instruction, the U.S. delegation proposed two new sections for inclusion in the draft then under consideration. One provided that "each party undertakes not to deploy ABM systems using devices other than ABM interceptor missiles, ABM launchers, or ABM radars to perform the functions of these components." The other added to the provisions banning testing and deployment a specific reference to "other devices to perform the functions of these components." Smith argued that the U.S. draft proposed a more complete prohibition, which would be in the interest of both parties specifically because it makes clear that the obligations in the relevant provision apply "also to possible future types of devices capable of performing the functions of these components."[41]

The Soviets rejected the U.S. wording, arguing that it would add an unnecessary element of vagueness to the treaty and that existing provisions for review and amendment would be sufficient. Karpov was reported to have expressed the belief that "it was wrong to limit means not known to anyone." The representative of the Soviet Ministry of Defense, Lt. Gen. Konstantin A. Trusov, objected that the United States was proposing limitations on "conjectural" systems.[42]

Smith replied firmly in support of the U.S. position that if the proposed changes were not adopted, "it would be a cruel illusion to the people of both nations to say that we had concluded an agreement on ABM systems. We should more properly say that there had been an agreement to limit ABM launchers, interceptors and radars." He "had a higher regard for Soviet weapon designers than to believe that they are content with ABM technology which dates back to the early 1950s."[43]

In Sofaer's view, then, the Soviet negotiators never abandoned their persistent opposition to a total ban on the development of future "devices." In accepting Agreed Statement D, they merely agreed that if such devices were developed (or "created") in the future, the intent of the parties to the Treaty was that such devices not be deployed before discussions between them, and that such discussions should be based on the express aim of the treaty to prevent the deployment of territorial defenses. This provision—coupled with the limiting language of Article II, which referred to ABM systems "currently consisting of" launchers, radars, and missiles—is therefore best understood not as a restriction on the testing of space-based systems incorporating new physical principles, but, on the contrary, as acknowledging that such testing would not be subject to the restrictions imposed on conventional technologies.

THE REBUTTAL OF THE "NEW INTERPRETATION"

A number of compelling, and in our view persuasive, responses have been made to Sofaer's reinterpretation.[44] Raymond L. Garthoff has responded in meticulous detail. The principal negotiator of the key changes made at the end of the negotiations on the "exotics" issue, Garthoff makes a particularly significant point by noting that, in developing the case for the reinterpretation, all of its advocates ignored the arguments advanced against it within the administration itself. In deliberately ignoring or bypassing opposition from responsible officials, the style of policy-making was, as Garthoff notes, disturbingly similar to that which produced the Reagan administration's Iran-*contra* fiasco. When Harris was invited by T. K. Jones to submit a study of the treaty testing provisions, two former negotiators, Col. Charles L. Fitzgerald and Sidney Graybeal, were also asked to submit a report. Their study, which reaffirmed the traditional interpretation, was not brought to Sofaer's attention when he was asked to do his original review. Earlier in 1985, moreover, the Office of the General Counsel of the Defense Department had reexamined the validity of the traditional interpretation and had also reaffirmed it. Even at the time Kunsberg's study was under review, the assistant general counsel of the Defense Department, John H. McNeill, "had written a memorandum rejecting it,"[45] a fact apparently not mentioned by Perle and Iklé at the October 11 meeting with the president. The reinterpretation was also rejected by the legal counsel of ACDA, Thomas Graham, Jr., and by one of Sofaer's own researchers, William J. Sims III, who subsequently moved to ACDA and submitted a rebuttal to Sofaer's 1986 classified report to Congress, resigning from his government position at the same time.[46]

The case against the reinterpretation rests essentially on several contentions. They are, first, that the text of the treaty supports the traditional interpretation; second, that the negotiators on both sides understood and explained the terms in accordance with the traditional interpretation both during and after the negotiations; third, that the terms were explained to the Senate in accordance with this interpretation at the time the treaty was ratified, and they were so understood by the senators who voted for and against; fourth, that subsequent official statements affirmed the traditional interpretation; and fifth, that the adoption of the so-called broad interpretation would vitiate the intent of the treaty and invite its violation, in express contradiction of the understanding in the treaty that it was to be permanently binding.

Of these, the single most important consideration is, as Sofaer himself points out, the treaty language itself, inasmuch as it expresses the intentions and understandings of the parties. Sofaer makes much of the fact that the phrase "currently consisting of," inserted into Article II, is used to describe the systems and components expressly regulated by the treaty. But as the critics of the reinterpretation point out, this language can more plausibly be interpreted as illustrative rather than limiting,[47] i.e., that the treaty bans the development and deployment of any and all systems and components that perform the same function as systems "currently consisting of" radars, launchers, and missiles. Garthoff, who was responsible for proposing the change, certainly so understood it.[48] Had the adverb "currently" not been inserted, the parties might have been free to interpret the language as Sofaer does—to permit testing of systems or components that did not fall under the designation of radars, launchers, and missiles. Agreed Statement D thus merely clarifies and reinforces the treaty's intent to permit development (or "creation") of *ground-based* ABM systems and components based on new physical principles. The provision opens the possibility of deployment after discussion insofar as the parties agree that such deployment could be made without endangering the treaty's central aim of preventing the deployment of territorial defenses. As Abram Chayes and Antonia Chayes have pointed out, to interpret an agreed understanding not as a clarification of treaty provisions but as a modification that significantly alters the scope and bearing of the text is to put more weight on such a statement than is warranted by its character and to contend, in effect, that the drafters were deliberately opening a loophole by which the parties could escape the intended limitations of the treaty—"making an absurdity out of the text of the treaty proper."[49]

As to the negotiating record, Garthoff points out that the U.S. delegation dropped its effort to get the Soviets to agree to ban the development of all conceivable ABM "devices." It was too broad a term, they decided, one that "could constrain and interfere with testing and development of multipurpose technologies." The delegation decided it would be preferable that the treaty "should refer only to ABM systems and components, including future systems or components based on other physical principles and capable of performing the functions of the then-current (1972) types of components of antiballistic missile systems." When the Soviets submitted a reformulation of U.S. proposals on future technology, the Soviet representative, Karpov, indicated that the new draft "took into account the wishes of the U.S. side" by using the word "components" to cover any and all ABM components. Graybeal, Garthoff notes, was asked to make sure that the new formulation was understood to cover future components using other physical principles. The negotiating record indicates that Karpov agreed with Graybeal's interpretation. Another Soviet negotiator subsequently agreed that the prohibition on various ABM systems other than those that were fixed and ground-based covered "the problem of future systems," contrary to Sofaer's reading of the Soviet understanding, which would have restricted the language of the treaty to future components based on known technologies and not to "unknown devices."[50]

Both subsequent statements and practice on both sides support Garthoff's interpretation. The reliance on the traditional interpretation in the annual ACDA arms control impact statements has already been noted. Although Reagan administration officials have sometimes construed a remark of Marshal Andrey Grechko (then the Soviet minister of defense) before the Presidium of the Supreme Soviet to mean that the Soviets themselves understood the treaty to allow space testing, Grechko's comment does not support such an interpretation. The treaty, he said, "does not place any limitations on the conduct of research and experimental work directed toward solution of the problems of defense of the country against nuclear-missile strikes."[51] Grechko made no mention of testing in space and there is no reason to assume that what he had in mind by "experimental work" was anything other than what is permitted under the terms of the treaty. So far as is known, Soviet experimentation on ballistic missile defense has been configured in accordance with the traditional interpretation. After SDI was announced, Soviet officials referred to the traditional interpretation in criticizing the initiative as a treaty violation. On the U.S. side, it is noteworthy that six former secretaries of defense (Melvin Laird, Harold Brown, Clark Clifford, Robert S. McNamara, Elliot Richardson, and James Schlesinger), three of them Democrats, three of them Republicans, have joined in urging that the United States adhere to the traditional, restrictive interpretation.

THE TREATY AND SDI EXPERIMENTS

As we have seen, some of the experiments planned for the SDI program would require revision or abrogation of the treaty. In the opinion of critics, "many of the demonstrations planned under the Strategic Defense Initiative . . . are almost certainly inconsistent with the terms of the Treaty."[52] Critics admit that some relevant considerations were not fully resolved in the negotiations. Despite numerous exchanges, the parties did not reach an agreed interpretation of "develop." The United States proposed that development be defined as the phase that follows research, understanding research to include conceptual design and laboratory testing, which precedes field testing. Development was understood to be associated with construction and testing of prototypes of a weapons system or its major components. The Soviets argued that the line dividing research from development should be placed where national technical means could identify specific systems as ABM-related.[53] "Testing in an ABM mode" is also not defined. The United States issued a unilateral statement explaining that, in its view, the term means testing against an RV with the flight trajectory of an ICBM, but the Soviets never agreed to the definition. Nevertheless, in the SCC in 1978 agreement was reached on criteria for defining testing in an ABM mode. (As previously noted, exact terms remain classified, but it appears that this agreement was similar to the United States' unilateral statement.) Similarly, because the two sides could find no easy formal definition for distinguishing air defense from ballistic missile defenses, this issue was left unresolved. The issue of the difference between a "component" and an "adjunct" also arose in the negotiations. It was agreed that a telescope used to calibrate a radar would not have meaningful ABM capabilities. But, again, no precise distinction was drawn between a component and an adjunct, no authoritative U.S. statement was issued, and no agreed definition was subsequently reached in the SCC.

There is disagreement between those in charge of the program and its critics as to whether current and proposed experiments conform to the treaty. The SDIO director, Lieutenant General Abrahamson, admitted in 1985 that "at some point . . . we would have to depart from the treaty." He thought that would be necessary "about the turn of the next decade."[54] Critics have argued that already the experiment to test an airborne optical system (AOS—formerly named "Adjunct") is inconsistent with the treaty. Administration representatives argue that a device is not a component if it does not perform the function of the component on a "stand alone" basis, or, in other words, if the technology is not sufficiently mature to be incorporated into a workable ABM system. Thus, development and testing of assemblies and subassemblies that do not constitute full ABM components are permissible. The AOS is a case in point. It is mainly an adjunct to a terminal imaging radar. To be considered a component, it would have to perform all the functions of sensing and battle management. The critics argue that the history of negotiations suggests that sensors need not perform the full spectrum of ABM battle-management functions in order to be considered components. Most missile-defense systems have more than one sensor component. The early Nike-Zeus had, not one or two, but four separate types of radars—for target acquisition, decoy discrimination, target tracking, and interceptor tracking. The AOS, they point out, performs a role similar to that of the perimeter acquisition radar (PAR) in Sentinel/Safeguard; these radars were clearly considered components and therefore are subject to strict limitations. The United States has officially contended that the Soviet Henhouse radars counted as components even though they played less of a role in the ABM system than did the PAR.[55]

With current verification capabilities, it is often impossible to distinguish between a component and an adjunct. Detailed knowledge of performance capabilities would be required—knowledge that cannot be ascertained by national technical means. It might be important to know that a large infrared telescope was being tested in the AOS in conjunction with strategic missile testing; the aperture of the telescope would also be useful information. National technical means cannot tell if the sensor hardware and computer software can perform an ABM mission. Meanwhile, development would be completed and the treaty circumvented. Current redesign of the AOS experiment has enhanced it so that it will include a laser range-finder and on-board computers, enabling the system to do virtually the entire range of ABM battle management.

By general admission, there are gray areas in the treaty—notably in the case of ATBMs and ASATs, but even in that of large phased-array radars (LPARs). Both the United States and U.S.S.R. "are deploying air defense systems that with some modifications could be upgraded to some anti-tactical missile capability" (the U.S. Patriot and improved Hawk and Soviet SA-10 and SA-X-12). ATBMs might be effective against "SLBMs which fly at a similar speed, flight trajectory, and reentry angle to MRBMs and IRMs,"[56] and in the SALT treaties, SLBMs are considered strategic missiles. The ABM Treaty does not prohibit development and testing of ASATs, but the technologies involved can also be applied in the development of space-based defenses. LPARs serve many functions. Distinguishing LPARs developed for one of these functions from those designed to be used in an ABM system is very difficult. Modernization of radars (involving replacement of old radars with PARs) might be inconsistent with the treaty, especially if this entails installations outside national territory. The United States' declared intention of modernizing the BMEWs facilities falls in this category. Because it is not clear whether the issue of modernizing a "grandfathered" early-warning system (i.e., previously constructed for a different purpose and ignored by the treaty) was settled during the negotiations, it is also unclear whether the BMEWs installed in Thule, Greenland, and Fylingdales, England, can be modernized without violating Article VII of the treaty.

The Boost Phase Surveillance and Tracking System (BSTS) experiments incorporate greatly enhanced infrared sensors that provide high resolution and precision for tracking missiles in their boost phase. But because MIRVed warheads are released, the system cannot give improved impact prediction or attack characterization unless it can also track the bus. BSTS could be a useful part of a layered ABM system, however. But some SDI opponents question these experiments because Article VI bans development and testing of space-based ABM systems or components. The technology, however, is not *intrinsically* ABM-related because the same technology could be used for early warning, long recognized as a legitimate goal for spaced-based technology, and thought by many also to have been "grandfathered into" the treaty.

The proposed Space Surveillance and Tracking System (SSTS) will use cryogenically cooled infrared sensors for midcourse detection and tracking. Initial versions are to be tested in space in the early 1990s. This system, too, would provide information that would be relayed to an interceptor. It may not be tested in an ABM mode; if tested against satellite targets, however, it might acquire an ABM capability prohibited in Article VI(a), which pledges the parties "not to give . . . radars . . . capabilities to counter strategic ballistic missiles."

Even terminal-imaging radars would violate the treaty if they are designed for deployment in a mobile mode to make them more survivable. Such a development would violate the provision in Article V(i) banning the testing and development of mobile components. The testing of space-based imaging radars and lasers would "raise questions" about compliance, because these devices could arguably perform exactly the functions "currently" performed by ground-based radars.[57] The successful Homing Overlay Experiment (HOE) in June 1984 also raised questions because the payload was carried aboard a modified Minuteman I ICBM. Article VI(a) stipulates agreement "not to give missiles . . . other than ABM interceptor missiles . . . capabilities to counter ballistic missiles or their elements in flight trajectory, and to test them in an ABM mode." In January 1984 the U.S.S.R. protested the use of Minuteman to test HOE in an aide memoir listing several dozen alleged U.S. violations. ACDA replied: "The test missile was observably different from Minuteman I, as were its performance characteristics. In any case, the Minuteman I is no longer deployable by the U.S." HOE experiments have used a single-intercept vehicle, but the program was originally designed to investigate the use of multiple-kill vehicles. The ACDA *Bulletin* noted that "the U.S. is not developing ABM interceptors with multiple warheads." Once ERIS is developed, however, pressure to deploy multiple warheads, which can significantly enhance kill prospects against a proliferated offense, will certainly be felt.[58]

Other experiments are also questionable. The supervelocity or advanced kinetic-energy launcher using an electromagnetic railgun could be considered a violation of the treaty's provision banning "rapid reload" because of its high rate of fire. Tests of the space-based kinetic-kill vehicle scheduled for early 1990s would be in blatant contradiction of Article VI(a), which forbids the development and testing of space-based ABM systems and components. The effort to develop a space-based laser via Talon Gold, LODE, and Alpha could also be inconsistent with the treaty. The Talon Gold project aims to attach a telescope to the laser to test pointing and tracking technologies. It was supposed to have been tested on the space shuttle in 1987 and 1988 but has been delayed both by the *Challenger* disaster and to allow for the addition of a second telescope. In 1984 congressional budget cuts reduced the scope of the study. Now, a new, more capable system is to be developed. Some officials argue that it is only a "generic" experiment, one that is not capable of substituting for an ABM component. This, however, is its purpose, and it will be ABM-capable. The LODE project (Large Optical Demonstration Experiment) would raise questions by putting mirrors in space that could be considered components of a BMD system. The Alpha project to develop a hydrogen fluoride chemical laser does not violate the treaty so long as experiments are made in a laboratory, but field testing may constitute a treaty violation inasmuch as the ultimate objective is to mount the lasers on space-based satellites for use in an ABM mode. The same would be true for experiments with neutral-particle-beam weapons to be deployed in space.[59]

The SDIO view is that because there was no agreed definition of some elements of the treaty, such as the definition of a component, it is necessary to infer specific standards. The DOD has adopted four working principles:[60]

1.   Compliance must be based on "objective assessments of capabilities" rather than on "subjective judgments of intent," so as to avoid a double standard of compliance.

2.   The treaty permits "research short of field testing of a prototype ABM system or component."

3.   New technologies should not be subjected to stricter standards than existing systems.

4.   The treaty does not apply to defenses against nonstrategic ballistic missiles or cruise missiles.

Under the DOD directive 5100.70 of January 9, 1973, the director of defense research and planning (DDRE) ensures that all military research programs comply with the treaty, on the advice of the Defense Department's general counsel. DOD Instruction S-5100.72 establishes general guidelines, and questions of interpretation are considered on a case-by-case basis. The DDRE undertakes to consult with general counsel, the office of International Security Policy in the Office of the Assistant Secretary of Defense, and the office of the Joint Chiefs. Military departments and agencies must certify compliance quarterly and, moreover, establish internal procedures to monitor and ensure it.

The DOD divides SDI research into several categories. The first, conceptual design or laboratory testing, obviously precedes field testing and is not verifiable by national technical means. It is therefore not subject to treaty limits. The second, field testing of devices that are neither ABM components or prototypes, is also said to be permissible. The DOD holds that for a device to be limited by the treaty, "it must constitute an ABM system or component (an ABM interceptor missile, ABM launcher, or ABM radar) or be capable of substituting for such an ABM component." In the third category are experiments involving field testing of fixed land-based ABM components. These must take place at "current" or "additionally agreed" test ranges. For the United States the authorized sites are the Kwajalein Missile Range (on an atoll in the Marshalls chain) and the White Sands Missile Range in New Mexico.[61] According to the DOD, most technology research projects for SDI fall in either category one or two; none falls in category three. Many are "under roof" experiments "using devices incapable of achieving ABM performance levels." Although some are designed to be based in space, the space environment is simulated in a laboratory.[62]

Laser systems currently under development are being designed to fit within the DOD guidelines. In the case of the Mid-Infrared Advanced Chemical Laser (MIRACL), or of the Sea Lite Beam Detector subsystems from a former navy program, the effort is to determine in a ground experiment whether a laser and beam director can be successfully integrated. Whether separately or combined, however, these cannot substitute for an ABM component because "the power, optics, and laser frequency are not compatible with atmospheric propagation at ranges useful for ABM applications."[63] The experiments are planned against ground-based static targets; another experiment is being planned in which a moving target will be launched from a point close to the MIRACL. Because MIRACL is ground-based, it would comply with the treaty. Other experiments involving acquisition, tracking, and pointing will demonstrate technologies but will not be capable of achieving ABM performance levels. For the time being, the free-electron laser will not have enough power to serve as an ABM weapon. But even if at a later stage it does obtain this power, the ground-based FEL will not violate the treaty, although it may have to be tested at an acknowledged test range. The High Brightness Relay (HIBREL) project involves experiments to demonstrate the feasibility of relay mirrors in space for beams from ground-based lasers. The mirrors will be able to handle light only from low-powered lasers and will use technologies that form just a part of what would ultimately be required for an ABM weapon; they, too, will not be able to achieve ABM performance levels. The neutral-particle-beam experiment will be tested in space to determine the technologies needed for midcourse discrimination or to detect nuclear material. The experiment will be conducted using nearby co-orbital targets at low average power; it will not be capable of "autonomously acquiring or tracking ballistic targets" and will therefore not have ABM capabilities, nor will the test be conducted in an ABM mode.[64]

SDIO also defends other experiments as treaty-compliant. The BSTS experiment will be designed to "determine if sufficiently sensitive tracking and signature data can be collected on-orbit against the earth's background." The BSTS will have only enough capacity to function as an early-warning system. It will collect ballistic-missile-plume data but will lack the real-time data-processing capacity needed to pass the data to a boost-phase interceptor. (Other capabilities will also be limited—by nature and resources.) The AOS experiment will test the feasibility of using an airborne infrared sensor to support a ground-based radar; it will involve only a single, passive sensor, and because of sensor and platform limitations it cannot substitute for an ABM component. The SBKKV project is designed to enable space-based kinetic interception by chemically propelled rockets, but the demonstration hardware for any space-based experiment will not be an ABM component, cannot substitute for an ABM component, and will not be tested in an ABM mode. (There will be no intercepts of strategic ballistic missiles or their elements in flight-trajectory in space, but intercepts of certain orbital targets simulating anti-satellite weapons can be compatible.) Otherwise, the planned experiments are said to raise no questions of compliance. The ERIS development concerns a ground-based ABM missile which will be provided with a single nonnuclear warhead; its terminal-imaging radar will be housed in a fixed site.[65]

But it is not clear that the development and testing in space of the space-based kinetic-kill vehicle system, now designated the space-based interceptor (SBI), would be allowable. It would use technology known at the time the treaty was adopted and incorporated into existing ground-based ABMs. Development and testing of this technology for purposes of a space-based ABM could therefore fall under the prohibitions in the provision on testing and development. Because the Reagan administration claimed an exception to the testing provisions only for technologies based on "other physical principles"—other, that is, than those incorporated into ABM systems when the treaty was signed—it would seem that SBI could not legally be tested, even under the "broad" interpretation. The only argument in favor of testing is that the adaptation of the technology for space-based purposes represents the use of "other physical principles." In 1987 and 1988 the Reagan administration was reported to be considering whether to adopt the view that while the ERIS ABM missile is based on traditional technology, the SBI is a "future" system, even though it relies on previously known kinetic principles. Plans have been made to conduct two suborbital flight tests of the SBI against a ballistic-missile target at Kwajalein Atoll between 1991 and 1992, and possibly earlier. Because these tests are suborbital, the SDIO asserts that they conform to the traditional interpretation of the treaty. The issue of whether or not these tests are legal has reportedly divided the experts in the administration, those in the Defense Department leaning toward approval, those in the State Department and ACDA toward opposition. Other critics have charged—correctly in our view—that all such development and testing are clearly prohibited.[66]

THE DISAGREEMENT AT REYKJAVÍK

Despite these efforts to argue that SDI research conforms with a restrictive interpretation of the ABM Treaty, the issue of what research is permitted under the treaty became the sticking point of the negotiations in Reykjavík. What happened at Reykjavík is in some dispute, but it appears that the two sides came close to a much broader agreement on arms reduction than had been anticipated by the United States. At most, U.S. negotiators had hoped to reach agreement with the Soviets on the removal of longer-range intermediate weapons from the European theater. When Gorbachev proposed a more sweeping agreement—which would have included the halving of strategic weapons in five years—followed by a total elimination of strategic offensive weapons, Reagan's response was encouraging (although the president appears to have proposed the elimination of strategic ballistic missiles rather than of all strategic weapons). The Soviet leader's proposal was associated with three others. One was that all longer-range intermediate weapons—the Soviet SS-20s and the U.S. Pershing Is and IIs and ground-launched cruise missiles—be removed from the European theater. Both sides would be free to retain up to one hundred of such launchers, but the

Soviets would keep theirs beyond the Urals and the United States would house its stock in the continental U.S. The second proposal was that both sides reaffirm the ABM Treaty by making a commitment to refrain from deploying defensive systems beyond what the treaty allowed for at least fifteen more years. During this time research on new systems might continue, but development and testing of space-based systems and components would be confined to the laboratory. The U.S. side, which had offered a seven-and-a-half-year commitment, compromised on ten years, which was acceptable to the Soviets, but would not accept the Soviet proposal for restrictions on development and testing. The third Soviet proposal was that all nuclear testing be banned, which the United States sought to defer pending further investigation of problems of verification.

The U.S. negotiators responded with two successive alternatives. The first committed each side "to confine itself to research, development and testing, which is permitted by the ABM treaty" for five years, during which time "strategic nuclear arsenals" would be reduced by 50 percent. Provided further reductions of offensive weapons took place, toward a goal of eliminating "all offensive ballistic missiles" by the end of a ten-year period, the same restrictions would hold. At the end of this ten-year period either side would be free to deploy additional defenses. When the Soviets declined this proposal, the United States tabled a second, pledging both sides not to exercise their right to withdraw from the treaty for ten years—adding, however, that the treaty "is of unlimited duration" (a change designed to meet the Soviet objection that the first draft would have changed the duration of the treaty to ten years). In addition, the draft added a comma after the word "testing," thus obviating the possible implication in the first draft that only the research, development, and testing specified in the treaty and further defined in the agreed statements and SCC clarifications would be permitted. In effect, the second draft left the United States free to adopt the "broad" interpretation of the treaty. In the event, however, this draft was also rejected by the Soviets, prompting Reagan to gather up his papers and end the negotiations.

The Soviet side was accused by Shultz and later by the president himself of trying to "kill" SDI by requiring that all development and testing be confined to the "four walls" of a laboratory—a point underscored by Foreign Minister Eduard Shevardnadze when he used his hands to describe the walls of a laboratory. In a television address from Moscow, Gorbachev repeated his assertion that the ABM Treaty banned development and testing of space defenses except in the laboratory, but he phrased it in ways that seemed somewhat less restrictive than U.S. representations. "We firmly stated," he observed, "that it was necessary to comply with the ABM Treaty of 1972 without any time limit. Moreover, in order to strengthen the regime of this Treaty, we proposed . . . mutual commitments . . . not to use our right to withdraw from the treaty for at least 10 years, until we finally eliminated the nuclear weapons." He said that the Soviet emphasis on the restrictions was intended to "strengthen the treaty," which seemed to bear out the U.S. contention that he was trying to add to or amend the treaty, but he made clear that the intention was to prohibit the testing of "all space elements of anti-ballistic missile defense" except in laboratories. "We did not demand or require," Gorbachev insisted, "that he stop work in this area, but with the understanding that all provisions of the ABM treaty be observed." Several times Gorbachev repeated that the terms of the treaty required that development and testing be confined to the laboratory. In one formulation, however, he introduced a possibly significant specification by observing that "testing of all space elements of anti-ballistic missile defense in space [is] prohibited except research and testing in laboratories."[67]

By introducing the term "space elements," the Soviets may have been deliberately attempting to broaden the scope of the treaty so as to eliminate any distinction between components and adjuncts, or they may simply have been intending to use a synonym for components. Conceivably, they may also have been signaling a willingness to discuss which types of experiments might be allowable on grounds that they are not elements of anti-ballistic-missile defense, or not exclusively that. If, for example, the U.S. side had asked if it was permissible to test improved sensors for early warning, even though such sensors could also be used in conjunction with ballistic-missile defense, it is conceivable that the Soviets would have agreed that such development could continue. That latitude would also have to apply, it appears, to systems designed to develop ASATs or to test ATBMs, the two acknowledged loopholes in the treaty.

Strangely, the U.S. delegation did not request clarification of the Soviet position. This may have been a result of exhaustion, for the issue came up at the end of an unexpectedly detailed and comprehensive set of negotiations. Conceivably, however, it may have reflected the United States' unwillingness to enter into any sort of compromise that would have restricted its testing and development. Perhaps the president and his advisors thought that, especially in the second five-year period, testing would have to go beyond the restrictive interpretation, which would certainly have been disallowed under the Soviet interpretation.

It is possible, but unlikely, that this was simply a missed opportunity, a failure on the part of both sides to recognize that they were not communicating their actual views. The Soviet position did not necessarily mean that the United States would be prevented from undertaking virtually all of the experiments on tracking, pointing, and acquisition planned for the SDI (because some of these could be justified as efforts to improve early warning) or for many other experiments that could be defined and configured as efforts to develop ASATs and to improve tactical air defense and anti-ballistic-missile defense. Because the Soviets were ready to drop their proposal for a comprehensive ban on nuclear testing, testing to develop the X-ray laser could also have continued as long as it did not involve the testing of the system in space. Even if the United States had accepted the Soviet formulation, much—arguably most—of what was planned for the SDI over the next ten years could apparently have been done in compliance with the treaty. It is also not clear why the Soviets introduced new language in speaking of "space elements." To find out what the Soviets intended, the United States could have proposed acceptance of the restrictive definition or, in other words, agreed that the treaty prohibits development and testing of ABM systems and components other than those that are ground-based. Given that the Soviets have an active program to develop ground-based lasers, they would presumably not object to such an interpretation and, indeed, may well have focused attention on space-based elements in order to distinguish them from the ground-based versions of new technologies they are developing.

Although it is intriguing to speculate about the possibility that the dispute might have been resolved if both sides had sought clarification, it would probably be a mistake to suppose that nothing more was at fault than fatigue and miscommunication. The same issue had been discussed in detail at the Geneva summit, but no final agreement could be achieved. The U.S. delegation went to Reykjavík without any expectation of an imminent breakthrough. The failure to reach an agreement was probably caused by more fundamental factors, not the least of which is that many of the Soviet proposals had not been anticipated, and thus not thoroughly studied, by any authoritative arm of the administration.

The president's fundamental concern centered on perceptions. He did not want to be seen as trading away SDI in return for an agreement on the reduction of offensive weapons. He did not want to disappoint his domestic supporters, who had come to see SDI as a unilateral U.S. move, based on superior technological ability, to ensure against any possibility of a Soviet preemptive strike and who would not have trusted the Soviets to adhere to any arms-control agreement—even one negotiated by Reagan. The president himself had come to see SDI as his legacy to the nation's defense and as an essential step away from the threat of nuclear catastrophe. He tried to persuade the Soviet leader at Geneva that strategic defenses would not pose an offensive threat and reiterated his willingness to share the system with the Soviets. (His own offer to share the technology was both clumsy and vulnerable to charges that it could hardly take place: (1) the United States would not be willing to share its most advanced technology with the U.S.S.R., and (2) knowing how to use the system means knowing how to defeat it. But Reagan may have had something else in mind, including the possibility that once the system were in place, both powers might at least use the data from sensors to identify third-party threats, or that the interceptors might be managed jointly or perhaps by some multinational entity.)

At Reykjavík, Reagan went out of his way to try to persuade Gorbachev that the only way to achieve total elimination of strategic weapons was to allow both sides to deploy defenses as an "insurance policy" against cheating or third-party threats. Presumably, as Fletcher and other proponents of strategic defenses (including Teller) have pointed out, such a defense need not be space-based, and some versions could be much less elaborate than a comprehensive layered shield, because they would need to defend only against a much smaller threat.[68] In any case, Reagan made clear that he was committed to the SDI and was unwilling to agree to any proposal that would prevent it from reaching a point at which a decision could be made ten years hence to deploy a system. Development would certainly require some forms of testing in space, though the experiments could be configured to conform to ABM Treaty restrictions—at least in the sense that the elements tested would not achieve ABM power levels or be tested against strategic launchers or RVs and could therefore not be used without further prototype development as BMD weapons. In effect, the official U.S. position has been that development and testing of the potential elements of a space-based defense are permissible, so long as they do not reach the point at which field testing of prototypes takes place. This seems to have been the president's own position. But he was also obviously aware of the danger that if an agreement were reached in his administration to reduce nuclear weapons and to restrict SDI research, forces in Congress would therefore be unwilling to fund it at a significant level.

There was apparently also a disagreement, or at least a difference of emphasis, among the president's counselors. Weinberger made it clear, before the Geneva summit and after Reykjavík, that he was prepared to have no arms-control treaties if the alternative meant constraints on the modernization of U.S. strategic forces and the development of strategic defenses. Because of this position, he and Perle may well have exaggerated the intransigence of the Soviets. Perle went so far as to suggest the Soviets were concerned with the offensive capabilities of strategic defenses because their own research is so advanced that they have discovered offensive uses of which the United States is unaware. Shultz, however, appeared to have been genuinely disappointed by the failure of the Reykjavík summit. He went to Geneva after Reykjavík in the hope of breaking the deadlock, but to no avail.

Reagan seemed to be immobilized between the contradictory views of Weinberger and Shultz. After Reykjavík, in early 1987, Weinberger sought to capitalize on the breakdown of negotiations by proposing that the "legally correct interpretation" be formally adopted as the basis for SDI experimentation and that the president endorse early deployment in the January 1987 State of the Union address. But the new national security advisor Frank C. Carlucci reportedly succeeded in dissuading the president from endorsing early deployment by pointing out that no decision had so far been reached on the issue within the administration. On February 3 a meeting was held with the key policymakers at which the president said he was ready to adopt the new interpretation but not to call for early deployment. Shultz, joined by Sofaer and Nitze, recommended that the president defer a decision pending a further review. Accordingly, Reagan approved National Security Decision Directive 261, which called for new studies on the interpretation. The minutes of this meeting were leaked to the press. Apparently, the participants discussed the likely Soviet reaction to an announcement that the new interpretation was to be adopted. The president is quoted as saying: "Don't ask the Soviets. Tell them," and "Why don't we just go ahead on the assumption that this is what we're doing and it's right?" [69]

At the Washington summit in December 1987, controversy over the testing provisions continued to pose an obstacle to a START agreement, but this time the leaders agreed to set the issue to one side. At first, Foreign Minister Shevardnadze insisted that the United States must agree to abide by the ABM Treaty as "signed and ratified." Secretary Shultz reportedly persuaded him that this formula was an inappropriate allusion to the debate over the interpretation of the treaty between the administration and members of the Senate. [70] A last-minute compromise was struck which enabled each side to claim that the other had accepted its position. In a prime specimen of diplomatic double-talk, the two leaders instructed their delegates in Geneva "to work out an agreement that would commit the sides to observe the ABM Treaty, as signed in 1972, while conducting their research, development and testing as required, which are permitted by the ABM Treaty, and not to withdraw from the treaty for a specified length of time."[71] In other words, the impasse over the kinds of testing that would be permitted was left unresolved, presumably to await further negotiation.

THE SOVIET POSITION

In the various meetings, the Soviets evidently did not make clear exactly why SDI was of such concern to them. Some Soviet statements indicated that they saw SDI as an offensive rather than a defensive program. Perhaps this explains their references to "space-strike" weapons. Some U.S. observers have observed that, in fact, these space-based weapons could be used for offensive purposes, i.e., for striking targets on the ground and in the air and for setting major fires.[72] These fears have been derided, however, by those who point out that there are far more efficient and inexpensive ways of mounting offensive strikes and that laser weapons cannot reliably penetrate the clouds to strike ground targets. Fires cannot readily be set in urban areas by the use of lasers, and in any case, the resulting exhaustion of fuel supplies for offensive purposes would render space-based defensive weapons useless for their primary purpose. Setting fires, moreover, would take time, and, by then, the Soviets would have ample warning of an attack and be able to launch their retaliatory strike.

The Soviet fear of SDI is more likely to be based on the general notion that it represents a major acceleration in the intensity of the technological arms race, which would only impose further strains on an economy already seriously handicapped by extravagant military expenditures. Furthermore, such a comprehensive program is virtually certain to produce technological advances that could be applied to nuclear and conventional weapons systems. Better sensors, computers, laser weapons, electromagnetic railguns, etc., could significantly increase the effectiveness of U.S. offensive weapons, forcing the Soviets to make substantial investments in similar modernization just to keep abreast. Their relative technological inferiority in most of the relevant technologies would put them at a disadvantage in this competition. The Soviets would have to do more than develop countermeasures to the SDI; the applicability of any research findings to offense would force them to undertake similar programs.

Another Soviet objection is that SDI could give the U.S. a first-strike option. The stated concern of the Soviets, since Premier Andropov first responded to Reagan's "Star Wars" speech, is that SDI would enable the United States to launch a first strike and then to absorb a "ragged retaliatory strike." Although at most a remote possibility, the thought has occurred even to SDI supporters. Weinberger has expressed horror at the prospect that the Soviets might obtain a significant defensive capability, because of the very scenario described by Andropov. "I can't imagine a more destabilizing factor for the world," Weinberger declared, "than if the Soviets should acquire a thoroughly reliable defense against these missiles before we do."[73] He has also said that he "cannot imagine that the Soviets, if they had a monopoly position, would do anything other than try to blackmail the rest of the world."[74] Why should the Soviets think the United States would behave any differently?

The Soviets may also reasonably fear that BMD weapons would find a ready use as ASATs. Satellites are not very difficult targets, so the products of SDI research will probably be more useful in this capacity than in defending against a massive missile attack. In a crisis, such weapons could be used as part of an offensive effort to destroy or blind enemy sensor and communication satellites. In this limited sense, it is plausible to think of them as space-strike weapons.

For all these reasons, the Soviets seem to have decided that they had to make SDI a central issue in the arms-control negotiations. If they were to agree to reductions in offensive arms without constraining the U.S. effort to design and deploy defenses, they would risk putting themselves in a strategically inferior position. Even if the U.S. program were only partially successful, the United States might decide to erect defenses (at the end of the ten-year extension of the ABM Treaty), challenging the parity they now enjoy because of constraints on defensive deployments. The Soviets claim that their position would make it unnecessary for either side to deploy defenses. They propose instead that both sides agree to eliminate all nuclear weapons. In that way, neither would face a nuclear threat and neither would therefore require defenses. The U.S. position is that a total elimination of nuclear weapons is an unrealistic expectation. The United States, at any rate, could not safely assume that the U.S.S.R. would not stockpile some undeclared nuclear weapons; even a few such weapons would be a formidable threat against a power with none. Defensive systems are therefore essential as "insurance" against cheating and third-party threats in conjunction with radical reductions in offensive arms.

BREAKING THE IMPASSE

Is there a way out of the impasse? One such way would be for both sides to agree on a more precise definition of allowable development and testing. Much of the work the SDIO has scheduled falls well within the customary, or restrictive, reading of the treaty. Some is in a gray area. The complexity of the proposed research makes it obvious, as various studies have shown in detail, that these technologies cannot possibly become candidates for deployment for many years—ten to fifteen at the very least. Restrictions on the testing of prototypes would therefore have no effect whatever on the pace of research. Restrictions on the testing in space of DEW satellites, however, or on satellites carrying beam generators with high power levels, would have some cramping effect. But, generally, much of the research on new physical principles can be done in the laboratory or in forms acceptable under the treaty. An agreement to abide by the restrictive interpretation for ten years would therefore not significantly delay the effort. In addition, it would assure the Soviets that ten years hence the U.S. effort could not possibly have reached the point where deployment could be implemented in a short period of time. Both sides are bound to continue their modernization of offensive weapons; provided SDI is not funded at extraordinary levels or surrounded by unrealistic rhetoric, the Soviets need not fear the likelihood of major breakthroughs that their own research and development could not possibly match.

In sum, the impasse can be broken if both sides finally come to realize that none of the systems being investigated under SDI is remotely likely to pose a threat to the current basis of deterrence for at least several decades. Certainly, there is no justification for supposing that the ABM Treaty must be violated within the next ten years to take account of new technological realities.

Nevertheless, in the absence of an arms-control agreement neither side is likely to rush toward a breakout from the ABM Treaty. Given that the technology of effective defense is so remote, the expense of early deployment cannot be justified. Early deployment of U.S. ground-based defenses is a possibility, but this could be done within the limits of the ABM Treaty. The Soviets have no incentive to abrogate the treaty unless

SDI testing blatantly disregards treaty limits. If either side decides to abrogate the treaty, however, the efforts to achieve negotiated strategic arms control are likely to collapse. Neither side would feel comfortable dismantling offensive weapons. Both would seek to develop force structures that would make the job of the defense more difficult, as both sides have already done. This could take the form of improving offensive penetration aids, shortening booster-burnout times, coating missiles, etc., and of efforts to develop defensive weapons, ground-based as well as space-based.

It is highly doubtful that either side would benefit from such a competition. As we have seen in chapter 3, history has shown that innovations by one side are easily matched by the other either by the development of a similar system or countersystem. In this case, another, more novel response might be attempted; the Soviets could decide to prevent the full deployment of a space-based defense. Striking at a satellite is not a clear violation of the international law that prohibits transgressing another state's territorial integrity because there is no established principle governing the deployment of a defensive satellite in what could be said to be an extension of the air space of another state. The state that did so could claim to have acted in self-defense, particularly if it warned that it viewed such satellites above its territory as hostile or invasive. Any state, furthermore, could disable satellites in ways that do not constitute outright attacks, such as blinding them or interfering with their mirrors by orbiting debris—a step that would not produce the equivalent of a smoking gun.

Another difficulty is that a shield in space would not protect against threats to go beneath it by attacking with depressed-trajectory weapons, tactical weapons, and air-breathing systems. The development of long-range, low-altitude stealthy cruise missiles is currently under active consideration in the United States. A separate initiative would be needed to produce an air defense and tactical BMD able to meet this kind of threat—including defense against the new stealth-type missile which, according to its promoters, is able to penetrate any known type of defense. Even if such an initiative were successful, it would not entirely remove the threat of a major nuclear attack. Even in the extremely unlikely event that all dangers from missiles and bombs could be averted, nuclear weapons could still be delivered to ports in the holds of cargo vessels, to major urban centers secreted in civilian aircraft, and otherwise smuggled in as suitcase bombs. Although such weapons would probably not have the devastating effect of a full-scale ICBM attack, they could nevertheless cause damage on a scale unprecedented in the history of warfare. A determined or desperate adversary would always have the means to threaten such an attack. Such delivery systems would not be adequate for attacking military targets, but they would be entirely adequate as threats against civil targets.

Similarly, there is little merit in the contention that a partially effective defense is better than none. Advocates of SDI argue that, at the very least, a defensive shield would create so much uncertainty in the mind of a potential attacker as to rule out any possibility of a preemptive attack. If the goal is to instill uncertainty, however, it can be achieved far more easily (and more reliably and cheaply) by increasing deployments at sea, on mobile launch platforms, and so forth, which unlike SDI, do not risk destabilizing the weapons balance. An enormously expensive program like SDI (or the follow-on deployment) is not needed if the only purpose is to instill uncertainty in the mind of the adversary.

The very fact of a breakdown in arms-control negotiations, coupled with the resumption of the defensive as well as the offensive arms race, could well promote insecurity on both sides. In such a situation, the side that thinks its position is worsening could be tempted to take actions that would prevent a further decline before it is too late, or it could take actions that could divert the other side from its program. Thus, a U.S. military buildup could be countered by a Soviet use of proxy forces against U.S. interests. The Soviet Union's ability to make trouble for the United States and its allies in the Third World is now well appreciated. Although the U.S.S.R. has resisted efforts to link arms control with détente in these areas, it would have an incentive to turn up the heat should the United States seek to threaten to gain a strategic advantage by developing weapons that the Soviets perceive as a direct threat to their security. Such a policy of provoking trouble for the United States may carry costs that the Soviets would not be willing to bear, but the United States has no interest in encouraging Soviet efforts to destabilize the international system.

In view of the potential for instability, a further development of the arms-control regime seems highly preferable. Such a regime would aim at continual steps to reduce nuclear arms to whatever level could be considered minimally acceptable. If defenses are to be deployed, they could be installed on the basis of agreed understandings, worked out on the model of the ABM Treaty, or by amending or renegotiating the treaty. As confidence grows, a cooperative deployment of defensive systems may become conceivable in which, for example, both sides would receive warning of any attack from sensor satellites. A multinational or transnational effort could then conceivably be mounted to administer certain peace-keeping devices, more or less in accordance with Reagan's belief that a shield could be shared with the Soviets. Unfortunately, these possibilities are undermined by the fact that so much new research—whether performed under military auspices or not—poses insuperable temptations to develop systems that confer temporary advantages but render cooperation with the other side more difficult. In the case of SDI, unilateral deployment would also jeopardize the unity of the Western alliance, for reasons we explore next.

CHAPTER 6

A "Maginot Line of the Twenty-first Century"?

SDI and the Western Alliance

Although the initial announcement of SDI came as an unwelcome surprise to the European allies of the United States, the project has so far not caused unmanageable difficulties for the Western alliance. Defense specialists in the European countries, who are as doubtful of the prospects for comprehensive defenses as most of their U.S. counterparts, discount the likelihood that SDI will have radical consequences for strategy and force structure in the near future. While the program remains in the research phase, they can be content to keep a watchful eye on its progress. As long as the United States continues to abide by the traditional interpretation of the ABM Treaty, the Soviets have no excuse to break out of it by deploying additional defenses that might diminish the credibility of the relatively small deterrent forces of Great Britain and France. Because SDI did not prevent the conclusion of the INF Treaty or hinder a resumption of negotiations to reduce strategic arsenals, it has not proved to be the obstacle to arms control that allied leaders feared it would become. Finally, the SDI budget has fallen far short of the levels initially called for, so it represents neither the major commitment of military R & D resources nor the economic challenge the allies feared.

There are nevertheless at least three foreseeable contingencies in which SDI could still have considerable effects on the alliance. One would arise if and when the United States were to decide to deploy on its own soil a first-phase defense system designed to protect military assets and to provide some marginal degree of population protection. Even if this decision were taken after consultation with the allies (but especially if taken unilaterally), many Western Europeans would regard it as a sig-

A Shield in Space?

nificant departure from the acceptance of shared risk of nuclear war. Until now, shared risk has been considered an essential guarantee of alliance solidarity. Apprehensions in the alliance that the United States is backing away from a commitment to the defense of Western Europe—already aroused by the loss of U.S. nuclear superiority vis-à-vis the Soviet Union—would be further reinforced.

The second contingency involves the link between SDI and NATO's interest in improving defenses against attacks from aircraft and short-range tactical ballistic missiles (TBMs). Although the INF Treaty has alleviated that concern, especially with respect to the highly threatening Soviet intermediate-range SS-20s, it has by no means been completely removed. Faced with improvements in Soviet attack aircraft and tactical missiles (carrying both conventional and nuclear warheads), NATO is actively pursuing "extended air defense." This rubric comprises efforts to develop better defenses against bombers, air-launched cruise missiles, and standoff weapons, as well as defenses against TBMs. An understanding has developed between the United States and its European allies whereby their military establishments and defense contractors will cooperate in the general program of SDI research while giving particular attention to (1) devising a "European architecture" for strategic defense and (2) integrating strategic defense with tactical defense for the European theater. If this cooperation results in deployable defenses (which would in all probability be ground-based), they could be viewed as a first step toward the deployment of comprehensive defenses. Their association with SDI, however, could well make a proposal to deploy active extended air defenses in Europe more controversial than it might otherwise be, if it was understood solely as a move to stabilize the existing form of deterrence.

A third contingency would arise if the United States' commitment to the pursuit of SDI should become the only obstacle to strategic arms reductions. So long as other obstacles remain, notably the difficulties surrounding verification, Western European concern over SDI will remain muted. If it should become the sole remaining obstacle, however, the West Europeans' keen interest in transcending the tensions of the cold war could easily revive and intensify the opposition aroused when SDI was first announced.

THE INITIAL SHOCK

When SDI was first announced in March 1983, allied reaction was almost uniformly negative. Support came from "High Frontier Europe," newly founded by such leading conservatives as Kai-Uwe von Hassel, former defense minister of the Federal Republic of Germany (FRG); Pierre Gallois, the French air force general who was instrumental in developing the rationale for France's nuclear forces; Robert Close, a retired Belgian general; and Air Vice-Marshal Stewart Menaul of Great Britain. In London, the Institute for European Defence and Strategic Studies, a newly created organization affiliated with the Heritage Foundation, opened its offices with the aim of promoting European cooperation with SDI. Otherwise, the major political leaders and military and scientific specialists were critical. President Reagan's closest political allies in Europe, Prime Minister Margaret Thatcher and Chancellor Helmut Kohl, were embarrassed that they were not consulted prior to the announcement of such a far-reaching departure from settled NATO policy. The United States' sudden rejection of continued reliance on nuclear deterrence struck Michael Howard, a highly regarded British writer on strategic issues, as altogether startling: "It's as if the pope announced that he no longer believed in original sin." [1]

In general, West Europeans were troubled by the strategic and economic implications they saw in SDI. Although the president might claim that its objective was to protect the allies as well as the North American continent, West Europeans reasoned that even a successful space shield could not protect them against the kind of attack with which they would continue to be threatened from tactical nuclear missiles, aircraft, and conventional ground forces. A U.S. space shield would have about thirty minutes in which to intercept an attack, but a Western European defense would have barely a few minutes to respond to launchings of Soviet short-range and intermediate-range missiles deployed in Eastern Europe. If the U.S. homeland were protected against Soviet ICBMs, then the United States' security would become even more "decoupled" from the defense of Europe than it had already become since the Soviets achieved strategic parity with the West. If the Soviets should respond to SDI by developing a more capable defense system of their own, the relatively small, independent nuclear deterrent forces of Great Britain and France, developed and maintained at considerable political and economic cost, might lose their credibility. As Trevor Taylor has pointed out, the governments of Great Britain and France "see nuclear weapons as the central element in their countries' defenses and allocate funds accordingly." Great Britain is currently procuring the Trident D-5 missile from the United States and building its own submarines and warheads for the system at a projected cost of almost $10 billion (in 1985–86 prices), an amount that will account for roughly 10 percent of the budget for new military equipment for several years. France spends even more on its nuclear *force de frappe,* which currently accounts for 30 percent of planned spending on new military equipment. Although not a member of NATO, France coordinates its strategy and conventional deployments with NATO while maintaining an independent ground-based, long-range nuclear missile force on the Plateau d'Albion, as well as eighteen Mirage IV aircraft equipped with standoff nuclear missiles, and six submarines armed with nuclear missiles, with a seventh on the way.[2]

A report prepared for the Assembly of the West European Union (WEU) expressed the concern of these and other West European governments: "If the idea spreads that the future depends on defensive weapons and that in the long run offensive weapons are destined to be relegated to the arsenal of obsolescent weapons, it is likely to become increasingly difficult to make an already hesitant public opinion accept the financial and other efforts necessary for the maintenance and development of nuclear weapons."[3]

The West European left was hardly ready to accept the Reagan administration's assurance that SDI would lead to nuclear disarmament. Moderate Socialists who accept the need for offensive deterrence saw it as a blow to the ABM Treaty and therefore to prospects for détente with the Soviet Union, as well as an effort to restore U.S. superiority over the U.S.S.R. in line with a dangerous commitment to a war-fighting policy. The views of more radical advocates of nuclear disarmament were reflected in the reaction of the historian E. P. Thompson, who heaped scorn on the Atlanticists in the European defense establishment for refusing to admit that SDI had revealed the glaring weaknesses of reliance on the U.S. nuclear umbrella:

> Star Wars made monkeys of the loyal NATO governments and their attendant defence experts. As Colonel Alford, of the International Institute for Strategic Studies, told *The New York Times:* "Europeans actually tend to like nuclear weapons." By this we must suppose that the good colonel did not refer to those Europeans who demonstrate against missiles or who answer opinion polls, but to another species of loyal Europeans—*Homo europus philatlanticus*—who staff the military services, defence ministries and the institutes for strategic research. This species really does like the Bomb. They have persuaded themselves that "the deterrent" truly is the only thing that prevents a major European war.
>
> The belief in "deterrence" is not dishonorable. . . . But the True Believers, who were the chorus who welcomed in cruise [missiles], were utterly confounded by Star Wars. They suspected that SDI signaled a strategic retreat which could de-couple Europe from Fortress America. If America alone had

an SDI shield, and could launch its missiles with impunity, they feared this might encourage American adventurism or could lead to a "limited" nuclear war being fought in Europe. Or if the Soviet Union built a shield also, then Europe would be left as a no-man's-land between the superpowers, with the laser-zapped nukes of both sides falling on its head.[4]

Thompson took pains, however, to distinguish his opposition to SDI from that of the Atlanticists: "The real message of Star Wars to west Europe is to get out from under America's hegemony—and umbrella—as soon as we can."[5]

Industrialists and economic policymakers saw SDI as another "American challenge" to Western Europe—a thinly disguised effort to subsidize U.S. high-technology industry that was bound to leave its competitors at a disadvantage. They feared SDI would enable U.S. high-technology companies to extend their dominance in major areas of civil as well as military technology, including computers, aerospace, lasers, and new materials.

Even after Thatcher had become reconciled to SDI, her foreign secretary, Sir Geoffrey Howe, was particularly forthright in criticizing the program. Although he sought to present a balanced response to the initiative by highlighting certain aspects of the projects he found attractive, Howe put far more emphasis on potentially negative consequences. On the positive side, he pointed out that the announcement had been useful in calling attention to the Soviet Union's "very considerable" investments in a range of defensive activities, in view of which it was sheer hypocrisy for the Soviets to call for the "demilitarization of space." Howe also suggested that in light of Soviet ASAT testing, a matching U.S. effort in space was "logical and prudent." But he said strategic defenses were another matter because the very effort to develop them would encourage the false view that the defense of the West need no longer rely on the traditional form of deterrence, even though the necessary technologies might not prove feasible or cost-effective against offensive countermeasures. "There could be no advantage," Howe said pointedly, "in creating a new Maginot Line of the twenty-first century, liable to be outflanked by relatively simpler and demonstrably cheaper counter-measures."[6]

Like critics in the United States, Howe noted that SDI raised new, disquieting problems for defense policy. Would the technology permit adequate political control, or would it lead to "a situation in which the peace of the world rested solely upon computers and automatic decision-making"? How would the costs be borne—costs that might run into "many hundreds of billions of dollars"? This was an issue, he noted, not only of whether the West could afford the costs of designing defenses but also of whether the "enormous funds might be better employed" in maintaining a "credible, sustainable and controllable mix of conventional and nuclear forces." In view of the dependence of both sides on satellites to gather intelligence, especially heavy in the case of the West, did it make sense to put those assets in jeopardy so that in a time of crisis either side might be "faced with the loss of its strategic eyes and ears"? Because such a development would be "gravely destabilizing," the British government's view was that negotiations for mutual constraint on ASATs would be preferable. Howe's fundamental concern was that the United States might be tempted to rely too much on technology and too little on negotiations. He feared that "research may acquire an unstoppable momentum of its own, even though the case for stopping may strengthen with the passage of years. . . . We must take care that political decisions are not pre-empted by the march of technology, still less by premature efforts to predict the line of march." The West must convince the Soviet Union that it is serious in wanting arms control, and the alliance must be sure that "the U.S. nuclear guarantee to Europe would indeed be enhanced as a result of defensive deployments." Although any cost-effective enhancements of defense would be welcome, Howe cautioned that these might be offset by Soviet moves "if unrestrained competition in ballistic missile defenses beyond the ABM Treaty limits were to be provoked."[7]

The reaction in France was somewhat different. President François Mitterrand accepted the idea that eventually warfare would become "spatial" and called upon Europe "to look beyond the nuclear era."[8] But Mitterrand was as skeptical as the other European political leaders that the U.S. program would actually lead to a defense transition. A senior official in the French Foreign Ministry, requesting anonymity, told a reporter that the idea behind SDI "absolutely stood the classical concept of nuclear deterrence on its head" and therefore undermined the effort of West European political leaders to rally support for the view that "nuclear weapons were a necessary cost." For the president of the United States to say suddenly that it is possible to get rid of the weapons altogether, he said, "is a very dangerous and unsettling notion, given the fragile public opinion outside of France on the nuclear issue."[9] On June 12, 1984, at the U.N. Conference on Disarmament in Geneva, France took a position independent of the United States, at least implicitly in opposition to SDI, by calling for an international conference to work out a ban, for a renewable five-year period, on the testing and development of directed-energy ABM systems, also proposing steps to ban ASATs and to guarantee the inviolability of the reconnaissance satellites of other nations in addition to those of the superpowers, which were covered by the ABM Treaty.[10]

Mitterrand initially responded to SDI by calling for European cooperation in a new high-technology research program. The proposal for a European Research and Coordinating Agency (EUREKA) was based on an analysis prepared by the Ministry of Foreign Affairs that concluded that European participation in SDI-related R & D would not have significant short-term benefits in nonmilitary applications, whereas in the longer run the inevitable favoritism of SDI contracting for U.S. firms would put Western Europe at a competitive disadvantage. EUREKA would allow for the pooling of resources in order to strengthen West European capabilities both in defense and civil technology, but the main emphasis would be in civil applications. The goal of EUREKA is to promote activities in a variety of fields, including computers, telecommunications, industrial lasers, robotics, new materials, and biotechnology. By the end of 1986, nineteen countries had agreed to participate in the venture (including four neutrals, Sweden, Finland, Switzerland, and Austria), which listed more than one hundred projects with total public and private funding of $4 billion.[11] EUREKA is designed to complement similar programs such as the European Strategic Program of Research in Information Technology (ESPRIT)—established in 1983 among universities, research institutes, and industries—and Research in Advanced Communication in Europe (RACE), established in 1985.

SDI aroused no greater enthusiasm in the Federal Republic. Chancellor Kohl was skeptical but eager above all to preserve good relations with the United States. Foreign Minister Hans-Dietrich Genscher, the leader of Kohl's coalition partner, the Free Democratic party, was openly critical of SDI, as was Finance Minister Gerhard Stoltenberg. Defense Minister Manfred Wörner was plainly less interested in SDI than he was in promoting initiatives aimed at providing defenses for Western Europe. Hans Rühle, director of the planning staff in the Ministry of Defense, expressed a view widely held among FRG defense planners and military officers when he pointed out that even if SDI were to succeed, Western Europe would remain vulnerable to a nuclear threat and to an intensified conventional threat:

> Should, as may be assumed, both superpowers follow the road charter by Reagan, their territories would become invulnerable sanctuaries, while Eu-

rope, even if it deployed a corresponding defense system, would be rid of few of its security policy concerns. Although in such a case protection from the Soviet ballistic missiles . . . [would be] guaranteed, Soviet cruise missiles, short-range missiles and low-flying bombers could not be prevented from penetrating into western Europe. What is worse, all conventional arms systems would regain in importance, recalling prenuclear times—not a particularly pleasant perspective in view of the existing conventional imbalance in favor of the Soviet Union.[12]

Some conservative West German political and military leaders— notably Franz-Josef Strauss and Alfred Dregger, both prominent in the Christian Democratic Union/Christian Social Union ruling coalition, along with colleagues in other West European nations—were at first more inclined to favor the pursuit of a separate "European Defense Initiative" (EDI) that would complement SDI but would be under the direct sponsorship and control of the European governments, would be solely addressed to European vulnerability, and in some versions might enable Western Europe to become "a third superpower" with its own defense strategy. Several military leaders, including Pierre Gallois, FRG Army Gen. Gerd Schmuckle, and Dutch Gen. G. C. Berkhof all supported the idea, as did France's former defense minister Charles Hernu. Von Hassel, former FRG defense minister, presented a sweeping version, ambitious even beyond President Reagan's dream, of a joint U.S.-European enterprise to develop defenses not just against threats from space and air but also on the ground: "By providing the scientific and technological prerequisites for the feasibility of SDI and EDI, a technological window is created for the first time which might neutralize both nuclear missiles in space and conventional weapons on the ground, without endangering human lives."[13] The aim, however, was not just to provide a European adjunct to the United States' SDI project but to develop a separate European perspective, if not a separate European military-political position, altogether. This undertone of separateness from NATO, coupled with the political sensitivity of the issue, led the FRG government to avoid endorsing calls for an EDI and instead to endorse NATO efforts to develop extended air defense.

Outside the ranks of the government, the leading spokesmen on foreign and defense policy in the Social Democratic opposition, including Helmut Schmidt, Willy Brandt, Hermann Scheer, Karsten D. Voigt, and Hans-Jochen Vogel, were sharply critical of SDI. The party officially urged that the ABM Treaty be tightened to eliminate all projects that might lead to space-based weapons, including ASATs, or to the development of anti-tactical ballistic missiles (ATBMs). The smaller and more radical Greens were even more caustic, arguing that the project was further evidence of the twin folly of allowing the United States to determine Europe's destiny and of succumbing to a delusory belief in the saving qualities of advanced technologies.[14]

European political leaders were equally upset by what the U.S. announcement portended for arms control. The START talks had been stalled for several years, and the United States' NATO allies were as inclined to blame the United States for the failure of these talks as they were the Soviet Union—with good reason, in view of the confusion in the U.S. position. The SDI seemed to signal the United States' readiness to abandon arms control altogether in favor of reliance on advances in military technology. The SDI was a direct challenge to the ABM Treaty, which was seen as the cornerstone of the arms-control process. The United States did not propose to negotiate a revision of the treaty, and the president's assurance that, once developed, the technology might be shared with the Soviets, was greeted with derision in view of the U.S. restrictions on technology transfers from NATO Europe to the Soviet Union under the Coordinating Committee for Multilateral Export Controls (COCOM). SDI seemed to confirm suspicions of a U.S. move to the right, in the sense that it reflected a revival of extreme cold war hostility toward the Soviet Union. Unlike the Reagan administration, West European governments were not convinced that the Soviets had flagrantly violated treaties, were still bent on world domination, and left the West with no choice but to develop the means to thwart their ambitions. Western Europeans, both on the right and the democratic left, were far more interested in reviving détente than the cold war. Although the governments had been anxious for the United States to reaffirm its commitment to Europe by adhering to the controversial two-track decision and deploying the Pershing II and cruise missiles as a counter to the Soviet SS-20s, they had to deal with strong reactions among European publics as these deployments were made. In addition, they had based their decision to deploy partly on the argument that the security of Europe rested on a balance of forces—a balance disturbed by the Soviet deployment of SS-20s.

But SDI was not part of this accepted strategic posture. By proposing to make nuclear weapons "impotent and obsolete," the president also threatened to make the strategic concepts on which Europe had come to depend just as impotent and obsolete. Even if the president's vision was unlikely to be realized, as the European leaders clearly believed, the effort to pursue it could well be destabilizing in several respects.

One concern was for the accepted NATO policy of "flexible response," or selective options. The West Europeans had been reluctant to accept flexible response in place of the previous commitment to threaten massive attack by nuclear weapons in the event a conventional defense in Europe were breached. But they finally came to accept it as a policy that would be more credible to the Soviets, even though it was never clearly understood exactly how such a policy would be implemented, in view of the enormous havoc that would be caused both by collateral damage and by retaliatory strikes. The allies had accepted it as one element of a formula that also included a continuing U.S. commitment to station significant ground forces in Europe and a willingness to pursue dialogue and détente as well as military preparedness—as enshrined in the 1967 Harmel Report. To the extent that SDI led to defensive deployments on both sides (which, while not leakproof, could provide an indefinite degree of protection, especially to military targets), the possibility of flexible response would be removed. Any U.S. retaliatory attack would therefore have to be massive and very likely be concentrated against cities. Thus, the major NATO strategy, over which a hard-won and fragile consensus had been achieved, was being put in serious doubt.

The French and British governments, as noted earlier, were particularly concerned about the possible effects of SDI on their independent deterrents. French defense policy, then Minister of Defense Paul Quilès emphasized, "is based on the nuclear deterrent." [15] France had built its deterrent forces in a deliberate effort to achieve and preserve great-power status and independence. Although the British had not done so in order to avoid reliance on the United States and were active NATO allies of the United States, they too had undertaken at considerable expense to develop and maintain a retaliatory force (relying mainly on Polaris submarines) that would deter a Soviet attack by itself. In order to preserve its independence and its security in the event the United States did not honor its commitments, Britain's established policy was that its own forces should be "able to hold at risk critical elements of Soviet state power," a deliberately ambiguous phrase that may "embrace a range of targets lying between hitting a large city and hitting a silo." [16] Similarly, the French, although they recognized they could not hope to match the firepower of the Soviet Union, could at least protect Paris by threatening Moscow and could even hold at risk the "vital works" of the Soviet Union. [17] Both countries had begun to modernize their forces to make them capable of penetrating any defenses the Soviets might erect in the foreseeable future. The British had made a commitment to acquire Trident D-5 missiles and submarines, a commitment that was sharply challenged by the Labour opposition. Even a partial Soviet defensive deployment of a significant new type, such as was suggested by the U.S. proposal of a layered defense, could have the effect of degrading and even nullifying the independent deterrents of Great Britain and France. SDI in effect put both Britain's Trident program and France's *force de frappe* in jeopardy.

Compounding these apprehensions was the concern for the economic harm that SDI might do to Europe. European leaders were already concerned about a growing "technology gap" between Europe and the United States and Japan. If the United States infused $26 billion into the high-technology sector of the U.S. economy over five years, Europe might find itself even further behind. Also the notion that the United States would allow the Europeans to participate as full partners was greeted with skepticism. Europeans knew from experience that U.S. firms would keep the lion's share of such contracts for themselves and treat the European firms as subcontractors. In the key technologies—computers, lasers, satellites—U.S. firms had significant advantages over their European counterparts, and security considerations would prevent the United States from sharing sensitive technology. Already, embarrassing technology transfers from the FRG had led to efforts to tighten the restrictions. Assistant Secretary of Defense Richard Perle, in particular, was leading an effort within the Pentagon and in Congress to tighten the existing restrictions. In addition, the ABM Treaty imposed restrictions on the transfer of ABM technology (and a later understanding included plans and blueprints in these restrictions), which would affect SDI cooperation.

In view of this skepticism, the French, who were officially opposed in principle to cooperating, attempted to develop support for EUREKA while quietly allowing their companies to compete for SDI contracts. French defense firms were uneasy about being excluded from the SDI, especially as it seemed more and more likely that other major European contractors would take part. As a result, while the French government did not abandon its official opposition, French firms, notably Thomson-CSF, Matra, and Aerospatiale, were permitted to take part in the program, and EUREKA began to take shape as a program in civil technology with military applications, that is, the reverse of SDI. A government study, the Delpech Report, concluded that by upgrading its offenses France could be assured for the indefinite future that its nuclear weapons carriers could penetrate any foreseeable Soviet defenses. Eventually, more effective defenses might be achieved, the report observed, but they were of no immediate concern: "Over a much longer period of time, the hypothetical realization of a sufficiently effective and not very vulnerable system could have strategic consequences for France, but this eventuality is remote and uncertain and a satisfactory modification of our strategic forces is not at all excluded." [18]

As Pierre Lellouche has explained, the French government found that by rejecting SDI, it had backed itself into a corner. The United States was not going to drop the program simply because the allies did not like it, and meanwhile, in the revived INF talks, the Soviets were demanding that France's strategic forces be constrained as part of a deal to reduce or eliminate U.S. and Soviet intermediate weapons. The French could not expect U.S. support for the exclusion of France's independent deterrent in the INF negotiation if France appeared to be siding with the U.S.S.R. on the SDI issue. "Given these realities," Lellouche observes, "France gradually moved to a more pragmatic attitude based on a clear-cut distinction between the strategic and technological sides of the SDI issue."

On strategic grounds, France remained opposed to SDI, arguing that it would destabilize European security and the superpower balance in nuclear weapons, in addition to undermining "what was left of Western consensus on deterrence after the Euromissile battle." On technological grounds, however, the French wanted to cooperate with the United States in order to make sure that their nuclear force retained its credibility in a rapidly changing technological environment. As a result, in the fall of 1985, Prime Minister Laurent Fabius and Defense Minister Quilès announced that France's opposition to SDI would not preclude French firms from entering into joint ventures with U.S. firms or from accepting contracts from the U.S. Defense Department. Thus, as Lellouche has noted, "France found itself in the somewhat bizarre position (its critics would call it hypocritical) of opposing SDI in principle while letting its firms—including the nationalized ones—run to Washington to secure contracts." [19] The vacillation was considerably reduced when Jacques Chirac became prime minister in 1986 and announced in his inaugural address that France would cooperate in European efforts to achieve tactical defenses in association with the U.S. program:

> Technological progress is leading to the emergence of defensive systems utilizing space. Their birth will not upset for many years to come, and may never upset, the fundamental basis of nuclear deterrence. Our American allies are actively working on this project, and important changes may thereby occur in the world balance, in the dialogue between the great pow-

ers, as in the defense of Europe. We must watch this evolution carefully, as well as the technological gaps that may result therefrom, proceed to the necessary adaptations and avoid missing the opportunities to strengthen European solidarity in this field as well.[20]

In Britain, Thatcher virtually ordered her cabinet colleagues to muffle their criticisms. She herself won considerable respect in Europe and at the same time mollified her colleagues by flying to Washington in December 1984 to secure President Reagan's agreement at Camp David to four points involving SDI: (1) it was to be a research program, and no decision to deploy defenses would be undertaken without an effort to negotiate the issue with the Soviets; (2) it was to be undertaken in conformity with the ABM Treaty in an effort to maintain strategic parity, not to achieve superiority; (3) efforts were to continue to negotiate arms reductions with the Soviets; and (4) SDI was to be undertaken to enhance deterrence, not to replace it. This agreement has sometimes been interpreted as a revision of the original plans for the SDI, especially insofar as it is formally described as an effort to enhance deterrence. In this way, Thatcher's supporters could claim that she forced a change in the program, away from the commitment to a leakproof area defense and toward a defense of retaliatory capacities.

From the perspective of the Reagan administration, this agreement was a small price to pay for calming European apprehensions, inasmuch as the program called for a long term defensive transition that might well result initially in enhancing deterrence by adding defense to offense. Both sides could interpret the agreement as they chose. In any event, given that deployment decisions could be deferred, any differences in interpretation would remain below the surface. A report of the House of Commons Defence Committee in 1985 sought to remove any apprehensions caused by SDI for the Trident program by emphasizing the improbable prospects for defenses: "After our discussions with representatives of the U.S. administration in March and April this year we were left in no doubt that the new era of strategic defenses that has been advocated is unlikely to arrive while Trident is in service—which suggests that the current excitement is being generated about a project unlikely to reach fruition before 2020."[21] Having thus determined at least to its own satisfaction that SDI was merely a long-range research program that would not interfere with its own strategic commitments, the British cabinet agreed to sign the memorandum of understanding with the United States on December 6, 1985, by which the two countries undertook to cooperate in the research.

In the Federal Republic, where, as one specialist put it, "attitudes toward SDI range from actual opposition to reluctant acceptance," [22] Kohl succeeded in persuading his cabinet that there was more to be gained by negotiating terms of cooperation than by refusing to follow the British example. He argued that the FRG would have more influence over the course of events by proving itself a loyal ally and cooperating with the Reagan administration's program, especially inasmuch as SDI was unlikely to produce any dramatically transforming technologies in the short run. By refusing, the government would play into the hands of both domestic critics of the alliance and the Soviets, who would take advantage of the split to brand the United States as an aggressive power and thereby undermine public support for NATO. On April 18, 1985, Kohl endorsed SDI "in principle." As U.S. officials emphasized that SDI was a research program whose benefits might redound to the civilian economy, FRG adherence to the U.S. program was made easier for the government to endorse. Even so, Kohl's cabinet feared that cooperation would be a one-way street and therefore developed a series of demands that would have to be satisfied in any negotiation. Pointedly, the Kohl government sent its economics minister, Martin Bangemann, to Washington to negotiate the terms of a joint agreement of principles committing West Germany to participate in SDI research. The United States made few concessions, but the West Germans agreed anyhow on March 27, 1986, opening the way for such major West German firms as Siemens and Messerschmitt-Bölkow-Blohm to participate in R & D contracts.

Other U.S. allies displayed varying degrees of receptivity toward the program. Only Israel was unabashedly enthusiastic, both out of an interest in benefiting from U.S. subsidies for military high-technology and out of a more specific need to counter the conventionally armed Soviet SS-21 missiles provided to the Syrians by their Soviet patrons—weapons the Israelis viewed as upsetting the balance of power in the region by threatening their airfields and marshaling points. In June 1988 Israel and the United States formally announced their cooperation in the Arrow project to develop an interceptor against tactical missiles. Israel would pay 20 percent of the cost, the United States 80 percent, out of SDI funds. In Italy, at the urging of Foreign Minister Giulio Andreotti, the government followed the lead of other European governments, waiting until April 1986 to agree to take part. Canada, Belgium, Portugal, and the Netherlands allowed their industries to take part. The Japanese government watched the moves in Europe toward cooperation and decided to join in. The Danes, Norwegians, and Australians, who had little to gain or to offer, chose not to participate.

From 1983 through the middle of 1986, the SDI issue loomed larger and larger in European debates. To some extent it became a left-right issue. In the Federal Republic the Social Democrats denounced it as inevitably destabilizing and a final blow to the prospects for détente with the Soviets. In Great Britain, although SDI did not revive the fortunes of the Campaign for Nuclear Disarmament (perhaps because, unlike cruise missiles, there were no deployments against which to rally opposition), it nevertheless reinforced the view of many on the left that the United States under Reagan was embarked on a highly dangerous course that could provoke a new phase of the arms race, both defensive and offensive, and that Europe needed to develop a position of its own, independently of the United States. Especially once the furor over INF deployments had died down, SDI served as a convenient stalking horse for a renewed assault on U.S. cold war policies and on conservative governments for their supposed willingness to remain dependent on the United States.

SDI was also grist for the mills of FRG leftists who were advocating a European "alternative defense," or "defensive defense," strategy to replace NATO and reliance on nuclear weapons. As Jonathan Dean has pointed out,[23] however, most of these proposals will probably not be adopted largely because they eliminate a front-line role for the United States and other European allies, thus weakening the deterrent effect and raising political difficulties. SDI served to revive the traditional themes of the left-right dispute in foreign policy, with those on the left arguing that Western Europe should pursue accommodation with the U.S.S.R. rather than confrontation and adopt a new Europeanism instead of remaining stuck in the middle of the superpower conflict. Alongside these themes there was also a more widely shared fear that European economic difficulties would be exacerbated by a new U.S. challenge. The disputes within the ruling conservative coalitions were of a narrower character, based on skepticism about the validity of the Reagan administration's technological hopes, as well as on fears of the consequences for NATO unity and the economic burdens that would be imposed in an effort to develop defenses while seeking to maintain nuclear deterrents and to modernize conventional forces. The European governments were much more inclined to want to see arms-reduction agreements that would relieve some of the burden of armament and promote a lessening of tensions, allowing increased trade between East and West and encouraging tendencies toward reform in the Soviet Union and the Eastern bloc.

Public opinion in Europe, while tending to mirror the uneasiness of the political elites, nevertheless did not react with marked hostility to the U.S. initiative. At least one poll, taken in Britain, showed that most respondents thought SDI was aimed to protect the United States rather than the alliance as a whole.[24] Like ordinary Americans, many West Europeans assumed that one way or another space would continue to be militarized, but they worried, more than Americans, that such a defense might increase the prospects of a conventional war fought in Europe with weapons even more destructive than those used in World War II. Europeans were not comforted by assurances that the "astrodome" would protect them as well as the United States, but they could take some comfort from the fact that the program was being promoted as nonnuclear, and at least some were aware that the Soviets had themselves made elaborate efforts to erect defenses against strategic nuclear attack. In the end, attitudes toward SDI were colored by more general attitudes toward the United States and the Soviet Union. There is some evidence to suggest, however, that SDI helped weaken confidence in the U.S. commitment to Europe and promote a desire to pursue an independent course, a trend that may well have been encouraged by the abruptness with which SDI was announced and the skepticism expressed by European leaders.[25] In the same British poll, most respondents thought the United States would go ahead with SDI even over European opposition, and a substantial number thought SDI had been created in order to induce the Soviets to negotiate about other matters.

On the whole, then, the initial reaction to the SDI in the allied nations was unfavorable and might have led to serious ruptures had the administration not mounted a major effort to soothe European feelings and relieve fears that SDI portended either an immediate lessening in the U.S. commitment to its allies or an unwillingness to negotiate arms reductions with the Soviets. As Wolfram F. Hanrieder perceptively noted: "Political costs have to be paid in advance, as it were, before the anticipated strategic benefits are realized in a distant future."[26]

MOLLIFYING WESTERN EUROPE

West European annoyance with the unilateral nature of the announcement of SDI and distress over its strategic and economic implications were only compounded by Defense Secretary Weinberger's seeming ultimatum in March 1985, in which allied governments were asked to indicate whether or not they were willing to cooperate within sixty days. Once the harshness of West European reaction became obvious, the

Reagan administration took steps to ease the situation for these governments. Reagan had readily agreed, as we saw earlier, to Thatcher's four points. The West Europeans could also take some satisfaction from the fact that Lieutenant General Abrahamson went out of his way to endorse these four points in testimony before Congress. In the administration's eyes, of course, the agreement had no substantial effect on the program. SDI had been designed as a research program, and it was acknowledged within the administration (and at least implied in the Fletcher report) that a defense transition would probably never become a practical option unless the Soviets agreed to reduce offensive weapons. Although the administration had not consulted with the allies prior to the decision (as it had not consulted even with the appropriate departments of the executive branch or with Congress), it was eager to help friendly leaders avoid trouble at home.

Part of the effort involved missions to explain the president's plan both to European government officials and journalists. George Bush, Shultz, Weinberger, Perle, U.N. Ambassador Jeane Kirkpatrick, and science advisor Keyworth were all pressed into service, along with the president himself. Technical specialists who supported SDI sought to show that the principles and technologies useful for strategic defense would also be useful in defending Western Europe. Teller told those who attended a *Wehrkunde* conference in Munich in February 1986 that laser beams reflected from mirrors popped up over the earth would make it "relatively easy" to destroy even such intermediate-range weapons as the Soviet SS-20.[27] Those sympathetic to the president's ideological views, or who were at least willing to give him the benefit of the doubt, found the explanations more impressive than they expected. Others, including high-ranking defense officials, remained skeptical. Their views were generally silenced, however, by the political leaders, who were anxious to maintain NATO unity. Opposition leaders in Great Britain and the Federal Republic of Germany seized on SDI as yet another example of the administration's susceptibility to illusion and the use of confrontation in its relations with the Soviet Union. They also tried to make the United States appear to be intent on developing a shield over itself which would leave Europe vulnerable to attack. United States officials, however, countered some of the effects of this campaign by promoting the idea that, if successful, SDI would protect Europeans and Americans alike.

Otherwise, the United States' primary effort to sell SDI concentrated on promising at least minimal economic inducements—prompting one "shrewd and worldly American bureaucrat to comment that although European government support could not be bought, it still might 'be rented.'"[28] U.S. government officials thus dangled the bait of significant contracts before the eyes of European industrialists, and the industrialists in turn pressured governments for permission to take part. They were mainly concerned that they be admitted on equal terms, and this theme was taken up by government representatives as the price of European cooperation. The West Germans in particular were concerned that they be allowed to market any civilian applications of the technology and that they not be unduly hampered in possible sales to East European countries. The U.S. negotiators offered to be conciliatory but in the end made few concessions, relying instead on European interest in not being shut out of the project. Initial funding was quite small—in the neighborhood of $30 million the first year—until, in the second year of the program, a series of larger contracts was let involving cooperative ventures by European and American firms.

The U.S. position vis-à-vis the allies improved considerably when the Soviets agreed in 1985 to return to arms-control negotiations, where they called for a 50 percent reduction in offensive weapons. Many West Europeans agreed with U.S. analysts that the Soviets had come back to the table in part because they became concerned that SDI might lead to unilateral U.S. deployments and might undercut the parity in offensive weapons they had won by considerable effort. This recognition of SDI's contribution to arms control was raised in the March 1985 ministerial meetings of NATO's Nuclear Planning Group and in Brussels in October of the same year. A communiqué issued at the close of the first set of meetings affirmed allied support for SDI but carefully couched that support in terms of the established NATO emphasis on offensive deterrence: "We support the United States research programme into these technologies, the aim of which is to enhance stability and deterrence at reduced levels of offensive nuclear forces."[29] In this formulation, the European allies of the United States in effect agreed to regard SDI primarily as a political question rather than as a new direction in alliance strategy. Although the leading partners were eager to stay abreast of U.S. research in case there might be any breakthroughs, their main motivation (and, even more, that of the other allies) was to exert influence on the direction of SDI so that it did not adversely affect the alliance. In particular, they wanted to make sure that it stayed a research program until they agreed to deployment, remained in conformity with the ABM Treaty, and did not jeopardize East-West arms control negotiations or destabilize the strategic balance.

THE "INTERMEDIATE OPTION" IN EUROPE: TOWARD A DIVISION OF LABOR

In addition to these various efforts to mollify the Europeans, the SDIO increasingly emphasized its willingness to cooperate with European efforts to develop defenses designed for the European theater. The Europeans had already taken steps in this direction before SDI was launched. The idea of a European Defense Initiative did not seem necessarily uncongenial to U.S. officials, who were already considering the possibility of initial theater deployment broached in the Hoffman report. Unlike the Fletcher report, which called for a long-term effort of research aimed at producing a layered defense, the Hoffman report emphasized that in view of the uncertainties attending the development of such systems, "partial systems, or systems with more modest technical goals, may be feasible earlier than the full system." These "intermediate" systems, the report stressed, might strengthen deterrence because they would "greatly complicate Soviet attack plans" and reduce Soviet confidence in a successful outcome at various sizes and levels of attack. The report called for an R&D program that would provide an option for early deployment while proceeding along the path toward the ultimate goal of layered defense.[30] The intermediate option could be of immediate utility in Europe and might later be integrated with a system to defend the continental United States:

> The advanced components, though developed initially in an ATM [anti-tactical missile] mode, might later play a role in continental United States (CONUS) defense. Such an option addresses the pressing military need to protect allied forces as well as our own, in theaters of operations, from either nonnuclear or nuclear attack. It would directly benefit our allies as well as ourselves. Inclusion of such an option in our long-range R&D program on ballistic missile defenses should reduce allied anxieties that our increased emphasis on defenses might indicate a weakening in our commitment to the defense of Europe.[31]

Intermediate deployment of ATBMs in Europe was also attractive for other reasons. First, they could be developed without violating the ABM Treaty. (The Hoffman report did not address the question of whether sharing technology with potential BMD applications would violate the provision against providing ABM information or blueprints to third parties; presumably, work on tactical defenses would be sufficiently differentiated from ABM research to conform to the provision.) Second, deployment of ATBMs in Europe would emphasize the coupling of U.S. and Western European security and would address the growing threat posed by improved Soviet offensive capabilities. Technically, the intermediate deployment option was within reach in the sense that it would not require major breakthroughs in technology. The deployment would represent a tangible commitment toward a comprehensive defense, a "first installment" that would ultimately serve as a sub-tier of a layered defense. (Alternatively, the recommendation could be read as a polite way of saying that although Reagan's vision of a comprehensive defense was not feasible, deployment of tactical defenses in Europe was both feasible and in keeping with perceived military needs.)

In discussing this option, however, the Hoffman report did not restrict the possibilities only to terminal systems that might be acceptable within treaty limitations. It also noted that even imperfect boost-phase defenses could have a significant effect against existing Soviet offensive weapons. Therefore, they might be worth deploying as an intermediate option—even before more advanced systems might be developed—presumably to cope with a Soviet offensive force designed to incorporate countermeasures. Soviet offensive improvements were eroding European confidence in the threat of U.S. nuclear response to Soviet attacks on Western Europe, the report noted, but a U.S. attempt to match the Soviet buildup by reversing the tendency to reduce arsenals and, instead, to increase stockpiles would only heighten public anxiety.[32]

The Hoffman report put particular stress on the possible contribution of defenses to NATO security. Soviet doctrine, it contended, emphasized operations designed "to bring large-scale conflict to a quick and decisive end, at as low a level of violence as is consistent with achievement of Soviet strategic aims." In a conflict involving NATO, a major goal would be to use intense initial attacks on critical military targets in the rear—particularly those relevant to theater nuclear capabilities and air power, but also those that would receive reinforcements from the United States. One purpose of such attacks would be to reduce the ability and resolve of NATO to initiate nuclear attacks if nonnuclear defense failed and to preempt a NATO attack. Tactical ballistic missiles would therefore play an important role in Soviet plans. If defenses were to deny the effective use of TBMs, the entire Soviet attack plan would be jeopardized, thus helping to deter theater combat, both nuclear and nonnuclear.[33]

Lieutenant General Abrahamson echoed this emphasis on the SDI mission in his first appearance before Congress on April 25, 1984: "We are not seeking only to build defenses for the United States. As Secretary Weinberger has indicated, our concept of an 'effective' defense is one which protects our allies as well as the United States."[34] When Weinberger invited eighteen allies to join in SDI research, he too stressed that "the SDI program will not confine itself solely to an exploitation of technologies with potential against ICBM and SLBM, but will also carefully examine technologies with potential against shorter-range ballistic missiles." [35] Under Secretary of Defense Fred C. Iklé informed Congress that the United States wanted "to provide the allies with the opportunity to become involved in SDI research projects that address some of the unique aspects of defending NATO-Europe against missile attack." [36] Nevertheless, the SDIO did not emphasize the benefits of the research program for tactical defense until two years had gone by. The system-architecture contracts did not explicitly address the need to consider system extension to Europe until September 1985. It was not until spring 1986 that plans for a competition were made for a European theater-defense architecture, and awards were made for these studies only in that year. In June 1986 SDIO awarded a $10-million contract to the British government to study theater defense, and in December of the same year contracts worth $2 million each were awarded to seven consortia, involving twenty-five European firms, for "architecture studies" of a missile defense for Western Europe.

Clearly, the difference of emphasis between the Fletcher panel, with its advocacy of long-term research and strategic defense, and the Hoffman panel, with its stress on intermediate deployments of relatively accessible technology, prefigured a conflict of goals within the Defense Department and SDIO. Congressional supporters of SDI also put pressure on SDIO to think more seriously about intermediate deployments. In October 1985 Rep. Duncan Hunter (R., Calif.) led a House Armed Services Committee delegation to Europe and reported that officials in France and the Federal Republic were ready to cooperate in developing ATBMs. The aim was to make the investment in SDI one that would have immediate benefits for U.S. regional commitments and would presumably at the same time demonstrate the real utility of SDI to the European as well as to the American public. An amendment prepared by Sen. John Glenn (D., Ohio) to bar the award of SDI contracts to firms not headquartered in the United States failed. But in the FY1987 authorization, a successful amendment introduced by then Sen. Dan Quayle (R., Ind.) "identified" up to $50 million in the SDI program (rising to $75 million in FY1988) to be used to accelerate ATBM technology development, looking to deployment in the 1990s. The amendment called on SDIO to cooperate with U.S. allies in developing the technologies. From the SDIO's point of view, ATBM work was valuable because it served to link Western Europe's interests in theater defense to the United

States' interest in strategic defense. In effect, there would be a cooperative division of labor in which the Europeans would emphasize ATBM
while the United States emphasized BMD. The Europeans were to be
encouraged—particularly the French and the West Germans—to design
their own systems for these purposes with U.S. support and cooperation. It is not clear that SDIO puts equal weight on the military significance of ATBM work as on strategic defenses, but it is well recognized
that the political benefits in assuring European support for SDI are
substantial.

As SDIO officials began to define the goals of SDI in more proximate
terms—that is, to emphasize its potential role in shoring up deterrence
by retaliation rather than making nuclear weapons obsolete—it came to
seem a better fit for European concerns with tactical defense and improved air defense. Although some Europeans sought to distinguish
sharply between Europe's need for extended air defense and for defense
against tactical ballistic missiles, the SDIO came to see the European
theater as a locus for a possible early deployment of missile defenses. In
effect, Western Europe would be encouraged to cooperate with the
United States in developing tactical defenses (thus avoiding ABM Treaty
restrictions) in order to take advantage of work already done there and
to reinforce European belief in the advisability of developing such defenses. In this way, a division of labor would develop in which SDI could
become an alliance commitment without raising the allies' hackles.
From SDIO's perspective, however, this division could not be a sharp
one, because tactical and air defenses could not be neatly separated
from strategic defenses. The same sensors that track strategic missiles
could be used against certain of the missiles fired by intermediate-range
launchers. Airborne detectors could be even more useful in tactical air
defense than in strategic defense.

This confluence of West European interest in air defense and ATBMs
and the United States' eagerness to claim European participation in SDI
has resulted in a kind of modus vivendi. Europeans emphasize work on
ATBM and air defense, cooperate with the United States on architecture
studies for the theater (which would include linking ATBM to BMD),
and play a lesser role in studies of exotic technologies that may eventually have applications both to ATBM and BMD.

THE ATBM ISSUE

West European cooperation with the United States on SDI reflects
concern among NATO strategists regarding a growing Soviet tactical

threat, both nuclear and nonnuclear. But the SDIO and European leaders differ sharply over the issue of linking SDI to tactical defense in Europe.

NATO strategists have become increasingly concerned about Warsaw pact threats to airfields, nuclear installations, and resupply depots because of improvements and additions to Soviet strength in aircraft and tactical ballistic missiles, conventional as well as nuclear. Assessment of the threat varies, as does assessment of the likely Soviet strategy for conducting a war in Europe, but there is general agreement that Soviet planners have taken account of the capacities of NATO's highly accurate conventional systems to avoid the introduction of nuclear weapons, thereby minimizing the possibility that NATO will escalate the conflict to a nuclear level. In the 1960s, as we note in chapter 4, Soviet strategy was predicated on the expectation that a theater conflict in Europe would automatically involve nuclear weapons. Soviet forces were therefore prepared to undertake massive nuclear strikes at the outset in order to preempt the expected Western use of such weapons. The Soviet doctrine was similar to the U.S. belief in massive retaliation. As a result, the Soviet Rocket Forces, formed in 1959, assumed a major role in Soviet battle planning and enabled some temporary cutbacks to be made in expenditures on conventional forces.

SHIFTING SOVIET STRATEGY

But just as massive-retaliation doctrine had encouraged the U.S.S.R. to adopt a greater reliance on the nuclear option, so the United States' move toward flexible response stimulated a renewed Soviet emphasis on conventional means of waging war. Military strategists under Brezhnev who favored greater flexibility received more of a hearing from the political leadership. The result was a shift of strategy in which tactical nuclear war and conventional war planning became guiding principles; emphasis was accordingly shifted in military production. During the 1970s the Soviets engaged in a military buildup that put these principles into effect. Belatedly, Soviet strategists explicitly acknowledged that the danger of introducing nuclear weapons was so great that all other means should first be exhausted. This recognition made Soviet force planning far more complex by introducing a need for a greater variety of weapons systems and requiring planning for varied military contingencies. Thus, in the mid-1970s the aim appeared to be to attain a diverse set of military options designed to dominate each level of escalation from conventional, to operational-tactical nuclear, to general nuclear war. This approach foresaw the need to preempt NATO's use of tactical nuclear weapons by striking those weapons with tactical nuclear weapons before employing strategic forces based in the Soviet Union. Gradually, however, another option began to appear plausible: the use of conventional attacks by frontal aviation, nonnuclear missiles, and conventionally armed bombers for the same purpose—an approach that might allow the Soviets to avoid introducing nuclear weapons, thus triggering a NATO response in kind.[37]

By the early 1980s Soviet military writers were discussing the possibility that major wars might be fought without nuclear weapons, a contingency that had earlier been ruled out as unrealistic. In these years, Soviet planners became more and more optimistic about emerging conventional technologies. This optimism mirrored that of Western technologists, who were also convinced that emerging conventional technologies, especially the advent of precision-guided munitions, would make it possible to use conventional instead of nuclear explosives against hard targets. The U.S.S.R. looked to longer-range, highly accurate, dual-capable delivery systems, which might be fitted with both conventional explosives and chemical weapons. The major aim of Soviet strategists in using these new armaments was to prevent NATO from using tactical nuclear weapons to respond to a Soviet conventional attack. Soviet defense forces were reorganized in order to take proper advantage of these new technologies. In particular, the Soviets emphasized the development of air operations as substitutes for initial nuclear strikes against major military targets. They also stressed the predeployment of munitions and other supplies in forward areas, so as to support rapidly mounted attacks by mobile groups whose mission would be to penetrate deeply into allied lines. In the 1970s new aircraft—including the SU-24 Fencer, the SU-17 Fitter D/H, and the MiG-27 Flogger D/J—gave the U.S.S.R. a frontal aviation power it had previously lacked. These aircraft were supported by other advances in target acquisition, all-weather operating capacity, and integrated theater command-and-control. The aim of the introduction of aircraft was to reduce reliance on longer-range air forces and nuclear missiles and to enable attacks on NATO military targets by frontal air assault making maximum use of surprise.[38]

At the same time, efforts were made to initiate new programs designed to improve short-range and intermediate-range missiles so as to provide them with accuracy great enough to deliver conventional munitions to military targets, including airfields. The SS-21 was given a conventional payload, and the SS-22 and SS-23 were to be developed for the same mission. According to U.S. sources, upgraded models of these missiles can deliver payloads to within 30 meters of their targets, evidently by using improved inertial guidance combined with terminal guidance. These accuracies are roughly the same as those reported for the U.S. Pershing IIs. The SS-21s, with a range of 120 km, have reportedly replaced the shorter-range Frog-7 missiles in Soviet divisions in the German Democratic Republic (GDR). The SS-23, with a range of 500 km, was to replace the older Scud missile, more than three hundred of which are located facing NATO and have a range of 300 km. The SS-12/Mod (formerly designated the SS-22), with a range of 900 km, was to replace the SS-12 Scaleboard. From locations in the GDR, it would have been capable of reaching Great Britain and would have greatly improved Soviet ability to mount a surprise attack.[39] By banning both Soviet intermediate-range missiles (the SS-20, SS-4, and SS-5) and two of the shorter-range missiles (the SS-12 and SS-23), the 1987 INF Treaty significantly reduced the threat the Soviets were mounting.

In addition to developing missiles with sufficient range and accuracy, the Soviets have also developed area munitions, such as cluster bombs and fuel air explosives that spread destruction over soft targets. The latter weapon has an explosive charge like that of the smallest nuclear weapons and is said to have been used by the Soviets in Afghanistan. So far, there is no firm evidence that the Soviets have deployed kinetic-energy or shaped-charge penetrators, such as the United States has been developing, to cause craters in runways or to penetrate the concrete used to shield headquarters or aircraft hangars, but these innovations may be in the offing.[40]

The military thinking behind these deployments is that the Soviet conventional force can be used to greatest advantage if it can take account of NATO's need for time to mobilize and disperse forces. In the event of war, the intention seems to be to use a combination of ground-launched missiles and aircraft, both using conventional munitions, to attack NATO forces in depth and to open corridors through which mobile ground forces can move in deep-penetration strikes. Soviet planners, heirs of a long-standing tradition that prizes massive artillery barrages, are attracted by the tactic of overwhelming critical enemy targets in a short time with a large fraction of their own offensive firepower. The emphasis is partly on the psychological demoralization to be achieved by heavy initial strikes. Successful blows against NATO airfields and the aircraft themselves could seriously damage NATO's ability to disrupt an attack—an ability on which NATO planners rely heavily. Although hardened shelters could protect aircraft from such attacks, the infrastructure necessary to enable planes to be refueled and rearmed, as well as to take off and land, is more vulnerable.[41]

A precursor missile attack aimed at airfields, taking advantage of the short flying times of missiles (from thirty seconds to five minutes) could help suppress NATO air defenses and improve the prospects of follow-on air attacks. Missiles cannot substitute for aircraft, which can carry much larger payloads, but serve rather to amplify, or compound, the effectiveness of reusable aircraft. If air defenses are suppressed, aircraft can use higher and deeper routes with heavier payloads, and face fewer allied interceptors. Thus, the use of conventionally armed missiles provides leverage for an air attack.[42]

Soviet respect for Western technological advances, coupled with concern over the adoption of counteroffensive strategies like NATO's Air-land Battle and Follow-On Forces Attack, has heightened interest in achieving surprise and in foiling NATO's efforts to carry out its ambitious plans. But the underlying motive is to be in a position to nullify NATO's nuclear threat (using tactical weapons and aircraft) by non-nuclear means.

POSSIBLE NATO RESPONSES

NATO could offset these plans by dispersing the targets, insofar as possible, to more locations and by developing mobile field units. Dispersal is an attractive option not only because it increases the chances that such forces could survive a preemptive strike but also because it lessens pressure to make early use of nuclear weapons. Critics warn, however, that sudden dispersal could be interpreted as provocative by the Soviets, who might respond by considering a preemptive attack, adding that it risks putting too much authority over nuclear weapons in the hands of field commanders. It is also not clear that dispersal could be accomplished rapidly enough upon warning of an impending attack. While dispersal is taking place, forces are exposed to attack. NATO is also vulnerable to an attack on its fixed surveillance radars, which provide early warning of an attack, and on the C[3] facilities that coordinate its defense,[43] although mobile radars are considerably more difficult to find and destroy.

In response to the Warsaw Pact's growing emphasis on conventional missile and air attack, NATO has given serious thought to active defenses. Air defense has been a long-standing NATO goal. What is new in the discussion is whether air defense can be "extended" or "expanded" to include defense against tactical ballistic missiles and cruise missiles, or, in other words, from all attacks from the air. From the NATO perspective, SDI is an outgrowth of the concern for air defense as it was initially extended, in the 1960s, to attacks from space. Recall that the United States had announced, toward the end of the 1960s, its intention of deploying a thin Sentinel shield in the United States. In the wake of that decision, some wondered if a similar BMD deployment should be made in Western Europe. The option was considered but rejected by the NATO Nuclear Planning Group as too expensive, not effective enough, and likely to hinder arms-control negotiations. Since then, however, concern for air defense has led to broader interest in defenses against tactical missiles as well—an interest that intersects with SDI: the general purpose is the same, and some of the technologies have overlapping functions. Airborne radar and optical-detection systems could track both long- and short-range missiles. Terminal interceptors could conceivably be designed for both types of attack. The principles involved in tracking, identifying, targeting, and destroying missiles are similar, if not identical, for the two classes of missiles.

The initial stages of the discussion of BMD in NATO were held in the ministerial-level Nuclear Planning Group from April 1967 to April 1968 and focused on ground-based systems equipped, like the earlier Nike-Hercules, with nuclear warheads, and designed to provide some measure of defense for population as well as military assets. In 1980 NATO's Advisory Group for Aerospace Research and Development (AGARD) produced a study endorsing the idea of extended air defense in the hope of achieving active defenses of critical military targets from either air or missile attacks. In the NATO context, defense systems were politically desirable because they demonstrated the indivisibility of the alliance in the event that the United States pursued ballistic missile defense, and they provided some protection against the sort of blackmail the Soviets had used effectively against Britain and France during the Suez crisis in 1956. West Europeans were hardly enthusiastic about pursuing BMD, which they thought would be ineffective, too expensive, and a barrier to arms control. But in 1986 Manfred Wörner called for a "process of incremental steps proceeding from existing air defense capabilities" in order to create a missile defense for Europe. The relevant technologies, he said, "could be harnessed to this process in complete conformity with current NATO guidelines covering the exploitation of new technologies for strengthening the conventional defenses of the Alliance." The defense need not be impenetrable, Wörner argued, nor would it need to protect Western Europe completely in order to have strategic benefit. Even a limited defense would introduce enough uncertainties into Soviet calculations regarding the success of an offensive attack to deter such an attack.[44] In May 1986 the NATO defense ministers approved the extended air defense concept, based on studies by AGARD, as a framework for developing both air defenses and ATBMs.

Thus, there has been a growing recognition among NATO strategic planners that the Soviet air and missile threat, particularly against fixed NATO installations, may require the development of hard-point defenses. At first, NATO planners emphasized the use of conventional offensive weapons, especially aircraft and precision-guided missiles, to interdict a Warsaw Pact attack by rendering command centers inoperative, striking at both forward and rear bases, and interfering with resupply efforts. As the Soviets improved their own capacities, the planners recognized that NATO's ability to launch such interdiction strikes was itself in jeopardy. Without point defenses to protect its own air and missile bases and command-and-control facilities, NATO would lack confidence in its ability to thwart a rapidly mounted Soviet attack except by early resort to nuclear weapons, and even these capacities might be denied by a massive initial Soviet attack on tactical-weapons launchers and bombers. For those in favor of emphasizing conventional war capabilities, the stress on ATBM is a way of promoting work (under the framework of SDI) designed to shore up the conventional idea of deterrence. From a West European perspective, it could be said to maintain existing options—i.e., to use conventional force so as to delay and possibly obviate the need to use nuclear force. On both strategic and political grounds, then, extended air defense using conventionally armed SAMs and ATBMs is attractive to West European military planners.

Skeptics point out, however, that the SDIO's interest in integrating European defenses with SDI "diverges starkly" from the approach prevalent in Western Europe, where the concern is for defense against a growing Soviet conventional threat.[45] The fear in Western Europe is that the Warsaw Pact forces may be preparing to use conventionally armed short-range missiles, along with intermediate-range bombers, to make a massive attack on NATO defenses. By using conventional munitions, the pact forces would minimize the risk of provoking a Western nuclear response. According to Wörner, the addition of this element could give the Soviets a decided military edge in the most likely form of conflict:

> By concentrating missile strikes on prime NATO targets over massively attacking Warsaw Pact air and ground formations, the Soviet Union could pre-

vent, delay or obstruct numerous NATO response options in the critical initial phase of a conflict. Thus, an orderly mounting of NATO defensive operations with emphasis on forward defense, the inflow of ground and air reinforcements from abroad, freedom of maneuver in the rear areas, as well as the Alliance's capacity for nuclear response—above all, the air-delivered components of that response—could be substantially disrupted and compromised, if not prevented entirely.[46]

Addressing the conventional threat poses very different requirements from those of intercepting nuclear weapons, which must take place at greater heights, requiring higher-velocity interceptors and stronger, more accurate radars. In effect, the difference is between SDI-type systems and upgraded SAMs. SAMs have been upgraded by the United States in the form of the Patriot missile, which was tested successfully to intercept a Lance missile in September 1986. The Europeans are also working on upgrading SAMs to replace the current Hawk system, which is part of a network of allied air defenses that includes NADGE (NATO air defense ground environment) for detection and SAMs and fighter interceptors.[47] Two French companies, Thomson-CSF and Aerospatiale, are at work in cooperation with France's Defense Ministry on the Surface-Sol-Air-Futur, a sea-based version of an ATBM; a land-based version is being planned. In the Federal Republic, Messerschmitt-Bölkow-Blohm is working on another system. The two governments are discussing the integration of these efforts.

The proposal for deploying ATBMs is also an appealing one to some elements in the U.S. military, notably the army unit responsible for the Patriot missile program. Although the Patriot was designed as an air-defense system, a commitment to extended air defense would bolster the Patriot's role and lead to increased expenditures on the system to give it defense capacities against tactical missiles as well as aircraft. In the competition for defense appropriations, the army can expect opposition from the air force to any request for greatly increased support of the Patriot. The air force would probably argue that incremental support should be designed to improve tactical offensive capabilities and provide better passive defenses for aircraft and radar systems. In view of the likelihood of conflict and the constraints on available incremental funding in the United States, the development of ATBMs for the European theater will be significantly affected by the level and pace of West European investment.

The desirability of major investments in ATBM is by no means universally accepted on either strategic or economic grounds. Many of the same strategic objectives can be served by passive defenses—in the form of hardening and dispersal and by greater reliance on counter-air activities. A technical study by Benoit Morel and Theodore A. Postol argues that relatively modest measures, such as burial of command posts, increased depth of "overburden" on shelters, along with hardening and dispersal, could readily negate the most severe threats from tactical ballistic missiles.[48] The cost of acquiring between fifty and seventy-five upgraded Patriot missile fire units has been estimated as $30 billion.[49] The high cost of Patriot is already inhibiting efforts to achieve air defense. Another technical study by two Rand Corporation analysts agrees that passive defenses are probably the best option in the near term but that "ATBM is an important, but longer-term, option for protecting airbases."[50] It is also not clear if defense should be designed to protect against nuclear as well as conventional attack. But calls like Wörner's for extended air defense have generated interest. The fact that investments have already been made in anti-aircraft systems like Hawk and associated AWACS surveillance systems and radar detection makes it all but inevitable that continued attention will be given to both air defense and defense against tactical missile attack. To the extent that arms-control agreements can eliminate or reduce the threat from missiles, that emphasis could be diminished.

SDI AND THE WESTERN ALLIANCE: THE PROSPECTIVE PROBLEMS

West European concentration on tactical defenses, even if they are designed to serve in conventional modernization, will not altogether alleviate the difficulties SDI has introduced into the Western alliance. As tactical defenses are developed, avoiding conflict with the ABM Treaty could become harder, inasmuch as many of the relevant technologies have applications for ABM as well as ATBM systems. By collaborating with SDI, moreover, the West European governments may be perceived to be lending encouragement to a development that would hamper prospects for East-West accord and jeopardize adherence to the ABM Treaty. Even ATBM defenses could become highly problematic for West Europeans, especially if they are to be armed with a nuclear kill mechanism. Such a development "would produce an avalanche of public and official opposition in Europe," as Hugh De Santis has noted, and raises the question of whether the United States would give prerelease authority to its allies.[51] At the same time, those Europeans who consider nuclear deterrence the best way of averting a Soviet attack might find that ATBMs would raise the nuclear threshold to an uncomfortable extent. As De Santis suggests, a conventional ATBM defense "might reduce deterrence if it contributed to the perception that NATO would not escalate to the use of nuclear weapons." [52]

By removing the threat posed by both intermediate- and shorter-range Soviet missiles, the 1987 INF Treaty seriously weakens the case for extended air defense in Europe. By prohibiting both conventionally and nuclear-armed tactical missiles with ranges between 500 and 5,500 km, the treaty significantly diminishes the Soviet threat to NATO. The threat is not altogether eliminated, however. Many of NATO's highest-value installations are within the 500-km range still permitted for short-range missiles, and the treaty limits may only encourage Soviet weapons designers to concentrate on improving the accuracy and yield of the theater missiles still permitted. NATO bases will remain vulnerable to attack by Soviet bombers, which are capable of delivering far larger amounts of conventional explosives than could be delivered by the missiles now being removed. Because treaties can be abrogated, a case can be made for developing ATBMs as a way of encouraging Soviet compliance with the INF Treaty.

Even with the intermediate- and short-range missile threat removed, however, the task of defending Western Europe against a possible Soviet attack, except by threatening nuclear retaliation, remains daunting. Soviet strategic missiles can be fired against European targets. Defenses must be able to intercept attacking warheads at high-enough altitudes in case they are salvage-fused (as Soviet warheads are now reported to be). Short-range tactical missiles do not have high apogees and therefore cannot be intercepted by interceptors designed to work in space. A Soviet attack combining ICBMs and low-trajectory SLBMs, coupled with precision-guided submunitions delivered by aircraft, short-range ballistic missiles, and cruise missiles, would easily overwhelm a tactical defense relying on technology available in the foreseeable future. Under these circumstances, a negotiated agreement to reduce the size and scale of the threat still further is a far more preferable option, especially because it would also prevent the development of corresponding defenses by the Soviets that could vitiate both NATO's strategy of flexible response and the credibility of the French and British deterrents.

In economic terms, SDI has so far been neither the roundabout subsidy for U.S. high-technology industry some Europeans feared nor the bonanza they hoped it might be for their own industries. By March 1987 Britain had won SDI contracts totaling just $34 million, a sum that was expected to rise to $100 million by the end of the year—but that would still amount to less than 2 percent of the SDI budgets for 1986 and 1987—a far cry from the hope expressed at the outset by Defense Secretary Michael Heseltine that contracts for Britain might reach $1.5 billion. Through June 1986 all European contractors had received awards totaling less than $100 million, or less than 1 percent of the total.[53] A report of the House of Commons Defence Select Committee found that despite promises, the United States was excluding foreign companies from "operationally sensitive work" and that, in any case, major spin-offs were unlikely. The committee noted that the most persuasive reason for Britain's continued participation was not any potential economic benefit but the chance to keep abreast of developments in strategic defense that might threaten the credibility of Britain's independent nuclear deterrent. The committee also warned against accepting the Reagan administration's "broad" interpretation of the ABM Treaty lest it jeopardize arms-control negotiations. The government, the committee asserted, ought to ensure that British research continue to adhere to the traditional interpretation "even in the event of the U.S. ceasing to abide by that interpretation."[54]

In the longer run, the anxieties initially generated by the announcement of SDI will persist so long as deployment remains a serious possibility. If both the United States and the U.S.S.R. should deploy defenses adequate to deal with relatively small-scale nuclear attacks, continued investments by the British and French in independent nuclear deterrents will become harder to justify. The plausibility of the flexible-response policy would also become more questionable. The line between a limited nuclear strike and a full-scale one would be fuzzier if defenses could be deployed to defend key military targets and command-and-control centers, especially the national-command authority in Moscow. Although a limited defense, designed to strengthen the credibility of NATO's retaliatory capacity (with some collateral protection of civil targets), would reassure the West Europeans, a fuller defense effort, especially if it were to involve the abrogation of the ABM Treaty in favor of the deployment of significant hard-point and population defenses, would presumably make them more dependent on the superpowers. The West Germans might hope to gain marginal political advantages by participating in the development of tactical defenses and, eventually, by deploying such defenses, but these gains would be more than offset by the likely growth in tensions between East and West. The FRG's interest in *Ostpolitik*, which is widespread, leads all West German parties to be as interested in détente as in defense. To the extent that defensive deployments would trigger a breakdown in the arms-control process and an intense competition in all military systems, the West Germans would certainly conclude that they would become worse off.

Another prospect that would seriously concern the West Europeans is that effective defenses—those that could eliminate or seriously reduce the role of nuclear weapons as deterrents—would increase the likelihood of conventional war. Insofar as they perceive themselves to be at a disadvantage vis-à-vis the Warsaw Pact in conventional forces, they would not welcome the loss of NATO's nuclear threat. U.S. officials have for years warned them that they have no real choice but to increase their contribution to defensive forces or suffer a dangerous inferiority that might tempt the Soviets to attack or, at the very least, to exert coercion. The West Europeans themselves have serious misgivings about moving out from under the U.S. nuclear umbrella and embarking on a costly and politically unappealing effort to upgrade conventional forces.

The preferred Western European strategy would therefore be for allied solidarity on SDI to contribute to greater willingness on the part of the Soviets to negotiate reductions in offensive forces in exchange for U.S. willingness to adhere to the ABM Treaty, at least until research demonstrates that a useful defense is deployable. An agreement to extend adherence to the treaty, such as the Soviets proposed at Reykjavík, would certainly be acceptable to the European leaders, however much they may have been disturbed by loose talk of a total abandonment of nuclear weapons or of a potential agreement on INF that took no account of Soviet short-range missiles and conventional forces confronting Europe.

From a West European perspective, the SDI is part of a U.S. effort to take the military and political initiative away from the Soviets and, possibly in the long term, to bring about a major change in strategy. In the short run, however, such an effort can only reestablish and reinforce European dependence on the United States. At a time when Western Europe is seeking greater economic and cultural integration, the U.S. initiative seems to threaten efforts to establish solidarity independent of the United States. It certainly threatens the effort of parties of the left, notably in the FRG, to seek accommodation with the Soviet Union as part of a campaign to put more stress on the integration of Europe and, in some versions, to create a third force between the two superpowers. The U.S. initiative, while it is not directly aimed at such efforts, is a forceful reminder that the United States sees itself as the leader of the alliance and that it will take unilateral decisions to develop technology that increases its military strength. The fact that the technology involves the use of space and the development of advanced technology, especially computers, is bound to be viewed as an effort by the United States to sustain its economic preeminence and to push outward into space without allowing either the West Europeans or the Soviets to challenge its military or technological leadership.[55] Ironically, however, while the SDI may have taken the wind out of the sails of the freeze movement in the United States, it has had the opposite effect in Western Europe by strengthening the case of those who oppose continued reliance on offensive weapons and who favor negotiations aimed at transcending reliance on force of all kinds to keep the peace.

Understandably reluctant to make SDI a critical alliance issue, West Europeans will be compelled to do so if it proceeds to the point of deployment. Their stake in a stable superpower relationship is almost as high as it is in preserving the alliance with the United States. Because of this ambivalence of objectives, the Europeans are bound to feel qualms about a U.S. program that in certain forms could challenge the Soviet feeling of parity. Insofar as the U.S. program is developed without attention to arms control or in an effort to substitute a military program for arms control, Europeans will grow increasingly wary. If a government should come to power in Britain committed to the denuclearization of the United States' closest European ally, and if SDI blocks arms-control agreements with the Soviets, the damage to the alliance could be considerable. If, conversely, the U.S. administration can negotiate agreed restrictions on testing and development of SDI systems so that an arms-reduction agreement can take place, with more reductions promised, West Europeans may well look on SDI as a blessing in disguise. If and when defensive systems become economically affordable and technologically feasible, however, the European allies may well be willing to adopt them on the grounds that an effective defense against nuclear weapons is preferable to no defense except for the nuclear deterrent. For the time being, they remain committed, on the whole, to the belief in the necessity of nuclear deterrence and wary of any new developments that threaten to upset the already precarious balance between East and West.

In the aftermath of the INF Treaty, the Western alliance will have to decide both on the course of NATO's military modernization and on the aims to be pursued in negotiations for conventional-arms reductions with the Warsaw Pact. On military and economic grounds, it is far from obvious that a major commitment to modernization is advisable, in view of the alternatives available in the form of passive defenses and further negotiated reductions in the Soviet threat. To the extent that SDI remains an obstacle in the strategic negotiations, it could also block progress on conventional reductions. Even a major commitment to pursue tactical defenses could complicate efforts to achieve détente in the European theater. The INF Treaty has considerably weakened the case for deploying tactical ballistic missile defenses. Further negotiated reductions could make the argument entirely obsolete. In the case of Europe, as in the East-West confrontation generally, the question is whether diplomacy can negate the need for costly and ultimately vain efforts to rely on even newer military technologies. If these diplomatic initiatives fail or are protracted, pressures could build for tactical deployments in Europe and early strategic deployments in the United States. These deployments would hearten advocates of SDI (who have good reason to fear that, otherwise, SDI would fall victim to détente and retrenchments in allied defense spending), but they should dismay those who recognize the futility of relying on new weapons to achieve security.

Decisions taken in the alliance framework could therefore have critical bearing on the question of whether SDI moves from research to deployment. The central decision, however, must still be made in the arena of American domestic politics—the subject to which we now turn.

Deploy or Perish

SDI and Domestic Politics

Like all other large-scale efforts to develop military technology, SDI is inevitably deeply enmeshed in domestic politics. Simplistic formulas by which such entanglements are sometimes measured—such as the suspicion that all military projects result from promotion on the part of a "military-industrial complex"—hardly describe the realities well enough.[1] This is certainly true in the case of SDI, which, as we have seen, was not promoted by any of the usual suspects. Although the project had some preliminary support among certain researchers in the national laboratories and defense firms, as well as among a handful of members of Congress, it became a high-priority national program only because a popular president embraced it and used his powers of persuasion to win support from the electorate. In order to sustain a project of this magnitude, especially when it moves from the research phase into the far more expensive and significant development and deployment stages, the support of a strong coalition of political forces is essential. The early history of SDI has been a struggle between those eager to build such a coalition and those determined to thwart and counteract their effort. It thus presents an instructive case study of how major projects in need of political support do or do not take hold, and how pressures for early deployment distort the research agenda.

DEMOCRATIC PRINCIPLES
AND THE COLD WAR

In democratic theory, a nation's commitment to shift to a radically new and exceedingly costly defensive strategy ought to rest on a widespread consensus that the change is desirable and feasible. In the United States, decisions are often made and sustained without such a consensus. Acquisition programs develop a momentum that makes them hard to stop, even when they are not justifiable in military terms. In very complex R & D programs, it is often difficult to know with a high degree of certainty whether what is envisioned in the program will be beneficial. Much depends on whether enough of those with influence believe in the desirability of a new weapons system strongly enough to press for its continuation and then, finally, for acquisition and deployment. Some of the will to believe comes from self-interest, some from conviction. The domestic politics of defense is to a large extent a struggle among forces motivated by a combination of self-interest and public interest—a struggle fought out in the budgetary process, in the press, in public-opinion polls, and during elections. The struggle is also influenced by changing perceptions of the international environment. If the Soviet Union is perceived to be mounting some new threat, and a particular program seems to be a plausible response, it is likely to gain adherents. If the Soviet Union does not appear to be mounting such a new threat, the quest for a technological fix becomes less appealing. The mistrust of the Soviets, and thus the competition for advantage, has been hard to overcome, so promoters of the continuing development of new military technologies have usually won out over resisters.

Whether or not the deployment of strategic defenses makes sense, therefore, there is some danger that the expenditure of considerable sums of money in developing them could lead to a point of no return, at which partial deployments would be made in the hope that they will eventually lead to a comprehensive system, even though there is no reason to believe that it will ever become a practical prospect. SDI has been restrained so far out of concern for its technical uncertainties and the high projected costs of development and deployment. Many also view it as unnecessary and unwise in view of the changes in Soviet foreign and military policy introduced under Gorbachev. The domestic struggle over the direction of SDI will be influenced, as it already has been, by the interplay of these international considerations with domestic politics.

SDI AND EARLIER MILITARY PROJECTS:
A COMPARISON

All major military projects have been "political" in the sense that those who decide to support them have policy objectives in mind. The United States' decision to develop the atomic bomb was a watershed in the degree to which the political authorities became committed to a program involving research as well as development. Unlike other projects aimed at perfecting existing weapons, this one was designed to conduct a complex series of experiments in an effort to discover whether a wholly new weapon (which was thought capable of introducing a radically new dimension to warfare) could be developed. The decision was made in conditions of secrecy at the highest level of the executive branch and was influenced by the fear that a wartime enemy, Nazi Germany, might be the first to develop such a weapon. Scientists played an important role in the decision—far more important than they had played in the initiation of military-technology programs in the past—because it depended critically, first, on their judgments of technical feasibility and, second, on their commitment to make the concept work.

The success of the Manhattan Project set two fundamental precedents. One was that national security was now closely coupled to progress in science and technology, at least in the physical sciences. Although the team that had developed the atomic bomb was dispersed at the end of the war, the project was revived a few years later because of a growing appreciation in the United States that a continuing effort had to be made to support science and technology for purposes of defense. This decision was not a result of domestic pressures from defense industry or the military services but was largely a reaction to the intensification of the cold war. The U.S. government, spurred on by public concern, was reacting to Soviet success in developing an atomic weapon, the Berlin blockade, creation of the Sino-Soviet bloc, and the outbreak of the Korean War. Even though the United States enjoyed a clear advantage in military technology over the Soviet Union, it seemed imperative that the partnership between the federal government and the military laboratories as well as with the research universities be maintained and strengthened in order to maintain that advantage, especially in view of the U.S.S.R.'s potential manpower and tactical superiority over Europe. This partnership represented a considerable break with a past in which the federal government was often constrained on constitutional and ideological grounds from either becoming an economic actor or from subsidizing private industry. Especially in the Progressive era, government had been conceived of as a watchdog over industry, a champion of free enterprise against combinations, trusts, and oligopolies. After World War II, however, concern for national security put the government in the unaccustomed role of underwriting the risk of private contractors and of reinforcing industrial oligopoly in order to support the most essential military contractors.

The United States has so far resisted pressures to go even beyond these arrangements. It has not created a cabinet-level department to co-ordinate science and technology, nor has it adopted a formula for national R&D expenditures based on the theory that overhead costs should be borne by the government. The United States' approach has been sectoral and pragmatic and has so far not engaged the federal government consistently and openly in the support of civil as well as military research and development. Despite the evidence that other countries have profited from government planning and direction, the United States has adhered to the classical liberal principle that private industry can do the best job of promoting innovation in the civil sector if left free of government interference. In the two principal areas of federal involvement, defense and space exploration, the U.S. pattern has been to emphasize work performed by private industry but subsidized by public R&D contracts and procurement. In supporting this R&D, the federal government relies on the "project system," except in the case of three nuclear-weapons laboratories—Los Alamos, Livermore, and Sandia—where research is supported on a nonprofit, "level-of-effort" basis—much as the Soviets do in their missile and other weapons-research facilities. Although some critics argue that the United States would be better off admitting that it had created a "contract state" or a "managed economy," and nationalizing those defense firms whose work is almost entirely dependent on federal contracts, such steps have been resisted on the ground that they violate traditional American norms and would be counterproductive.

Despite such disputes about methods, it was well recognized, especially in the late 1950s, that national security required a wide range of activities in R&D of all sorts. Various factors influenced decisions on research priorities: the perceived military need, technical feasibility, and the comparative cost vis-à-vis other existing or new systems. In an effort to achieve better control of the process, Secretary of Defense Robert S. McNamara introduced cost-benefit analysis for comparing weapons systems rather than allowing the services to pursue their own needs and to iron out priorities by interservice bargaining. Although the need to reconcile economic and strategic goals with the priorities set by each of the services continues to bedevil defense planning, McNamara's efforts at least compelled the planners to think about the interrelationships of weapons and their roles in general strategic doctrine.

Although it would be too much to say that strategic doctrine alone fueled the quest for new military technology, it is certainly true that the advent of the atomic bomb gradually led to the adoption of the belief in strategic deterrence, and that this belief influenced the development of offensive forces.[2] The decision to employ intercontinental ballistic missiles as delivery vehicles for atomic weapons was only a more efficient way to implement a strategy already in place. The Soviet Union undoubtedly had something to do with this decision, but it probably would have been made anyhow. The decision to build the thermonuclear bomb was different. It was not obvious in 1949, when the matter was first considered, either that the bomb could be designed or that it would confer some military advantage not supplied by the atomic bomb. Accordingly, the scientists on the General Advisory Committee (GAC) to the Atomic Energy Commission recommended almost unanimously against a crash program to develop the new, more powerful bomb. President Truman overruled the GAC on the advice of a small group of scientists committed to the idea. Truman and his political advisors were uneasy that the Soviets had developed an atomic bomb of their own, fearing that they might develop a thermonuclear bomb ahead of the United States and use their resulting superiority to achieve advantages, much as Secretary of State James F. Byrnes had tried to do with "atomic diplomacy."

The H-bomb decision deviated from the wartime pattern in that the president decided to proceed over the opposition of key scientific advisors, who had warned that a crash program was not only premature but would also be costly in terms of other military needs, such as a continental air defense and tactical atomic weapons. Nevertheless, the president did not reach his decision arbitrarily or in defiance of informed opinion. In fact, the administrators of the Los Alamos Laboratory had recommended that research on the H-bomb be accelerated, along with other projects. Karl T. Compton, head of the country's highest-ranking defense-science advisory body, the Research and Development Board, which was attached to the Department of Defense, had recommended going ahead with the effort to develop the H-bomb. This decision, then, was based on recommendations of those with operative responsibility and on the opinion of senior scientific advisors, even though it had been opposed by the GAC. Congress's role in this decision was almost as limited as it had been in the case of the atomic bomb, except that one senator, Brien McMahon (D., Conn.)—who had a key role in such matters as chairman of the Joint Congressional Committee on Atomic Energy— worked with the air force in promoting the case for a crash program.[3]

Since then, the general pattern in weapons development has been that new ideas have percolated up, from the industrial contractors, the DOD laboratories, and the federally funded research centers. The ideas move up through a hierarchy of decision makers, including those in charge of military R & D and the military planners, and are reviewed—if they reach the top levels of the Pentagon—by special outside advisory committees made up of experts from industry and academia, in addition to senior officials, elected as well as appointed. Ideas that involve new weapons that either parallel new Soviet developments or act to counter them are especially likely to run this entire gauntlet. In 1954, for example, a U.S. ICBM program *both* paralleled the Soviet ICBM project *and* seemed to solve the problem of how to penetrate Soviet air defenses. The ICBM's unique speed was also an important consideration. Such proposals reach the White House only after lengthy, thorough, and iterative reviews in the defense establishment. When proposals come to the attention of the president without undergoing this process, they have rarely if ever been acted upon.

THE "IRON TRIANGLE"

In general, the dynamic system now in place generates so much work and so many new ideas that it is sometimes accused of promoting projects for which there is no real military need. Hence, President Dwight D. Eisenhower's warning against the "military-industrial complex" and the scientific-technological elite, and the indictment of the Pentagon as a kind of state within the state, nurturing new weapons in order to perpetuate the cold war and the "warfare state." Recurrent scandals involving kickbacks, exorbitant consultant fees, and "revolving door" employment of civilian and military-procurement personnel by defense contractors have reinforced this suspicion. Nevertheless, the reality is more prosaic. The profit motive and corrupt practices oil the wheels, but they do not drive the machine. Cold war anxieties, coupled with the rapidity of technological change in modern times, provide the main impetus for weapons innovations, as is apparent in the fact that the Soviet Union, even without a private-sector economy, has developed a thriving military-industrial complex of its own.

More and more, this system has also come to involve Congress in detailed decisions on R & D and procurement. Although Congress has rarely if ever shaped new strategic or defense policy (such as the "New Look" or "Massive Retaliation," which have typically been introduced by the executive), both houses and their committees take a keen interest in the allocation of federal funds for defense R & D and procurement. Much of this is a pork-barrel interest. Members of Congress are eager to secure new projects for their districts and to preserve those already created. Key legislators on key committees are in the best position to control the distribution of the largesse, resulting in an "iron triangle" that links the military services, the contractors, and the key members of Congress.[4] Their combined efforts create a formidable force in favor of the perpetuation of military spending and the initiation of new programs. When there is conflict, it is often because those in the triangle perceive their interests differently. When one aircraft has to be chosen from among several candidates, different constituencies become rivals, and the prime contractors seek to reduce political risk by spreading the work over as many congressional districts as possible. When the interests of one branch of the service have to be chosen over those of one of its rivals, the same kind of competition ensues. Congress sometimes plays a more constructive role when individual members expose scandals and use the legislature's investigative power to expose kickbacks, inflation of costs, and other forms of fraud and waste. The General Accounting Office, a major watchdog agency of Congress, has also achieved significant reforms in contracting procedures after discovering that contract reviews in negotiated R&D contracts were often inadequate and unduly influenced by relationships between the contractors and the military-procurement officers. But the opportunities and temptations have proved hard to control or police, and collusive practices persist.

To characterize the military R&D and procurement processes as a triangle, however, is to miss some of its dimensions. Much of the incentive for new programs comes from service rivalries, sometimes even within particular branches of the services. Thus, "bureaucratic politics" involving competition between two services, as in the conflict between the army and air force in the Thor-Jupiter controversy,[5] weighs heavily in the outcome of such struggles. The Defense Department's effort to gain a measure of control over such rivalries is also a factor in the picture, yet the DOD is itself a bureaucratic actor. It has sometimes promoted weapons systems and modernization out of its own "organizational imperative."

Disentangling self-interest from public interest is difficult. When the services and the DOD propose some pattern of military spending, it is not necessarily, or even usually, the case that they are acting purely out of organizational self-interest. These organizations tend to develop a concept of a public interest in national security that is presumably being served by the policies they advocate. They argue, often plausibly, that they cannot carry out their policies unless they can count on help from others in the executive branch, especially the president, and unless they receive enough backing from public opinion to influence Congress to vote the funds in accordance with their priorities, rather than those dictated by political pressures.

Nevertheless, the general pattern of support for new military projects is one in which the laboratories tend to initiate ideas, the services become committed to particular projects and strive to have them adopted and brought to completion, the Defense Department reviews them and determines which of them make sense, and the secretary of defense, in collaboration with the contractors and Congress, decides whether or not to pursue them. By no means are all plausible candidates supported, and the evidence suggests that the contractors alone cannot carry the day unless they can succeed in forging a strong enough coalition with at least one of the armed services and interested politicians. A good example is the B-1-bomber program. When President Carter decided to shelve this program in favor of upgrading the older B-52 until the Stealth bomber would come into production, the proposal for a major new military program was temporarily defeated. This happened even though the prime contractor, Rockwell, had a great deal at stake and had assembled a formidable coalition of industrial subcontractors who stood to benefit from the adoption of the program. The formidable B-1-bomber lobby spent heavily on behalf of the cause and eventually succeeded, but it would not have done so without the election of Ronald Reagan, who was committed to a broad program of strategic modernization, including the B-1. Thus, the B-1 cannot be viewed as an example of a lobby's strength alone. In this case, the key to its success was the election of a president with a political mandate to support the program.[6]

THE POLITICAL AUSPICES OF SDI

Political auspices were equally critical for the initial success of SDI. The SDI was promoted by a very small coalition of military officers, scientists, strategists, and politicians, but it enjoyed nothing approaching the support for the B-1 bomber. SDI did not carry the immediate promise of lucrative procurement contracts, and it did not arouse much enthusiasm among military researchers, who had come to rely more on continued modernization of offensive weapons. Because there seemed to be no effective defenses against nuclear attack, the important goal, in their view, was to assure that the nuclear-deterrent forces could be protected from attack, could penetrate prospective defenses, and would be accurate enough to do whatever was required. Although there had long been a significant level of support for basic research into technologies that might have defensive applications, the 1972 ABM Treaty had ruled out their development. Indeed, as we note in chapter 1, early in the Reagan administration's first term, even the Defense Department's own internal review of the High Frontier proposal on strategic defenses had led to the conclusion, announced by Secretary Weinberger, that the project was premature at best, because it could easily be defeated and overwhelmed.

The president's decision to make SDI his own pet project made all the difference. As an air force general with planning responsibilities observed: "All other systems stem from some statement of operational need. SDI was generated by the president. We didn't have that operational requirement before the president's vision of a world with no nukes."[7] As we note in chapter 1, Reagan did not seek prior approval from the defense establishment because he had been warned that SDI would be resisted. He also did not consult the White House Science Council. When a broad review committee was finally established (the Fletcher Committee), it was not asked "whether," but "how." Instead, Reagan chose to listen only to enthusiasts and to trust his own judgment about what was desirable. That judgment was based on a faith in U.S. science and technology as well as on a personal frustration with the existing strategic situation and concern that a future U.S. president might not be able to rely on being able to deter an attack by threatening unacceptable retaliation. As we saw in chapter 1, this belief, coupled with skepticism about the prospects for negotiating a reduction of the nuclear threat and a dislike for the very notion of mutual U.S.-Soviet nuclear deterrence prompted the president's decision. It was successfully implemented not because the president could count on support in Congress, the DOD, and the contractors—or, in other words, from all points of the "iron triangle"—but rather because he went over the heads of the "establishment" and appealed to the electorate. His simplistic vision of a space shield against nuclear weapons aroused precisely the strong public approval that he needed and that his political instincts told him he could expect.

Once he advanced this vision and the people responded favorably, Reagan could count on enlisting institutional support among the contractors whose interests would be served, within the services where special divisions would be created with responsibility for the program, and among those who would develop the strategic rationale for the program. Although he could anticipate opposition to the program, he could calculate that most of it would come from political liberals, whom he had defeated before. By couching the issue in ideological terms, as a test of his hardheaded conservatism versus his critics' supposed weak-kneed liberalism, the president could hope to fashion a foreign policy issue that would serve as a focal counterpart to his campaign for the domestic conservative agenda. SDI had a particular appeal for his ideological supporters because it represented an effort to achieve national security by relying on U.S. military-technological initiatives rather than on negotiations with the Soviets. At the same time, it undercut the moral case of freeze advocates and went them one better by proposing a nonnuclear defense that would make nuclear weapons "impotent and obsolete." In short, it was in many respects well calculated to (1) evoke the same fervor that other elements of the conservative crusade had elicited among Reagan's most ardent following and in the general public, and (2) buttress and institutionalize this appeal by building a coalition of support among contractors, the defense laboratories, and influential figures in the media. Opposition, the president knew, could easily be labeled as evidence of the liberals' eagerness to make lopsided concessions in order to achieve agreements with the Soviet Union. Ironically, liberal opposition would only make the cause of SDI that much more formidable politically.

PUBLIC SUPPORT FOR SDI

According to opinion polls, SDI has been favorably received by the American public. This general assessment may be deceptive, however. Polls measure simplified responses to complex and sometimes ambiguously worded questions, and some of the data suggest serious confusion and reservations among the respondents, especially in response to questions that link SDI to issues of arms control and expenditure. Public support never seemed to grow firmer than at the time of the 1984 presidential election; but even that support was ambiguous. During the campaign, the Democratic candidate, former Vice-President Walter Mondale, accused the president of wanting to "militarize the heavens" with a scheme that would not work and would prevent progress in arms control and cause grave destabilization. The public seemed to sympathize both with Reagan's proposal and with Mondale's doubts. Among viewers of a televised debate between the candidates, 57 percent of those polled found Reagan more persuasive on SDI; 23 percent found Mondale more persuasive.[8] A week before the election, however, another poll showed that 48 percent of registered voters concurred with Mondale that SDI would "just speed up the arms race," while only 30 percent thought it would "make us more secure."[9] After the Reagan landslide, the confusion remained just as evident. Early in January 1985, 62 percent of respondents thought a defense in space could prove workable, compared with only 23 percent who thought it could not. In the same poll, however, 60 percent said that having such a system in space would worry them, whereas only 25 percent thought it would make them feel more secure.[10]

The failure of the meeting at Reykjavík to produce agreement on arms control or on SDI-testing seemed to strengthen public support. The public overwhelmingly supported the president's stand at Reykjavík. In one poll, 56 percent approved the president's refusal to trade away SDI for an arms-control agreement, compared with 16 percent who disapproved.[11] Another showed 62 percent supporting the president against 22 percent opposing him.[12] Still another showed a still larger disparity of 66 percent to 21 percent.[13] And when a poll stressed Reagan's leadership role by asking whether he did "the right thing" in "refusing to change his ideas for the development of 'Star Wars'"— 72 percent agreed and only 18 percent disagreed. Asked in the same poll if they continued to favor SDI, a majority indicated approval by a margin of 60 percent to 26 percent.[14]

Several polls revealed considerable apprehension about the possible effects of SDI. In a November 1985 poll, 71 percent of the respondents agreed that negotiations for a reduction in nuclear missiles were preferable to developing SDI.[15] In October 1985, 74 percent of those polled said that it was more important for the United States and U.S.S.R. to agree to arms reduction than for the United States to develop space-based weapons to defend against nuclear attack.[16] Asked the same year about Gorbachev's proposal that both sides cut their missiles by 50 percent and negotiate a "total ban" on the development of space-based defenses, 47 percent approved, 32 percent did not.[17] Respondents in another poll that year agreed, 46 percent to 39 percent, that "some limits" on SDI should be accepted if no treaty could be negotiated otherwise.[18] By 53 to 33 percent, those questioned said they would choose negotiations over development of "Star Wars," if these were the only choices.[19] Almost a year after Reykjavík, in September 1986, by a slight margin of 47 to 43 percent, respondents favored cutting back on "Star Wars" in order to achieve an arms-control agreement.[20]

In addition, despite support for SDI, before and after Reykjavík, there was evidence of concern over the costs of the project. In January of 1985, 46 percent said SDI would not be worth the money it would cost, while 40 percent said it would prove worthwhile.[21] In October 1985, 48 percent said they would favor spending the "many billions" it would cost, but 46 percent were opposed.[22] In November 1985, by a margin of 59 to 27 percent, respondents agreed that the president's proposed budget of $26 billion over five years was too high.[23] In January 1987, however, after an election in which the president failed to persuade the electorate to send back members of Congress who would support SDI, 50 percent still thought SDI was "worth the amount of money it would cost," against 37 percent opposed.[24]

If any conclusions can be drawn from these responses, the most fundamental would seem to be that the president did succeed in persuading most respondents that his proposal was a good one, but that many remained concerned that SDI was blocking prospects for arms control and could turn out to be more expensive than it was worth.[25]

CREATING A SPECIAL OFFICE: SDIO

In order to give SDI better definition and better protection against cuts in the defense budget, and probably just as much to protect it against doubters in the defense establishment, the Reagan administration decided to establish the Strategic Defense Initiative Organization (SDIO) within the Department of Defense. The office initially succeeded in preventing the program from fragmenting and in providing a focus for the direction of research and public information. It has been less successful, however, in protecting the program from budget restraints imposed by Congress.

In appointing a military officer with a background that included direction of the NASA space shuttle program, Lieutenant General Abrahamson, the administration gained the assistance of an experienced manager who had shown himself able to work with a variety of agencies and congressional committees. The office drew upon the services of industrial and government laboratory scientists and engineers and immediately launched a major effort to invite proposals from hundreds of industrial laboratories. SDIO recognized from the outset that the agency needed to establish itself within the military services and in the laboratories in order to widen its base of support and to mobilize the degree of cooperation that would be necessary to implement the complex agenda.

Accordingly, funding authorities were set up in the various services through which SDIO channeled its contracts, creating a network of military officers whose careers would be affected by the success of the project. An Office of Innovative Science and Technology was established to encourage submissions from university researchers, thereby blunting the outspoken opposition that was emerging on the campuses. Over the first several years of the project, contracts were let to hundreds of prime and secondary contractors and university-based researchers.

While SDIO benefited from strong support of Weinberger and the president (who ordered that SDI be protected from defense-budget cuts required under the 1985 Gramm-Rudman Deficit Reduction Act), it had less success in establishing its credibility in Congress. A small group of strongly supportive congressmen tried valiantly to resist budget cuts and to trumpet the significance of the program's achievements. SDIO set its own technical milestones, and each time these were met, the claim was made that they vindicated the aims of the project and showed progress even more rapid than had been anticipated. Critics were not impressed, however, claiming that the milestones were publicity stunts. To some extent, perhaps, SDIO suffered from public disillusionment with high technology owing to the disastrous accident at the Chernobyl nuclear power plant, the debacle of the *Challenger* space shuttle, and the failure of the AEGIS system aboard the USS *Vincennes* in the Persian Gulf. Congressional opponents were able to cite the OTA reports that warned of technical and other barriers to the success of the project, as well as the opposition of leading scientists. Neutral members of Congress were influenced by negative assessments from within the defense establishment, openly advanced before the March 1983 speech but expressed confidentially thereafter.

In response to the urgings of its supporters and in the hope of counteracting the criticisms of its opponents, the SDIO decided to shift its strategy in 1986 to put more emphasis on near-term deployable systems and less on longer-term research. Although the office formally denied any such change, analysis of actual allocation of funds belies the SDIO's claim: constraints on expansion of funding had been met by shifting the allocations to nearer-term technologies. Both supporters and skeptics in Congress had joined in urging the SDIO to identify near-term prospects. The supporters were eager to show that the project was succeeding in order to prevent their opponents from voting low levels of funds and "researching it to death." The critics were convinced that SDI could not achieve the president's goal, but some thought that a deployment of mainly terminal defenses for retaliatory weapons had merit. Hoping to weaken popular support, some of the critics were undoubtedly also interested in putting SDIO in the position of abandoning the president's vision of protecting population. SDI could then be attacked as an unrealistic and overly expensive way of protecting missiles. The issue became confused because some in Congress wanted to redefine the program so that it would lead to the deployment of silo defenses, while others believed that the goals of the program should continue to be defined in accordance with the president's vision of population defense.

Meanwhile, SDIO was also caught in the crossfire between the executive branch, which was forwarding a reinterpretation of the ABM Treaty, and an outraged Senate. SDIO originally assured Congress that its experiments would be configured so as to conform to the treaty, although Abrahamson and other DOD officials pointed out that at some point testing in space would have to take place if the validity of developing space-based systems were to be established. Then, when the administration wanted support for its reinterpretation, SDIO was asked to prepare a list of experiments that could not be done under the "narrow" interpretation. The SDIO therefore reported that the narrow interpretation would result in the waste of billions of dollars by prohibiting experiments that could save time and effort. Beset on two sides, Abrahamson had to walk a tightrope so as to satisfy supporters and influential critics alike, supporting the administration's policies with one hand while promising with the other to obey congressionally mandated restrictions.

Abrahamson probably became a more credible figure by allowing SDIO officials to disagree publicly. Thus, when others were urging early deployment of a partial shield, Louis Marquet, SDIO's technical director, said that by the time an early deployment of kinetic-energy satellites could be made, the Soviets could counter it by going to fast-burn boosters.[26] Marquet's comments contradicted arguments of SDI supporters, including a former deputy to Abrahamson, Col. Simon P. Worden, urging early deployment and contending that it would take the Soviets longer to build countermeasures and cost them more than they could afford. Marquet's candor, coupled with the care taken by Abrahamson not to enter the policy thicket himself, helped to preserve the credibility of the program in Congress, even though it did not prevent substantial and increasing cuts in appropriations requests.

In the longer run, it remains to be seen whether SDIO can survive as a separate entity. The more the defense budget is restricted, and the more skepticism is generated about SDI, the more pressure is likely to be felt to reintegrate the elements of SDI into DARPA and the services so that the Department of Defense can make better judgments about trade-offs between SDI and other R & D programs. In the short run, however, the establishment of SDIO was a politic move. It prevented the losses caused by such integration and enabled the program director to create a network of cooperative officials and agencies, more or less along the lines of the successful ICBM and Polaris projects of the 1950s and 1960s. In an effort to reinforce its status and perhaps to help assure longevity, SDIO has proposed the creation of a Strategic Defense Initiative Institute, in the belief that such a body would undertake useful, arm's-length reviews of contractors' work—much along the lines of the Aerospace Corporation, which reviews work done for the air force. Critics in Congress charge that the real aim is to create a public-relations agency for SDIO's activities. The proposal has so far been rejected.

THE DEBATE AMONG THE SCIENTISTS

In the debate over SDI, as in the earlier controversy over ABM, opposition from scientists has played an important role in shaping legislation and public opinion. Disagreements over defense policy within the nation's scientific community have become commonplace since the end of World War II, when scientists and engineers began to play a regular and important role in the nation's defense effort. Many scientists and engineers are employed in defense work—25 to 30 percent by one rough estimate [27]—and even those who are primarily engaged in non-defense employment contribute indirectly to the defense effort because their work has military applications and because some consult for defense agencies. In view of the importance of their contributions, many have come to feel a special responsibility for taking part in policy debates. Some have gone further, either deciding to opt out of military work or out of all science on the ground that their work could be misused. A few have taken matters into their own hands and practiced resistance, particularly during the controversy over the Vietnam War. Generally, however, most members of the scientific community acknowledge that their expertise gives them no special knowledge of matters of foreign and defense policy. A leadership elite, however, has been very active. Those who generally seek to limit the arms race or openly oppose many new weapons tend to join such organizations as the Federation of American Scientists and the Union of Concerned Scientists. Those who generally support modernization tend to serve on official committees or to work for government and industrial laboratories; they sometimes support candidates for office who favor a strong defense program.

SDI's most vocal promoters have been a small group of physicists who work at the two major weapons laboratories—Los Alamos and Lawrence Livermore. There is also strong (though much dispersed) support in industry, "think tanks," and in the government. At Livermore, Edward Teller has been an inspiring leader of some of the key researchers in part as director of the Hertz Foundation, through which some of the most talented young physicists have been recruited to the laboratory.

The role is one to which Teller has grown accustomed. He has long been a believer in the exploitation of technology for military purposes without restraint. While the fission bomb was still under development, he agitated at Los Alamos for permission to work on the next stage, the thermonuclear bomb. This permission was granted by the laboratory director, J. Robert Oppenheimer, once the key theoretical task involved in the fission bomb was sufficiently accomplished. A few years later, when Oppenheimer chaired the GAC (which recommended against a crash program to develop the H-bomb), Teller criticized him passionately, accusing him not only of bad judgment (which, as he would later testify at Oppenheimer's security hearing, was ground for concluding that he was a "security risk") but also of interjecting political and moral views when asked his scientific opinions. He believes that the United States is in a life-and-death struggle with Soviet communism and that the best U.S. strategy would be the unrestrained pursuit of technological advantage.

Teller also believed in the virtues of defense, as we note in chapter 1. In the 1950s, he was an advocate of civil defense at a time when it was thought the Soviets were developing a bomber force that could strike at the U.S. mainland. As the Soviets developed a large ICBM force capable of devastating U.S. urban centers, most of those who had become interested in civil defense abandoned the cause, convinced that it would be a futile, tremendously expensive way to protect even a fraction of the population. Some also argued that building defenses would be interpreted as provocative because a commitment to do so could indicate willingness to contemplate a first strike. Teller disagreed and urged the adoption of a serious program to build shelters and to disperse industry and population.

Teller has remained consistent in his support for continuing improvements to defensive and offensive weapons. He has argued that some defense is better than none, and that all forms of defense, including both passive and active measures, are desirable and even critical to the credibility of a deterrent posture. He opposed the limited test ban of 1963 because it would seriously interfere with U.S. development of an ABM (then always thought of as employing nuclear explosives). More generally, he has opposed the proposal for a comprehensive nuclear-test ban on the ground that it would inhibit research to develop newer atomic weapons of all kinds, including types that would produce less fallout and be configured for greater accuracy and thus less collateral damage. He also opposed the ABM Treaty on the ground that it would prevent the United States from developing new systems that might be more effective than those known in 1972 for intercepting nuclear attacks.

As we have noted, however, Teller did not endorse the Fletcher Committee's recommendation that a decision on deployment be deferred pending further research. He argued that elaborate space-based systems were vulnerable to countermeasures and were far too expensive as well as unlikely to provide a truly leakproof defense. For the same reason, he also declined to endorse High Frontier's space-based KEW system, arguing instead for terminal defenses, which were feasible and would provide affordable protection to some degree, and for a high-priority development program, mainly involving the X-ray laser.

The main political push for the president's program had come initially from the High Frontier organization, which was the brainchild of Lt. Gen. Daniel O. Graham, and which came to include a small group of relatively second-rank industrial military researchers. In 1984 a document marked "not for release" and apparently prepared under the auspices of the Heritage Foundation (though an official of that organization later attributed it to High Frontier) was obtained and widely circulated by SDI critics. It was seized upon with relish by these critics because it seemed to reveal a cynical and conspiratorial strategy for promoting SDI, which bore at least a superficial resemblance to actual events. The document, reportedly prepared by a consultant, set three goals for the campaign: to achieve "initial startup" of deployment during the second term of the Reagan administration, to develop sufficient momentum behind the project so that "it could not be turned off by a replacement or successor Democratic administration," and to foster the creation of "a broad political constituency favoring a new U.S. arms-control strategy featuring major BMD deployments at an early time." The strategy called for a unilateral U.S. effort to develop BMD to be couched as a "new approach to nuclear arms control" which "could be represented as a bilateral effort—one with Soviet reciprocation and participation." Among the virtues of this approach, the author argued, was that it could "disarm BMD opponents either by stealing their language and cause (arms control), or . . . [put] them into a tough political corner through their explicit or de facto advocacy of classical anti-population war crimes." The author recommended that High Frontier enlist an "off-shore" constituency among major allied governments and find some institutional "home" for the project outside its own ranks. This might be done by identifying a "forceful personality" who might champion the cause (Henry Kissinger was mentioned as a possible candidate), by inspiring the creation of a summer study group, or (in the author's opinion the best option) by organizing a group across the political spectrum in order to remove the perception that "BMD is primarily a 'right wing' cause." Earmarked for recruitment to the cause were conservative columnists, members of Congress, and defense analysts, "neutral" groups such as "pro-Israel political circles," financial and professional organizations, and—most ambitious of all—even such already committed groups as the FAS, SANE, freeze groups, and the Center for Defense Information.[28]

Graham did not succeed in enlisting nearly so broad a constituency, but he did find allies in Congress and in the White House. Defense Department officials turned a polite but deaf ear to High Frontier proposals until the president adopted the cause. From then on, the DOD reversed course until, in short order, its leaders were arguing that an intermediate deployment such as that advocated by High Frontier would make sense and that eventually beam weapons would be added to the system.

When critical reports began to appear, starting with the report for the Office of Technology Assessment prepared under commission by the physicist Ashton B. Carter[29] and a report prepared by the Union of Concerned Scientists,[30] under the direction of physicists Hans Bethe, Kurt Gottfried, and Richard Garwin, other defenders of SDI began to be heard from. One spokesman was Robert Jastrow, a professor at Dartmouth who had been director of the NASA Goddard Space Flight Center. Using data supplied by the pro-SDI scientists at Los Alamos, Jastrow disputed the figures that the UCS used to show that an SDI system would be impossibly expensive.[31] The UCS had calculated that in order to achieve adequate coverage against the existing Soviet ICBM force, the United States would have to orbit a fleet of more than two hundred satellites. Jastrow claimed the real number was closer to one hundred. The UCS conceded that its original calculation was in error, pointing out that the mistake had been corrected before its testimony was presented to Congress, but it also argued that Jastrow's numbers rested on unrealistic assumptions about the brightness that could be achieved by chemical lasers and other relevant parameters. This phase of the debate was soon superseded, when attention shifted away from chemical lasers based on battle satellites toward a combination of kinetic weapons parked in "garages" in space and beam weapons fired from ground-based systems such as the free-electron or excimer laser using presumably cheap mirrors capable of being proliferated at low cost.

The anti-SDI forces were spearheaded by the UCS and the FAS. The FAS maintained a resident space specialist, John E. Pike, to comment on the program and to study its various facets, including the relationship of SDI to the ABM Treaty, the pattern of contracting, and the relationship of SDI to arms control. Both the UCS and FAS issued a drumbeat of reports critical of the project.

A subsidiary theme in the quarrel over the SDI has long been the question of its applicability to the nation's civil industry. Supporters, notably Keyworth, argue that SDI would be a tonic for U.S. high-technology industry. Knowledgeable skeptics like Harvey Brooks complain that SDI is an altogether inadequate substitute for a national science policy. Brooks notes that military projects tend to be directed toward narrow objectives and to yield products and processes that are of limited value in the civil economy, partly because of security restrictions but also because of the growing incompatibility of military (especially space) technology and civil needs.[32] John P. Holdren and F. Bailey Green argue that far from promoting useful spin-offs, SDI is likely to divert critically needed talent and resources from the civil sector and make the country even less competitive in civil markets.[33]

The anti-SDI forces also gained strength from the circulation of a variety of petitions and opinion surveys. A petition circulated by a group of physicists at Cornell University and the University of Illinois at Urbana-Champaign among physics departments in the nation's universities was signed by some 6,500 faculty members and graduate students, who pledged not to accept funds for research on SDI. The signers included majorities of the faculties at the nation's twenty leading departments.[34] In response to a questionnaire sent to members of the prestigious National Academy of Sciences (NAS) a large majority of respondents declared SDI's goals neither feasible nor desirable.[35] Another petition, initiated at AT&T Bell Laboratories and circulated among researchers employed in government and industrial laboratories, called for a curb on appropriations for SDI (but did not commit the signatories to boycott SDI-related projects). This petition, which had 1,600 signatures, took the form of an open letter to Congress urging that support for SDI be limited "to a scale appropriate to exploratory research."[36] A poll taken by the UCS of 549 randomly selected members of the American Physical Society found that SDI was criticized as "a step in the wrong direction" by 54 percent of the respondents who did not oppose other military R & D; 29 percent were in favor.[37]

A counterpetition was circulated by a group of eighty scientists and engineers led by Frederick Seitz, a former NAS president. This petition chided those who opposed SDI for being unfaithful to the scientific method. Instead of condemning the project in advance, "hastily, unscientifically, or ideologically," the petitioners urged their fellow scientists to allow it to continue until the prospects for strategic defense could be fairly evaluated.[38]

Conflict over SDI also flared dramatically into the open in 1988 when Roy D. Woodruff, associate director of defense systems at Livermore, made public his complaint that Teller and others at the laboratory were passing on their own overoptimistic assessments of progress on the X-ray laser to senior officials, including Nitze and McFarlane, as though they reflected the views of the laboratory. In October 1985 Woodruff had resigned his position in protest, charging that he had been put in an "untenable position" because he had been denied an opportunity to show that Teller and Wood were "overselling" the program. Although Woodruff was subsequently reassigned to a new post, and a General Accounting Office inquiry found that several Livermore officials, including Woodruff himself, had made statements about the X-ray laser that had been no less optimistic than Teller's, it was also reported that Woodruff had specifically taken issue with Teller's claim, as early as December 1983, that research had been so successful that the laser was ready "for engineering." Woodruff eventually decided to file a personal grievance with the president of the University of California (which operates the laboratory under contract to the Department of Energy) that he had been "constructively demoted" because Teller and Wood "undercut my management responsibility for the X-ray laser program and conveyed both orally and in writing overly optimistic, technically incorrect statements regarding this research to the nation's highest policy makers."[39]

SCIENTIFIC JUDGMENT
AND POLITICAL COMMITMENT

What significance should be attached to the expressions of dissent among scientists not at work on SDI is an intriguing and difficult question. In what proportions does the controversy among the scientists and

engineers reflect scientific judgment or political commitment? Many of
the physicists who signed the Cornell-Illinois petition are probably not
directly conversant with defense research and receive their research support from the National Science Foundation and other nonmilitary agencies. Strong opposition at the universities has not prevented SDIO from
placing a large number of projects with university scientists. SDIO officials even claimed to have set up university-industry consortia, though
this claim aroused protests from university administrators who noted
that contracts accepted by individual researchers did not imply institutional endorsement. Some of the opposition among scientists clearly
does not arise solely from scientific judgment. Many university physicists were apt to oppose the Reagan administration and its policies, including SDI, on political grounds. Even many of the critics agree, moreover, that some level of expenditure on strategic-defense research is
warranted as a hedge against the possibility that the Soviets might stage
a breakout from the ABM Treaty and might deploy certain space-based
defensive technologies. Some also suggest that the United States might
profitably consider the deployment of defenses aimed at protecting
retaliatory capacity and command and control.

A similar division of scientific opinion was expressed in congressional hearings on the proposed deployment of ABMs in the 1960s.
Then, too, as Harvey Brooks notes, policy views were couched in the
form of technical judgments to suit political purposes:

> Many of the technical witnesses, on both sides, were really motivated by
> strategic policy considerations, or their personal evaluations of the inter-
> national situation, or the supposed intentions of the Soviets, but their politi-
> cal allies found it more politic for them to couch their arguments in narrow
> technical terms, partly because technical experts are often automatically re-
> garded as having nothing useful to say on policy matters. Furthermore, tech-
> nical testimony appears more "objective" and politically neutral, and it is
> thus thought to carry more weight with those politicians who have not yet
> made up their minds.[40]

Professional and personal interests are also at play. Some of those
who do military R & D are no doubt committed to SDI because they see
it as a source of continued funding, especially if the need for research on
offensive weapons tapers off. In view of the many technical problems
that remain to be addressed in order to perfect offensive systems, however, such self-interest seems an unlikely explanation for the attitudes of
researchers—although industrial laboratories and firms may have their
eyes on the vast potential represented by defensive procurement con-

tracts. Some scientists may believe, as David L. Parnas has charged, that even if nothing militarily useful can come of SDI, something beneficial can come for the specialties in which they work.[41] In that sense professional curiosity and self-interest may be a motivating factor for some of the scientists. In the case of some of the younger scientists, it is also possible that a desire to do something new and better than their elders is at play. Some of the scientists who work on military projects generally, including SDI, believe they have a duty to contribute to the national security of the United States and the security of the West generally, because, generally speaking, the United States has used its power for benign purposes whereas the Soviet Union is an aggressive, expansionist power whose leaders cannot be trusted. Still others view the world as a system of sovereign states with little law and no law enforcement governing the relations among them, and they argue that even if they did not do the research, someone else would. Motives are undoubtedly as varied and complex in this area as they are in others.

On the side of the critics, there seems to be a more explicit political motivation. Generally, those who are ready to renounce funding for SDI and are otherwise dubious about the motivations behind SDI argue that the political forces promoting it are eager to avoid arms control because they do not fear nuclear war as much as they fear Soviet superiority. In their view, the aim of SDI is not the president's benign goal of making nuclear weapons "impotent and obsolete" (because that is widely recognized to be unattainable) but a panoply of much less benign motivations: to challenge the Soviets to an expensive race in high-technology weapons development that they would lose, to establish a military presence in space for offensive as well as defensive purposes, and to sustain the military-industrial complex by promoting a new phase in the military competition between the superpowers. Whatever the goal, they argue, the result of the competition would be to make the world less stable and to promote the chances of nuclear war, because the Soviet response would include the development of a stronger offensive force and resistance to any proposals for arms control. In general, they perceived the Reagan administration to be guided by an obsessive anticommunism and mistrust of arms control, ironically at a time when, because of a major change in the Soviet leadership, the U.S.S.R. is more open than ever to the possibility of serious arms reduction and a renewal of détente with the West. If SDI had not been deliberately contrived for aggressive purposes, they suggest, the administration should have been willing to trade it away as a bargaining chip in negotiations.

The report prepared by a panel appointed by the American Physical Society (APS) suggests that despite these very real political differences— which produce powerful effects in promoting policy commitments—the structure of scientific evidence and thinking is such that consensus is possible on a good many, if not all, of the main technical points. Scientists are apt to disagree about what can be accomplished over what span of time and at what level of effort, but they do not disagree much about what is known and what is yet to be accomplished. The APS report makes it clear that some of the proposed technologies are at least theoretically conceivable, but it also points out that the most important of them are still orders of magnitude away from producing the energies or power necessary to be useful in defensive systems. Even if the technical parameters are met, the report cautions, it remains to be seen whether the devices will prove feasible as weapons or will be less expensive to deploy than offensive systems that could overwhelm or evade them.

In political terms, the APS report was widely considered hostile to SDI. Journalistic accounts emphasized the report's conclusion that it would be many years before the feasibility of space-based beam weapons could be demonstrated. That much was correct, and insofar as SDI has been perceived as a program that promises a quick answer to the question, the report was properly considered critical. If SDI is perceived as a research program, however, the report is not so much a critique as a status report. Nevertheless, it did not satisfy enthusiasts for SDI. In a presentation to the House Republican Research Committee in May 1987, two active SDI researchers, Lowell Wood and Gregory Canavan, criticized both the press coverage of the APS report and the report itself.[42] As we note in chapter 3, their charges provoked a rebuttal that left the report's findings undisturbed.

The SDI is only the latest chapter in a division among physicists that opened once the atomic bomb was developed and used against Japan. Until then, disagreements had been muted for the sake of winning the war against Nazi Germany. Once the war was over, a split developed that reflected differing appraisals of the need to gain control over atomic warfare and the possibility of rapprochement with the Soviets. Scientists took different views of defense policy, first with respect to containment, then with respect to the strategy of deterrence and arms control. Many have continued to work on weapons even though they may have disagreed with various aspects of government policy. They do so partly to continue to have some access to policymakers and thus to have influence over policy, partly because they are fascinated by the technology, but in general because they are committed both to the design of military technology and to the effort to achieve their different policy goals. When Hans Bethe came to Livermore and acknowledged that the idea behind the X-ray laser was scientifically sound, Teller felt vindicated. In an open letter to Bethe in 1986, Teller criticized the scientists who had opposed SDI in the NAS poll, lamenting that the "World War II unanimity of the scientific community" in developing nuclear weapons had been lost. "I am writing this letter," Teller asserted, "in the hope that you and others may find some way to move from polemic debate and confrontation toward technical criticism, understanding, and cooperation."[43] Behind the show of indignation, however, lies a reluctance to acknowledge that more is at stake than the accuracy of a scientific theory or line of work. Teller and Bethe—and the scientists who align themselves with both— disagree about what is to be done with such weapons and how their use can be prevented. Both sides are inevitably enmeshed in a political struggle to organize constituencies for and against SDI.

ORGANIZING A CONSTITUENCY: SDIO AND THE CONTRACTORS

As Erik Pratt, John E. Pike, and Daniel Lindley have pointed out, although the formal rationale for SDI is that it is a research program to determine whether comprehensive strategic defenses are feasible and desirable—a program that is not intended to lead to a decision to develop or deploy until after the term of the Reagan administration—the expenditure of funds in this phase of the project will help build a constituency in favor of its continuation:

> Before a formal deployment decision can be made, SDIO will have spent billions of dollars and involved hundreds of institutions and thousands of individuals. In the process, many of these people and organizations will have acquired vested interests in SDI and in the deployment of strategic defense systems. For many government organizations, research labs, and universities, SDI will provide a large share of the budget. For defense firms, SDI will be the source of significant profits. For some individuals, careers and promotions will be determined by the progress of the strategic defense program. As a result, these vested interests will become part of the "Star Wars constituency," seeking to influence policy and control decisions concerning strategic defense.[44]

This statement puts the argument sharply, perhaps too sharply. Not all of the institutions and individuals engaged in SDI work have an *exclusive* interest in its perpetuation. They are often also engaged in other types of military research. For instance, the nuclear-weapons laboratories did not expand to accommodate work on SDI. As the program grows, it attracts people from elsewhere in the laboratories and, as an SDI project is completed, they may well shift to other work, so they do not necessarily have the same vested interest in SDI as other organizations would whose entire raison d'être is predicated on it. It is misleading to suggest that corporations engaged in SDI work depend on it for profits. Whereas military procurement has had a "critical role" in the growth of defense industries, military R & D spending has had "a much more modest role."[45] It is only insofar as R & D work may lead to procurement that profits enter the picture in a significant way, and in some cases the firms that are likely to secure the procurement contracts are not the same as those that carry out the R & D. Nevertheless, there is good reason to suppose that the expenditure of large sums of money on SDI will create a constituency interested in perpetuating it. By the time a decision must be made to move to the stage of development, at least $20 billion is likely to have been spent on the research phase. The development stage would involve far higher expenditures.

For most of the contractors, SDI's importance is accentuated by the fact that several of the large strategic programs, such as the B-1B, MX, and Trident II, are now being completed. New "black" or secret programs—like "stealthy" bombers, fighters, and cruise missiles—have been taking up any slack. Had it not been for SDI, however, funding of military R & D might have been reduced. As the new systems are deployed, SDI could become the major source for continued military R & D funding and for deployment contracts. Because deployment could involve much larger sums—estimates range from hundreds of billions to a trillion or more dollars—the stakes could be very high.[46] Interest in the defense contracting community in SDI has been keen. The contractors sent 1,200 representatives to an initial classified briefing. During the first three years of the project, 2,210 SDI-related contracts were awarded to 510 different entities.[47] These entities are located in the private, university, and government sectors and also include federally funded research and development centers (FFRDCs) as well as foreign contractors. Some 331 business firms and 15 nonprofit corporations have been engaged in SDI research, along with 14 of the 38 FFRDCs, entities that perform research on behalf of government agencies but are administered by nonprofit organizations. Two such FFRDCs are the Livermore and Los Alamos laboratories, both of which have played leading roles in SDI research. SDI work has also been performed at eighty-one campuses and in sixty-seven U.S. government agencies. The largest share of the funds—almost three-quarters—has gone to the private contractors. Another 20 percent has gone to the FFRDCs. The remaining 5 percent is divided among the others, with universities accounting for 2.7 percent, U.S. government agencies for 2.3 percent, and foreign contractors for only .4 percent.[48]

Among the private contractors, awards tend to be concentrated among relatively few firms that inevitably develop an interest in promoting various SDI programs. The top one hundred SDI contractors account for 95 percent of the total, the remaining four hundred plus for less than 5 percent. This concentration is even higher than is generally the case in defense work, where the top one hundred contractors receive 88.3 percent of total prime contract awards. Ten firms alone account for 53.1 percent of total SDI awards, five for 42 percent.[49] More than 90 percent of space weapons' prime contracts in FY1983 went to four states: California (45 percent), Washington (22 percent), Texas (13 percent), and Alabama (10 percent); 77 percent went to states or districts represented by House and Senate members who sit on the armed services committees and appropriations defense subcommittees. Thus, the program promotes possibilities for conflict of interest for both legislators and contractors. Contractors with much to gain "have been assigned the task of both developing and assessing the technical feasibility and strategic advisability of proceeding beyond the research and development phase."[50]

As the program moves out of the concept-definition stage—in accordance with the "horse race" scheme adopted by Abrahamson—fewer contractors are selected for the succeeding stages, and the value of the contracts grows larger. The horse-race idea was originally employed for the study and development of alternative architectures. Contractors would be eliminated when a particular architecture (or a smaller set) was chosen for more detailed analysis. Four contractors were awarded Phase I contracts for the development of the National Test Bed. Two teams, one led by Martin Marietta, the other by Rockwell, were selected for the second phase, and Martin Marietta was chosen as prime contractor for the construction of the facility, possibly worth $1 billion. Because the prime contractors distribute some of these large amounts to subcontractors, the constituency remains fairly large, despite the concentration of the awards, as measured by prime contracts.

Although SDI support for university research remains relatively small, it contributes to a growing trend toward increasing dependence of university researchers on military R&D support. As a fraction of all federal support for university R&D, the DOD share rose from 11.6 percent in FY1980 to 16.7 percent in FY1986. In constant dollars, DOD funding for university research during the Reagan years nearly reached the level attained in the peak years of the Vietnam War.[51] This dependence could dampen university protests against SDI, particularly in view of the comments by at least one DOD official, Donald A. Hicks, under secretary for research and engineering, who pointedly noted that although university researchers may be free to criticize DOD programs, the DOD is free not to provide them with support. During his Senate confirmation hearing on July 25, 1985, Hicks said: "I am not particularly interested in seeing department money going in someplace where an individual is outspoken in his rejection of department aims, even for basic research." In an interview with a reporter from *Science,* Hicks confirmed his belief that critics of defense policy should not expect research support from the DOD: "If they want to get out and use their role as professors to make statements, that's fine. It's a free country, [but] freedom works both ways. They're free to keep their mouths shut, [and] I'm also free not to give money." The DOD later claimed that Hicks was expressing his own views rather than department policy,[52] but the warning had been delivered.

The general point properly made by critics is that all support, even in relatively modest amounts, can serve to co-opt potential critics, or at least generate self-interested acquiescence, both domestically and abroad. But the point should not be exaggerated. An offsetting factor is that many of the largest firms are so large that SDI work constitutes only a small fraction of their total budgets. General Motors (GM), the second-largest SDI contractor, had net sales in 1985 of more than $102 billion. Less than one-tenth of 1 percent of the total came from SDI work done by Hughes Aircraft, a division then newly acquired by GM. Even for Hughes, however, which had annual sales of $6 billion, SDI became more significant in 1985 and could become still more so. For a number of other firms, SDI already represents 20 percent or more of their R&D contracts. By "buying in" early, they can hope to receive even larger amounts in the future and thus gain an inside-track position from which to compete for far more lucrative procurement contracts. For smaller firms, SDI contracting can be a very substantial part of their business—without which they would not survive. One such company, Sparta, whose president had served on the Fletcher Committee, had a nearly 1600 percent sales increase between 1981 and 1985, owing in large part to SDI contracts. Close to half the companies highly dependent on SDI

R & D funding are located in Huntsville, Alabama, near the army's Strategic Defense Command.[53]

Four FFRDCs perform 96.2 percent of all SDI work awarded to these institutions: Livermore, Los Alamos, Sandia, and Lincoln laboratories. At the first two, SDI-funded work grew to about 12 percent of the budget by 1985; at Lincoln, which does virtually all of the work on SATKA, the SDI budget grew to 22 percent of the total.[54] At these laboratories, government-established priorities set the pace for research efforts, and SDI is considered a major challenge, particularly for younger researchers. The competition among the laboratories, especially between Livermore and Los Alamos, is clearly evident in their competing designs for a free-electron laser. This rivalry is helpful because it provides critical reviews of ongoing programs and a stimulus to advance the project. Los Alamos scientists, for example, raised questions about the quality of Livermore's X-ray laser research and testing. The involvement of the various laboratories and industrial contractors makes it inevitable that those involved in the work will have a significant degree of influence over the evaluation of what has been achieved and the decision to move on to the next stages. Defense-review panels rarely include critics. At the same time, the greater the involvement, the less likely that laboratory representatives will favor terminating the projects altogether.

In addition, conflicts of interest arise because so many former military officers and DOD civilian employees enter employment with defense contractors once they leave their Pentagon positions. Although federal law requires that such employees notify the DOD if they join a defense contractor within two years of leaving the government's employ, a GAO study in 1986 concluded that only 30 percent of those who were required to file a report actually did so and that many others were exempt from reporting on technical grounds. The DOD, which has no institutional interest in closing the revolving door, has not been active in enforcing the requirement. In 1985, of the ten contractors with the most former DOD employees, nine were major SDI contractors. Several key figures in SDIO had previous jobs with defense industries and have taken subsequent positions with firms heavily engaged in SDI work. Although this flow between DOD and the laboratories and industrial firms is inevitable as both seek to obtain the best-qualified personnel, the result is that a strong relationship of shared assumptions is created, which is bound to affect judgments about research priorities. Thousands of jobs are already at stake, and a drastic cutback in SDI would have serious consequences.[55]

The existence of such a constituency is certainly a real enough phenomenon, and its potential role is evident from previous cases, when defense contractors helped to stimulate initiation and perpetuation of projects that might have languished on purely military or economic grounds. Whether such constituency pressure will be enough to promote an increase of support for SDI is at least questionable, at this stage, especially in view of the opposition SDI has met in Congress. The existence of a constituency is not an automatic guarantee of its success, especially given the general interest of that constituency in defense funding, which can be spent on systems other than those under study in SDI. Even with respect to strategic defense, this constituency has actually restrained the more radical proposals for SDI. Staunch supporters of SDI have argued that the program is suffering in the hands of defense officials who do not share Reagan's belief in the possibility of a fundamental shift away from offense to defense, and a leakproof defense at that. Thus, the constituency could just as well frustrate the more radical dreams of SDI advocates as promote them. By emphasizing near-term options that can serve mainly to protect retaliatory capacities, they may actually be undermining support for the president's emphasis on a long-term effort to develop population defenses.

It is equally a mistake to suppose that all those who are in the employ of FFRDCs and industrial contractors are venal and will thus support any program that promises to provide them with research funding. They must recognize that funds for one program may come at the expense of others. They may have conflicting interests, which could lead them to prefer non-SDI programs to SDI, particularly if they work on technologies that lose out in the research phase. Those who work at FFRDCs are presumably freer to put their professional judgment ahead of their vested interests, if only because they cannot benefit from follow-on procurement contracts. When decisions have to be made to enter into development and procurement, their independent judgment could be crucial in blocking efforts by industrial contractors to promote the adoption of programs that are not likely to work.

Still, the actual experience of such costly failures as the division air defense (DIVAD) anti-aircraft gun suggests that the DOD does not have adequate mechanisms for ensuring unbiased appraisals and may be too reliant on the judgments of contractors who work closely with procurement officers. Both groups have a vested interest in not canceling expensive projects, even though they are not performing as expected. In order to assure that decisions with respect to development and deployment of strategic systems are not unduly influenced by the assessments of their sponsors, better reviewing mechanisms may well be needed. The experience with DIVAD indicates that the influence of supporters can keep a program going even though it is not meeting prescribed goals. But it also shows that the truth cannot be suppressed indefinitely. Experience with strategic defenses is similar. Twice before, the United States has gone a long way down the road of deploying defenses. Each time, the effort was strongly supported by vested interests. Each time, however, the nation drew back when technical considerations as well as military and strategic factors made the efforts seem unattainable.

CONGRESS AND SDI: THE BATTLE FOR
THE FUTURE OF THE PROJECT

The Reagan administration's campaign for SDI ran into difficulty for several reasons. It was launched at a time when Congress was generally eager to assert a stronger constitutional role in foreign policy—an attitude originally generated by the Vietnam War but strengthened during the nuclear-freeze campaign when many members of Congress came to feel that they alone represented their constituents' concerns at a time when the administration was ignoring them. Arms control was so low on the agenda of the Reagan administration that many Democrats in Congress came to feel that if it were to be promoted actively, they would have to be the ones to do so. Members of Congress were influenced by the strong opposition to SDI from the scientific community and by the skepticism they knew prevailed within the Pentagon itself. In addition, their own Office of Technology Assessment produced reports that cast serious doubts on the project. Many in Congress seemed to conclude that although they might risk the ire of the voters by challenging the entire basis of SDI, they would be safe in taking a skeptical attitude by keeping appropriations below those requested and by insisting that the program conform to the ABM Treaty. Although the president was able to quiet some of the opposition in Congress by arguing that it ought not to tie his hands in negotiations with the Soviets before Reykjavík, the failure of that meeting to produce an agreement and the administration's insistence on promoting its reinterpretation of the treaty provoked a strong response from the Democrats, especially after they gained control of both houses of Congress in the 1986 election during which the president had made SDI an issue. When the voters ignored his request for support, SDI critics were all the more emboldened.

In the immediate aftermath of the president's SDI speech, both support and opposition appeared in Congress, but neither was very strong. The division developed along party lines, particularly as the issue was injected into the 1984 election campaign. When Mondale charged that the proposal would militarize the heavens, the president responded that SDI was a research program—something even Mondale admitted was advisable—and argued that it was right to try to replace mutual assured destruction by a system that promised mutual assured survival. The president's personal popularity was a major factor in his reelection, but his policies were also popular. On the domestic front, the economy had revived after a shaky start, and the tax cut was widely approved. In foreign affairs the president's bold approach had restored a sense of direction and patriotism, even though there were significant failures not only in arms control but also in the abortive peace-keeping effort in Lebanon in 1983. SDI did nothing to detract from the president's electoral appeal. Accordingly, congressional opposition was muted.

As SDI became a more contentious issue, both in arms-control negotiations and domestically in the appropriations process, a group of Republicans emerged as strong champions. Senators Wallop, Quayle, and Pete Wilson, and Representatives Kemp (N.Y.) and Jim Courter (N.J.) came to be known as the "Gang of Five." In 1986 they became convinced that the anti-SDI forces had settled on a strategy of not attacking SDI directly and vigorously but, instead, of allowing it to proceed at only a low level of support. If no decision were made during the Reagan administration to exceed the testing limits of the ABM Treaty or to schedule deployment, a new administration might kill the program altogether. Otherwise, the program might simply wither away, as momentum was lost and public enthusiasm waned. The same fear was shared by others sympathetic to SDI. SDIO's former chief scientist, Gerold Yonas, wondered if the U.S. public had the patience to support a long-term project that had no immediate payoff. "It's the ultimate Catch-22," he observed: "Congress won't provide the funding unless you are serious. And yet you can't be serious without funding. The fundamental problem is with organizational psyche. We want instant gratification. Rather than discuss early deployment, the nation should debate capability, survivability, and feasibility—those are the real issues." [56] Experienced legislators like former president Gerald R. Ford warned that Congress would not continue to vote large amounts of money for SDI unless it could be assured that the research phase would be followed by deployment. [57]

To counter the presumed strategy of the Democrats, congressional supporters of SDI urged the administration to adopt the "broad interpretation" of the ABM Treaty so as to permit advanced testing and, if necessary, to consider abrogating the treaty altogether. Late in 1986 Senator Wallop and Representative Kemp wrote a letter to the president in which they noted that to defer a deployment decision for five to seven years, as originally contemplated, "would place the United States in a no-win position and the Russians in a no-lose position." In an article in the conservative *National Review*, Kemp argued that SDI was the most important single initiative of the Reagan administration and that it would be the key issue of the 1988 presidential campaign. He made it clear that he at least was prepared to make it the key issue in his campaign for the Republican nomination. Kemp argued that the Democrats in effect should be "smoked out" on the issue, forced to reveal their true opposition to SDI rather than be allowed to appear supportive when in fact they were attempting to starve the program and stretch it out.[58]

Among the opponents of SDI, the leading figures were a number of Democrats, including Alan Cranston (California), J. Bennett Johnston (Louisiana), William Proxmire (Wisconsin) in the Senate, and George Brown (California) and Thomas Downy (New York) in the House. Proxmire and Johnston, along with senators Lawton Chiles (D., Fla.) and Dale Bumpers (D., Ark.), instructed members of their staff to prepare reports on the actual progress of the program. Three reports were prepared in consecutive years. The first, submitted March 17, 1986, reported on the basis of interviews with researchers that, contrary to some reports, there had been "no major breakthroughs" that promised to make deployment in the 1990s of comprehensive defenses any more feasible than it had been at the start of the project. The staff members found that the "schedule-driven" nature of the research had, in fact, aroused apprehensions among scientists at the national weapons laboratories by threatening to compromise long-term research to suit an arbitrary schedule and to promote a public-relations style of research. (SDI, said one senior Livermore scientist, was degenerating into "a series of sleazy stunts.") The results so far, they reported, had shown that the job of creating a boost-phase defense would be even harder than initially thought, and that other problems, such as the logistics of orbiting the needed hardware, were even more daunting because of the shuttle accident. In general, the report noted that although SDI continued to have broad bipartisan support as a research project, the pace at which it ought to be pursued and the direction it should take remained contentious issues.[59]

On March 19, 1987, the three staff members submitted a second, updated report, in response to a request from Proxmire and Johnston, who specifically asked them to examine the effort to commit the country to a "near-term" deployment. They reported that if the president were to announce such a decision, there would be nothing ready to deploy, but they noted that SDIO was indeed reorienting the program to pursue near-term deployment, possibly in the 1994–95 time frame, even without a formal presidential request. Accordingly, SDIO had cut back its directed-energy program drastically and increased the kinetic-energy weapon budget. In a number of cases, more innovative technologies were being scaled down to permit greater emphasis on the near-term option. In particular, the office was emphasizing the rapid development of the space-based kinetic kill vehicle (SBKKVs) to pursue a near-term deployment in the mid 1990s. Such a system would have a more limited capability than the one previously discussed as essential for boost-phase interception. They had been informed that SDIO had a "black" program for "developing a reference architecture for a near-term deployment of strategic defenses"—a program hidden from most members of Congress. Based on what they claimed was a careful review, the staff members estimated that the near-term system contemplated by SDIO would have an effectiveness of no more than 16 percent against Soviet ballistic missile warheads. The system would comprise SBKKVs—since renamed space-based interceptors (SBI)—and ground-based ERIS missiles. Again they reported that SDI researchers were extremely unhappy over the reorientation of the program toward near-term deployment. While noting again that progress had been made in the research, they found no significant breakthroughs in the effort to achieve a comprehensive defense.[60]

After the second report was presented, the issue of adherence to the Nitze criteria became a bone of contention between the SDIO and its congressional critics, as the third Senate staff report, issued in June 1988, made abundantly clear. Formally, the Nitze criteria were endorsed by administration officials. "Within the SDI research program," a State Department report asserted, "we will judge defenses to be desirable only if they are survivable and cost-effective at the margin. . . . We intend to consider . . . the degree to which certain types of defensive systems by their very nature, encourage an adversary to try simply to overwhelm them with additional offensive forces."[61] In congressional testimony on October 30, 1985, Lieutenant General Abrahamson also endorsed the Nitze criteria: "We will not proceed to development and deployment unless the research indicates that the defenses meet strict criteria: Within the SDI research program, we will judge defenses to be desirable only if they are survivable and cost-effective at the margin." [62]

To ensure that the administration would adhere to these commitments, Congress enacted them into law in 1985 in the Department of Defense Authorization Act of 1986 (P.L. 99-145), adopting an amendment introduced by Senator Proxmire. The provision spells out the meaning of the criteria and requires presidential certification of their observance as a condition for recommending deployment:

> A strategic defense system developed as a consequence of research, development, test, and evaluation conducted in the Strategic Defense Initiative program may not be deployed in whole or in part unless—
> (1) the President determines and certifies to Congress in writing that—
>   (A) the system is survivable (that is, the system is able to maintain a sufficient degree of effectiveness to fulfill its mission, even in the face of determined attacks against it); and
>   (B) the system is cost effective at the margin to the extent that the system is able to maintain its defense at less cost than it would take to develop offensive countermeasures and proliferate the ballistic missiles necessary to overcome it; and
> (2) funding for the deployment of such system has been specifically authorized by legislation enacted after the date on which the President makes the certification to Congress. [63]

Senate and House conferees agreed that the terms of the law would permit deployment of particular systems that might form parts of a future strategic defense, provided that their primary purpose was not strategic defense at the time of initial deployment. Thus, sensor satellites could be deployed for conventional surveillance purposes without assurance that the Nitze criteria were being observed.

As the SDIO sought to press ahead with plans for early deployment, however, its officials sought to broaden the meaning of the criteria and to treat them as guidelines rather than restrictions. In May 1986 Abrahamson suggested that the criteria ought not to be construed so narrowly as to defeat the larger goal of national policy:

> The reason that many people, including us, were worried about cost-effective at the margin is for the fundamental principle: we are trying to get the Russians to modify their behavior. . . . There may be many reasons for wanting to make a positive judgment that we can or cannot go forward. And it shouldn't be our criteria; it should be our best judgment about what will produce the best results for our nation both in terms of Soviet behavior and our capability. . . . [The Nitze standard] shouldn't be defined so narrowly as to preclude a deployment that would be sound for other reasons. [64]

The 1986 SDIO annual report ignored the Nitze criteria altogether and instead laid down four different criteria, much easier to meet, that would justify deployment:

Potential role in U.S. strategy

Deterrent to surprise attack and enemy escalation

Contribution to our arms control objectives

Technical feasibility

In lieu of cost-effectiveness at the margin, the report asserted that "affordability" ought to be the economic standard. By this measure, the trade-off between the comparative cost of U.S. defenses and Soviet countermeasures could simply be ignored. When SDIO was criticized in Congress for failing to maintain the second of the Nitze criteria, its rebuttal came in a May 1987 report. Here the agency restated its adherence to the criterion but sought to diminish its significance as a basis for a deployment decision by observing that it is "much more than an economic concept." As the Senate staff report noted, this formulation was a rather obvious effort on the part of the organization to gain some maneuvering room. Nevertheless, it could not escape the requirement laid down by Congress that in order to request any deployment of strategic defenses, the president must certify that both of the Nitze criteria have been met.[65]

The Senate report reaffirmed an earlier finding that SDIO had altered the program's original mandate: "The goal of completing the research by the early 1990s to determine if comprehensive ballistic missile defenses were feasible has evolved into making a decision by the early 1990s as to whether a 'thin' ballistic missile system embodied in Phase I is feasible."[66] The report charged that contrary to the agency's claim that programs earmarked for Phase I deployment would receive only 14 percent of the FY1989 budget request, these programs would actually be consuming 50 percent of the budget, if relevant program elements carrying other designations were counted. The report contended that the agency was sacrificing long-term research projects to promote near-term candidates for deployment. Furthermore, although SDIO officials had advised Congress that the costs of the contemplated Phase I deployment would be between $40 to $100 billion or more, the SDIO's own figures indicated that life-cycle costs for Phase I would be as high as $171 billion—an estimate virtually identical to the one arrived at in the

Marshall Institute study, whose authors claimed to be relying on SDIO calculations.[67]

The Senate report found that the proposed deployment could not be justified either on technological grounds or on grounds of survivability. The decision to press for early deployment—or, as the SDIO preferred, "phased deployment"—was not made because of technological breakthroughs: "The brightness proposed for a prototype chemical laser [under consideration for Phase I deployment] is exactly that described in the Fletcher report as 'not worthy of early deployment.'" As to survivability, the report noted that even proponents of the initiative worry that the large satellites contemplated as weapons carriers would be extremely vulnerable—"the aircraft carriers of space."[68]

Both the early-deployment issue and the interpretation of the ABM Treaty came in for a great deal of attention in the winter and spring of 1987. On March 11 Senate Minority Leader Robert Dole (R., Kan.), along with senators Quayle, Wallop, and Wilson, wrote to Weinberger advising him that he must submit a report on near-term applications of SDI or find funding "much more difficult." This request was formally mandated in the 1987 Defense Authorization bill. One Democrat, Sen. Ernest Hollings (D., S.C.), joined the Republicans in criticizing his fellow Democrats who called for a compromise on the ABM Treaty to permit a strategic-arms-control agreement with the Soviets. To compromise on the treaty, he argued, is to compromise and end SDI.[69]

The major development in Congress, however, was the decision of Sen. Sam Nunn, chairman of the Senate Armed Services Committee, to challenge the new interpretation of the ABM treaty. Nunn had become the Democrats' bellwether on defense, along with Les Aspin (D., Wis.) in the House. A political centrist, he had been known for supporting most of the Reagan strategic-modernization efforts, concentrating on examining the particulars and the implementation of the program. In March of 1987 he took to the floor of the Senate to attack the administration's effort to reinterpret the ABM Treaty, arguing that when the Senate ratified the treaty, it did so on the understanding that contrary to the administration's reinterpretation, testing in space was prohibited. For the administration now to reinterpret the treaty would therefore provoke a "constitutional confrontation" with Congress. The administration, said Nunn, was "wrong in its analysis of the Senate ratification debate, wrong in its analysis of subsequent practice . . . and wrong in its analysis of the negotiating record itself." Nunn castigated the State Department's legal advisor, Judge Sofaer, for not conducting a rigorous study of the ratification process, and Sofaer subsequently conceded that Nunn was correct in this aspect of his complaint, but blamed the failure on inexperienced staff members. After examining the record of the negotiations, Nunn concluded that although there were ambiguities in the negotiating record, these were not as important with respect to the interpretive issues as either the treaty itself or the interpretation of the treaty by both U.S. and Soviet officials and that both the United States and the Soviet Union had, in fact, adopted the view that the treaty banned the development of space-based systems. Nunn also pointed out that the space-based kinetic kill vehicles contemplated for early deployment could not be deployed within the terms of the treaty because they would include a mobile system incorporating technology not in use when the treaty was signed.[70]

A new phalanx of opposition to early deployment and the broad interpretation coalesced around Nunn, including Johnston, Proxmire, Carl Levin (D., Mich.), and Paul Simon (D., Ill.). Budget resolutions were introduced in both the House and Senate stipulating that funding for SDI be made conditional on adherence to the traditional interpretation of the ABM Treaty. In the Senate, thirty-four Republicans signed a letter urging the president to veto any such provision—enough to sustain a veto. The Democrats rejoined that in the event Reagan decided to veto and the veto was sustained, they would move to cut funding in retaliation. Eventually a tacit understanding was reached and a confrontation was avoided.

These stirrings on Capitol Hill were not the result only of concern over SDI. They also reflected a desire on the part of many lawmakers to play a more active role in defense policy. This interest had been building for some time. Until the Vietnam War, Congress generally was content to accept a more passive role in defense and foreign policy. From World War II to Vietnam, as Edward Weisband observes, presidents were "formulating bold and forward-looking policies for the nation while an unimaginative Congress appeared to be hindering those efforts and defending special interests."[71] Many came to believe, even on Capitol Hill, that Congress was too decentralized and that individual members were too independent and too parochial for the legislature to play more of a role in formulating foreign policy—a role that was in any case assigned by the Constitution primarily to the executive. In 1973, however, Congress passed the War Powers Act sharply limiting the power of the executive to commit troops to battle. In 1974–75 it conducted a review of intelligence activities, which led to legislation affecting covert actions.

From 1974 to 1978 it prohibited military sales to Turkey over the objections of the Carter administration. In 1979 congressional opposition contributed to President Carter's decision not to submit the SALT II Treaty for ratification. In the Reagan administration, congressional opposition to arms sales to Saudi Arabia compelled the president to undertake an extraordinary lobbying effort.

Well before the advent of the Reagan administration, Congress's increasing activism in foreign policy led a number of observers to predict that Congress would be a force to be reckoned with in this area, and their predictions have been amply borne out. Thus, in 1976 Graham Allison and Peter Szanton observed that "congressional involvement will make the largest single difference between foreign policy making in the last quarter century, and that of preceding decades."[72] In terms of the scrutiny of the defense budget alone, the change has been dramatic. Congressional staffs have grown larger, and the number of hours devoted to hearings has also increased substantially. The use of staffs to investigate and requests for OTA to prepare reports on SDI gave the Senate the information it needed to review the program in detail. The decision to legislate a ban on testing ASATs against objects in space reflected the confidence gained by Congress and represented an extraordinary departure from previous congressional procedure. This precedent was followed by attempts to require executive adherence to the ABM Treaty.

How far Congress will go in asserting its role in foreign policy will depend on how successful presidents are in asserting leadership. If presidents can achieve arms-control agreements, they will certainly steal Congress's thunder. Even a president who does not favor arms control is in a position to rally national sentiment behind programs like SDI by arguing that the Soviets have prevented agreement, and that to inhibit any of these programs is, as Reagan put it in a State of the Union address, to enact Gorbachev's wishes into law.

DRAWING THE POLITICAL LESSON

If there is a single lesson to be drawn from the political debates over SDI, it is that although a popular president can gain support for a new venture in military technology by "going public" or by using the mass media to appeal directly to the electorate,[73] the representative system allows opponents of the policy to keep it under control by restraining expenditures, casting doubt on its technical prospects, and warning of its potentially destabilizing effects on international relations. In view of the widespread alarm over the failures of technology in the Chernobyl and *Challenger* disasters, there is ample opportunity to play on public fears, counterbalancing efforts to play on the public's hopes. But even without trying to contest the president in the arena of public opinion, opponents of SDI have discovered that they can have considerable effect by aiming their efforts at Congress. The defense budget is the largest single part of the federal budget subject to congressional review, and although it is composed for the most part of fixed expenses, special programs like SDI are tempting targets for budget cutters.

Some of the efforts of the opposition would therefore have been effective despite public approval of SDI, but the weakening of Reagan's presidency, owing to difficulties in the conduct of other dimensions of foreign policy, made the rest of his program more vulnerable. The SDI probably suffered from the general loss of public confidence in Reagan's leadership following his much criticized "arms for hostages" deal with Iran. By refusing to compromise on SDI in the arms-control negotiations with the Soviets, moreover, the president triggered anxieties on that front as well, both domestically and among allies. These anxieties, coupled with criticisms generated by the decision of pro-SDI forces to push for early deployment, played into the hands of the opponents.

Political considerations will continue to influence SDI in the Bush administration. President George Bush will probably want to make less of an issue of SDI, but if the START negotiations falter, SDI's supporters will undoubtedly press him to give it renewed emphasis. The most likely prospect is that the new administration will be no more able than its predecessor to impose a reinterpretation of the treaty and an early-deployment decision over the opposition in Congress, and that SDI in general, because it has become so much identified with Reagan, will be much less of a political issue than it was during his term in office. Progress in arms-control negotiations with the Soviets would counteract pressures for early deployment. Even without such progress, however, concern over the economic implications of moving to development and deployment—the subject of the next chapter—could dampen enthusiasm, especially in view of mounting concern for reducing the U.S. budget deficit.

Calculating the Costs and Benefits

The question of whether to proceed with SDI beyond the research phase into development and deployment depends not only on a determination that the various technologies are feasible but also on a calculus of costs and benefits. To attempt such a calculus, especially at this stage of the project, is to become aware of the difficulties in making plausible economic projections for complex technological projects with so many unknowns and variables.

The difficulties arise at every level of complexity. Even estimates based on the use of "off the shelf" technologies show wide variations. As we noted in chapter 1, advocates of the High Frontier scheme claimed in 1982 that its proposed space-based kinetic interceptor scheme would cost between $15 billion and $30 billion to deploy, but DOD analysts thought the same system would end up costing between $200 billion and $300 billion. Advocates of the three-layer Marshall Institute scheme estimate costs of development and deployment at $121 billion, but critics consider this estimate overly optimistic. Experienced analysts have produced projections of the cost of a full-fledged, multilayered comprehensive system that vary between almost $700 billion and $1 trillion.

Although cost projections of certain of the near-term technologies, especially those that would be ground-based, are apt to be less disparate than those for technologies still in a conceptual stage, all the calculations are based on assumptions that remain to be put to a practical test. The economics of space-based systems are the hardest to determine because there is simply no adequate basis for making firm estimates of the cost of deploying and operating advanced sensors, weapons, and data processors in space—especially when the calculations involve "life cycle" costs, including launching, maintenance, replacement, and periodic renovation. Many of the most critical components are still undergoing testing and refinement in the research phase, which precedes development or engineering. Until the physical specifications can be spelled out in an "RFP"—the standard "request for proposals" by which the government invites bids from contractors—costs cannot even be approximated. Even then, estimates are apt to be uncertain, because unanticipated problems often arise in the development phase that raise cost estimates and delay completion. Military development projects typically end up costing substantially more than originally estimated—sometimes two or three times as much—and usually take longer than originally planned. SDI costs will also be affected by the expense of launching satellites into orbit, which could become lower as technology advances.

In view of these uncertainties, about all that can be done with any assurance now is to compare the original research strategy with the one that has actually been pursued. The more speculative prospects must also be examined in order to identify the issues that will need to be resolved before a commitment is made to development and deployment. Among the critical issues to be addressed, if development and deployment become feasible, are these:

• Can a defensive shield be "cost-effective at the margin" in the sense that it could not be defeated or overcome by less-expensive offensive increments, improvements, and countermeasures?

• If not, would the United States nevertheless be well-advised to spend more to deploy defenses than the Soviets would be willing or able to spend on offenses?

• Would an effort to develop and deploy SDI draw national resources away from other military programs to a degree that would lead to imbalance between the development of defenses and the modernization of offenses?

• Will the effort divert qualified technical personnel and other resources away from the civil sectors so as to cause serious harm at a time when efforts are needed to make the civil sector more competitive internationally?

• Will SDI provide such important "spin-off" benefits to civilian high-technology industry as to offset any such harm?

Definitive answers to these and other related economic questions are inherently out of reach, and even educated guesses are doubtful while so many parameters cannot be quantified. At this stage, it is realistic only to raise the questions and consider some of the preliminary answers.

THE RESEARCH PHASE:
PROJECTIONS AND ACTUAL APPROPRIATIONS

When the Fletcher panel was asked to prepare a detailed research agenda, it was also asked to provide two sets of cost estimates—one for a project that would be "technology limited" (or, in other words, that would allow the pace of research alone to determine allocations), the other for a "resource constrained" approach. Accordingly, the panel proposed a "technically aggressive" budget calling for the expenditure of $26 billion over five years beginning in FY1985, and an alternative, fiscally limited, budget of $14.3 billion. The panel endorsed the higher figure, which was announced publicly and incorporated into the DOD's five-year defense budget.[1]

Had this projection been followed, the annual budget for SDI would have reached $8 billion by FY1989, approximately twice as much as Congress actually allocated. Over the five-year period actual appropriations for SDI, including those for work administered by the Department of Energy, have totaled $16.2 billion, or almost 40 percent less than the announced projection, and somewhat more than the lower, unannounced projection (see Table 3).

Although SDI has already cost as much in inflation-adjusted dollars as the Manhattan Project, it is not yet the "big ticket" item its advocates hoped, and its opponents feared, it would become. Still a research project, SDI does not yet carry as great a financial commitment as other military projects, which have passed into development and procurement. The Stealth bomber project, for example, could cost more than $60 billion if it is carried to full completion as presently planned. As a component of the Pentagon's budget for research, development, testing and evaluation (RDT&E), SDI currently accounts for 10 percent of the total—a large fraction, but one that was anticipated and is not so high as to deprive other high-priority projects of necessary support. The DOD had projected that spending for SDI would rise from 3.69 percent of defense R&D in 1984 to 13.06 percent in 1989. If the SDI budget had achieved that rate of increase, and if it were to continue to rise to an even higher proportion of total R&D expenditures, it would be taking

TABLE 3.   PROJECTED AND ACTUAL EXPENDITURES
ON BALLISTIC MISSILE DEFENSE[a]
(in millions)

	Projected by DOD Prior to SDI		Projected by SDIO as of 1985	Authorized by Congress	
	DOD	DOE	DOD	DOD	DOE
1984	991	NA	991	991	120
1985	1,527	210	1,397	1,397	224
1986	1,802	295	3,722	2,759	303
1987	2,181	365	4,908	3,213	317
1988	2,699	439	6,165	3,610	279
1989	2,982	505	7,300	3,821	262
TOTAL	12,182	1,814	24,483	15,791	1,505

SOURCES: App. F, "BMD and the Military R&D Budget," in *Ballistic Missile Defense Technologies*, U.S. Congress, Office of Technology Assessment (Washington, D.C.: OTA, 1986), p. 292, and Alan Sweedler, "Congress and the SDI," in *Lost in Space: The Domestic Politics of SDI*, ed. Gerald M. Steinberg (Lexington, Mass.: Lexington Books, 1988), table 4-1, p. 59, and Gordon Adams, Defense Budget Research Project.

[a] Prior to the announcement of SDI, the DOD had projected that planned expenditures on BMD from 1984 through 1989 would total $14.626 billion, including the DOE projection. SDIO's initial projection (for FY1984 through FY1989) called for $24.488 billion for the DOD portion alone, and for a total of $26 billion, including the DOE allocation. Actual appropriations for the six-year period were $17.3 billion. For the five-year period from FY1985 through FY1989, the Fletcher panel called for the expenditure of $26 billion, and Congress actually appropriated $16.2 billion.

the lion's share of new resources for advanced projects—about 45 percent of cumulative increases projected for FY1987–1991.[2]

Given the reluctance of Congress to allow the SDI budget to increase as planned, the immediate future is cloudy. An in-house concept paper on the strategic defense system issued August 1, 1987, ignored the political controversy and projected total research costs through a Milestone II decision on development of Phase I—presumably now to be reached in the mid-1990s—at about $50 billion. This presupposes a very sharp increase in the level of funding, one that would make the SDI research effort much larger than other DOD programs. As a Senate staff report pointed out: "If SDI proceeds on schedule by FY1992 the annual SDI budget request would be $11.5 billion or more than the Army or Navy now spend[s] on RDT&E for *all* their programs."[3]

THE PRESENT STATUS OF SDI

According to its original rationale, SDI was supposed to be designed to determine the feasibility of moving to the next stage of development. But because of the crosscutting political pressures (described in chapter 7), the project has acquired a more ambiguous character. The timetable originally called for a decision to be made on development in the early to mid-1990s. In 1987 there were indications that the timetable had been moved up to enable a decision on development *and simultaneous initial deployment* to be made in 1991. The original plan also called for a full exploration of technical options so that the system to be considered for deployment would be one that would meet the announced goal of a comprehensive shield for population and not only for military targets. This goal has been significantly altered, under various pressures, to emphasize options for near-term deployment of a system that would be only partially effective (estimates range from 11 to 30 percent) in intercepting Soviet warheads. Because the proposed near-term system involves boost-phase interception by space-based kinetic kill vehicles (the space-based interceptor, or SBI) and by terminal ABMs with large footprints, it can be said to serve Reagan's announced goal of providing population defense, based on the "random subtractive" principle—i.e., the enemy RVs intercepted might be aimed either at military or civilian targets. Because this limited deployment cannot provide more than partial interception, however, it can hardly guarantee the safety of the population, much less promise to render nuclear missiles "impotent and obsolete."

Changes and uncertainties of this sort make it particularly hard to discuss the economic implications of SDI. Lieutenant General Abrahamson has been reluctant, for various reasons, to make cost estimates of future systems. The SDIO designed a "strawman" estimate based on a possible Phase I system. Its general view of what this option would cost is thought to be close to that of the pro-SDI George C. Marshall Institute, whose plan calls for a larger system that, it is claimed, would be more than 90 percent effective against the present Soviet missile force, at a cost of $121 billion—not counting the cost of air defense. The first SDIO estimate was more modest, calling for expenditures of $40–$50 billion, but this amount would buy only a very limited "first installment."

The most direct reason SDI has not met its projections is that it has encountered stiff resistance in Congress. But this opposition reflects a skepticism that is widespread within the defense establishment itself, counterbalanced only by the self-interest of some defense contractors. Most technical specialists consider the project either not feasible at all or at too early a stage to warrant a commitment to development, let alone deployment. Military leaders are apprehensive that great increases in the SDI budget might deprive other strategic and conventional programs of the research support they need for improvements that are far more likely to be attained in the near term. Defense contractors are more supportive not because they are more optimistic about the technical prospects but because they fear that funding for research on strategic offensive weapons is likely to decline. During the Carter administration support for R & D on strategic offenses was running at about $2 billion a year. It has risen under the Reagan administration to about $8 billion—most of which has supported development of the B-1 and Stealth aircraft. If, as expected, that part of the budget should decline during the next few years, SDI could take up the slack and would therefore be particularly welcome to those dependent on military R & D contracting. Military industry clearly welcomes SDI, but mostly for its longer-range potential as a basis for future procurements. Procurements for strategic offensive forces rose to almost $20 billion in 1985 but are expected to decline to less than $5 billion annually by the late 1990s.[4] Whether SDI's procurement potential will be realized depends on political decisions yet to be reached. The long-term implications of SDI thus remain highly speculative. Although the program has acquired some momentum because of the number and size of the research contracts, SDI's march into development and deployment is not a foregone conclusion.

REORIENTING THE "INVESTMENT STRATEGY"

The SDIO breaks down its expenditures in several different ways. One is by distinguishing basic research, exploratory development, advanced and engineering development, management support (including funds for installations like test ranges), and operational-systems development (or engineering development for systems already deployed). It is typical for DOD programs that only a small fraction—2.5 percent in the FY1985 request—is committed to basic research. All the research done by SDIO is classified by the DOD as "advanced development" for its purposes. Another breakdown, by type of work, divides the support among programs to develop kinetic-energy weapons (KEWs), directed-energy weapons (DEWs), "SATKA" (surveillance, acquisition, tracking, and kill assessment), and battle management. The separate DOE budget supports research on the X-ray laser as well as on the SP-100 program— an effort to develop a 100 kw nuclear reactor suitable for space applications. In addition to the DOE budget, SDI also benefits from funds separately allocated to NASA for efforts to reduce launch costs.

The SDIO has defined its "investment strategy" as having three major directions. The first is to bring the most mature technologies to a point at which the implementation of a decision to deploy "would be largely one of engineering." The second is to pursue "emerging technologies" with potential for major improvements. The third is to ensure that investment is also made in "innovative ideas." The overall goal is to demonstrate technical feasibility and provide the broadest possible range of options. The office warned in 1986 that continued shortfalls in meeting its budget requests would have a substantial detrimental effect on the program. Further reductions would place SDIO in a position "where simply scaling back alternatives is no longer viable."[5] Already, some programs have had to be canceled, others deferred and scaled down. In FY1987 a choice had to be made between the boost surveillance and tracking system and the satellite surveillance and tracking system. Because the first was designed for boost phase and the second for midcourse, the agency decided to support the former. Thus, what was conceived to be a more pressing need for a deployable first-phase system was chosen over a project that would be vital to a more comprehensive system. More generally, the shifts favor programs necessary for near-term deployment at the expense of those designed to enhance the "technology base."

In 1987 SDIO's budget was altered to reflect congressional budget cuts and to support increased emphasis on initial or early deployment. SDIO acknowledged in its budgetary analysis that its projected milestones reflect a change of relative emphasis away from countering the responsive threat and to support early-deployment options. The budget for near-term options was cut less than that for long-term options. In 1987 the request for KEWs was 20.8 percent, compared with the previous year's 20.5 percent. DEW meanwhile dropped from 33.6 percent of the FY1986 request to 26 percent of the 1987 request, and to 21.2 percent of the FY1988 request.[6]

In this process of reorientation, the original criteria have been loosened. In defining its idea of the requirements of a defensive system, SDIO has not simply endorsed the Nitze criteria but has instead "reinterpreted" them. Nitze laid down only two: survivability and cost-effectiveness at the margin. SDIO has made another consideration, "military effectiveness," the first criterion, contending that a defensive system must be able to destroy enough of an attacking force to make any adversary reluctant to try a preemptive strike. This objective would include the ability to deny the aggressor the opportunity of destroying a "militarily significant portion of the target bases he wishes to attack." The system must be capable of evolving over time to counter "responsive threats" or countermeasures and should be capable of deterring a strong offensive response.[7] In other words, the aim is not to achieve population defense, at least at the outset, but to defend military assets so as to complicate an enemy's plans for a preemptive strike.

The second requirement is that the defensive system must possess "*adequate* [N.B.] survivability." This is said to mean that the defenses must maintain enough effectiveness to fulfill their mission even in the face of determined attacks and the loss of some components and not therefore present an appealing target for defense suppression. The offense must be forced to pay a penalty for trying to negate the defense. "This penalty would be sufficiently high in cost and/or uncertainty . . . that such an attack would not be contemplated seriously."[8] In other words, the system need not be altogether survivable but only sufficiently so to enable it to perform its mission under attack.

The third requirement is that the defensive options generated "discourage" an adversary from overwhelming them with additional offense. The aim is to achieve defensive systems that could be maintained, protected, and proliferated more easily than an adversary could install reliable countermeasures: "This criterion is couched in terms of cost-effectiveness at the margin; however, it is much more than an economic concept."[9] In other words, this restatement does not meet the Nitze criterion squarely but relies on a rough approximation emphasizing non-economic considerations.

Contrary to this reformulation, cost-effectiveness at the margin is usually understood to mean that it must be less *expensive* (not just technically easier) for the defense to proliferate added defenses or otherwise add protection than it is for the offense to improve its threat whether by developing countermeasures or by adding more launchers and warheads. In the ideal case, a defensive system would have such a high kill ratio in each of its layers that the offense would have to proliferate missiles at an unacceptable rate to achieve sufficient penetration. Thus, a battle station should not cost more than the cost of the number of boost-

ers it can destroy. If a battle station could account for thirty boosters, as
an OTA study suggests, "a cost of $50 million per booster would mean
that the defense could spend $1.5 billion per battle station, and still
keep up with the offense in the cost-exchange race." [10] The trouble in
applying this approach is that no such formula can be used to compute
the actual future costs of development, deployment, and maintenance,
because there is no comparable experience from which to derive cost
estimates. In the case of offensive missiles, there is solid experience to
serve as a guide. In the case of the defensive systems, it is necessary to
make simplifying assumptions and estimate likely costs by extrapolat-
ing from an experiential base that is not fully comparable. As another
OTA report aptly observes: "Nobody knows how to calculate, let alone
demonstrate to the Soviets, the cost-exchange ratio between offense and
defense." [11]

Another problem is that what may prove to be an acceptable cost for
one society may not be for another. Even though defenses may not be
cost-effective at the margin in the narrow economic sense, the United
States might be willing to pay for them on the theory that it could afford
to spend more to defend itself than the Soviets can to maintain their
threat. At the same time, because the Soviet Union is a more centralized
society and demonstrably eager to maintain parity with the United
States, it may be able and willing to spend more to improve its offense
than U.S. taxpayers may be willing to commit to defenses.

GAUGING THE DIRECT AND INDIRECT
COSTS OF DEPLOYMENT

Ashton B. Carter has identified three ways of comparing the relative
costs of offense and defense:[12]

1.   The cost of a new defense versus the cost of a new offense needed
to counter it.

2.   The full cost of a new defense versus the marginal cost of improving present offensive capabilities to defeat it.

3.   The marginal cost of improving a deployed defensive capability
to defeat marginal improvements to a fixed offensive capability.

The Council on Economic Priorities (CEP) adds a fourth: a net cost
assessment that includes complications caused by a Soviet deployment
of defenses.[13] (Thus, for example, a Soviet defense of strategic forces and

C^3 could require a costly U.S. offensive response that must be added to the cost of a U.S. defense, insofar as the United States believes it advisable to maintain an offensive threat to those elements of the Soviet military forces.)

Although these formulas are useful, they do not preclude significant disagreements over cost estimates. Carter contends that fuel, in the form of chemical reactants necessary to pump chemical battle lasers, would require a full shuttle load to be orbited—a cost that, in comparison to Soviet cost per warhead intercepted, would not be favorable to the defense. SDIO analysts dispute this estimate, which they believe overstates the required weapon ranges and the power needed to fire a lethal beam at each target. Launch costs are potentially critical in view of the assumed weight of the battle stations to be orbited. In estimating costs, much would depend on the characteristics of the systems. If the Soviets elected to deploy missiles with less accuracy in order to threaten cities, costs would go down.[14]

As Carter also points out, the offense can "stress" the defense by putting all its missiles in one region and increasing their number. Because of the need to provide continuous coverage, the defense is compelled to greatly increase—by as much as two or three times—the number of satellites needed to assure a successful rate of interception in the boost phase. Everything depends on assumptions made about the number of intercepts the battle satellites could perform in a given time and the time available during boost and post-boost phases. Countermeasures could also stress the defense, for example, by decreasing its effectiveness and increasing the weight that would have to be put in orbit.[15]

Is SDI affordable? As the CEP study points out, in an economy producing more than $3 trillion worth of goods and services each year, a $32 billion six-year research program "is not likely to bankrupt our nation." But there is a significant opportunity cost to be paid, as the study also notes. Money invested in SDI is money that could be invested elsewhere, or, if unspent, would reduce the budget deficit. The costs could be significant for the balance of the economy, especially because of the possible effects on the distribution of technical employment in military and civil industries. Although the supply of engineers is affected by rising and falling demand in other defense and nondefense sectors, the supply of physicists is relatively fixed in the medium term. Efforts to draw physicists into work on directed-energy weapons, for example, would create shortages and reduce the effectiveness of R & D efforts elsewhere. Some of the slack might be taken up by encouraging immigration, as higher U.S. salaries and better research opportunities attract qualified scientists from other countries. In general, the recession of the early 1980s cooled demand for qualified scientists and engineers, but the renewed growth in the economy took up this slack. Higher salaries in industry have already affected Ph.D. programs in the natural sciences. In 1971, 3,498 new Ph.D.s were awarded in the natural sciences. In 1981 the number was 2,528. An increasing percentage of Ph.D.s is being earned by foreign students (51.5 percent by 1981 compared to 29.8 percent in 1971). In the fall of 1980 universities reported that 10 percent of their faculty positions were vacant. While undergraduate enrollments in engineering increased by 66 percent from 1969–70 to 1981–82, faculty increased just 11 percent. Teaching loads were increased and schools were unable to offer courses in some areas. More of the actual teaching load has fallen on teaching assistants and part-time faculty.[16]

The deep recession that began in 1981 mitigated the problem. Companies found it easier to recruit qualified personnel, and starting salaries fell back. In examining the cost of SDI deployment, the question for the future is what will happen if economic growth persists and accelerates and funding for SDI draws qualified researchers away from other employment. A study prepared for the NSF indicated that between 1982 and 1987, new entrants and immigrants would match or exceed the demand created by economic growth and attrition in all but three of the twenty-one occupational groups of engineers and scientists: computer specialists, aeronautical/astronautical engineers, and electrical/ electronic engineers. If demand is high in both the civil and military economy, demand for computer specialists would exceed supply by 30 percent—or 138,200 people. But if demand is low, the problem would be much less serious. The most likely difficulties will be found in certain sectors, such as aerospace, where demand in both military and civil programs is expected to be high.[17]

To gauge how many engineers, scientists, and technicians the SDI would absorb, if funding met original projections, the CEP team constructed a rough mathematical estimate, based on assumed yearly outlays for SDI, which were converted into production per industry. Then the average number of jobs per billion dollars of RDT & E expenditure was computed for each industry, on the assumption that SDI will require the same levels of production as the average in military RDT & E, which the CEP study admits is a questionable assumption, in view of the fact that SDI involves technological exploration rather than full-scale development. The result is likely to underestimate the number of scientists, engineers, and technologists (SETs) required. The CEP study estimates that in 1984 the SDI required about 4,800 SETs, a figure that would have risen to 18,400 if projected spending over the next five years had materialized. Although SDI would remain only a small fraction of overall national and DOD demand, SDI could have used about 5 percent of the total SET personnel employed by the Pentagon and roughly 0.5 percent of the national total. The CEP estimated that between 1984 and 1987 the DOD would require roughly a third of all new engineers, of whom SDI would account for about 12 percent. SDI's impact would be particularly acute in the areas in which its work is concentrated: computer professionals and aeronautical/astronautical engineers.[18]

By comparison, as the study points out, the Apollo program took up 13.5 percent of national funding for R & D, and NASA as a whole accounted for about 21 percent of total national R & D. SDI could take up 5.1 percent of total R & D by 1990. In marginal terms, however, SDI is already as significant as Apollo. Apollo received 40 percent of new R & D funding in 1965 and 20.8 percent in 1966. If SDI had met its projections, it might have used roughly 34.6 percent of new R & D funds during 1986. Even though the federal government encouraged university students to become space scientists and layoffs owing to defense cuts provided a pool of qualified people, by 1966 there were indications, nevertheless, of a severe shortage of scientists and engineers; the unemployment rate for engineers fell to 0.7 percent. As a result, R & D labor costs grew rapidly, and basic industries, forced to compete with aerospace and electronics industry salaries, found R & D investments less attractive. Similarly, increased demand for skilled manpower in the SDI could draw away skilled personnel from other fields, imposing higher costs on industries also requiring those specialties. The CEP study estimated that at the projected level the SDI could require 4 percent of all new engineers between 1984 and 1987 and that the DOD would likely take up a third of all engineers, with SDI requiring more than 12 percent of the total.[19]

PROJECTING THE COSTS
OF INITIAL DEPLOYMENT

The projected cost of Phase I deployment has been a subject of some confusion. On March 19, 1987, Abrahamson testified to a Senate appropriations defense subcommittee that this deployment would cost be-

tween $50 and $60 billion in 1985 dollars. In a September 1987 interview, however, he gave a considerably higher estimate, noting that it
would cost at least $70 billion and perhaps well over $100 billion for an
"initial, partially capable but very impressive deployment"—presumably one that was more capable and impressive than the initial deployment he was referring to in his congressional testimony. The second estimate was reportedly based on analyses prepared by SDIO for the
Defense Acquisition Board in its Milestone I review. In February 1988
Abrahamson addressed the same issue and this time said that the cost
would be between $75 and $150 billion (in 1988 dollars)—a figure that
evidently included demonstration, validation, full-scale engineering development, and production.[20] In the summer of 1988, he reported that
technical progress would enable SDIO to construct a somewhat scaled-
down version at a cost of $69 billion.

In reporting these changes, the Senate staff report of June 1988 noted
that briefings given to the staff and confirmed by SDIO documents
showed that the SDIO had come up with the higher estimate at least as
early as June 1987. The report also points out that the panel reviewing
Milestone I was aware of these estimates, pointing out that "by the time
the necessary system and underlying technology work is complete, the
design may change considerably and costs [may] change as well." As the
staff report notes, in addition to these development costs, SDI would
simultaneously incur other costs in support of ongoing research, estimated for FY1988–92 at more than $28 billion. Operation and mainte-
nance costs for the Phase I system are estimated to be from $2 billion to
$4.2 billion per year, and the Advanced Launch System to be used by
SDIO would be developed jointly with the air force, which would contribute more than $1 billion dollars from other funds for this project.
The budgetary impact would be sustained, as the report points out, because Phase II deployment is scheduled to begin "right on the heels of
Phase I deployment." Directed-energy weapons would be deployed only
two to four years after an initial deployment of kinetic weapons. The
result would be "a mind-numbing annual expense," which, counting
life-cycle expenses for both Phase I and Phase II, "could approach three-
quarters of a trillion dollars."[21]

These projections have been all but ignored in the political effort to
build momentum behind SDI. The Reagan administration sought to
keep the project on schedule by making the cuts required by the
Gramm-Rudman-Hollings deficit-reduction law. This suggests an effort
to keep SDI from economic comparisons, on the grounds that the pre-

liminary research is critical and must be undertaken within a short time frame, but it can also be interpreted as an effort to establish a momentum behind the program that will make it hard to terminate. Can Congress simply write *finis* to a program on which upwards of $30 billion will have been spent for exploration, or will it be tempted to provide at least some funds for development and deployment, even though the research does not result in a system that promises a virtually leakproof defense? Indeed, the pressure for early deployment of a limited or intermediate system suggests that this concern for tangible results is already being felt well before the research phase was supposed to terminate and make possible a decision regarding development and deployment. Now, the question is whether to proceed with deployment while the research phase continues.

BLECHMAN AND UTGOFF'S FOUR "NOTIONAL" SYSTEMS

Barry M. Blechman and Victor A. Utgoff suppose that cost estimates need to be made for four possible strategic-defense architectures. These are, first, a system aimed at providing terminal defenses, assisted by airborne surveillance and interceptor aircraft and designed to make U.S. nuclear retaliatory forces less attractive targets; second, adding a light, terminal area defense to the first system; third, protecting the entire population of the United States and Canada from ballistic missiles and aircraft by adding a space-based KEW component to the ground-based and airborne components used for the first and second systems; and fourth, addition of a space-based DEW component designed to destroy Soviet missiles in the boost phase with chemical lasers. These are designated, respectively, Alpha, Beta, Gamma, and Delta.[22]

There are problems with this choice of options. The Delta system uses satellite-based chemical lasers, which have come into disfavor on various grounds. There is also no attempt to estimate costs for ground-based free-electron lasers, using space-based mirrors—an option considered more attractive than space-based lasers in critical respects—nor is there any consideration of the possible role in midcourse of neutral particle-beam discriminators. The study assumes that an initial, least expensive deployment would omit the boost-phase and aim for defense of military targets, whereas some actual proposals for an intermediate deployment would include boost-phase defenses and more than defense of military targets alone. Nevertheless, the exercise is a useful one. The notional systems enable the analyst to make reasonably realistic estimates of the costs of putting satellites in orbit and maintaining them, hardening missile silos and satellites, and of the corresponding opportunity costs.

In developing their estimates, Blechman and Utgoff make certain critical assumptions. One is that interceptor missiles can be built—both the ground-based missiles and the space-based interceptors—that would have a probability of .9 of destroying their targets in any single engagement. If this is not possible, costs would rise considerably. A second assumption is that relatively inexpensive measures would be sufficient to protect the space-based components by hardening and orbiting as many as five decoy satellites for every space-based satellite deployed. A determined effort by the Soviets to develop effective ASATs could require more costly measures for defending satellites (including proliferation). Another assumption is that key components of all the systems would be built in sufficient numbers and according to the same design so as to capture the learning effects of manufacturing. They assume a 90 percent learning curve, or, in other words, that the marginal costs would decrease by 10 percent every time the quantity to be procured (e.g., of missiles) was doubled. If the assumed learning curve is only slightly higher or lower, the results would vary considerably. (For example, an 85 percent learning curve in one case would reduce costs by 25 percent of what they would otherwise be.) They also assume that during the fifteen or more years before a U.S. system could become operational, the U.S.S.R. could replace its force of offensive missiles and tailor its characteristics to make it less vulnerable to the defenses selected by the United States. Thus, the Soviets would deploy their missiles in an area roughly one-third the present size and would reduce boost times and harden their missiles against DEW.

The cost estimates of these four notional systems range from $160 billion for the Alpha to $170 billion for Beta, $770 billion for Gamma ($600 billion added to the cost of Beta), and $670 billion for Delta. The most expensive of the systems, Gamma, would therefore cost on the order of $44 billion annually during its ten peak years. Although this would represent a 15 percent real increase in the current level of defense outlays and a commitment of roughly 1 percent of the nation's resources for a considerable period of time, defense expenditures would increase from their current level of about 6 percent to only 7 percent. As they point out, this figure has been far exceeded in wartime and been matched or exceeded during all but a few of the peacetime years from 1945 to

1970. Only the first two systems could be financed within historical levels of spending for strategic offensive forces; the space-based systems would require greater levels than have been historically committed for strategic forces. Trade-offs will also have to be made, no matter which level of expenditure is chosen, with other defense requirements. The $160 billion required for the Alpha system is equivalent to the cost of eight aircraft-carrier battle groups or twenty-seven wings of F-15 fighters or fourteen armored divisions. The more expensive systems would cost far more than the army now spends on development and procurement and would be roughly comparable to the air force budget for development and procurement.

If strategic defenses were to be financed without harming other defense programs, cutting civilian programs might be an alternative, but the cuts would have to be significant. Peak expenditures for the Alpha system would be roughly the same as current federal outlays for higher education. The Delta and Gamma costs of $44 billion and $37 billion per year, respectively, are comparable to the $25 billion devoted to farm price stabilization in 1986, the $30 billion for health care services, and the $71 billion for Medicare. Funding the Delta system in its peak years would require cutting about 20 percent of the current $180 billion in so-called discretionary nondefense federal spending.

Another possible alternative for financing strategic defenses would be to increase federal revenues. This would require, for the Gamma system, roughly an 11 percent increase in federal revenues from individual income taxes, based on 1985 returns, or about $570 for the average family earning between $30,000 and $50,000 per year. Alternatively, the system could be financed by raising corporate income taxes by 50 percent. Either step would cut individual consumption and saving and affect economic growth, employment, and inflation.

Blechman and Utgoff note, however, that increasing the share of federal expenditures allocated to strategic defense would not necessarily have adverse economic effects. As they point out, history suggests that the effects of defense expenditures can be influenced by monetary policy and by international economic circumstances in such a way as to counterbalance negative effects. They agree with the CEP group, however, that specific industrial and scientific sectors could be affected by the manpower and resource requirements of SDI. A large program "could strongly impact on the availability and price of certain kinds of scientists and engineers, computer programmers, and other specialists" and distort markets for specific types of raw materials and manufactured goods. Such adverse consequences could be minimized by cooperation between the federal government and affected industries and federal encouragement of related occupations.[23]

The notional Alpha system—a terminal defense—would be based on known technology and could be developed within seven years and be fully deployed in roughly double that time. It would render the U.S. deterrent force more resistant to attack by raising the cost of attacking the facilities where the forces are based—more nuclear weapons would be required to destroy each base than could be expected to be found at the base at the time the attack was executed. Potential attackers would thus lose the incentive to attack because they would use up more warheads than they could reasonably expect to destroy. The system would employ ground-based interceptors (HEDI and LEDI) to provide two layers of defense and would be assisted by ground-based radars and airborne systems for surveillance, target acquisition, and battle management. Early warning would be provided by surveillance satellites in geosynchronous orbits and ground-based over-the-horizon radars. The surveillance systems would require no incremental expenditures.

The missile-defense system would be accompanied by an airborne system to defend against bombers and cruise missiles. Surveillance aircraft would continuously patrol a barrier well to the north and off the coasts of the United States. Shorter-range interceptor aircraft guided by AWACs-type aircraft would intercept enemy bombers. (Airborne air defenses were chosen because they would be less costly than ground-based systems and more flexible in that they could intercept at the points of attack, whereas SAMs would have to be deployed in sufficient numbers all along potential attack corridors.) Because the terminal-defense system is designed to function within the atmosphere, the decoy problem is ignored, and it is assumed that any warheads that escape interception by the high-endoatmospheric system would be destroyed by high-acceleration, low-endoatmospheric interceptors before they could explode close enough to military targets to destroy the missiles, bombers, and submarines at which they are aimed.

The sizing of the air defense assumes that the U.S.S.R. deploys a force of two hundred Bear F and Blackjack strategic bombers carrying an average of ten cruise missiles each. Estimating that two-thirds of the bombers would participate in the initial attack, Blechman and Utgoff add that by the turn of the century the Soviets might also be able to launch 350 cruise missiles from submarines off the U.S. coasts. The United States' defense would require three hundred shorter-range interceptors and ten AWACs already planned for continental air defenses in the 1990s. New air bases would be required, and these bases would also have to be defended against both air attack and ICBM attack.

According to their estimates, the total number of U.S. weapons considered vulnerable to air attack would be 2,943, assuming that silo-based missiles will have been launched before cruise missiles launched by bombers could hit. Because the Soviets would have available 1,700 bomber and submarine-launched cruise missiles, the defender could expect to kill 600 of the attacking cruise missiles by interceptors, assuming that 300 U.S. aircraft were available each carrying four missiles and that the alert rate of the aircraft and the kill probability of each missile were both .7 ($300 \times .7 = 210$; $210 \times 4 = 840$; $840 \times .7 = 588$). The remaining 1,100 would have to be destroyed by aircraft in the outer barrier. If one calculates expected kill ratios, sixteen alert surveillance aircraft would be required, in addition to the already-planned air defense forces. To allow coverage of the entire 4,500 nautical-mile-long perimeter, a total force of fifty aircraft would be required (assuming a 40 percent strip alert rate). Because of the submarine threat, however, additional planes would be needed, raising the inventory requirement to seventy-five armed surveillance aircraft. The effectiveness of the aircraft would be greatly improved by aerial refueling; tanker aircraft would also be needed, totaling thirty-five, the equivalent of the KC-10A. The air bases for this defending force would have to be dispersed and as well defended as the missile silos. Thus, thirty-two bases might be advisable for the 275 strategic-defense aircraft of the Alpha system, in addition to the ten already available. Each base would need to be defended by 122 HEDI and 20 LEDI and 1 ground-based radar. The targets would have to be hardened against salvage-fused missiles lest nuclear effects destroy targets such as hangars and aircraft.

Of the total cost of $160 billion, somewhat more than half would go for air defense. If the aim were to defend only silo-based ballistic missiles, and to defend them only from attacks by ballistic missiles, the total ten-year cost for a terminal system would be roughly $30 billion. This system could be less expensive if only ground-based radars and a single layer of defense were employed.

THE SDIO/MARSHALL INSTITUTE
PHASE I SYSTEM

By comparison, the strawman concept advanced by the SDIO in 1987 contemplated a system using three thousand space-based kinetic-kill vehicles carried on several hundred satellites—and both ERIS and HEDI terminal defenses supplemented by airborne tracking systems but not by an air defense. Such a system—which was not put forward as just a defense of military targets but, instead, in a random subtractive mode—would cost between $40 billion and $60 billion, according to SDIO estimates, and could be deployed as early as 1994 and 1995. The system was estimated to have an effectiveness of 11 percent against the current Soviet ballistic missile threat. A representative for Lockheed Missiles and Space claimed that the company's ERIS missiles could be deployed within a few years and could provide effective interim defense against the current Soviet threat at a life-cycle cost of $1 million per intercept.[24]

The Marshall Institute proposal, which is thought to be closely modeled after the one SDIO is contemplating (and therefore warrants more scrutiny than it might otherwise merit), calls for a more extensive deployment than the SDIO strawman proposal. Arguing against the common view that terminal defenses are the most feasible in the near term, followed by midcourse defenses, the proposal contends that technical progress achieved under SDI had "invalidated this traditional view." Instead, the proposal suggests that a boost-phase defense can be deployed in the same time frame as the ground-based layers.[25]

The Marshall defense would be based on homing interceptors—nonnuclear, heat-seeking missiles using the same technology developed for air defense. The system would have three layers, boost phase, late midcourse and terminal interception. All would rely on kinetic weapons in view of the fact that beam weapons lag "a few years" behind KEWs. Deployment of the full defense could be achieved seven years after the decision to deploy, assuming "streamlined management and procurement procedures are followed." Deployment of the ERIS layer would begin five years from the date of the decision to deploy. A decision to proceed with an incremental deployment would provide the earliest possible protection against "accidental or irrational" launches and a useful degree of deterrence against limited attacks on key military sites. The institute cites SDIO's success in completing the Delta 180 experiment in fourteen months from initiation, claiming that normal procedures would have required twice as long.[26]

The level of effectiveness of the three-layer defense is calculated to be approximately 93 percent against a "threat cloud" of 10,000 warheads and 100,000 decoys. With decoy discrimination in the ERIS layer, the proposed defense is presumed to have an effectiveness "well in excess of 99 percent."[27] Defenses of this level of effectiveness "will virtually foreclose the possibility of a nuclear first strike against the United States." The detailed calculations supporting this conclusion are based on the assumed present strength of the Soviet strategic force as well as the assumed kill probabilities of the proposed U.S. defense. The Soviets are believed to deploy eight thousand to ten thousand strategic ballistic missile warheads—a total that may grow to as many as fifteen thousand in the mid-1990s, according to CIA estimates. Currently, if the Soviets were to assign two warheads to each target in the United States, they could be confident of destroying it. With a U.S. defense in place, an attacker would have to devote more than two warheads to each target to achieve the same kill probability. The Marshall study calculates that if the defense is 90 percent effective, thirty-eight warheads would have to be assigned to each of the targets to assure the same level of destruction. The statistical calculation supporting this estimate is not provided, but presumably it is based on the assumption that because the attacker cannot know which of the warheads he launches will be intercepted, he must compensate by greatly increasing the size of the attack. Because the United States has more than one thousand high-priority military targets, this calculation leads to the conclusion that the Soviets would have to launch more than 38,000 warheads to achieve the same results that they could now expect in the absence of U.S. defenses. This would be more than three times the present Soviet inventory and "an impractically large number." Even so large a force, moreover, would not be capable of destroying the U.S. arsenal on submarines at sea or bombers on alert. Thus, the proposed defensive deployment would introduce "a paralyzing degree of uncertainty" into an adversary's strategic calculus, virtually ruling out consideration of a possible preemptive strike.[28]

The cost of such a system to the point of initial operating capability (IOC) or partial deployment is estimated to be $54 billion; full operational capability (FOC) would cost $121 billion. Thus, the annual cost during development and deployment would be in the range of $10 to $15 billion annually, or between 3 and 4 percent of probable DOD annual budgets through the mid-1990s. The most expensive of the three layers would be the space-based one. The cost to manufacture each SBKKV is estimated at $1.5 million, based on independent studies by three contractors and the DOD. The cost to launch for each SBKKV is put at $.75 million, based on launch costs of 500 lbs. at $1,500 a lb.; the launch cost of the satellite that carries the SBKKV is also estimated as $.75 million. Cost of operations and maintenance for a ten-year life cycle is projected to be $1.5 million per SBKKV. The sensor satellites in low earth orbit (LEO) are estimated to cost $1 billion each, for a total cost of $10 billion for the ten sensor satellites. Cost of four sensor satellites in geosynchronous orbit (GEO) is estimated to be $2 billion each, or $8 billion for all four. The space-based layer, comprising eleven thousand SBKKVs and supporting sensor satellites would cost $68 billion. The ERIS layer would cost a total of $32 billion for ten thousand interceptors, including the aircraft carrying the airborne optical system (costing $10 billion). Each ERIS interceptor would cost $1.5 million along with $.75 million for launch facilities and operation and maintenance costs for ten years of $.75 million. The HEDI layer would cost a total of $18 billion. Each HEDI would cost about twice as much as an ERIS missile, $3 million each, because a costlier rocket is required to produce the higher acceleration and to cool the interceptor detector window. IOC would include deployment of sensor satellites, AOS aircraft, ground radars, and one-quarter of the full complement of SBKKVs.[29]

The institute calculates that the system would enjoy a favorable marginal cost ratio compared to Soviet ICBMs because their cost is approximately $20 million per warhead. In the boost phase a U.S. defense consisting of eleven thousand U.S. SBKKVs, estimated to cost about $68 billion, would in theory destroy boosters and buses carrying a total of nine thousand warheads, costing the Soviets $180 billion, giving the defense a marginal cost ratio of 3 : 1. For ERIS, the equivalent cost of each missile is approximately $3 million. But its effectiveness is estimated to be 70 percent, so its net cost would become $4.2 million. Cost of the incoming warheads is $20 million each. If ten decoys are deployed per warhead and decoy discrimination is not available, $42 million in ERIS missiles must be expended to destroy one warhead, with a marginal cost ratio of approximately 2 : 1 in favor of the offense. With effective decoy discrimination, the cost ratio shifts to 5 : 1 in favor of the defense. For HEDI, including ten-year life-cycle costs, each interceptor and its launchers are conservatively estimated to cost $6 million. At an average effectiveness of 70 percent, the cost would be $12 million per interceptor, or a cost ratio of 1.7 : 1 in favor of the defense. Against submarine-launched missiles on flat trajectories, HEDI effectiveness would rise to 100 percent and the cost ratio would be 2 : 5 in favor of the defense.[30]

Former secretary of defense Harold Brown says that the proposal for a three-tier defense is "unrealistic and would not lead to an effective capability." The KKV architectures, he observes, appear to be too easily countered by a reactive offense. The 1993–94 initial deployment date, moreover, is "difficult to credit." Six years is the same time that elapsed between the decision in 1981 to produce the B-1 bomber and its initial deployment. Seven years is about the time it will take to deploy an aircraft carrier if Congress appropriated funds for it. An SDI system, even in its initial form, is far more complex and unprecedented. Although the Soviets are not now developing a fast-burn booster, a U.S. decision to deploy a boost-phase defense would provide a strong motivation for such a development—along with space mines and other countermeasures. According to Brown, the countermeasures can be developed more cheaply and deployed more easily than fast-burn boosters.[31]

In contrast to the Marshall Institute plan, the study by Blechman and Utgoff estimates that space-based interceptor missiles "could probably be fully deployed around the year 2012."[32] These are the same SBKKVs the Marshall study sees as fully deployable a decade sooner. The study assumes that by the time the U.S. defense could be deployed, the Soviets would have altered the characteristics of their offensive arsenal so that their missiles would spend only 90 seconds in boost phase, that the post-boost phase would also be shortened to 60 seconds, and that Soviet missiles would be deployed in a more compressed area. On the U.S. side, the main difference in architecture between the Blechman and Utgoff study and the Marshall proposal is that the latter provides for no special battle-management satellites—eliminated presumably because the decentralization of the system would make them unnecessary. Blechman and Utgoff also assume that the interceptors would be capable of achieving a kill probability of 0.9 against any Soviet missile within range, but in their scheme the battle-management system would serve a critical function of assigning targets and ordering second strikes against targets not killed in the first wave.

The Blechman and Utgoff study also assumes a 5 kg homing warhead with an initial missile weight of 150 kg in order to achieve a burnout velocity of 10 km per second. The study estimates that 60,800 interceptors would be needed against the current force of Soviet ICBMs, 86,900 if intermediate-range missiles are also considered. The estimate calls for placing no more than 175 interceptor rockets on one satellite against only ICBMs—250 if intermediate weapons are included. Because the Soviets could cut a hole through the defense by destroying as few as nine to twelve of these battle satellites, it is probable that no more than fifty rocket interceptors would be placed on one pod. This also guarantees that enough interceptors would be close enough to the offensive missiles to enable a timely arrival of the second wave of interceptors. The system would also include decoy satellites—five for each battle satellite. In all, a total of 1,335 battle satellites and 6,675 decoys would be required to defend against Soviet ICBMs and SLBMs; 1,915 satellites and 9,575 decoys against a total force, including intermediate missiles. The payload weight would be 7,500 kg, the total satellite weight that would have to be placed in orbit would be 15.3 million kg, or 21.9 million kg to deal with the entire Soviet missile force. Given the roughly 16,000 kg payload the current space shuttle could put in orbit, launching these weights would require approximately 960 and 1,370 shuttle-equivalent flights respectively. Repairs and "rolling renewal" would require annual launches of about 10 percent of the initial weight.[33]

In contrast to the launch estimates of the Marshall Institute, Blechman and Utgoff contend (on the basis of a study by R. G. Finke and others)[34] that the initial lift requirement for this system would not be great enough to justify the high costs of developing and installing a new, large unmanned booster and would be better met by accepting the marginal costs of upgrading the shuttle. An upgraded shuttle would be capable of launching twice as much payload as the current shuttle: 60,000 kg in a low earth orbit required for the interceptors, 33,000 kg into the polar earth orbit required for the battle management satellites. Some 580–820 flights would be required over a four-year period, and approximately 50 or 70 per year thereafter. Based on the cost of producing ASATs now being manufactured by the LTV Corporation—taking into account reductions for increased numbers—the study estimates that the cost of producing the 73,600 interceptors needed (including 10 percent extra for testing and ground-based maintenance) would be $180 billion; $246 billion for the larger system. This represents an average cost of $2.5 million per missile. Research and development would cost $3 billion, including $2 billion for the battle satellites. The cost per satellite would be $85 million, with reduction of cost as the design was standardized. The cost of producing battle satellites would therefore be about $42–$50 billion for the entire system, and another $20 billion for twenty battle-management satellites. It would cost $33 billion to launch and sustain the space-based component, or $8 billion for the larger system. Launch costs thereafter would be $2.8 billion to $4 billion. Thus, the total cost for the space-based element would be between $460 and $600 billion (roughly 60 percent of the cost attributable to interceptor missiles). And it would cost an additional $170 billion for the ground-based system that would complement it. Given other marginal costs, the total system cost would be between $630 billion and $770 billion, or far more than the Marshall proposal contemplates.

THE SPIN-OFF ISSUE

As to the possible spin-off benefits, the CEP study noted that it is difficult to ascertain the value of such spin-offs even from the space program, where the effects can be studied. It seems clear that NASA investments have paid off handsomely in promoting the commercial use of communications satellites. Other examples could also be cited, notably the use of satellites for mapping and exploration for minerals as well as weather forecasting. But the quantitative economic benefits are hard to measure, particularly because many of the benefits are captured by world users in general, rather than solely by the United States.

Most analysis seems to show that government-supported R & D is less likely to promote economic efficiency than industry-sponsored R & D. Government support may help develop products for particular uses, but these may not be commercially applicable. Some studies also suggest that firms cut back on private funding of research when they receive government research support. Economists also generally assume that basic research is likely to have more favorable spin-offs than applied research, whereas SDI emphasizes applied research. Private commercial applications of high-energy lasers, particle beams, large optics, and infrared sensors are "not immediately obvious," as the CEP study by William D. Hartung and others notes.[35] Potential spin-offs are also limited by extremely tight security. SDI has tried to alleviate these problems, as NASA did, by setting up a special office to promote commercial spin-offs and by allocating funds, in the case of the X-ray laser, for research into medical applications, but it is not clear that SDIO can do much to resolve any problems of dissemination that might result from the concentration of this funding on military projects.

In its 1987 report to Congress, SDIO addressed this issue in discussing the work of its Office of Civil Applications. Emphasis was placed on the development of a referral data base containing synoptic data regarding new and unique SDI-generated technologies, which would be made available by computer modem to qualified business and academic clients approved by the DOD. In addition, a subcommittee is to be established for the SDIO Advisory Committee, with technology applications panels to function on a continuing basis "in reformatting technology into industrial technology profiles, identifying potential applications, reviewing client inquiries, and recommending further development of research." These panels are being established in several generic areas: biomedical applications, electronics, communications and computer applications; power-generation, storage and transmission applications; and materials and industrial-process applications. In 1984 Congress included a program for medical applications of the free-electron laser in the SDI program. Five regional medical free-electron centers are being established: three at universities and two at nonprofit laboratories (Brookhaven and the National Bureau of Standards). Other laboratories are being involved in the general effort.[36]

According to SDIO, a number of key areas for civil applications have been identified: computer data-processing speed and efficiency enhancements through improved components, circuitry, and software; lighter, smaller, more capable and energy-efficient electronic components; software with artificial intelligence that would allow computer systems to learn from experience and to make realistic deductions; optical computing using laser light; electrical power systems that are more efficient, and less expensive sensors that are lighter, smaller, more sensitive, and less expensive for medical applications, manufacturing, research, control systems, and many other applications; cryogenic cooling systems that are lighter, smaller, and more efficient for food preservation, medical applications, etc.; lightweight mirrors with computer-controlled adaptive alignment for laser applications to manufacturing processes; electrical systems hardening techniques applicable to reducing or eliminating noise and other interference in communication systems; tracking and pointing technology that might be useful in commercial aircraft guidance and control and ground-traffic monitoring; tomography-assisted technology to enhance medical diagnosis; free-electron applications for noninvasive surgery and diagnosis; integration of laser technology, robotics, and computerized precision control into industrial and biomedical applications.

Again, however, the opportunity costs need to be included in the balance. SDI could have a significant impact on R & D resources. The Apollo program consumed a much larger fraction of total U.S. R & D, especially in its peak year of 1966, than SDI will. NASA as a whole took up 20.8 percent of all research and development spending in the United States. In 1965 and 1966 Apollo required 40 and 20.8 percent respectively of new R & D resources. In 1990, even in the unlikely event that original projections are met, SDI would take up only 5.1 percent of all national R & D. Prior to the Apollo program, NASA did not significantly compete with private industry for scientists and engineers, nor did NASA's early growth strain the labor supply because of an economic slowdown in 1960–61. And NASA made a major effort to expand the labor pool so as not to compete with the private sector by establishing cooperative training and recruiting relationships with major universities. By 1966, however, there were unmistakable signs of a severe shortage of scientists and engineers. This competition, according to the CEP study, "exacted a high toll on U.S. industry during the 1960s." The cost per employed scientist and engineer rose for civilian industry. Labor costs expanded as much as 80 percent for one industry, and almost as much for others.[37] A greatly expanded SDI project could have similar results.

Still, if the NASA experience is repeated, SDI could also have significant economic benefits. NASA's R & D is thought to have been "strongly associated" with rising productivity in the economy between 1960 and 1974. NASA's R & D was said by a Chase econometrics study to have yielded a high rate of return in increased productivity; this study was performed for NASA. A GAO account of it, however, found that the claim was based on sensitive assumptions. The GAO did not claim to have disproved the study but only suggested that macroeconomic studies were hard to validate. Case studies are more persuasive, but they are inevitably too particularistic to allow for generalization. A study by the Midwest Research Institute in 1971 found a variety of innovations derived from NASA efforts. NASA's research provided the basic knowledge that made possible geostationary satellites now used for civil and military communication. NASA was the initial user of many industrial products. NASA assisted industry by evaluating alternative technologies, demonstrating new devices, and reducing uncertainty. "Nowhere," as the CEP notes, "is the value of NASA efforts more evident than in the development of communications satellites." Satellite communications is an application that would certainly not have been developed as rapidly or as well if not for NASA's pioneering efforts.[38]

Such anecdotal evidence cannot prove that NASA's overall impact has been positive for the economy or that defense research is also of net benefit to the civil economy. Econometric analysis has shown, for example, "that while industry-financed R & D is significantly related to productivity, government-supported R & D is not statistically connected to increased economic efficiency." And industries that are major recipients of federal R & D funds have the lowest productivity return on R & D from both sources. The reasons are several. Government R & D may lower the marginal cost to the firm of performing R & D and thus expand the amount of R & D that the firm can perform. Most of the government's R & D dollars are spent in R & D-intensive industries. In this way, government support could stimulate civil R & D. Second, most of the government's R & D goes for developing products for its own use, such as aircraft and communications equipment, not on improving the production, for example, of commercial foods. There is an important distinction between product and process improvements. Product improvements are useful only for the specific product; process improvements tend to be diffused throughout the economy. For this reason, government defense R & D is "a rather inefficient way to increase economic efficiency" because Pentagon products are not designed in a cost-minimizing environment. Another study has shown that increases in federal R & D were associated with reductions in company-financed research, contradicting the supposition that federal R & D stimulates greater private R & D. Instead, it tends to crowd out commercial research. A federally funded increase of one hundred R & D scientists and engineers one year will result in a decrease of company sponsorship of thirty-nine within a year, essentially no change the next, and an increase of seven the year afterward. Thus, the evidence is inconclusive.[39]

Another issue raised by the CEP study is the contention that spin-offs result more from basic research than from applied research in defense R & D and that most of the work done under SDI will be applied. Most economists tend to believe that if the effort is aimed at producing new technologies for specific uses, fewer commercial spin-offs will result. All of the SDI programs are designed to produce specific items for the layered defense against ballistic missiles. If in the process progress is made in developing lasers, sensors, and computers, that progress will not necessarily be transferable to commercial products and processes. There are instances where parallel uses are apparent and significant, notably the development of very high speed integrated circuits (VHSIC), which are necessary for real-time data processing for strategic defenses and have already found commercial markets. But there is far less likelihood that research on an electromagnetic railgun will prove adaptable to civil transportation, for example. Another problem inhibiting technology transfer to civil products is security classification. This concern with security has already blocked the transfer of VHSIC technology to civil applications lest the Soviets use a prototype to "reverse engineer" a device incorporating it.

Because SDI has not received the level of funding called for by the Reagan administration, it has not had the impact on defense spending or on the civil economy that has aroused the keenest controversy. If a decision is taken to deploy even a modest BMD system involving space-based defenses, the likely expenditures would be very high, whether one accepts the estimates of the advocates of such systems or of those who can claim to be more objective. It is evident that any full-scale space-based system would cost hundreds of billions of dollars to deploy, and billions more for a complementary air defense. Over a period of years even expenses in the range of hundreds of billions of dollars can be assimilated, but only if other military and civil programs are constrained. Such a program is not likely to have great positive benefits for the civil sector but is more likely to draw talent and other resources away from it and to raise factor prices in a strong economy. It could also generate a momentum in favor of continued expenditures, which would perpetuate dependency on defense spending in key industries and regions. Thus, even if deployment eventually becomes advisable for strategic and political reasons, there should be no illusions about the likely costs or about the potential spin-off benefits.

CHAPTER 9

Security Through Technology

An Illusory Faith

In the preceding chapters, we have tried to present a comprehensive review of the proposal for the development of strategic defenses, limiting commentary and interpretation to specific issues. Here we review the evidence and offer a general evaluation of SDI and reflections on the larger issue it raises: the proper role of science and technology in the quest for national and international security.

Both with respect to strategic defenses and other aspects of national security policy, the fundamental point we wish to emphasize is that research and development are best understood as means to a variety of ends, not as means that can or ought to determine ends. To expect advances in technology to provide security, in and by themselves, is to ask more than they can possibly provide. In touting SDI, President Reagan's science advisor (himself a reluctant convert) repeated an argument often used by promoters of new military systems: "We must start to play our trump—technological leverage." Amb. Gerard C. Smith offered a reply to this argument with which we fully agree: "In fact, we have played this card again and again in the strategic competition, with the H-bomb, with MIRVs, with the cruise missile, believing that our new weapons developments would make us secure. In every case, the Soviets matched our developments, and we ended up less secure."[1] To adopt this illusory faith that technology alone can achieve national security is also to ignore the need to address the political sources of insecurity by diplomatic means. SDI is only the latest in a series of fundamentally misguided efforts by both superpowers to achieve security by unilateral reliance on technological initiatives.[2] Invariably, these efforts have only exacerbated tensions and encouraged offsetting efforts on both sides with no increase in security.

THE EFFECTS OF POLITICIZATION: REVIEWING THE EVIDENCE

As we show in chapter 1, the proposal for a major effort to achieve a comprehensive strategic defense—one that would protect whole societies against nuclear attack and even make nuclear weapons "impotent and obsolete"—was not an inevitable result of scientific progress but, instead, a personal decision made by a president of the United States with the advice of a small group of nongovernmental counselors. The decision did not reflect the evolution of military technology or the judgment of what was possible or required by the "defense establishment"—the civilians responsible for advanced research, the chiefs of the military services, the leaders of the major weapons laboratories, and the research directors and other officers of the major defense contractors. It was arrived at largely by bypassing this establishment, in the belief that specialists in positions of authority would resist such a radical departure from conventional thinking.

In this respect, the decision smacked of the same mix of populism and conservatism that helped elect Ronald Reagan. Both as a candidate and in office, his stock in trade was the populistic complaint that government was "part of the problem, not the solution." The new administration pledged to "get government off the backs of the people" by curbing its intrusive role in the economy, eliminating two cabinet-level departments, reducing the size of the federal bureaucracy, and cutting taxes to curtail government spending. Although its attitude toward defense was far more positive, the disdain for bureaucracy and for the conventional wisdom of consensus-oriented foreign policy also affected its view of the defense establishment—and helped produce SDI. In keeping with its conservative leanings, this administration took office convinced that the Soviet Union would stop at nothing to fulfill the Marxist-Leninist dream of overthrowing Western capitalism and installing Soviet-style socialism throughout the world. Oblivious to the historic moves toward retrenchment and restructuring that the Soviet leadership was preparing, the new administration set out to do battle with the view that the United States should be content to contain Soviet expansionism rather than try to "roll back" and defeat communism.

This general impulse to develop U.S. military power and to use it to thwart the perceived threat of Soviet imperialism led the administration to paint Soviet progress in military technology as a grave menace and an already successful effort to achieve not just military parity with the United States but primacy. In response, the Reagan administration called for a "strategic modernization" of U.S. forces that would meet the supposed challenge. Thus, the B-1 bomber program, deferred under the Carter administration, was resurrected at considerable cost, even though many experts argued that the plane would soon become obsolete because of the development of the Stealth bomber. A vast expansion of naval power was planned, aimed at implementing a new "maritime strategy" requiring a 600-ship navy capable not just of deterring a Soviet attack but also of fighting a conventional and nuclear war. The increasingly costly Trident submarine program—already under way and designed as a key element of the strategic deterrent—was sustained at the planned pace, but a new emphasis was simultaneously placed on carrier battle groups and battleships to implement the maritime strategy. New manpower policies were adopted to help all three services to attract and train the needed personnel. Expensive high-technology projects were promoted, some of which, like the DIVAD anti-aircraft gun, turned out badly, partly because of their technological complexity but also because of an administrative failure to require that new projects be properly tested, as the General Accounting Office reported in 1988. The Reagan administration did not initiate the process by which the military services came to rely more and more on high-technology weaponry, but it encouraged the belief that the United States should compensate for Soviet quantitative advantages by using the qualitative multipliers that technological superiority could provide. Thus, a continued emphasis was also placed on precision-guided munitions, along with other "emerging technologies," as a response to Soviet emphasis on increased firepower and nuclear weapons.

With respect to strategic weapons and arms control, the administration took the view that the United States was lagging behind the Soviets and that previous arms-control agreements had only made it easier for them to press their strategic advance in heavy missiles—missiles whose throw-weight accommodated very large payloads and which, because they were launched from silos, were more accurate than SLBMs on which the United States relied most. Richard Perle, a strong critic of the SALT II agreement largely on the ground that it enabled the Soviets to retain this advantage, was accordingly appointed assistant secretary of defense for international security affairs and was able to exert considerable influence in shaping arms-control policy. Another hard-liner, Edward L. Rowny, a retired army general who had resigned from the delegation when the SALT II agreement was negotiated, was appointed chief negotiator in the strategic arms control talks.

Meanwhile, the administration pressed for the deployment of the MX missile, a weapons system developed by the Carter administration as part of its effort to gain support for SALT II. The Reagan administration argued that the Soviets were capable of destroying more than 80 percent of the fixed, land-based Minuteman force in a first strike, and that the only way to close this "window of vulnerability" was to install MX in some shelter mode that would enable it to ride out a first strike. Although the administration was no more successful than its predecessor in winning support for a basing scheme for MX, it nevertheless persisted in campaigning for the construction of a large number of the new missiles, even though they were to be deployed in existing silos only marginally modified to resist blast pressures. The president's own Scowcroft Commission supported his policy of proceeding with the MX emplacement, but only as an intermediate step before the development and deployment of the smaller, single-warhead mobile Midgetman. The administration was never of one mind on the Midgetman proposal and even made the unexpected demand (before the meeting with Gorbachev at Reykjavík) that the Soviets agree to dismantle hard-to-target mobile missiles. This position ran directly contrary to the advice of the Scowcroft Commission, whose view was that mobile missiles promote stability because they lessen the chances of a successful first strike and could carry fewer warheads of lower explosive power than heavier fixed missiles.

To these efforts at promoting the adoption of new military systems while treading water on arms control, the administration added some venturesome new thoughts on military doctrine. U.S. forces, Secretary Weinberger suggested, should be configured so that the United States could "prevail" in an extended nuclear exchange in the event deterrence failed. Although he did not go so far as to claim that either side could win a nuclear war, he did suggest that the United States should regard nuclear weapons not merely as instruments with which to deter war, but as weapons to be used like other weapons if it became necessary to fight a war. The expectation was that the side best prepared for battle would have the best chance of surviving or of being able to recover afterward. Other high-ranking officials revived the belief in the desirability of civil

defense as a way of improving prospects for prevailing. One was imprudent enough to suggest that "with enough shovels," the population
could save itself from nuclear attack by digging shelters against fallout.[3]

These moves appeared to many observers—particularly foreigners
inclined to take bellicose statements by a president of the United States
as more than domestic propaganda—to signal a far-reaching new ag-
gressiveness in U.S. foreign policy. The new administration, it seemed,
was once again changing the course of U.S. strategic and foreign policy,
this time away from any belief in combining détente and deterrence (as
enshrined, especially for West Germans, in the 1967 Harmel Report)
toward a much more adventurous policy aimed at restoring U.S. military superiority in the cold war that had been lost in the 1970s. This
new superiority would certainly be used, critics suggested, to intimidate
the U.S.S.R. and to extend U.S. hegemony.

Although the rhetorical flourishes did herald a commitment to increased defense spending, none of the Reagan administration initiatives
had a fundamental effect on the strategic foundations of the superpower
conflict. Modernization efforts begun earlier and carried forward in the
Reagan years have significantly diminished the numerical size and the
megatonnage of the U.S. nuclear arsenal. In this reduction, the biggest
single factor has been the arming of bombers with standoff weapons
rather than gravity bombs in order to assure penetration of Soviet air
defenses—a point worth emphasizing because it suggests that U.S. efforts to achieve strategic defenses would be met by corresponding Soviet
efforts to assure penetration. In addition, the adoption of the ABM
Treaty and voluntary adherence to the SALT II limits on offensive weapons restrained both sides from expanding nuclear arsenals to the maximum made possible by the MIRVing of warheads. Otherwise, the Reagan administration's "strategic modernization" program resulted in
increased appropriations, both for strategic and conventional forces,
but did not change the strategic situation or remove any of its dangers.

For the future, however, SDI will remain problematic insofar as it
arouses expectations of a fundamental change in the status quo. Its supporters will continue to paint it in the visionary colors Reagan used
when he first introduced SDI in 1983. Skeptics will continue to say that
the population defense central to the president's vision is not feasible
and that SDI will only destabilize an already precarious balance of
power. But those who cling to Reagan's vision will continue to expect
strategic defenses to make nuclear weapons obsolete. To its most faith-
ful advocates, SDI promises something far better than a freeze, some-

thing much more productive than the tedious and partial arms-control negotiations.

That promise, as has become clear in SDI, is to be realized by building a shield in space to intercept nuclear weapons. Would such a shield be used only to protect Americans? In his March 1983 speech, Reagan declared that his intention was to protect the United States and its allies but not to threaten the Soviet Union. He was prepared, he claimed, to share the technology with the Soviets, provided they would agree to reduce and eventually eliminate nuclear weapons in exchange for defenses. Again, critics scoffed and agreed with the Soviets themselves[4] that so long as the United States refused to sell the Soviets more conventional products—on the ground that they would somehow enhance the Soviet's war-making abilities—the United States was scarcely likely to provide them with the secrets of its most advanced weapons systems— secrets that might well be used to develop countermeasures effective enough to defeat the system. Nevertheless, Reagan insisted that he was sincere and proposed that both sides cooperate in a defense transition. During this transition they would agree to radical reductions in offensive arsenals while they both developed defenses. If and when it became feasible to deploy defenses, they would try to negotiate a joint deployment of some sort, failing which the United States would feel free to deploy defenses on its own. They would proceed in the expectation that defenses would promote the abolition of nuclear weapons, if only by demonstrating that they were no longer useful or as economical a form of deterrence as a space shield. However unrealistic the goal, its supporters are likely to cling to this vision so long as they continue to suppose that there must be a technological answer to the anxieties of the nuclear age.

Experience has not shaken this faith in technology since 1983. As we have seen, the president ran into difficulties at the outset in his attempt to persuade the U.S.S.R. that his intention was benign, but his insistence on pursuing the SDI did not prevent resumption of arms-control negotiations. Although the Soviet Union contended that SDI was a transparent U.S. effort to achieve "space-strike weapons" with which to militarize space and to enable the United States to intimidate the Soviet Union by threatening to develop a credible first strike, it nevertheless agreed to resume arms-control negotiations, provided space weapons were discussed. The Soviet leaders evidently concluded that in view of the president's reelection, he would be in a position to pursue his plans. They regarded these plans as threatening not necessarily because they promised to create an effective space-based defense—Soviet scientific authorities publicly expressed the same skepticism on this score as most Western experts—but probably because they feared the overall impact of the technological advances on improving the West's military forces. The ABM Treaty had not prevented the Soviets from deploying a significant strategic defense against aircraft, from deploying and improving the one allowed ABM system around Moscow, or from undertaking research not only on other BMD weapons using beam technology but also on other space systems, such as the ASAT. The SDI threatened to remove the barriers imposed by the ABM Treaty on the U.S. capacity to exploit technological superiorities, notably in computers and miniaturization, and to make more use of space for military purposes. The Soviets did not look on this development with equanimity and were therefore eager to engage the United States in negotiations that would tie reductions in offensive weapons to constraints on SDI. They were prepared to make reductions anyway because they, too, were modernizing their forces to promote greater emphasis on mobile missiles and submarine-launched cruise missiles. SDI therefore turned out to be a stimulus to negotiations rather than a barrier.

Reagan also ran into difficulties with the United States' European allies, but these were managed relatively easily by assuring the Europeans that SDI was still a research program and that no decision would be made to develop and deploy an SDI system without consulting them and without negotiating the issue with the U.S.S.R. In addition, the administration offered the allies an opportunity to participate in the program, an invitation they could ill afford to turn down, especially because it involved a U.S. subsidy and carried an implicit threat that they might be left out of a major leap in advanced technology. Besides, the West Europeans were also concerned about developing defenses against aircraft and short-range missiles, which the United States was quite ready to accommodate—in effect agreeing to a division of labor in which the allies pursued this element of the problem with greatest emphasis.

With the help of an overwhelming victory in the 1984 election, in which his Democratic opponent tried unsuccessfully to use the Star Wars issue against him, Reagan was in a strong position to press Congress for budgetary support. As a result, the program gradually took shape, and instead of appearing to be mostly the president's uninformed vision, it acquired real advocates and implementers, with budgets and contracts to dispense. From then on, the main focus of concern shifted to the technology of SDI. What exactly would the space shield consist of? How feasible were laser weapons and elaborate battle-management software? What countermeasures could be adopted, and how could the system be kept effective and survivable against them?

The formidable difficulties and uncertainties of the technology, described in chapter 3, have gravely diminished support for the program, forcing changes of direction. Expectations have shifted dramatically under various pressures—technical as well as political and economic—during the few years the program has been in existence. Whereas at first it was designed to explore all possible technical options, it was soon altered to put the highest emphasis on near-term options when political pressures began to be felt in 1986 and 1987. Funding for directed-energy weapons, which are potentially the most effective but the furthest from realization, was cut back, while support for kinetic-energy weapons and improved techniques for surveillance and detection, which are the nearest to realization, was given higher priority. Whereas, at first, officials like the president's first science advisor disdainfully insisted that a defense of missiles was not even in the path of the president's objective, by 1988 SDIO was giving high priority to the development of such defenses as an immediate step that might keep the program alive and eventually lead to the full-scale system.

The fact that the program was politically driven from the outset has critically affected its development, despite efforts to insulate it from political debate. The Fletcher panel tried to overcome this political liability by calling for a broad-spectrum research effort that would not presuppose eventual deployment but would aim to provide the knowledge upon which a decision might be made first to develop, then to deploy a defensive system. The panel was particularly anxious that an early decision be avoided, lest the nation be locked into a system that would not be as effective as one that might be devised after a more complete inquiry. But the pressures for early deployment built up from two sources, Congress and the executive branch.

The congressional Republicans who strongly supported the program were anxious that it move from the phase of pure research into a more practical mode as soon as possible—even if that were too soon to know about the utility of beam weapons—so that the program could continue to receive public support. They feared that if nothing practical came of it in the short term, the opponents of SDI would succeed in keeping support at a low level until it was sacrificed for the sake of arms control, if not by Reagan, then by a successor. By gaining an early commitment to development and deployment, they could prove that the program was already having some benefit and was not the "pie in the sky" project its critics claimed. By showing that early deployment would not cost anything near the trillion dollars some critics claimed it would, they hoped to defuse that criticism. Some Democrats in Congress also contributed to the pressure for early deployment because they were interested in redirecting the program from its long-term goal of providing population defense to the goal they considered more realistic of developing terminal defenses for missile silos.

Like the Republicans in Congress, the champions of SDI in the executive branch were eager to overcome efforts to curb its budget. By supporting early deployment, they could hope to show that the program was succeeding beyond expectations and that it could serve a real military purpose by adding to the uncertainty of an enemy contemplating an attack, even if it could not promise to intercept more than a fraction of a massive attack. Such an installation would be a first step toward a more comprehensive defense, drawing on future technologies. In addition, they were interested in forestalling an arms-control agreement to reduce offensive systems, especially one that was tied to constraints on the testing and development of BMD. By promoting SDI, many of them hoped to force the abrogation of the ABM Treaty, along with the SALT II Treaty, and very likely to prevent an agreement on offensive-arms reduction. This faction operated on the assumption that arms control was inevitably more in the Soviet Union's national interest than the United States', because the Soviets would exploit every opportunity such an agreement provided to modernize their nuclear weapons and, just as important, to enhance their conventional forces, while the United States would take arms control as a signal to cut back on military preparedness and modernization. Preventing arms-control agreements was therefore essential to maintaining national security by means of strength rather than trust in Soviet intentions.

This position was not unambiguously shared by all in the highest councils of the administration. It was not shared, for example, by Nitze, who made it clear that he still regarded the SDI as a research program and did not believe that enough progress had been achieved to warrant a decision to develop and deploy a near-term system. He contended, in contrast to Weinberger, that the research had not yet yielded a basis for concluding that a system could be built that would satisfy the stiff criteria he had set. Such an assurance, he suggested, would not be available until at least ten years after the project had been begun, or the mid-1990s, as originally contemplated. Like the drafters of the Fletcher report, moreover, he recognized that the prospects of achieving a successful defense would depend heavily on also achieving, by political means, an agreement to constrain offenses. He therefore saw SDI as an important lever in bargaining with the Soviets—not a bargaining chip to be foregone, but an instrument by which to persuade the Soviets to enter into a cooperatively managed defense transition. For Nitze, an arms-reduction agreement was not an alternative to SDI but a natural complement. There is reason to suppose that his view was shared by others in the State Department, including Shultz, who was clearly disappointed by the failure to achieve a radical arms-reduction agreement at Reykjavík and who also saw no contradiction between continued pursuit of SDI and the achievement of such an agreement. The common point of consensus between both factions in the administration was the issue of the broad interpretation of the ABM Treaty. Nitze supported the correctness of this interpretation, and so did Shultz, at least publicly, even though it has been an obstacle to the conclusion of an agreement with the Soviets.

Ironically, one reason the advocates of early deployment have not succeeded is that they have been unable to enlist strong support from the military services. So long as the SDI effort was confined to research and did not detract from other planned military research, the leaders of the services and others in the defense technology community saw no important reason to object to it, especially because they were grateful to Reagan for his strong commitment to defense spending. Support for SDI was a small price to pay, even for those skeptical of the program. Early deployment is another matter, however, because it would be so expensive as to jeopardize other programs. The Joint Chiefs have been noticeably cool to the idea, and there have been warnings from other military figures to the effect that it must not be permitted to bring about reductions in other programs. Already in 1985 Gen. Bernard Rogers, then supreme allied commander in Europe, warned that overemphasis on SDI would be harmful for NATO: "If from now on we turn all our attention to SDI, we then fail to undergird our efforts in the more mundane areas such as sustainability of conventional forces and modernization of nuclear weapons."[5] As early deployment was being promoted in political circles, military leaders expressed decided skepticism. Adm. William J. Crowe, Jr., chairman of the Joint Chiefs, noted that people had begun to talk about an SDI system as though it were actually "out there in the parking lot waiting to be deployed."[6] Lt. Gen. Harley Hughes, air force deputy chief of staff for plans and operations, told an

Air Force Association symposium that deployment of strategic defenses should not come at the expense of modernizing offensive nuclear and conventional weapons. "We have got to raise the money independently of ongoing strategic and conventional force modernizations."

The issue of "affordability" obviously looms larger as deployment of a marginally effective Phase I system, costing at least $69 billion, is proposed. Military leaders, including the Joint Chiefs, were reported to consider even this estimate too high a price to be paid for a "brand-new weapons system." Hughes did not deny that a strategic defense would be valuable. An SDI system would be the "perfect countervailing strategy" to the Soviet Union's stress on land-based ICBMs. But he warned that no one should be under the illusion that defenses could be chosen in place of offensive weapons: "There are those walking around, some in positions of influence, that say SDI is so close that we don't need to look at the triad. That's hogwash." Similarly, Gen. John Chain, commander-in-chief of SAC, argued that deployment of strategic defenses would only increase the importance of air-breathing forces: "If the U.S. deploys SDI, the Soviets will deploy their SDI. ICBMs, perhaps through negotiations or through choice on each side, will be reduced in importance in the triad. At the same time, I see air-breathers increasing significantly." [7]

Such reticence on the part of the military, combined with exceptionally strong criticism from university based physicists and the cautionary APS report, helped to strengthen the hand of those in Congress who sought to restrain the program. Their aim has been to head off premature deployment, prevent it from jeopardizing progress in arms control, and restrain the growth of the budget deficit. Congressional opposition, its hard core mainly composed of Democrats, included many who were critical of the program because they saw it as an effort by conservatives to derail the prospects for détente with the Soviets. Others, notably Sen. Sam Nunn, also saw it as a threat to the balance of the military program as well as a challenge (in the form of the "broad interpretation") to the treaty-ratifying role of the Senate. This pronounced opposition made it easier for doubters in the defense establishment— including members of the Defense Science Board—to press their own criticisms and reservations.

The result has been that SDI has been maintained, but at a level of funding far short of the steeply rising rate of increase called for by the administration. In its most ambitious version, SDI has fallen victim to political opposition, just as its initial success was made possible by the political popularity of its principal sponsor. The difficulties experienced by the program reflect both the decline of the president's popularity and the fact that once a program is initiated, it becomes subject to all the pulls and counterpulls that affect all forms of defense appropriations. SDI pitted the wishes of the political directors of the Defense Department against the judgment of staff specialists and the interests of the military services in other projects. Partisan differences affected the congressional consideration of the issue. Within the executive branch itself, foreign policy considerations inhibited the president from supporting the pro-SDI movement as strongly as he might have liked to do. Although Reagan was tempted to order deployment and let the chips fall where they may, he was restrained by strong protestations from U.S. allies as well as by fear that such a decision would have jeopardized the conclusion of the INF agreement with the Soviets that he wanted to achieve.

Such political considerations are inescapable when what is at stake is either a large-scale research effort or one that also includes a commitment to deployment. So long as research is relatively low-key and long-term it is conducted with only minimal political scrutiny. Strategic defense was given a distinctly higher profile than other Pentagon research objectives because the president chose to stress the importance of the research and to point it toward a radical strategic and foreign policy objective. By making extravagant promises, he politicized the project, making it a major public question around which both support and opposition crystallized. Had the research been conducted with less fanfare, it would have been assured of at least some Democratic support. (Under different auspices, one can even picture liberals rallying to the SDI as a peaceful alternative to an offensive arms race, and Republicans viewing it with suspicion as a devious ploy intended to justify the curtailment of offensive military programs.) But once the program was launched by a conservative president without prior consensus in the military establishment, it was bound to be put in a precarious position. SDI's fate so far has reflected the conditions of its inception, but under any circumstances, a technological program of this magnitude and with these implications is bound to arouse contentious political forces.

How much momentum such a program can create is hard to estimate. The Apollo project was different because it was directed toward a particular objective and pitted man against nature, not against man. SDI is still a research program whose only objective is to ascertain the feasibility of a military mission. Whatever commitments are made by contractors and others in expectation of follow-on contracts will still have to be integrated with foreign policy interests and decisions and will have to overcome resistance on other grounds—including the defense establishment's fear that a major procurement program in strategic defenses will come at the expense of other military priorities. Although partisans have certainly hoped they could built this momentum, and critics have feared they would succeed, the evidence so far suggests that the program is far from irreversible, particularly if the remarkable swing toward U.S.-Soviet cooperation initiated by Reagan and Gorbachev inhibits potentially destabilizing moves on both sides.

PROSPECTS FOR U.S.-SOVIET AGREEMENT

This new cooperation has created a momentum of its own, which could lead to an agreement to control the development of space weapons, even though a total prohibition is probably impossible to achieve. Given the commitments of both the Soviet Union and the United States to the exploitation of space, it is hard to imagine an agreement that would completely prevent the further militarization of space. Space programs are to a large extent inherently dual-purpose. To build large rockets, launch capacity, and even space platforms is to provide for future uses that may be civil or military. It may still be possible, nevertheless, to regulate the testing and development of space weapons—as distinct from systems and components with military roles—such as surveillance and communications satellites. An agreement is also conceivable under which strategic defenses might be deployed that would have only minimal components in space, such as sensors.

The opportunities for such agreements, however, may grow fewer with time. As each nation pursues major programs to achieve dual-purpose uses in space, the investments represent long-term commitments that neither will be willing to write off. As the United States develops space-based weapons, the U.S.S.R. is bound to seek to develop systems for countering those weapons as well as space-based weapons of its own. Failure to achieve agreements for restraint and cooperation will lead to an intense competition. The notion that there would be an opportunity to limit the militarization of space while this competition is under way is wishful. More likely, the defensive competition will resemble the offensive one. Both sides will develop and deploy their systems, and only then will they seek to arrange some form of parity and noninterference, such as "rules of the road" in space to prevent war by accident. The need to carry out intrusive investigations in order to determine whether a particular satellite contains a weapon or a weapons system will make verification of elaborate agreements very difficult, once such weapons are tested and deployed. The only effective way to prevent deployment of space-based weapons is to prevent their testing. Even that may not be sufficient, inasmuch as certain of the weapons can be well tested in the atmosphere or on earth, particularly if they involve lasers or for that matter kinetic weapons.

But why make a major commitment to develop space-based defenses? Apart from the question of whether such systems are feasible, there are two related policy questions: Is it worthwhile to expend the considerable sums that will be needed to achieve them? If the effort succeeds, can the result possibly represent a gain in national or world security?

Before these policy questions can be answered, however, it is first necessary to pose another question. Is there something so fundamentally wrong in the current defense posture that the search for a technological alternative should be accelerated? In chapter 4, we review several of the serious problems associated with the current reliance on retaliatory deterrence. These problems can be remedied, at least in part, by radical reductions in the quantity of nuclear arms deployed, especially those most likely to be used in a first strike, and by other measures, such as improving the safety of weapons to make them less prone to accidental discharge. These measures will not altogether eliminate nuclear weapons, but they might pave the way toward a virtually complete elimination of the threat of nuclear war by greatly improving mutual confidence and cooperation. Unfortunately, however, radical reductions of nuclear weapons will have to be accompanied by other agreements designed to reduce the threat from conventional weapons. Otherwise, the West will be unwilling to relinquish the threat of nuclear weapons to offset presumed Soviet conventional superiority in Europe, and neither side will be willing to deplete its nuclear arsenals lest they be needed in order to meet some contingency stemming from an escalation of a conventional conflict. Reductions are not inconceivable, however, especially as geopolitical lines of separation between superpower spheres of influence, like those acknowledged for Europe in the Helsinki Final Accords, are achieved elsewhere as well. The key to this sort of arms reduction and conflict resolution lies in the mitigation of political mistrust by progressively enhanced mutual security. The greater the sense of security, the more arms reduction will be acceptable. There is no prospect that mutual confidence will become so great that all arms can be eliminated, but deterrence can be stabilized by the removal of the threat, first of all, of a nuclear first strike, and second, of a major war in which nuclear weapons might be used. Paradoxically, while radical arms control requires mutual willingness to cooperate, that willingness can best be achieved by incremental progress in arms control.

This attempt to make deterrence more stable need not preclude any role for strategic defense. On the contrary, as confidence is established, it is entirely possible that limited forms of defense could be substituted for some elements of offense. The danger is that defenses will be *added* to offense, in which case deterrence could be destabilized. How much destabilization would occur would depend on the quality of the defenses. The highest likelihood is that in the short term there will be little destabilization, simply because for the time being no system can be conceived, regardless of cost, that will accomplish the total defense of population against nuclear attack in view of the enormous capacities for population overkill that both sides have and are likely to keep. It must be remembered that these capacities include not only ballistic missiles but also the air-breathing threat. Given modern technology, or any reasonable extrapolation, it is simply not possible to construct such a defense, not in six or seven years, not in ten, not at all. This means that offensive weapons will not be eliminated by the deployment of defenses. If they are not eliminated, they must somehow be integrated with defensive deployments. Short of an agreement to integrate them, there will be synergism between the programs to develop and deploy them, producing greater instability than now exists, as Harold Brown has explained:

> Such measures as antiballistic missile defense of urban industrial areas and massive civil defense programs may well destabilize the situation. They might reduce the likely number of deaths in case of a thermonuclear war, but they might also stimulate a responsive buildup of the other side's offensive forces that would more than overcome their damage-limiting effect—especially because damage-limiting measures are less likely to work than the countering offensive steps. They may then, in the end, result in more casualties in a thermonuclear war than if they had not been undertaken.[8]

What sort of agreement is conceivable? An agreement might well be entered into on the lines of what was proposed at Reykjavík and has been under consideration since then, whereby both sides would be free to continue to do research on defensive systems, but by which they would commit themselves not to deploy any defensive systems other than those permitted under the ABM Treaty. This agreement would be accompanied by another one reducing offensive arsenals, at first by roughly half, with agreed sublimits. While this would still leave both sides with more than enough for a devastating retaliation, and with some potential first-strike capability, it would reduce the likelihood that either side could contemplate a "successful" first strike, i.e., one that could destroy so much of the adversary's retaliatory force that a devastating counterattack would be impossible.

This first phase of reductions would not radically change the nature of the nuclear confrontation. Nevertheless, its significance should not be minimized. Both sides would have overtly recognized the present capacities for overkill and would have thus committed themselves to a reduction of nuclear arsenals, not simply to their limitation, as was mainly the basis of the SALT I and SALT II agreements. Because the arrangement would also commit both sides to observe the terms of the ABM Treaty for at least a certain number of years, it would reinforce the framework of the entire process. Neither side would have to consider the advisability of retaining offensive weapons to offset deployment of strategic defenses. Without such an assurance, giving up these weapons might be imprudent. If the moratorium on deployment is for a considerable period of time, such as the ten years discussed at Reykjavík, both sides could well consider that the weapons in question would become obsolete in any case, especially if there was a need to protect them from a potential space-based defense. The Soviets already appear to have decided to shift to single-warhead mobile missiles, which would be harder to detect than the heavy MIRVed ground-based missiles. They also have an additional incentive to develop fast-burn boosters because of SDI. The moratorium on deployment of defenses would enable them to move away from reliance on their present ICBM force without having to do so on a crash basis and without corresponding concessions by the United States. For its part, the United States could also afford to lower or to eliminate its present dependence on fixed ICBMs in favor of mobile ground-based missiles, as recommended by the Scowcroft Commission. Thus, the intermediate phase of the defense transition, as envisioned by Nitze, would be achieved.

The next phase is less certain.[9] If both sides should succeed in developing defenses in which they have confidence, they could conceivably agree to further offensive reductions accompanied by a relaxation of the ABM Treaty limitations on the deployment of defenses. A partial defense, such as the scheme proposed by the Defense Science Board task force in 1988, might be deployed. This kind of defense would be designed to provide not only a degree of population defense but also partial protection for ground-based missiles, other retaliatory forces, and national-command authorities. It would be primarily ground-based, with airborne sensors supplementing ground-based radar and space-based surveillance and tracking systems. Even without such defenses, it is at least conceivable that both sides would agree to further reductions of offensive nuclear forces on the understanding that one thousand to two thousand nuclear warheads, if based on relatively invulnerable launch platforms, would be more than adequate to deter a first strike. Now that both countries have embarked on a high-priority inquiry into defenses—assuming the Soviets have made this a high priority in response to SDI if it was not one already—they are unlikely to agree to such reductions unless they can be confident of what the other will do in deploying defenses. Further reductions would be possible only if the defenses to be deployed would not provide much more protection than a leveraged defense of hard-point targets. In order to achieve this level of confidence, however, a firm, verifiable agreement would be needed to assure that only certain types and numbers of defenses would be deployed for at least a fixed period of years.

THE CONSEQUENCES OF A FAILURE
TO ACHIEVE AGREEMENT

What is likely to happen if such an agreement cannot be concluded? This is perhaps the most difficult question of all, because it entails so much that is necessarily conjectural. What if the United States and the U.S.S.R. should fail to achieve an agreement to cut offenses, either in the intermediate phase envisioned by Nitze or in a subsequent one? Presumably, if by some unexpected chance the SDI produces strategic defenses that meet the Nitze standards, the Soviets would be compelled to accept the logic of the defense transition. They might not choose to negotiate the terms of the transition, but they would be forced to recognize that the threat posed by their offensive weapons was losing credibility. They would therefore have to develop and deploy defenses against U.S. offenses, and the result would be that, independently, both sides would be participating in a transition. The trouble with this expectation is that the technological prospects for a truly effective defense have yet to be validated. A more likely expectation is that competition and mutual suspicion might lead one or both sides to abrogate the ABM Treaty in order to deploy defenses that would be acknowledged to provide only incremental benefits. This decision might be taken on sheer strategic grounds. If there is concern about the vulnerability of land-based assets—not only missile silos but also submarine bases and airbases—and especially about a decapitating attack directed against the national-command authorities, then active as well as passive defenses may be advisable. Such defenses would not of themselves transform the situation but could be regarded as stabilizing on the basis of existing notions of deterrence. They might be undertaken in a calculated effort to improve offensive capacities, or as an effort to move the country away from a commitment to international accommodation and toward a more aggressive policy. It is less likely, though not impossible, that a deployment would be made because of inertia or from the momentum of previous commitments. This is so simply because the jump from a low-level research program to a multibillion dollar deployment would not be a light commitment or one that could be made incrementally. The recent debate over whether to commit almost $70 billion over a seven-year period for an intermediate deployment of a three-layered defense makes it obvious that such a decision is likely to be reached only after major soul-searching and after, not before, there is a clearly felt breakdown in U.S.-Soviet relations.

In the immediate future, the likelihood that SDI will continue to be supported only as a research project, to be conducted in conformity with the ABM Treaty, is far higher than the prospects for development and deployment. The very fact that the 1987 INF Treaty was negotiated and concluded by an administration that had come into office insisting that the Soviets could not be trusted to observe any arms-control agreement will make it easier for its successor to move forward in other negotiations. Under these circumstances, there will probably be little public support for the view that the ABM Treaty should be abrogated in order to rush to deploy a system that can make only incremental improvements in the existing form of deterrence. The possibility of achieving many of the same benefits by passive measures—including the dispersal of offensive forces—will be a strong argument against the wisdom or necessity of deploying active defenses. At most, Congress is likely to approve the activation and modernization of the defenses once deployed at Grand Forks, North Dakota, a move that would be permitted within the terms of the treaty. An alternative would be to emplace a ground-based defense around the national capital to match the Soviet deployment around Moscow and to gain experience with modernized ABM systems. For this option to be adopted, however, political leaders will need to overcome the popular resistance to the idea of protecting Washington, D.C., while leaving the rest of the country unprotected—a sentiment expressed in response to an earlier proposal to defend only the capital. Another alternative is to deploy a ground-based system located in the center of the country with a footprint large enough to protect Washington, D.C. This option, however, is considered doubtful both on technical and political grounds—especially since it would violate the ABM Treaty by providing a territorial defense.

Given all these difficulties, it would seem in the best interests of both sides to refrain from deploying defensive systems that would require an abrogation of the ABM Treaty without providing more than a partially effective defense of military targets and, at most, a marginal defense of population. Such a defense would invite the other side to build up rather than build down its offensive forces and to concentrate its efforts on countermeasures that could easily provoke hostile confrontations. One side may decide not to allow a deployment of space weapons over its territory. Even once deployed, defensive satellites would be countered by ASATs, space mines, or more surreptitious forms of interference. The character of this confrontation could not be confined to the surface of the earth but would involve a competition in measures and countermeasures, actions and reactions, in space as well as elsewhere—the outcome of which can hardly be foreseen.

One incidental result would be to sour the prospects for cooperation in civil space efforts. Whereas the Soviets are now eager to encourage cooperative efforts, they would certainly become less welcoming if they became convinced that the United States was making no distinction between efforts to operate in space for peaceful and for military purposes. It may well be that the Soviets have similar intentions, and that space platforms designed for peaceful purposes can easily be turned to military uses. But if there is no agreement to restrict such activities, the effort to make military use of space will become more and more deliberate on both sides, to an extent that will preclude cooperation.

The harm that a unilateral U.S. decision to deploy space weapons would do is not restricted to U.S.-Soviet cooperation. In view of the apprehensions of U.S. allies, it is hardly farfetched to suppose that the strains long evident in NATO would become too much for the alliance to bear were the Soviets to counter the United States' partial defenses by erecting defenses of their own that would effectively degrade and perhaps nullify the British and French independent deterrents and make the U.S. commitment to flexible response even less reassuring than it already is. As things stand, West Europeans are ambivalent, wanting both U.S. protection and better relations with the Soviets, fearing both U.S. abandonment and entrapment in U.S. efforts to contain Soviet expansion outside Europe. The combination of deterrence and détente, however ambiguous it may be at times, serves that interest well. Compelling West Europeans to rely solely on U.S. military strength would strengthen forces already demanding "European initiatives"—a vague notion that encompasses quite opposite tendencies, one aiming for cooperation with the Soviets, the other for building new defenses against the Soviets. In any case, the stability of the alliance might be sorely tested and possibly be damaged irreparably.

In the long run, it is possible that the research efforts being pursued under the aegis of SDI and in other space-related activities could transform the character of warfare so that it would inevitably have a full spatial dimension, somewhat as anticipated by such films as *Star Wars*. The advocates of SDI could eventually be vindicated, as advances in technology make it possible to intercept ballistic missiles effectively and economically and to supplement a BMD shield with an affordable air defense that would be similarly effective against cruise missiles and short-range low-trajectory ballistic missiles. If these technological prospects should come to pass, and if it should prove possible to arrange some sort of joint operation of defenses between East and West, or even a grander international scheme, nuclear weapons might indeed become a thing of the past. But without international cooperation the likelihood is very small—perhaps even infinitesimal—that such a technology can be achieved. In a world with determined and equally capable adversaries eager to defeat each other's defenses, there could never be certainty that any system would work. In any case, the need to modify it continuously so that it could cope with successive offensive improvements could make deployment prohibitively expensive.

A far better way to achieve security—less costly, much more reliable—would be for both East and West to recognize the futility of relying on military and technological means alone, or even primarily, and to come to terms on political accommodations that would make it unnecessary to suppose that weapons alone confer security. Is such a prospect utopian? The record does not inspire great confidence, it is true, that in the immediate future the United States and the Soviet Union will overcome their differences to such an extent that they will cease to fear each other's hostile intentions, or that the Soviets will be willing to withdraw from territories beyond their borders that they have come to consider vital for their security and ideological confidence, any more than the U.S. would be prepared to look the other way if not only Cuba and Nicaragua but also the whole of Central America and the Caribbean were to become a Soviet foothold in the Western Hemisphere. The primacy of the concern with national security will dictate insistence on protecting spheres of interest and access to critical resources—a concern that is bound to pose opportunities for conflict and rivalry. Nevertheless, the fact that there has so far not been a direct conflict between the two superpowers, and that both have carefully refrained from entering into conflicts where such a confrontation could occur is an indication that the threat of nuclear war may be having a sobering effect. As the complexities of modern warfare impress themselves on generals as well as politicians, the futility of relying on technology to provide security or advantage may grow ever more apparent, despite the fascination with improving military technology. There is no technological imperative that makes it impossible or illogical to reverse course and constrain the deployment of ever newer and more sophisticated weapons systems. What is missing is the will and skill of leaders in working out political accommodations.

MOTIVES AND CONSEQUENCES

Even granting that Reagan launched the SDI with the best of motives—humanitarian concern to provide an alternative to relying on the threat of nuclear war—it does not follow that the consequences must be equally benign. Our examination of the prospects for strategic defenses does not lead to any certain conclusion as to their ultimate technological feasibility; we can only conclude that the question will not be fully resolved for many years. The very effort to develop space-based defenses could be self-defeating, however, if the lure of a new technology leads politicians and ordinary citizens to suppose that there is a technological fix for the very complicated problems involved in preventing political conflicts from erupting into major wars.

For that, after all, is the real issue—not whether a space-based defense will be feasible or affordable but whether and how it is possible to make the world safer now that nuclear weapons exist. As has often been said, nuclear weapons cannot be uninvented. For forty years, humanity has had to come to grips with the reality of warfare in the nuclear age. Although the advent of nuclear weapons did not immediately alter the character of warfare—nuclear bombs delivered by airplanes were at first only extrapolated versions of blockbusters, and it was not yet obvious that they would be decisive—the development of far more explosive thermonuclear warheads that can be delivered by intercontinental missiles has fundamentally changed the character of warfare. Total war has already obliterated the old distinction between battlefield and home front. Total nuclear war poses a still more terrifying menace. Whether weapons are directed at "counterforce" (military) or "countervalue" targets (populations and the fabric of civil life), this very mode of warfare threatens a scale of damage so horrendous for attacker as well as victim as to make it altogether profitless, altogether senseless. And, yet, the fact that it has become a self-defeating activity has not meant that people have come to feel any safer or that states have concluded they do not need vast, ramified military establishments. On the contrary, the arsenals of warfare have grown ever more elaborate, indeed baroque. It is now taken for granted that delivery systems must be continually improved to assure that nuclear weapons will penetrate defenses and will serve a variety of military purposes and that conventional capabilities must be as effective and elaborate as may be necessary to forestall resort to nuclear weapons until there is no alternative. In view of this reality, it may be asked, why not try to develop a space-based defense? If nothing else can work to remove the scourge of nuclear weapons, why not try to develop a technology that is itself nonnuclear and that promises to minimize the damage from nuclear attack and perhaps ultimately to make such attacks so risky for the attacker that it will have no incentive whatever to launch them? Besides, does not even a limited nuclear defense promise to protect against a small-scale attack, such as might be launched by some "crazy state" or mad ruler who supposes he has nothing to lose?

The temptation to accept this line of reasoning is strong, and many have done so. Many more would agree, we among them, that even though we strongly doubt a defense against nuclear attack is now conceivable, efforts to determine the feasibility of such a defense deserve support. The danger with this approach is that it can become an alternative to other means of addressing the problem and can foster costly illusions. A commitment to develop comprehensive defenses, especially if undertaken without regard to the effect on existing and prospective arms-control treaties, would only make matters worse than they are now by precipitating an unconstrained competition in which both sides have no incentive to restrain their offensive armaments. In that event, whatever limited security obtains when both sides feel they enjoy a parity in such weapons and are therefore equally vulnerable to attack, could be lost. If either side thinks itself more vulnerable than the other or sufficiently superior, it may be tempted to take steps either to relieve that vulnerability or to take advantage of its superiority. The essential lesson of the nuclear age has been that it is perilous for one side to feel threatened by the other—perilous because the threatened side becomes insecure and makes every effort to do damage to the other's interest short of risking nuclear war and meanwhile makes every effort to overcome its perceived inferiority. Sometimes the perception of inferiority has nothing to do with the reality, as in the case of the phantom "missile gap" of the 1960s, but the consequences are the same. The side that perceives itself behind takes steps to catch up. The other side, which knows it is not ahead, concludes it has no choice but to match or defeat the other side's efforts. A climate of mutual suspicion produces a qualitative arms race—a race aimed not only at increasing the lethality of armaments but also at improving the technical efficiency with which they can be hidden, delivered, and made more accurate.

In such an arms race, which has gone on with varying degrees of intensity during the forty years of the cold war, neither side can feel secure, despite the possession of nuclear weapons against which there is no defense. The reasons are, first, that each side fears the other may be developing a capacity to launch a disarming preemptive attack—whether one that cripples the retaliatory capability or that "decapitates" the enemy and thereby prevents an effective response—and, second, that one side, perceiving the other as weaker, may exploit its superiority in order to extract concessions, or in other words to blackmail the other. This, at any rate, is how the Soviets interpreted the U.S. blockade of nuclear-weapons shipments to Cuba, even though it resulted in a U.S. concession in the form of a commitment to respect Cuba's sovereignty. It is also what U.S. analysts fear would happen to the Western alliance, particularly to its NATO partners, if the Soviets were perceived to have military superiority and were to use it to "Finlandize" Western Europe.

The SALT process was an effort to alleviate the insecurities by arresting the arms race. It was premised on the idea that, by a series of steps, both sides would agree to limitations on testing and deployment of weapons. Such limitations would, first of all, assure essential parity in offensive systems and in its more refined phases eliminate weapons that were particularly useful in a first or preemptive strike—those that were sufficiently fast and accurate to cripple the adversary's retaliatory capacity. When defensive systems came into the picture and both sides, the Soviets first, decided to field defenses against ICBMs as well as air attack, those who believed in arms control argued that defenses would only lead to an effort to build offenses that could overcome them—which was precisely what happened when MIRVed warheads were designed—and would thereby undermine the entire process. It was for this reason that a limitation on territorial defenses was proposed. And the signing of the ABM Treaty reassured those who believed in arms control that the process was once again on track and could reduce nuclear arsenals on both sides by mutually agreed steps and at the same time introduce qualitative restrictions on the types of weapons deployed as well as on further testing. The failure to make much progress was a reflection of the entanglement between arms control and other aspects of political conflict. The United States' failure to ratify SALT II was partly a result of the suspicion that it was inequitable and enabled the U.S.S.R. to cheat, but even more the result of the Soviet invasion of Afghanistan and a general perception that the Soviet Union was continuing to modernize its armaments out of an intent to expand its empire at the expense of the West.

If the revival of arms control produces a verifiable agreement to reduce strategic arsenals, it should not be rejected in the hope that defenses will offer an alternative. Comprehensive defenses are simply not available. Limited defenses are only of limited value. They may offer some security against accidental attack, but they cannot fully eliminate the danger of nuclear terrorism. Unfortunately, atomic bombs can be made small enough to be moved, even smuggled, across borders by a variety of means that no strategic defense can prevent.

RESISTANCE TO ARMS CONTROL: THE MINDSET BEHIND SDI

Those who support SDI most strongly continue to feel, in spite of the advent of Gorbachev and the willingness of the Soviets to resume the arms-control process by actually reducing the size of nuclear arsenals, that the Soviet interest in arms control is insincere, indeed, hypocritical. They also argue that arms-control measures have so far not impeded the buildup of the arms both sides want to develop and that the Soviets see it largely as a propaganda exercise and a way to prevent the West from taking advantage of its technological and economic superiority. Arms control, according to this line of reasoning, is merely a Soviet technique for disarming the West, and the Soviet Union's calls for the demilitarization of space ring hollow as it continues singlemindedly to make military use of space while engaging in propaganda attacks against similar efforts by the West. The U.S.S.R., SDI proponents claim, is deceiving the world by making it appear that its space program aims mainly at civilian accomplishments and that only the United States aims to "militarize space."

These opponents of arms control contend that instead of being content with paper guarantees, which in any case cover only peripheral and obsolete systems, the United States should rely instead on exploiting its own resources to build a formidable military system that can deter the Soviets from contemplating an attack, reassure our allies of the United States' ability to come to their defense, and at the same time provide the basis for conventional strength, under a nuclear shield, that may be necessary to deter attacks aimed at affecting vital interests of the West. The militarization of space, they argue, is inevitable because the U.S.S.R. would get there first if the United States does not. So, it is imperative the United States not accept any limitations, including those of the ABM Treaty, that inhibit an effort to compete with the Soviet Union and seize the "high ground" of space ahead of them. From this point of view, the ABM Treaty ensures that "mutual assured destruction" will continue to be the effective basis of national security. As a writer for the conservative journal *Human Events* observed: "As the ABM accord embodies MAD, so strategic defense as proposed by Reagan would repudiate it. If Reagan is successful in promoting SDI, a strategic revolution will be accomplished, and Mutual Armed Destruction and the ABM accord will go by the boards." [10]

No one could be said to have been a more convinced advocate of this point of view than Ronald Reagan was both before and during his first term. It is not surprising, therefore, that his promotion of SDI was quite enough to arouse opposition from those who believe in arms control and détente and who see the crusade against communism as an obsolete and oversimple response to the more complicated reality of revolutionary movements in the less-developed regions of the world. Had SDI been proposed by a different administration, it is at least conceivable that it would have been met with less skepticism, especially if it had been made clear at the outset, as the president tried to argue, that it would be a research project to be pursued in conformity with the ABM Treaty and that the purpose was to achieve defenses that would not be threatening to anyone but would save mankind from the threat of nuclear extinction. (The fact that even so pronounced a critic of nuclear deterrence as Jonathan Schell could have endorsed the aim of a defense transition [11] is an indication that it might well have had broader support had it been issued under other auspices.)

As it was, however, there was good reason to be suspicious that there was more to SDI than the president maintained, or that he may have understood. This interpretation is especially warranted in view of the administration's brazen reinterpretation of the ABM Treaty. The attempt to rewrite the treaty in order to enable testing outlawed in the negotiations made it clear that the administration did not respect the arms-control process and was not prepared to accept the ABM Treaty as the keystone of the arch. A second blow to any benign interpretation of the motives for SDI came when a high-level faction within the administration, led by Weinberger, called for a decision by the president to support early deployment of a partial system. Such a deployment would assuredly mean the end of the treaty. The fact that the administration was prepared to use the "broad interpretation" at Reykjavík to prevent a compromise on testing, which might have led to a major agreement on the reduction of long-range systems, was yet another indication of its fundamental opposition to arms control as a process by which agreements could be reached with the Soviets—agreements that might eventually extend to conventional warfare and to the sources of superpower conflict. This evidence suggests that, far from intending to pursue only that research allowed under the treaty in order to bring about a cooperative transition to defenses, SDI's strongest supporters within the administration saw the initiative as a unilateral military-technological challenge to the Soviets. Their assumption was that only superiority in force would persuade the Soviets to respect Western interests and to refrain from expansionism.

To criticize the Reagan administration for its deceptive policy in pursuing SDI is not to defend the Soviet leaders. Their *glasnost* on this issue is still far from complete. They have denied, untruthfully, that they have any program to develop strategic defenses, when, as we have seen, they have a significant program in strategic defense. So far, it involves deployments aimed mainly at a U.S. air attack, but attacks in space and on space systems such as satellites are also being contemplated. Their strategic modernization program has involved massive expenditures and has taken a highly threatening form in Europe. They are certainly to blame in large part for creating a climate in the West in which military efforts of all sorts, including space-based defenses, could be thought to be necessary to cope with the "Soviet threat."

But the Soviet efforts are in a sense beside the point. They have been and can continue to be offset by offensive countermeasures. Indeed, one of the criticisms of SDI is that it threatens to divert resources needed to improve both strategic and conventional offensive systems. Modernization can take many forms, and in view of the need to choose among them, it is not obvious that emphasizing strategic defense is the best bet, especially in view of the great uncertainty that such defenses can ever be more than partial. Other investments, including those designed to assure penetration of Soviet defenses (but premised on the view that the best defense against attack will remain deterrence by threat of retaliation), may make better sense.

These uncertainties are compounded by others that involve Soviet perceptions. Theorists have often noted that the United States and the Soviet Union are trapped in a kind of prisoners' dilemma. Although they can communicate, unlike the prisoners in the hypothetical dilemma, they are either unable or unwilling to settle for solutions that are less than optimal but much better than those that could result if they refuse to compromise altogether. Soviet leaders fear a modernized version of capitalist encirclement. Despite their relative success in establishing Soviet power in the Russian motherland and in Eastern Europe, they may recognize that the loss of China's adhesion to their Socialist bloc represents an erosion of Soviet power, and a dangerous precedent for further defection. They may well suspect that the West, by developing an opening to China, aims to exploit the loss by weaning China altogether away from the Socialist path and to extend its influence to include China, as it now includes Japan, South Korea, and many other countries in the developing world. Some Soviet leaders may entertain a more confident vision, based on the fact that China is at least a Communist society and that other countries, including India, are not taking the capitalist road. But whatever their beliefs and whatever their mental reservations, they cannot escape the same recognition that must animate the minds of Westerners—which is that a conflict between these two systems can easily escalate to the level of a nuclear war, and that in such a war there can be no winners. Recent Soviet leaders have often stated their recognition of this principle. Whether they actually believe what they say cannot be ascertained, but one of the critical tests is willingness to conclude and to observe arms-control agreements. These agreements are the instruments by which mutual understanding can be developed and confidence maintained. An ever larger, more varied arsenal only increases the danger either of inadvertent use or of the escalation of a conflict into a nuclear exchange. Arms-control measures that aim to constrain the development of such weapons and to maintain parity and stability between the two blocs are essential if this dangerous competition is to be arrested.

Nor is there a practical substitute for negotiated arms control. It is sometimes argued that the two sides can signal their intentions to each other by a process of reciprocal unilateral initiatives. While this technique has sometimes been useful—notably in the reciprocal unilateral moratoria on testing that eventually led to the Limited Test Ban Treaty—too much should not be expected of such informal bargaining. When a conflict is fueled by mistrust, it is not likely to be resolved by unilateral initiatives that treat only certain aspects of the military preparations of the two sides but do not alleviate suspicion. Only treaties, which involve verifiable undertakings across a fairly broad spectrum, can allay suspicion. Such treaties, moreover, have important symbolic value, in that they demonstrate to populations saturated with propaganda designed to inflame hatred and fear that relations of amity exist between the governments. These symbolic understandings can be translated into more structural arrangements, such as those involving trade and travel. They do not necessarily create conditions for linkage between arms control and a broader form of détente, but they create an atmosphere in which such understandings and cooperation become more likely than they would be otherwise.

As we have already indicated, we suspect that many of those who strongly support SDI see it as one more way to defeat the arms-control process. Why else would they be prepared to see the ABM Treaty abrogated and further reductions of offensive arms stymied? They claim that arms control has been of little or no benefit, and that it has created only the illusion of détente—an illusion behind which the Soviets develop their military capacities with cynical indifference to agreements. The truth is, however, that both sides have behaved questionably with respect to the existing treaties. Although the United States can rightly point to the building of the Krasnoyarsk radar as a blatant violation of the ABM Treaty—in spite of the transparently false Soviet claim that it is allowable under the treaty provision for space tracking—the United States does not have altogether clean hands. The Reagan administration's decision to replace the mechanically steered radars at Fylingdales and Thule with phased-array radars also rests on arguably flimsy grounds. The testing that has been undertaken for SDI under a supposedly narrow interpretation of the treaty also raises questions about compliance, and the United States' failure to use the SCC as it was intended to be used—to resolve conflicting treaty interpretations—indicates bad faith on the part of the Reagan administration.

More important, the refusal to negotiate an agreement based on continued adherence to the narrow interpretation betrays a desire to break the treaty without appearing to do so and misses an opportunity to do precisely what the Reagan administration claimed was its goal—to achieve a cooperative transition to greater reliance on defensive systems by reducing offensive weapons while research proceeds to determine what can be done defensively. There is no good technical reason to proceed to early space testing, certainly not to deployment of an expensive and altogether inadequate and easily countered space-based kinetic system. The only rationale for proceeding with such efforts is that they make arms-control agreements impossible to achieve. For those for whom such agreements are anathema, this makes perfect sense. Otherwise, it makes no sense at all. As Nitze has emphasized, it is altogether premature to move to a stage of development that would require breaking the ABM Treaty, much less to the stage of deployment. A great deal can be done in laboratories and at fixed, allowable test ranges to test technology. Much of this testing can be done for other purposes, which the treaty does not cover—the development of ASATs, of ATBMs, and of sensors for the detection of attack. Only if both sides can agree to constrain their development and testing can they be reasonably secure that there will be no extraordinary breakout from the existing form of parity. It remains to be seen whether the exceedingly complex technologies being worked on for the advanced stages of a space-based defense will ever become feasible and affordable. To sacrifice the possibility of major arms reduction in the short run for the sake of some unknown future development would be foolhardy.

It would be foolhardy even though the United States may enjoy technological superiority over the U.S.S.R. The advocates of unrestrained development for SDI seem to be counting on the fact that the Soviets are inferior to the West in most areas of technology. But mounting a challenge to their security in the form of an accelerated SDI could well be counterproductive by stimulating the Soviets to make corresponding advances in other areas of military technology. The supposed menace of SDI could be a stick with which Soviet leaders can beat Soviet workers into accepting sacrifices in consumer satisfaction for the sake of military progress. Besides, as lumbering as it is, the Soviet economy has shown itself quite capable of matching the West in key areas of military power. What reason is there to suppose that an accelerated U.S. program would either compel the Soviets to accept the reinterpretation of the treaty the United States is insisting on, as the price for a moratorium on deployment, or leave the Soviets at such a grave military disadvantage that the United States could impose a *Pax Americana?* On the contrary, the evidence suggests that the Soviets will refuse to entertain arms-control agreements that would handicap their ability to rely on a quantitative offensive response to a space-based defense or to match the developments in the United States' space-based effort and build countermeasures. Given the U.S.S.R.'s well-established achievements in laser technology and other exotic weapons, it would be arrogant vanity to suppose that the Soviets cannot achieve rough equivalence, or at the very least develop countermeasures that would make a U.S. SDI system prohibitively expensive so that it will lose all of its appeal.

Meanwhile, the very effort of challenging the Soviets to a competition in the full militarization of space, beginning with the deployment of ASATs, not only risks putting U.S. space assets in jeopardy—assets on which the United States relies even more than the Soviets—but also carries serious political costs. The Soviet Union can plausibly claim that the United States' fixation on offensive and defensive modernization prevents agreements that can reduce the threat of nuclear war without requiring the development of leakproof defenses. In Europe and elsewhere, Soviet propaganda has already had an easy time exploiting this apparent contrast. Although this propaganda conveniently neglects the Soviet Union's own responsibilities for contributing to Western anxieties by building up its armaments—including defenses—it is nevertheless perceived to be justified. The United States stands to lose support among friends and allies if it persists in refusing to accept a strategic arms control agreement in which the traditional understanding of the treaty is honored.

Ironically, it is not just overseas but even at home that the supporters of the SDI are risking their own cause. Judged politically, they went too far by promoting the reinterpretation of the treaty and by calling for early deployment—further than public opinion was willing to go. By trying to show that the critics were "wrong" in suggesting that an SDI defense would cost a trillion dollars and, instead, by arguing that an interim defense, which would not protect against an upgraded Soviet system, would cost as much as $121 billion (and, in addition, upwards of $70 billion for air defense of the United States and billions more for an upgraded air and tactical defense in Europe), they have only forced the voters to recognize that this scheme cannot be a cheap technological fix.

THE POLITICAL SYSTEM AS A CORRECTIVE

Some comfort can be taken from the way in which the U.S. political system serves as a corrective to unthinking enthusiasms. The same public that is prepared to endorse the idea of a Star Wars defense has second thoughts when it looks at the price tag that will show up on its tax bills. Some comfort, but not very much. One of the most troubling aspects of the SDI controversy is what the issue has revealed about public ignorance of defense issues. The fact that a large majority of those surveyed in public opinion polls either do not know whether the United States already has a defense against nuclear attack or suppose that one already exists [12] is one glaring example of this ignorance. Although it is too much to expect, perhaps, that in a society that relies on representative government, voters should feel obliged to become familiar with every detail of a defense project or of an arms-control treaty, such a dismal lack of knowledge makes it impossible for many voters to decide when its leaders are credible or deceiving. How can support be mobilized for arms-control measures—measures that are easily attacked, no matter how carefully they are drawn, as one-sided or not perfectly verifiable— unless there is public appreciation of what is at stake?

A representative system of government, it is true, is designed to provide a filter for public opinion in the form of legislators who have both the ability and the opportunity to familiarize themselves with the issues and to explain them to their constituents as well as to vote on their behalf. In this instance, the representative process has worked well. Congress has reacted with interest to the vision of a defensive system, reflecting the generally favorable public response but has also responded with skepticism as doubts have been raised by credible scientific specialists. In this connection, the work of Congress's own Office of Technology Assessment should be singled out, along with studies by congressional staff. The OTA was established in order to make the kind of balanced evaluations of the potential impact of new technologies it has in fact provided in this case. The three OTA reports have been models of good research and careful judgment. Staff studies prepared for several senators have also helped by bringing the views of working defense scientists directly to the attention of legislators. These studies, coupled with the more impassioned skepticism of the sort found in the writings of the Union of Concerned Scientists and the Federation of American Scientists, have been very influential in restraining congressional support for SDI. The APS report probably had an even more powerful, if less direct, role because of its influence on public opinion. The work of members of Congress on both sides of the issue has also been exemplary. Senator Nunn's insistence on looking carefully at the ABM Treaty himself to determine whether the administration's "broad interpretation" was justified and whether it represented an unconstitutional reinterpretation of a treaty ratified by the Senate is also one of the saving graces in the story of SDI. SDI is certainly one of the most political of major defense programs, both in the sense that it was launched in an appeal to public opinion, over the heads of the bureaucracy and Congress, and that it has been held back because of skepticism it has aroused there.

THE MYTH OF TECHNOLOGICAL DETERMINISM

These political factors point to a larger consideration. It is sometimes supposed, even if rarely put forward so boldly, that in matters of defense policy, technological momentum is an irresistible force. A "technological determinism" is thought to hold sway, according to which whatever can be done will be done. The examples sometimes cited in support of this view are the decision to proceed with the development of the atomic bomb, even after it was learned that Germany was far behind and on the verge of collapse and even though Japan could not possibly achieve it in time to avert defeat, or the decision to proceed with the thermonuclear weapon even though it was not obvious that the additional lethal force of this new nuclear weapon would serve any strategic purpose. The same charge has been made concerning the development of the ABM and the MIRV, both of which have been said to represent no great strategic benefit but rather to reflect the sheer force of the momentum created by a commitment to military R & D. Strategic defense has raised the same suspicion. But it is far too simple to attribute the arms race to sheer technological momentum.

It is too simple—in the case of SDI certainly—because, as we have seen, the decision to embark on the project was not determined by technological advances. It was very much a political decision made with factors other than the advances themselves exclusively in mind. Had the decision been left up to the technologists, it would certainly not have been taken. As we have noted, a study requested by the White House science advisor before the president's "Star Wars" speech concluded that there was no technological reason to suppose that defenses were more advisable now than they had been in 1972, when the ABM Treaty was negotiated. Scientists in the Pentagon were no less skeptical. The president made his decision, it is true, having in mind Edward Teller's warning that the Soviets were working on an X-ray laser and might achieve this technology before the United States, but Teller himself did not advocate a move toward defense out of any belief that nuclear weapons were about to be made obsolete. Teller wanted strategic defenses for the same reason he had earlier wanted civil defense—to give the United States the maximum protection possible against nuclear attack and to enable it to take advantage of defensive technologies to enhance its military and political position vis-à-vis the Soviet Union. These were undoubtedly the same considerations that preoccupied the president and his kitchen-cabinet colleagues when this decision took shape. Indeed, Reagan acknowledged that no such defense was yet available when he called on the scientific community to provide one.

This call represented a considerable faith in the powers of science and technology, a faith no doubt inspired by previous successes. In this sense, the achievements of the Manhattan Project, of Project Apollo, of ICBMs and MIRVs, lay behind the decision. The president and his immediate supporters were confident that if the United States used its strong suit—its advantage in science and technology—it could overcome what he and they saw as a frustrating obstacle to escaping the perilous dilemma posed by nuclear weapons. This hope, born of frustration, may well have been naïve, but, in any case, it was not an expectation grounded on scientific advice.

The president did indeed receive encouragement or reinforcement for this hope from the technical panel he set up under Fletcher once the decision was announced. Even this panel, however, recognized that there were major obstacles to be overcome before the goal could be achieved, and at least some of the members, including the chairman, recognized that without the cooperation of the Soviets, a defense transition would be impossible in an environment unconstrained by limits on the offense. Many of those who have worked on the SDI since the Fletcher report have argued that although a perfect defense against nuclear attack is inconceivable, even an imperfect defense is desirable because it would discourage nuclear attack. This argument lends support to Reagan's objective, but it is scarcely an endorsement of a program to make nuclear weapons impotent or obsolete or to achieve his stated goal of saving lives rather than avenging them.

A corollary of the belief in the momentum of technology is that the machinery of destruction—the military-industrial complex—needs ever newer weapons systems to feed its insatiable desire for contracts. But the industries were not campaigning for SDI. They were receptive to the administration's general views, to be sure, and very supportive of its military modernization program, but that support did not involve much active lobbying for a program in strategic defense. Indeed, because the first years of strategic defense would mostly be absorbed in research, the industries could not hope to profit enormously from it—in contrast to the major procurement programs. At best, it would have been for them a source of support for preparatory work that could lead to procurement in the future—on a massive scale—but the actual announcement of SDI was as much a surprise to the defense contractors as it was to everyone else.

AVOIDING THE ILLUSORY FAITH IN
SECURITY THROUGH TECHNOLOGY

The technology required for a comprehensive strategic defense is extremely complex and full of uncertainties. Indeed, extraordinary advances are needed in so many areas that one can hardly predict success for such a system with confidence. In order for a boost-phase defense to work against the most obvious countermeasures employed by a determined enemy (such as adopting fast-burn boosters capable of achieving separation in 60 or 90 seconds), kinetic-energy weapons (which have been proposed for interim deployment on space-based satellites) would be inadequate. They might still have some utility against the bus that carries the warheads, if the bus continues to require additional time before discharging the warheads on their free flight to their targets. But against the rockets themselves, which are much the easiest targets, directed-energy weapons would probably be essential. DEWs might be "popped up" from submarines in close enough range of Soviet missile trajectories, but the time constraints would probably rule out such launches. Maintaining orbiting satellites with laser weapons or mirrors to reflect hybrid ground-based laser weapons seems a more plausible alternative. To achieve the levels of brightness required for killing the launchers, even as they are presently shielded, however, will require lasers several orders of magnitude brighter than have so far been attained. Such brightness is not precluded by laws of physics, but it may be precluded by the power requirements, which would impose such weight on the satellites as to increase the cost of launching and producing the satellites to a prohibitive degree. The coordination of firings and sightings is itself no mean problem, even assuming that the surveillance techniques can be achieved and that the surveillance satellites can be made safe from attack, at least until they have done their assigned job. To coordinate hundreds or thousands of battle stations means having the ability to identify targets, assess the damage done to them, keep track of them as they continue to hurtle through space, hand them on from one layer to another, and, of course, protect them from attack. Although the problem can be compared to the coordination of a sea, land, or air battle, with scouts, communication, and defensive measures all integrated with the actual battle stations, the task of performing these integrated steps in space is especially daunting—all the more so given that the consequences of performing all these functions in a battle environment likely to be affected by nuclear explosions are unknown. The possibility that each adversary would orbit systems designed to interfere with and to attack the other's defense means that each must contend not only with the enemy's offensive forces in the usual sense but also with its counterdefensive systems as well.

So far, all efforts to design such defensive systems have been defeated by improvements in offensive forces that have effectively maintained the ability to penetrate to the target. There is good reason to suppose that on technological grounds the advantage will remain with the offense for the foreseeable future. Because of the "absentee" problem, discussed in chapter 3, an orbital defense must be larger than an engagement would actually require. The offense need not destroy the entire defensive complex, but only punch a hole through the defensive screen, which can be done by concentrating forces against those elements of the defense in the requisite location at any given time. Orbiting defenses can be destroyed by space mines or ASAT weapons; even by drawing the protective fire of the defensive systems, an offense would compel the defender to divert valuable energy away from intercepting launchers. Once through the boost-phase screen, an attacking force could employ decoy and diversion techniques that greatly tax the remaining defense layers. The midcourse layers would have to use techniques of discrimination, such as space-based particle beams that have yet to be developed in adequate form. Only the terminal layers can be identified with any confidence, and these by themselves cannot prevent a massive attack from achieving assured destruction of urban targets.

Thus, from a purely technological point of view, all that can be said in favor of strategic defenses at this point is that further research may refine the techniques currently conceivable. However, none of these techniques can be developed and deployed as an effective system in any foreseeable time frame. The case for a more limited hard-point defense, especially one that relies on preferential defense and is expected only to assure partial survival of offensive forces and command and control authorities, is more technologically credible. Here, the improvements achieved since 1972 could be applied with good effect. If all that is desired is assurance of the survival of retaliatory forces, however, an agreement to dismantle threatening first-strike weapons and to disperse or harden those that remain is a far less costly alternative. Such an agreement, moreover, would not be seen as a first step toward a possibly unilateral and therefore destabilizing deployment of more comprehensive defenses. Even the feasibility and desirability of terminal defenses depend on the readiness of both sides to reduce offensive forces drastically. Without such reductions, defenses for prime military targets could not be relied on, and the offense might have additional incentive to attack more vulnerable civilian targets. Even a small-scale attack on these targets could have devastating consequences.

In view of all these uncertainties, difficulties, and potential ramifications, there can be little doubt that the current prohibition on the deployment of territorial defenses, coupled with further reductions in offensive arsenals—nuclear as well as conventional—is the more prudent path to national security. In the earlier phases of East-West competition, cold war hostilities and a blind faith in technological initiatives prevented agreements to limit advances in military technology. The militarization of space for purposes of war has not yet gone so far that it cannot be stopped, at least in the most destabilizing respects. If SDI stimulates an effort to achieve a cooperative regime in space, it will have served a purpose far more valuable for national and international security than yet another extension of the arms race. Such a regime can be achieved only by practical and persistent efforts of international negotiation involving not only the United States and the Soviet Union but the entire world community—for the risks of warfare in space could well turn out to be universal.

The demand for change now being felt not only in the Soviet Union but also in China and other Communist countries arises mainly from domestic discontent, but domestic reforms are incompatible with an aggressive foreign policy. The pragmatists who are coming to power in these countries recognize the need to pursue foreign policies of accommodation rather than of unsupportable expansion and belligerence. At this historic juncture in the cold war, when the possibility has arisen of greatly minimizing the risks of confrontation, or possibly even of transcending the conflict altogether, it would be senseless and an act of gross irresponsibility to embark unilaterally on an effort to build space-based defenses. Before that fateful step is attempted, every effort should be made to achieve political understanding rather than to count on the faith, so often betrayed in the past, that technology can ensure national security.

Notes

1. WHY SDI?

1. Robert S. McNamara, excerpts from a speech delivered September 18, 1967, in San Francisco before a meeting of journalists, reprinted in *ABM: An Evaluation of the Decision to Deploy an Antiballistic Missile System,* ed. Abram Chayes and Jerome B. Wiesner (New York: New American Library, 1969), p. 237.

2. For the role of the refugee physicists, see Richard G. Hewlett and Oscar E. Anderson, Jr., *A History of the United States Atomic Energy Commission,* vol. 1: *The New World, 1939–1946* (University Park: Pennsylvania State University Press, 1962), pp. 14–19; Martin Sherwin, *A World Destroyed* (New York: Knopf, 1975), pp. 18–30; and J. Stefan Dupré and Sanford A. Lakoff, *Science and the Nation: Policy and Politics* (Englewood Cliffs, N.J.: Prentice-Hall, 1962), pp. 91–93.

3. Truman reached his decision after the question had been well aired within the executive branch. The General Advisory Committee to the Atomic Energy Commission had recommended against a crash program, but the commissioners themselves favored proceeding with it by 3 to 2. Truman asked a subcommittee of the National Security Council, composed of AEC chairman David E. Lilienthal, Secretary of Defense Louis Johnson, and Secretary of State Dean Acheson, to review the matter for him. The subcommittee was in favor by 2 to 1. Truman's decision was supported by prominent nuclear physicists, including Karl T. Compton, Edward Teller, Ernest O. Lawrence, John von Neumann, and Luis Alvarez. See Herbert F. York, *The Advisors: Oppenheimer, Teller, and the Superbomb* (San Francisco: W. H. Freeman, 1976).

4. Studies of defense policy making provide support for each of these factors. The role of "bureaucratic politics," i.e., the interplay of departments and agencies in the executive branch, acting out of organizational interest and perspective, is often stressed. Thus, in *The Polaris System Development: Bureaucratic and Programmatic Success in Government* (Cambridge: Harvard Uni-

versity Press, 1972), Harvey M. Sapolsky notes that the success of the Polaris project was a result of the skill of its proponents in bureaucratic politics: "Competitors had to be eliminated; reviewing agencies had to be outmaneuvered; congressmen, admirals, newspapermen, and academicians had to be co-opted" (p. 244). In examining the controversy between the army and air force over which service should get responsibility for intermediate-range ballistic missiles, Michael H. Armacost also notes the importance of lobbying by the services and the applicability of the pressure-group model of analysis. He points out, however, that the services found it necessary to build consensus among journalists, members of Congress, analysts in quasi-autonomous "think tanks," and "an extensive network of scientific and technical advisory committees located within the Executive branch," and that this "very pluralism assured the government of a broad base of scientific and technical advice, and, superimposed upon service rivalries, this provided additional insurance that criticism of weapons programs was persistent and far from perfunctory" (*The Politics of Weapons Innovation: The Thor-Jupiter Controversy* [New York: Columbia University Press, 1969], p. 256).

Ted Greenwood, in a study of the decision to adopt the MIRV principle for warheads, argues persuasively against adoption of any single-factor analysis, noting that the decision to adopt MIRV resulted from "the complex interplay of technological opportunity, bureaucratic politics, strategic and policy preferences of senior decisionmakers, and great uncertainty about Soviet activities" (*Making the MIRV: A Study of Defense Decision Making* [Cambridge, Mass.: Ballinger, 1975], p. xv). Other studies, such as Gordon Adams, *The Politics of Defense Contracting: The Iron Triangle* (New Brunswick, N.J.: Transaction, 1982), emphasize the role of the "iron triangle" (the federal bureaucracy, the key committees and members of Congress, and the defense contractors) in promoting military expenditures. Seymour Melman, in *Pentagon Capitalism: The Political Economy of War* (New York: McGraw-Hill, 1970), contends that the managers of DOD "sell weapons-improvement programs to Congress and the public" (p. 70). None of these factors played a significant role in the decision to begin SDI, though they may well become important when and if the research phase is succeeded by a commitment to develop and deploy an SDI system, when the stakes will be much higher.

5. McNamara, in *ABM: An Evaluation*, p. 236. Graham T. Allison has suggested, however, that "U.S. research and development has been as much self-generated as Soviet-generated." See his "Questions About the Arms Race: Who's Racing Whom? A Bureaucratic Perspective," in *Contrasting Approaches to Strategic Arms Control*, ed. Robert L. Pfaltzgraff, Jr. (Lexington, Mass.: Lexington Books, 1974), p. 42.

6. Herbert F. York, *Race to Oblivion: A Participant's View of the Arms Race* (New York: Simon and Schuster, 1970), pp. 238–39.

7. Paul B. Stares, *The Militarization of Space: U.S. Policy, 1945–84* (Ithaca: Cornell University Press, 1985), pp. 190–92.

8. Testimony of Robert S. Cooper before the U.S. Congress, Senate Committee on Armed Services, *Hearing on Strategic and Theater Nuclear Forces*, 97th Cong., 2d sess., pt. 7, March 16, 1982, pp. 4845–76.

9. Reagan's solicitation of advice on SDI from "a highly selective group" that was, in addition, intensely loyal to him has been contrasted with Eisenhower's submission of the proposal for a nuclear test ban to a broadly representative group of scientists in the President's Science Advisory Committee in G. Allen Greb, *Science Advice to Presidents: From Test Bans to the Strategic Defense Initiative,* Research Paper no. 3 (La Jolla: University of California Institute on Global Conflict and Cooperation, 1987), p. 15.

10. For a detailed account of how Eisenhower reached these decisions, see Samuel P. Huntington, *The Common Defense* (New York: Columbia University Press, 1961), pp. 326–41.

11. Interview in *Newsweek,* March 18, 1985, quoted in *Star Wars Quotes* (Washington, D.C.: Arms Control Association, 1986), p. 26.

12. *National Party Platforms of 1980,* comp. Donald Bruce Johnson (Urbana: University of Illinois Press, 1982), p. 207. Richard V. Allen, who was to become President Reagan's first assistant for national security affairs, was influential in the adoption of the plank, according to his colleague, Martin Anderson, who was responsible for pressing Reagan's views on domestic policy with the platform drafters. See Martin Anderson, *Revolution* (San Diego: Harcourt Brace Jovanovich, 1988), p. 87.

13. See Garry Wills, *Reagan's America: Innocents at Home* (Garden City, N.Y.: Doubleday, 1987), p. 361, and Michael Paul Rogin, *Ronald Reagan, the Movie and Other Episodes in Political Demonology* (Berkeley and Los Angeles: University of California Press, 1987), pp. 1–2. The finale of the movie recapitulates the classical myth in which Phaeton, claiming to be the son of Apollo, nearly destroys the world by driving Apollo's chariot of the sun erratically until Jupiter rescues the earth by loosing a thunderbolt and arresting the flight.

14. Quoted in Anderson, *Revolution,* p. 83.

15. Text of interview in Robert Scheer, *With Enough Shovels: Reagan, Bush, and Nuclear War* (New York: Random House, 1982), pp. 232–33.

16. Anderson, *Revolution,* pp. 85–86.

17. The air force's "Space Master Plan" was publicized in July 1983 by *Aviation Week & Space Technology.* Stares, *Militarization of Space,* p. 219.

18. Quoted in Frank Greve, "Star Wars," *San Jose Mercury News,* November 17, 1985.

19. *Weekly Compilation of Presidential Documents,* vol. 19, no. 13 (Washington, D.C.: White House, April 4, 1983), p. 453. Reagan had also used the same image years before: "As early as 1976, when he was challenging Gerald Ford for the Republican nomination, he criticized deterrence, comparing the arrangement to two people with guns cocked at each other's head." Michael Mandelbaum and Strobe Talbott, *Reagan and Gorbachev* (New York: Vintage, 1987), p. 126.

20. Daniel O. Graham, "Towards a New U.S. Strategy: Bold Strokes Rather Than Increments," *Strategic Review* (Spring 1981): 9–16.

21. Daniel O. Graham, *High Frontier, A New National Strategy* (Washington, D.C.: High Frontier, 1982), pp. 9, 18, 20.

22. Cooper testimony, Senate Armed Services Committee, p. 4635.

23. GAO, "DOD's Space-Based Laser Program—Potential, Progress, and

Problems," Report by the Comptroller General of the United States (Washington, D.C.: GAO, February 26, 1982), pp. iii–iv.

24. In 1982 DOD established a space laser program, as recommended by DARPA, in cooperation with the air force and the army. The plan called for the expenditure of $800 million over the period from FY1982 through FY1988, under the supervision of the office of the assistant secretary for directed energy weapons.

25. Gregg Herken, *Cardinal Choices: The President's Science Advisers from Roosevelt to Reagan*, draft of chap. 6, p. 21. A substantial part of this chapter has been published as "The Earthly Origins of 'Star Wars,'" *Bulletin of the Atomic Scientists* (October 1987), pp. 20–28.

26. Pete V. Domenici, "Towards a Decision on Ballistic Missile Defense," *Strategic Review* (Winter 1982): 22–27.

27. William J. Broad, *Star Warriors* (New York: Simon and Schuster, 1985), pp. 39–40.

28. Edward Teller, "SDI: The Last Best Hope," *Insight* (October 20, 1985), pp. 75–79.

29. Broad, *Star Warriors*, p. 122. "In all," according to Broad, "Teller met with the President four times over the course of little more than a year." Teller, in a letter to the authors (September 21, 1987) claims to have had little direct influence on the president's decision: "Before the President's announcement of SDI, I had two very brief meetings with the President. I expressed no more than my general support and good hopes." In the September meeting, he recalls, "defense was mentioned but no subject like the X-ray laser was explicitly discussed." With respect to the X-ray laser, Teller's recollection does not jibe with Keyworth's. See Herken, *Cardinal Choices*, p. 23.

30. Quoted in Greve, "Star Wars."

31. Quoted by Broad, *Star Warriors*, p. 73.

32. Edward Teller with Allen Brown, *The Legacy of Hiroshima* (Garden City, N.Y.: Doubleday, 1962), pp. 128–29.

33. Edward Teller (Address to the Faculty Seminar on International Security at the University of California, San Diego, December 12, 1983).

34. Anderson, *Revolution*, p. 95.

35. Ibid.

36. Greve, "Star Wars."

37. Statement by the assistant for directed energy weapons to the under secretary of defense for research and engineering before the U.S. Congress, Senate Subcommittee on Strategic and Theater Nuclear Forces of the Committee on Armed Services, 98th Cong., 1st sess., March 23, 1983.

38. Richard DeLauer, quoted in *Arms Control Reporter* (November 10, 1983).

39. Richard DeLauer, interview in *Government Executive* (July–August 1983), quoted in *Star Wars Quotes*, p. 34.

40. Greve, "Star Wars."

41. Ibid.

42. Herken, *Cardinal Choices*, chap. 6, pp. 46–47.

43. John Bardeen, letter to the editor, *Arms Control Today* (July–August 1986), p. 2.

44. Greve, "Star Wars."

45. Hedrick Smith, *The Power Game: How Washington Works* (New York: Random House, 1988), pp. 612–14.

46. Anderson, *Revolution,* p. 43.

47. Greve, "Star Wars."

48. Ibid.

49. Anderson, *Revolution,* p. 97.

50. Greve, "Star Wars."

51. Testimony of Robert C. McFarlane before the U.S. Congress, Defense Policy Subcommittee, House Armed Services Committee, May 17, 1988, type script, pp. 167–68.

52. Ronald W. Reagan, interview, *U.S. News and World Report* (November 18, 1985), p. 30.

53. Text of the "Star Wars" speech, *New York Times,* March 24, 1983.

54. McFarlane testimony, Defense Policy Subcommittee, pp. 165–66; Mr. McFarlane's testimony was not altogether clear at this point. We have therefore supplied (in brackets) some punctuation and the subjects of unclear pronoun referents not supplied in the original transcript yet needed for sense.

55. The CIA view was presented in the testimony by Robert M. Gates and Lawrence K. Gershwin before a joint session of the Subcommittee on Strategic and Theater Nuclear Forces of the Senate Armed Services Committee and the Defense Subcommittee of the Senate Appropriations Committee, June 26, 1985. The Joint Chiefs' view is reported in Strobe Talbott, *Deadly Gambits: The Reagan Administration and the Stalemate in Nuclear Arms Control* (New York: Knopf, 1984), p. 224.

56. Helmut Sonnenfeldt (Address at Lawrence Livermore National Laboratory, November 29, 1986).

57. Thomas C. Schelling, "What Went Wrong with Arms Control?" *Foreign Affairs* 64 (Winter 1985–86): 217–33.

58. See Michael Novak, "Moral Clarity in the Nuclear Age," *National Review* (April 1, 1983), pp. 354–62, and "The Bishops Speak Out," *National Review* (June 10, 1983), pp. 674–81.

59. "Star Wars" speech, *New York Times.*

60. Herken, *Cardinal Choices,* chap. 6, p. 49.

61. "Star Wars" speech, *New York Times.*

62. Ibid.

63. Excerpt from an interview with Andropov in *Pravda,* March 27, 1983, quoted in Sidney D. Drell, Philip J. Farley, and David Holloway, *The Reagan Strategic Defense Initiative: A Technical, Political, and Arms Control Assessment* (Stanford, Calif.: Center for International Security and Arms Control, Stanford University, 1984), appendix B, p. 105.

64. McGeorge Bundy, George F. Kennan, Robert S. McNamara, and Gerard Smith, "The President's Choice: Star Wars or Arms Control," *Foreign Affairs* 63 (Winter 1984–85): 270–72.

65. Reagan interview with six journalists, *Weekly Compilation of Presidential Documents,* vol. 19, no. 13 (Washington, D.C.: White House, April 4, 1983), p. 471.

66. A 1985 Sindlinger Poll found that 85 percent of the U.S. public favored

development of a missile defense "even if it can't protect everyone." Jeffrey Hart, "A Surprising Poll on Star Wars," *Washington Times,* August 9, 1985. A Gallup Poll in November 1985 found 61 percent in favor of the United States proceeding with SDI. *Christian Science Monitor,* November 21, 1985.

67. *Soviet Strategic Defense Program* (Washington, D.C.: U.S. Department of Defense and Department of State, October 1985).

68. On December 7, 1983, Secretary Weinberger was quoted in the *Wall Street Journal* as saying: "I can't imagine a more destabilizing factor for the world than if the Soviets should acquire a thoroughly reliable defense against these missiles before we did." Cited in *Star Wars Quotes,* p. 52.

69. See Colin S. Gray, "Air Defence: A Sceptical View," *Queens Quarterly* 79 (Spring 1972): 9, where he notes that boost-phase interception of ICBMs "would take the lion's share of the current U.S. defence budget."

70. Colin S. Gray, *American Military Space Policy: Information Systems, Weapons Systems, and Arms Control* (Cambridge, Mass.: Abt Books, 1982), pp. 15–16.

71. "The low incremental costs per kill . . . could make lasers effective against other targets, such as bombers and cruise missiles. Given the ability to detect them, either could be attacked from space for the incremental cost of the fuel required. Space lasers could engage tactical aircraft at cost advantages of about 100 : 1." Gregory H. Canavan, "Defense Technologies for Europe," in *Strategic Defense and the Western Alliance,* ed. Sanford Lakoff and Randy Willoughby (Lexington, Mass.: Lexington Books, 1987), p. 49.

72. "A defended America could more reasonably make security guarantees to NATO-Europe because it would face fewer risks in doing so. A U.S. deterrent threat on behalf of its allies would be much more credible if that threat did not enable the potential destruction of the U.S." Keith B. Payne, *Strategic Defense: "Star Wars" in Perspective* (Lanham, Md.: Hamilton, 1986), p. 214.

73. See William D. Hartung et al., in *The Strategic Defense Initiative: Costs, Contractors, and Consequences,* ed. Alice Tepper Marlin and Paula Lippin (New York: Council on Economic Priorities, 1985); John P. Holdren and F. Bailey Green, "Military Spending, the SDI, and Government Support of Research and Development: Effects on the Economy and the Health of American Science," *F.A.S. Public Interest Report* 39 (September 1986); and Daniel S. Greenberg, "Civilian Research Spinoffs from SDI Are a Delusion," *Los Angeles Times,* September 9, 1986.

74. The potential economic benefits were stressed in Graham, *High Frontier,* pp. 89–98, and more recently in SDIO, *Report to Congress on the Strategic Defense Initiative* (Washington, D.C.: SDIO, April 1987), pp. viii, 2–5.

75. "You know, we only have a military-industrial complex until a time of danger, and then it becomes the arsenal of democracy. Spending for defense is investing in things that are priceless—peace and freedom." President Ronald Reagan, State of the Union Address, February 6, 1985, *Weekly Compilation of Presidential Documents,* vol. 21, no. 6 (Washington, D.C.: White House, February 11, 1985), p. 143.

76. For a presentation of this conservative view, see Norman Podhoretz, *The Present Danger* (New York: Simon and Schuster, 1980), pp. 56–57.

77. Ibid.

78. For an exposition of the "Reagan doctrine" see Jeane J. Kirkpatrick, "The Reagan Doctrine and U.S. Foreign Policy" (Washington, D.C.: Heritage Foundation, 1983) and "Implementing the Reagan Doctrine," National Security Record no. 82 (Washington, D.C.: Heritage Foundation, August 1985). The doctrine is examined critically in Stephen S. Rosenfeld, "The Guns of July," *Foreign Affairs* 64 (Spring 1986): 698–714.

79. Garry Wills, *Reagan*, p. 360. The broad appeal of SDI is noted in Kevin Phillips, "Defense Beyond Thin Air: Space Holds the Audience," *Los Angeles Times*, March 10, 1985.

80. Fred S. Hoffman, study director, *Ballistic Missile Defenses and U.S. National Security* (Summary report prepared for the Future Security Strategy Group, October 1983).

81. "Given the drastically changed strategic balance and the developments in offensive arms control and BMD technology since the signing of the ABM Treaty, an important question is whether it serves a useful purpose." Payne, *Strategic Defense*, p. 161.

82. "We would see the transition period as a cooperative endeavor with the Soviets. Arms control would play a critical role. We would, for example, envisage continued reductions in offensive nuclear arms." Paul H. Nitze, "On the Road to a More Stable Peace" (address to the Philadelphia World Affairs Council, February 20, 1985); published as Current Policy no. 657 (Washington, D.C.: U.S. Department of State, Bureau of Public Affairs).

83. Ibid.

84. Alvin M. Weinberg and Jack N. Barkenbus, "Stabilizing Star Wars," *Foreign Policy* 54 (Spring 1984): 164–70, and Weinberg and Barkenbus, eds., *Strategic Defenses and Arms Control* (New York: Paragon House, 1987).

85. "To achieve agreements drastically reducing numbers of offensive weapons, and to provide assurance against clandestine violations of such agreements, some deployment of missile defenses may be helpful. In the long run, the transition from a world of assured destruction to a world of live-and-let-live must be accompanied by a transfer of emphasis from offensive to defensive weapons." Freeman Dyson, *Weapons and Hope* (New York: Harper and Row, 1984), p. 281.

86. Reagan, quoted in *New York Times*, October 15, 1986.

87. See Thomas K. Longstreth, John E. Pike, and John B. Rhinelander, *The Impact of U.S. and Soviet Ballistic Missile Defense Programs on the ABM Treaty* (Washington, D.C.: National Campaign to Save the ABM Treaty, March 1985), pp. 42–51, and Peter A. Clausen, "Transition Improbable: Arms Control and SDI," in *Empty Promise: The Growing Case Against Star Wars*, ed. John Tirman, Union of Concerned Scientists (Boston: Beacon, 1986), pp. 191–92.

88. Robert C. McFarlane, in a television interview, quoted in *Arms Control Reporter* (October 1985).

89. Ambassador Smith made this comment on October 6, 1985; quoted in *Arms Control Reporter* (October 1985).

90. Gerard C. Smith, letter to the editor, *New York Times*, October 23, 1985.

91. George P. Shultz (Address to the North Atlantic Assembly, San Francisco, October 14, 1985), quoted in *Arms Control Reporter* (October 1985).

92. *Report to Congress on the Strategic Defense Initiative* (Washington, D.C.: SDIO, June 1986), appendix C.

93. Thus, Sidney D. Drell has called for "a prudent, deliberate, and high-quality research program . . . within ABM Treaty limits" at a level of roughly $2 billion per year. "Prudence and the 'Star Wars' Effort: Research Within the Bounds of ABM Treaty Can Aid Safer World," *Los Angeles Times,* March 10, 1985.

94. See especially Yevgeni Velikhov, Roald Sagdeyev, and Andrei Kokoshin, eds., *Weaponry in Space: The Dilemma of Security* (Moscow: Mir Publishers, 1986), chap. 4, pp. 69–77, chap. 7, pp. 106–27.

95. "The Department of Defense Directed Energy Program and Its Relevance to Strategic Defense," statement by the assistant for directed energy weapons to the under secretary of defense for research and engineering before the Subcommittee on Strategic and Theater Nuclear Forces of the Committee on Armed Services, U.S. Senate, 98th Cong., 1st sess., March 23, 1983, p. 3.

2. THE ELUSIVE QUEST FOR STRATEGIC DEFENSES: LESSONS OF RECENT HISTORY

1. The International Institute for Strategic Studies, *The Military Balance, 1986–1987* (London: IISS, 1986), p. 33.

2. Jeffrey Richelson, "Ballistic Missile Defense and Soviet Strategy," in *The Soviet Calculus of Nuclear War,* ed. Roman Kolkowicz and Ellen Propper Mickiewicz (Lexington, Mass.: Lexington Books, 1986), p. 71.

3. Robert S. McNamara, *Blundering Into Disaster: Surviving the First Century of the Nuclear Age* (New York: Pantheon, 1986), p. 42.

4. R. L. Maust, G. W. Goodman, Jr., and C. E. McLain, *History of Strategic Defense,* report prepared for Defense Science Board (Arlington, Va.: System Planning Corp., September 1981), pp. 11–12.

5. Edward Randolph Jayne II, "The ABM Debate: Strategic Defense and National Security" (Ph.D. diss., Massachusetts Institute of Technology), p. 32.

6. Ibid., pp. 41–42.

7. Ibid., p. 45. McElroy was originally quoted in Jack Raymond, *New York Times,* November 21, 1957.

8. Ibid., pp. 52–53.

9. Maust, Goodman, and McLain, *Strategic Defense,* p. 15.

10. McNamara, *Blundering Into Disaster,* p. 57.

11. Excerpts from a speech delivered by Robert S. McNamara on September 18, 1967, in San Francisco, in *ABM: An Evaluation of the Decision to Deploy an Antiballistic Missile System,* ed. Abram Chayes and Jerome B. Wiesner (New York: New American Library, 1969), p. 242.

12. See Anne Hessing Cahn, "American Scientists and the ABM: A Case Study in Controversy," in *Scientists and Public Affairs,* ed. Albert H. Teich (Cambridge: MIT Press, 1974), pp. 41–120.

13. Maust, Goodman, and McLain, *Strategic Defense,* pp. 18–19.

14. Richelson, "Ballistic Missile Defense," p. 70.

15. Quoted in Sayre Stevens, "The Soviet BMD Program," in *Ballistic Mis-*

sile Defense, ed. Ashton B. Carter and David N. Schwartz (Washington, D.C.: Brookings Institution, 1984), p. 194. The Malinovsky quote is from *Pravda,* October 25, 1961; Khrushchev was quoted in Theodore Shabad, *New York Times,* July 17, 1962.

16. Department of Defense, *Soviet Military Power 1986* (Washington, D.C.: U.S. Government Printing Office, 1986), p. 44.

17. Ibid., p. 43.

18. Stevens, "Soviet BMD," p. 199; Richelson, "Ballistic Missile Defense," p. 71.

19. Robert M. Gates and Lawrence K. Gershwin, testimony before U.S. Congress, Defense Subcommittee, Senate Committee on Appropriations, June 26, 1985, quoted in David S. Yost, "Alliance Strategy and BMD," in *Strategic Defense and the Western Alliance,* ed. Sanford Lakoff and Randy Willoughby (Lexington, Mass.: Lexington Books, 1987), p. 71.

20. DOD, *Soviet Military Power,* p. 45.

21. Michael MccGwire, *Military Objectives in Soviet Foreign Policy* (Washington, D.C.: Brookings Institution, 1987), pp. 243–44.

22. DOD, *Soviet Military Power,* p. 54.

23. Ibid., p. 57.

24. Ibid., pp. 54–57.

25. Ibid., pp. 54–55.

26. The Reagan administration's complaint about the Soviets' new tracking radar was made in President Reagan's February 1985 report to Congress on Soviet noncompliance with arms-control agreements. Cited in David S. Yost, "Strategic Defenses in Soviet Doctrine and Force Posture," in *Swords and Shields: NATO, the U.S.S.R., and New Choices for Long-Range Offense and Defense,* ed. Fred S. Hoffman, Albert Wohlstetter, and David S. Yost (Lexington, Mass.: Lexington Books, 1987), p. 133.

27. DOD, *Soviet Military Power,* p. 57.

28. Yost, "Alliance Strategy," pp. 79–80.

29. DOD, *Soviet Military Power,* p. 53.

30. Ibid., p. 57.

31. Ibid., p. 46.

32. Ibid., p. 47.

33. Report in William J. Broad, *New York Times,* October 23, 1987, p. 11. See also Broad, "The Secrets of Soviet Star Wars," *New York Times Magazine,* June 28, 1987, pp. 22–28.

34. Yost, "Alliance Strategy," p. 75.

35. Stevens, "Soviet BMD," p. 219.

36. MccGwire, *Military Objectives,* p. 36.

37. Stevens, "Soviet BMD," p. 187.

38. MccGwire, *Military Objectives,* p. 242.

39. Bhupendra M. Jasani, ed., *Space Weapons—The Arms Control Dilemma* (London: Taylor and Francis, 1984), p. 5.

40. Paul B. Stares, *The Militarization of Space: U.S. Policy, 1945–1984* (Ithaca: Cornell University Press, 1985), pp. 55–57.

41. Ibid., p. 76.

42. Paul B. Stares, *Space and National Security* (Washington, D.C.: Brookings Institution, 1987), p. 2.
43. Stares, *Militarization of Space,* p. 200.
44. Ibid., p. 232.
45. *Science* 240 (June 12, 1987).

3. MEASURE FOR MEASURE:
THE TECHNOLOGICAL PROSPECT

1. Except for the quote by Haldane, these pessimistic predictions are cited in Kenneth Adelman, "Setting the Record Straight," Current Policy no. 730 (Washington, D.C.: U.S. Department of State, Bureau of Public Affairs, August 7, 1985), and in Keith B. Payne, *Strategic Defense: "Star Wars" in Perspective* (Lanham, Md.: Hamilton, 1986), pp. 56–67. See J. B. S. Haldane, *Callinicus* (London: Kegan Paul, Trench, Trubner, 1925), p. 17, for his comments.
2. J. Robert Oppenheimer, the physicist who directed the Los Alamos Laboratory when the atomic bomb was developed, epitomized this sense of challenge and vocation when he later recommended against a crash program to develop the thermonuclear bomb, at least partly on moral grounds, but abandoned his opposition when he learned of a promising new approach: "When you see something that is technologically sweet," he explained, "you go ahead and do it and argue about what to do about it only after you have had your technical success." *In the Matter of J. Robert Oppenheimer, Transcript of Hearing Before Personnel Security Board,* Atomic Energy Commission (Washington, D.C.: U.S. Government Printing Office, 1954), p. 81. See also Sanford Lakoff, "The Trial of Dr. Oppenheimer," in *Knowledge and Power: Essays on Science and Government,* ed. Sanford Lakoff (New York: Free Press, 1966), pp. 80–82, and "Moral Responsibility and the 'Galilean Imperative,'" *Ethics* 91 (October 1980): 100–106.
3. William J. Broad, *Star Warriors* (New York: Simon and Schuster, 1985), p. 88.
4. U.S. Congress, Office of Technology Assessment, *Ballistic Missile Defense Technologies* (Washington, D.C.: U.S. Government Printing Office, September 1985), p. 139.
5. McGeorge Bundy, George F. Kennan, Robert S. McNamara, and Gerard Smith, "The President's Choice: Star Wars or Arms Control," *Foreign Affairs* 63 (Winter 1984–85): 267.
6. *Report to the American Physical Society of the Study Group on Science and Technology of Directed Energy Weapons* (New York: American Physical Society, 1987).
7. James T. Bruce, Bruce W. MacDonald, and Ronald L. Tammen, "Star Wars at the Crossroads: The Strategic Defense Initiative After Five Years" (U.S. Congress, staff report to senators J. Bennett Johnston, Dale Bumpers, and William Proxmire, typescript, June 12, 1988), p. 34.
8. Ibid., pp. 30–31.
9. Ibid., pp. 21, 41–45.

10. For a given payload weight, and certain other simplifying assumptions, a final velocity of 6 km per second (more precisely, twice the exhaust velocity) minimizes the SBKKVs' total weight in orbit. See Christopher T. Cunningham, Tom Morgan, and Phil Duffy, Lawrence Livermore National Laboratory, "Near-Term Ballistic Missile Defenses" (Draft paper, 1987; private communication with the authors), and "Kinetic Kill Vehicles," *Energy and Technology Review* (July 1987), p. 16, and Christopher T. Cunningham, "The Space-Based Interceptor," Lawrence Livermore National Laboratory, UCRL-99768, October 1988.

11. Marshall Institute, *Report of the Technical Panel on Missile Defense in the 1990s* (hereafter *Marshall Report*) (Washington, D.C.: George C. Marshall Institute, February 1987), pp. 17–28.

12. *Report to the APS*, p. 4.

13. Ibid., p. 5.

14. Ibid.

15. The countermeasures of proliferation, maneuvering, decoys, and deception are described at length in a special addendum to the *Marshall Report* written by Edward Geary.

16. Michael M. May, "Safeguarding Our Space Assets" (Paper prepared for the Aspen Strategy Group, August 13, 1985), p. 11.

17. One such false alarm, discussed in Daniel Ford, *The Button* (New York: Simon and Schuster, 1985), pp. 78–79, occurred on June 3, 1980, when a computer disk costing forty-six cents malfunctioned, sending Strategic Air Command pilots racing to their planes.

18. Bruce, MacDonald, and Tammen, "Star Wars at the Crossroads," p. 52.

19. David Lorge Parnas, "Software Aspects of Strategic Defense Systems," *American Scientist* 73 (September–October 1985): 434–35.

20. From a statement by Dr. Frederick P. Brooks before the U.S. Congress, Senate Subcommittee on Strategic and Theater Nuclear Force, Committee on Armed Services, 99-933, p. 54, quoted in U.S. Congress, Office of Technology Assessment, *SDI: Technology, Survivability, and Software*, OTA-ISC-353 (Washington, D.C.: U.S. Government Printing Office, May 1988), p. 221.

21. Philip M. Boffey, "Software Seen as Obstacle," *New York Times*, September 16, 1986, p. 15.

22. OTA, *SDI*, p. 4.

23. *Report to the APS*, p. 1.

24. Letter of the review committee to the APS council (April 20, 1987), *Report to the APS*.

25. *Report to the APS*, p. 2.

26. Statement issued by the APS council, April 24, 1987.

27. Transcript of press conference, April 23, 1987, at the Pentagon.

28. Statement by Dr. Frederick Seitz before the U.S. Congress, House Armed Services Committee, Defense Policy Panel and R&D Subcommittee, September 15, 1987.

29. *Congressional Record*, May 20, 1987, p. 2005.

30. Quoted in Colleen Cordes, "6,500 Scientists Vow to Boycott Studies Aided by 'Star Wars,'" *Chronicle of Higher Education* 32 (May 27, 1986): 7.

368   Notes to Pages 111–26

31. "Joint Opening Statement of Drs. Lowell Wood and Gregory Canavan Before the House Republican Research Committee," May 19, 1987, typescript.

32. "APS Directed Energy Study Group Responses to Critiques by Wood and Canavan," June 8, 1987, typescript.

33. Ibid.

34. Ibid.

35. Ibid.

36. "Joint Statement of Wood and Canavan," p. 4.

37. "APS Study Group Responses," p. 5.

38. Ibid.

39. As paraphrased in SDIO, *Report to Congress on the Strategic Defense Initiative* (Washington, D.C.: SDIO, June 1986), p. VII-F-13.

40. Ibid., pp. VII-F-14–15.

41. Addendum to letter from Joseph F. Salgado to Rep. Edward J. Markey, October 28, 1987.

42. *Marshall Report,* p. 6.

43. Text of Robert R. Everett's memorandum to Under Secretary Godwin was published in *Strategic Defense* 2 (July 30, 1987): 3.

44. Quoted in *Strategic Defense* 2 (July 5, 1987): 5.

45. Ibid., p. 6.

46. Philip J. Klass, *Aviation Week & Space Technology* (May 23, 1988), p. 23.

47. Colin Norman, "SDI Deployment Program Up in the Air," *Science* 241 (June 17, 1988): 1608–09.

48. *Marshall Report,* pp. 6, 8.

49. Everett memorandum, *Strategic Defense,* pp. 1–2.

50. Cunningham, Morgan, and Duffy, "Near-Term BMD."

51. Ibid.

52. Bruce, MacDonald, and Tammen, "Star Wars at the Crossroads," p. 104.

53. Cunningham, Morgan, and Duffy, "Near-Term BMD."

54. Bruce, MacDonald, and Tammen, "Star Wars at the Crossroads," p. 104.

55. Ibid., p. 105.

56. Paul Mann, "Nunn Redirects Antimissile Debate, Proposing Accidental Launch Shield," *Aviation Week & Space Technology* (January 25, 1988), p. 19. The OTA has reached a similar conclusion: "Insofar as the ERIS ground-launched interceptor relied on fixed, ground-based early-warning radars for launch-commit information, its effectiveness could be greatly reduced by nuclear or jamming attacks on those radars." OTA, *SDI,* p. 16.

57. Dan Stober, *San Jose Mercury News,* August 19, 1988.

58. Lowell Wood, "'Brilliant Pebbles' Missile Defense Concept Advocated by Livermore Scientist," *Aviation Week & Space Technology* (June 12, 1988), pp. 151–53.

59. Richard L. Garwin, "Enforcing BMD Against a Determined Adversary?," in *Space Weapons and International Security,* ed. Bhupendra Jasani (Oxford: Oxford University Press, 1987), p. 78.

60. Richard L. Garwin, letter to Howard Ris, Union of Concerned Scientists, August 15, 1988.

4. A DEFENSE TRANSITION?
SDI AND STRATEGIC STABILITY

1. "The requirements process should be broadened to include an analysis of the desirability of deployment which includes a consideration of a two-sided BMD deployment." Memorandum for the Under Secretary of Defense (Acquisition) from the Defense Science Board Task Force Subgroup Strategic Air Defense—Strategic Defense Milestone (SDM) Panel, published in *Strategic Defense* 2 (July 30, 1987): 1.

2. B. H. Liddell Hart, *Strategy: The Indirect Approach* (London: Faber & Faber, 1968), p. 334. Quoted in Lawrence Freedman, *The Evolution of Nuclear Strategy* (New York: St. Martin's, 1981), p. xvii.

3. Benjamin S. Lambeth, "Soviet Perspectives on SDI," in *Strategic Defenses and Soviet-American Relations,* ed. Samuel F. Wells, Jr., and Robert S. Litwak (Cambridge, Mass.: Ballinger, 1987), p. 70. Emphasis in original.

4. For Zbigniew Brzezinski's views on strategic defense, see his "Mutual Strategic Security and Strategic Defense," in *Promise or Peril: The Strategic Defense Initiative,* ed. Zbigniew Brzezinski (Washington, D.C.: Ethics and Public Policy Center, 1986), pp. 64–66, where he recommends a "limited strategic defense." Henry Kissinger, in "Reducing the Risk of War," *Promise or Peril,* p. 98, argues that "a foolproof defense of civil population . . . is a mirage" but that the existence of some active defenses would strengthen deterrence by adding greatly to the uncertainty of a potential attacker's calculation.

5. See Edward Teller, *Better a Shield Than a Sword: Perspectives on Defense and Technology* (New York: Free Press, 1987).

6. See Alvin M. Weinberg and Jack N. Barkenbus, "Moving to Defenses Through the Defense Protected Build-Down (DPB)," and Alvin M. Weinberg, "Speculations on a Defense-Dominated World," in *Strategic Defenses and Arms Control,* ed. Weinberg and Barkenbus (New York: Paragon House, 1987), pp. 23–65, 89–110. For a responsive commentary on their views, see Sanford Lakoff, "Toward a Broader Framework for U.S.-Soviet Agreement," in ibid., pp. 66–88.

7. See Peter A. Clausen, "Limited Defense: The Unspoken Goal," in *Empty Promises: The Growing Case Against Star Wars,* ed. John Tirman, Union of Concerned Scientists (Boston: Beacon, 1986), esp. pp. 154–59.

8. Richard Ned Lebow, "Is Crisis Management Always Possible?" *Political Science Quarterly* 102 (Summer 1987): 182.

9. Fred C. Iklé, "Can Nuclear Deterrence Last Out the Century?" *Foreign Affairs* 51 (January 1973): 267–85, cited in Colin S. Gray, "The Missile Defense Debate in the Early 1970s," in Brzezinski, ed., *Promise or Peril,* p. 45.

10. *The President's Strategic Defense Initiative* (Washington, D.C.: U.S. Government Printing Office, 1985), p. 4. David S. Yost suggests that, for Soviet strategists, a combination of offensive and defensive superiority is advantageous because it offers a way to defeat NATO's flexible-response strategy. Such superiority could be used to "persuade NATO governments either not to initiate the use of nuclear weapons or not to engage in more extensive use in the event selective strikes failed to achieve their intended purpose." "Alliance Strategy and

Ballistic Missile Defense," in *Strategic Defense and the Western Alliance,* ed. Sanford Lakoff and Randy Willoughby (Lexington, Mass.: Lexington Books, 1987), p. 73.

11. "I cannot envision any circumstance more threatening and dangerous to the free world than one in which our populations and military forces remain vulnerable to Soviet nuclear missiles while their population and military assets are immune to our retaliatory forces" (Address by Secretary of Defense Caspar W. Weinberger before the National Space Foundation, Colorado Springs, Colorado, January 22, 1987), news release, Office of Assistant Secretary of Defense (Public Affairs).

12. Strategic Defense Initiative Organization (SDIO), *Report to Congress on the Strategic Defense Initiative* (Washington, D.C.: SDIO, April 1987), p. II–11.

13. Paul H. Nitze, "On the Road to a More Stable Peace" (Address to the Philadelphia World Affairs Council, February 20, 1985); published as Current Policy no. 657 (Washington, D.C.: U.S. Department of State, Bureau of Public Affairs), p. 3.

14. Harold Brown, *The Strategic Defense Initiative: Defense Systems and the Strategic Debate,* Discussion Paper no. 104 (Santa Monica, Calif.: California Seminar on International Security and Foreign Policy, March 1985), pp. 3–4.

15. Brent Scowcroft, *Report of the President's Commission on Strategic Forces* (Washington, D.C.: U.S. Department of Defense, April 6, 1983), pp. 7–8, 17.

16. Robert S. McNamara, *Blundering Into Disaster: Surviving the First Century of the Nuclear Age* (New York: Pantheon, 1986), p. 92.

17. Michael MccGwire, "Why the Soviets Are Serious About Arms Control," *Brookings Review* (Spring 1987): 11. For a different view, see Rebecca V. Strode, "Space-Based Lasers for Ballistic Missile Defense: Soviet Policy Options," in *Laser Weapons in Space: Policy and Doctrine,* ed. Keith B. Payne (Boulder, Colo.: Westview, 1983). She contends that the Soviet leadership has not accepted the notion that mutual vulnerability is desirable and that the Soviet military leadership "retains a keen interest in the potential military advantages of reduced homeland vulnerability" (pp. 134–35). Statements by Soviet leaders, beginning with Leonid Brezhnev (acknowledging that no country can win a nuclear war), differ from those appearing in the Soviet military press and reflect either a propaganda effort to allay Western alarm over the Soviet military buildup or the views of some in the leadership who have not yet been able to bring about "major alterations in Soviet operational strategy" (p. 138).

18. For a good review of the various casualty estimates, see Paul P. Craig and John Jungerman, *Nuclear Arms Race: Technology and Society* (New York: McGraw-Hill, 1986), chap. 19, pp. 307–28.

19. *The Challenge of Peace: God's Promise and Our Response: A Pastoral Letter on War and Peace* (Washington, D.C.: United States Catholic Conference, 1983), pp. 56–58.

20. Iklé, "Nuclear Deterrence," p. 281.

21. As Michael Walzer observes, in *Just and Unjust Wars* (New York: Basic

Books, 1977), "deterrence and mass murder are very far apart. We threaten evil in order not to do it. . . . The threat seems in comparison to be morally defensible." Cited in Gregg Herken, *Counsels of War* (New York: Knopf, 1985), n. 11, chap. 21, p. 372.

22. Leon Wieseltier, *Nuclear War, Nuclear Peace* (New York: Holt, Rinehart and Winston, 1983), p. 73.

23. Cited in Robert Jervis, *The Illogic of American Nuclear Strategy* (Ithaca: Cornell University Press, 1984), p. 15.

24. Admiral Gayler's remarks on nuclear deterrence are quoted in McNamara, *Blundering Into Disaster,* p. 112.

25. Department of Defense, *Soviet Military Power* (Washington, D.C.: U.S. Government Printing Office, 1986), p. 25.

26. See Herbert F. York, *Making Weapons, Talking Peace* (New York: Basic Books, 1987), pp. 183–94, and 337, and Richard L. Garwin, "Launch Under Attack to Redress Minuteman Vulnerability?" *International Security* 4 (Winter 1979–80): 117–39.

27. McNamara, *Blundering Into Disaster,* p. 49.

28. See the discussion of low-endoatmospheric technologies in Gregory H. Canavan, "Defensive Technologies for Europe," in *Strategic Defense,* ed. Lakoff and Willoughby, pp. 44–45.

29. McNamara, *Blundering Into Disaster,* p. 109.

30. U.S. Congress, Office of Technology Assessment (OTA), *Ballistic Missile Defense Technologies* (Washington, D.C.: OTA, 1985), pp. 95–98.

31. Ibid., p. 104.

32. Ibid., p. 113.

33. Ibid., p. 114.

34. The Reagan administration's attitude toward arms control, at least during the first term, has been well described by Strobe Talbott: "Until the buildup in Western defenses was well under way, nuclear arms control would be a matter of keeping up appearances, of limiting damage, of buying time, and of laying the groundwork for agreement later," in *Deadly Gambits: The Reagan Administration and the Stalemate in Nuclear Arms Control* (New York: Knopf, 1984), p. 3.

35. Paul H. Nitze, "The Impact of SDI on U.S.-Soviet Relations (Address to a seminar sponsored by American Enterprise Institute–National Defense University, April 29, 1986); published as Current Policy no. 830 (Washington, D.C.: U.S. Department of State, Bureau of Public Affairs), p. 3.

36. Ibid.

37. Ibid., p. 4.

38. Weinberg and Barkenbus, eds., *Strategic Defenses.*

39. The difficulties with the proposal for a defense-protected build-down are described in more detail in Sanford Lakoff, "A Framework for U.S.-Soviet Agreement," in ibid., pp. 67–69.

40. OTA, *BMD Technologies* (Executive Summary), p. 13.

41. Freeman Dyson, *Weapons and Hope* (New York: Harper and Row, 1984), pp. 280–81.

42. McNamara, *Blundering Into Disaster,* p. 108.

43. James T. Bruce, Bruce W. MacDonald, and Ronald L. Tammen, "Star Wars at the Crossroads: The Strategic Defense Initiative After Five Years" (U.S. Congress, staff report to senators J. Bennett Johnston, Dale Bumpers, and William Proxmire, June 12, 1988, typescript), p. 92.

5. "DON'T ASK THE SOVIETS. TELL THEM": SDI AND ARMS CONTROL

1. Paul H. Nitze sees the development of strategic defenses in the context of a cooperative "defense transition." See his "On the Road to a More Stable Peace" (Address to the World Affairs Council, February 20, 1985); published as Current Policy no. 657 (Washington, D.C.: U.S. Department of State, Bureau of Public Affairs). James C. Fletcher stresses the need to link deployment of defenses to agreements to reduce offensive arsenals. See his "The Technologies for Ballistic Missile Defense," *Issues in Science and Technology* 1 (Fall 1984): 15–26. Although he stops short of endorsing arms control, Zbigniew Brzezinski has called for unilateral U.S. efforts to achieve "limited strategic defense" in order to make the U.S.-Soviet relationship more stable and to improve prospects for "mutual accommodation." See his "Mutual Strategic Security and Strategic Defense," in *Promise or Peril: The Strategic Defense Initiative*, ed. Zbigniew Brzezinski (Washington, D.C.: Ethics and Public Policy Center, 1986), pp. 64–67.

2. See in particular the brief account of the McNamara-Brezhnev exchange at the Glassboro summit in Robert S. McNamara, *Blundering Into Disaster: Surviving the First Century of the Nuclear Age* (New York: Pantheon, 1986), pp. 56–58.

3. Robert W. Buchheim and Philip J. Farley, "The U.S.-Soviet Standing Consultative Commission," in *U.S.-Soviet Security Cooperation: Achievements, Failures, Lessons*, ed. Alexander L. George, Philip J. Farley, and Alexander Dallin (New York: Oxford University Press, 1988), p. 263.

4. Thomas K. Longstreth, John E. Pike, and John B. Rhinelander, *The Impact of U.S. and Soviet Ballistic Missile Defense Programs on the ABM Treaty* (Washington, D.C.: National Campaign to Save the ABM Treaty, March 1985), p. 5.

5. Abraham D. Sofaer, "The ABM Treaty and the Strategic Defense Initiative," *Harvard Law Review* 99 (June 1986): 1972.

6. John Newhouse, *Cold Dawn: The Story of SALT* (New York: Holt, Rinehart, and Winston, 1973), p. 230.

7. Office of the Legal Advisor, Department of State, "The ABM Treaty" (Washington, D.C.: U.S. Department of State, May 11, 1987), appendix A, p. 503. Typescript.

8. "Military Implications of the Treaty on Limitations of Anti-Ballistic Missile Systems and the Interim Agreement on Limitation of Strategic Offensive Arms," Hearings before the U.S. Congress, Senate Committee on Armed Services, 92d Cong., 2d sess. (June 6, 1972), pp. 40–41.

9. Ibid.

10. Ibid., pp. 274–75.

11. Ibid., p. 275.

12. Sen. Sam Nunn, "Interpretation of the ABM Treaty," *Congressional Record* 133, no. 38 (March 11, 1987): 8.

13. Ambassador Smith's written clarification for the Senate Armed Services Committee is quoted in Longstreth, Pike, and Rhinelander, *Impact of BMD on the ABM Treaty*, p. 26.

14. Office of the Legal Advisor, State Department, "ABM Treaty," A-503.

15. *Congressional Record* 118 (1972): 26,700, cited in ibid., pt. II, appendix B, p. 55.

16. Ibid., 26,682, cited in Office of the Legal Advisor, State Department, "ABM Treaty," pt. II, appendix B, p. 54.

17. U.S. Congress, *Fiscal Year 1985 Arms Control Impact Statement*, 98th Cong., 2d sess., 252 (1984), quoted in Abram Chayes and Antonia Handler Chayes, "Testing and Development of 'Exotic' Systems Under the ABM Treaty: The Great Reinterpretation Caper," *Harvard Law Review* 99 (June 1986): 1969.

18. Robert McFarlane was quoted in Nunn, "Interpretation," p. 6.

19. Donald G. Brennan's letter to John Rhinelander is quoted in Raymond L. Garthoff, *Policy Versus the Law: The Reinterpretation of the ABM Treaty* (Washington, D.C.: Brookings Institution, 1987), n. 6, p. 6.

20. Raymond L. Garthoff, letter to *International Security* 2 (Summer 1977): 106—09.

21. Garthoff, *Reinterpretation*, n. 6, pp. 6—7.

22. Ibid., p. 7.

23. Ibid.

24. Perle's reaction to the legal review cited in *Arms Control Reporter* (1985), 603.B.75.

25. Garthoff, *Reinterpretation*, p. 8; Nitze had changed his mind about the interpretation of the treaty, according to Garthoff, because he "had no doubts about the traditional interpretation in 1977, or even in May 1985," ibid., n. 6, p. 7.

26. Ibid., pp. 8—10.

27. Quoted in Lou Cannon, *Washington Post*, July 10, 1985, and in *Arms Control Reporter* (1985), 603.B.72.

28. Quoted in ibid., 603.B.73.

29. Quoted in ibid.

30. Gerard C. Smith, "A Dangerous Dream: Why Reagan's Plan Threatens the Nuclear Balance," *Baltimore Sun*, March 29, 1983, and cited in Alan B. Sherr, *Legal Issues of the "Star Wars" Defense Program* (Boston: Lawyers' Alliance for Nuclear Arms Control, June 1986), p. 10.

31. Spurgeon Keeney, quoted in *Arms Control Reporter* (October 11, 1985), 603.B.73.

32. George P. Shultz, "Arms Control, Strategic Stability, and Global Security" (Address before the North Atlantic Assembly, San Francisco, October 14, 1985), later published in *State Department Bulletin* 85 (December 1985): 23.

33. Quoted in Garthoff, *Reinterpretation*, p. 100.

34. Office of the Legal Advisor, State Department, "ABM Treaty," p. 3.

35. Ibid., pp. 11—12.

36. Ibid., pp. 29—37, 75—82.

37. Ibid., pp. 14–16.
38. Ibid., quoted pp. 16–17.
39. Ibid., quoted p. 17.
40. Ibid., quoted p. 18.
41. Ibid., quoted p. 19.
42. Ibid., quoted p. 23.
43. Ibid.
44. In addition to Garthoff, *Reinterpretation,* see Chayes and Chayes, "'Exotic' Systems"; Sherr, *Legal Issues;* and Committee on International Arms Control and Security Affairs, Association of the Bar of the City of New York, *The Anti-Ballistic Missile Treaty Interpretation Dispute* (New York: Association of the Bar of the City of New York, 1987). In March 1985 (before the reinterpretation was developed) DOD commissioned a study by two former members of the SALT negotiating team, Col. Charles L. Fitzgerald and Sidney Graybeal, which turned out to be supportive of the traditional interpretation: *SALT I Negotiating History Relating to Limitations on Future ABM Systems and Components Based on "Other Physical Principles"* (Arlington, Va.: System Planning Corp.: March 1985).
45. Garthoff, *Reinterpretation,* n. 7, p. 8.
46. Ibid.
47. See especially Chayes and Chayes, "'Exotic' Systems," pp. 1963–64.
48. Garthoff made his view clear in his response to Becker's letter, *International Security* 2 (Summer 1987): 107–08.
49. Chayes and Chayes, "'Exotic' Systems," pp. 1963–64.
50. Garthoff, *Reinterpretation,* pp. 33–37.
51. Marshal Grechko's statement, published in *Pravda,* September 30, 1972, is quoted in Garthoff, *Reinterpretation,* p. 76.
52. Longstreth, Pike, and Rhinelander, *Impact of BMD,* p. 23.
53. Ibid., pp. 23–24.
54. Lt. Gen. James Abrahamson, testimony before the U.S. Congress, House Armed Services Committee, February 27, 1985, quoted in ibid., p. 28.
55. Ibid., pp. 28–30.
56. Ibid., pp. 34–35.
57. Ibid., p. 43.
58. ACDA, quoted in ibid., p. 45.
59. Ibid., pp. 48–49.
60. U.S. Department of Defense, *Report to the Congress on the Strategic Defense Initiative* (Washington, D.C.: Department of Defense, June 1986), p. C-3.
61. Ibid., pp. C-5–8.
62. Ibid., p. C-11.
63. Ibid., pp. C-9–11.
64. Ibid.
65. Ibid., pp. C-12–13.
66. See, in particular, Thomas K. Longstreth, "Space-Based Interceptors for Star Wars: Untestable Under Any Interpretation of the ABM Treaty" (Prepared for the Federation of American Scientists, October 1, 1987; draft).

67. *New York Times,* October 15, 1986.

68. James C. Fletcher, "The Technologies for Ballistic Missile Defense," *Issues in Science and Technology* (Fall 1984): 15–26.

69. The president made this comment at a meeting with the National Security Planning Group, also attended by Weinberger and Shultz, on February 3, 1987, according to minutes leaked to the press, as reported in Gregory A. Fossedal, "NSC Minutes Show President Leaning to SDI Deployment," *Washington Times,* February 6, 1987. Cited in Garthoff, *Reinterpretation,* p. 13.

70. Michael R. Gordon, "How the U.S. and Soviet Officials Agreed to Disagree on 'Star Wars,'" *New York Times,* December 12, 1987, pp. 1, 8.

71. R. W. Apple, Jr., "Reagan and Gorbachev Report Progress on Long-Range Arms; Mute Quarrel over 'Star Wars,'" *New York Times,* December 11, 1987, p. A-22.

72. The physicist Peter Zimmerman has argued that "the kinds of kinetic kill vehicles that have been proposed for use in a first-generation SDI system can be redesigned and rejiggered for offensive purposes." Quoted in William J. Broad, *New York Times,* February 22, 1987.

73. Quoted in *Wall Street Journal,* December 7, 1983, cited in *Star Wars Quotes* (Washington, D.C.: Arms Control Association, July 1986), p. 52.

74. Quoted in *Washington Times,* May 13, 1985, cited in *Star Wars Quotes,* ibid.

6. A "MAGINOT LINE OF THE TWENTY-FIRST CENTURY"? SDI AND THE WESTERN ALLIANCE

1. Michael Howard, quoted in David Ignatius, *Wall Street Journal,* October 15, 1985.

2. Trevor Taylor, "The Implications of SDI for the Independent Nuclear Forces of Europe," in *Strategic Defense and the Western Alliance,* ed. Sanford Lakoff and Randy Willoughby (Lexington, Mass.: Lexington Books, 1987), p. 107.

3. Assembly of the Western European Union, "WEU and the Strategic Defense Initiative—the European Pillar of the Atlantic Alliance," document 1034, November 5, 1985, p. 10. Cited in Taylor, "Implications of SDI," p. 115.

4. E. P. Thompson, "Folly's Comet," in *Star Wars: Science-Fiction Fantasy or Serious Probability?,* ed. E. P. Thompson (Harmondsworth, England: Penguin, 1985), pp. 106–07.

5. Ibid., p. 148.

6. Geoffrey Howe (Address to the Royal United Services Institute for Defence Studies, March 15, 1985). Excerpted in the *Times* (London), March 22, 1985.

7. Ibid.

8. President Mitterrand, quoted in Pierre Lellouche, "SDI and European Security: A View from France," in *Strategic Defense,* ed. Lakoff and Willoughby, n. 6, p. 145.

9. Senior official, French Foreign Ministry, quoted in Judith Miller, "Allies in West Lend Support to 'Star Wars,'" *New York Times,* December 30, 1985.

10. John Fenske, "France and the Strategic Defence Initiative: speeding up or putting on the brakes?" *International Affairs* 62 (Spring 1986): 233.

11. Heinz Riesenhuber, "Die EUREKA-Initiative zeigt eine beachtliche Dynamik," *Die Welt,* December 13, 1986. Riesenhuber was FRG minister for research and technology. Cited in Michael Lucas, "The Economic and Technological Impact of SDI on Western Europe," typescript.

12. Hans Rühle, quoted in North Atlantic Assembly, "General Report of the Scientific and Technical Committee" (San Francisco: North Atlantic Assembly, November 1984), p. 27.

13. Kai-Uwe von Hassel, "Uberlegungen zu einer Europaischen Verteidigungsinitiative" ["Reflections on a European Defense Initiative"], December 31, 1985, p. 24; also quoted in Thomas O. Enders, *Missile Defense as Part of an Extended NATO Air Defense* (St. Augustin, F.R.G.: Sozialwissenschaftliches Forschungsinstitut der Konrad-Adenauer-Stiftung, May 1986), p. 6.

14. See Michael Lucas, "SDI and Europe," *World Policy Journal* 3 (Spring 1986): 229; Ernst-Otto Czempiel, "SDI and NATO: The Case of the Federal Republic of Germany," in *Strategic Defense,* ed. Lakoff and Willoughby, pp. 157–58; and Hans Günter Brauch, ed., *Star Wars and European Defense, Implications for Europe: Perceptions and Assessments* (New York: St. Martin's, 1987).

15. Interview with French Defense Minister Paul Quilès, *Jane's Defence Weekly,* March 8, 1986, p. 411, also in Taylor, "Implications of SDI," p. 108.

16. Michael Quinlan, senior civil servant responsible for nuclear issues, quoted in Lawrence Freedman, "British Nuclear Targeting," *Defence Analysis* 1 (June 1985): 94.

17. See David S. Yost, "France's Deterrent Posture and Security in Europe, Part I: Capabilities and Doctrines," Adelphi Paper no. 194 (London: International Institute for Strategic Studies, Winter 1984–85), p. 15.

18. Commission d'Etudes sur les Armes Spatiales, *Rapport de Synthèse présenté au Ministre de la Défense,* January 30, 1986, trans. U.S. Congressional Research Service, p. 12. Cited in Taylor, "Implications of SDI," p. 81. This report is known as the "Delpech Report" because the commission was chaired by Jean François Delpech, director of research at the Centre National de la Récherche Scientifique.

19. Lellouche, "SDI and European Security," pp. 129–30.

20. Jacques Chirac, inaugural address before the National Assembly, reprinted in *Le Monde,* April 11, 1986, and quoted in Lellouche, ibid., p. 145.

21. Quoted in Taylor, "Implications of SDI," p. 113.

22. Czempiel, "SDI and NATO," p. 152. See also Hans Günter Brauch, "The West German Debate on the ABM Treaty" (Paper presented at the annual meeting, International Studies Association, Washington, D.C., April 14–18, 1987), and Brauch, ed., *Star Wars and European Defense.*

23. Jonathan Dean, *Watershed in Europe: Dismantling the East-West Military Confrontation* (Lexington, Mass.: Lexington Books, 1987), pp. 262–63.

24. Gallup Poll, Ltd., February 1985. Fifty-eight percent of those polled thought defensive weapons were being developed mainly to defend the United

States, 23 percent thought they were intended to defend both the United States and Western Europe.

25. Between June 1982 and January 1986, the percentage of West Germans preferring to cooperate with the United States rather than the U.S.S.R. shrank from 52 percent to 32 percent. Among the young, support for unilateral disarmament rose from 44 to 55 percent. Czempiel, "SDI and NATO," p. 152.

26. Wolfram F. Hanrieder, "SDI: Strategic Disengagement and Independence," in *Arms Control, the FRG, and the Future of East-West Relations,* ed. Wolfram F. Hanrieder (Boulder, Colo.: Westview, 1987), p. 125.

27. Hugh De Santis, "An Anti-Tactical Missile Defense for Europe," *SAIS Review* 6 (Summer–Fall 1986): 101.

28. Quoted in George W. Ball, "The War for Star Wars," *New York Review of Books,* April 11, 1985, p. 41.

29. NATO Nuclear Planning Group Final Communiqué, text in *Survival* 27 (May–June 1985): 129.

30. Fred S. Hoffman, study director, *Ballistic Missile Defenses and U.S. National Security* (Summary report prepared for the Future Security Strategy Study, October 1983), p. 2.

31. Ibid., p. 3.

32. Ibid., pp. 3–5.

33. Ibid., p. 10.

34. U.S. Congress, Senate Committee on Foreign Relations, Hearings, *Strategic Defense and Anti-Satellite Weapons* (Washington, D.C.: U.S. Government Printing Office, 1984), p. 17.

35. Text of Weinberger letter in *Survival* 27 (May–June 1985): 128.

36. U.S. Congress, House of Representatives, "U.S. Plans for Anti-Tactical Ballistic Missiles," p. 5, cited in Ivo H. Daalder, "A Tactical Defense Initiative for Europe?" *Bulletin of the Atomic Scientists* 43 (May 1987): 34.

37. Dennis M. Gormley, "A New Dimension to Soviet Theater Strategy," *Orbis* 29 (Fall 1985): 541–54.

38. Dennis M. Gormley, "Emerging Attack Options in Soviet Theater Strategy," in *Swords and Shields: NATO, the U.S.S.R., and New Choices for Long-Range Offense and Defense,* ed. Fred S. Hoffman, Albert Wohlstetter, and David S. Yost (Lexington, Mass.: Lexington Books, 1987), pp. 90–94.

39. Ibid., see also De Santis, "Anti-Tactical Missile Defense," 103–04.

40. See Andrew H. Cordesman, "SDI and Europe: Where Does Theatre Defense Fit In?," *International Defense Review* 20 (April 1987): 411.

41. Gormley, "New Dimension," 561–66.

42. Ibid., p. 563.

43. Ibid., p. 567.

44. Manfred Wörner, "A Missile Defense for NATO Europe," *Strategic Review* 14 (Winter 1986): 13–20. Similar views were advanced earlier by military analyst Uwe Nerlich in "Taktische oder erweiterte strategische Raketenverteidigung für Europa" ["Tactical or Extended Strategic Missile Defense for Europe"] (Ebenhausen: Stiftung Wissenschaft und Politik, January 1985).

45. See Daalder, "Tactical Defense," p. 34.

46. Wörner, "Missile Defense," p. 15.

47. Daalder, "Missile Defense," p. 36.

48. Benoit Morel and Theodore A. Postol, "A Technical Assessment of Potential Threats to NATO from Non-Nuclear Soviet Tactical Missiles." This paper and another by the same authors, "Anti-Tactical Ballistic Missiles and NATO," prepared in 1987 for the Center for International Security and Arms Control, Stanford University, were subsequently published in Donald Hafner and John Roper, eds., *ATBMs and Western Security: Missile Defenses for Europe* (Cambridge, Mass.: Ballinger, 1988). See also Benoit Morel, "ATBM—A Solution in Search of a Problem," *Bulletin of the Atomic Scientists* 43 (May 1987): 39–41.

49. According to a calculation by the *Economist,* January 12, 1985, pp. 30–40, cited in De Santis, "Anti-Tactical Missile Defense," p. 112.

50. David Rubenson and James Bonomo, "The Role of ATBM in NATO Strategy," *Survival* 24 (November–December 1982): 518–19.

51. De Santis, "Anti-Tactical Missile Defense," p. 112.

52. Ibid.

53. *Science and Government Report* (U.K.), June 1, 1987.

54. *Times* (London), June 19, 1987.

55. See Michael Lucas, "The United States and Post-INF Europe," *World Policy Journal* 5 (Spring 1988): 183–233.

7. DEPLOY OR PERISH: SDI AND DOMESTIC POLITICS

1. For theoretical and empirical analyses of the involvement of the defense industries in government procurement and R&D, see Steven Rosen, ed., *Testing the Theory of the Military-Industrial Complex* (Lexington, Mass.: D.C. Heath, 1973). C. Wright Mills, in *The Causes of World War III* (New York: Ballantine, 1958), suggests that the concept applies both to the United States and U.S.S.R. in the sense that in both countries an alliance exists between heavy industry and the military services, buttressed by a commonly held ideological commitment to the cold war, which exerts strong influence in perpetuating high levels of military procurement and R&D. As a general structural principle, the concept undoubtedly has some merit. As an explanatory theory, however, it fails to account either for specific decisions or for incremental changes in overall defense expenditures. In some versions, the concept implies that military contracting is more lucrative than ordinary business, but a recent study indicates that although the data are not available to support a definitive analysis, no clear-cut evidence exists that defense industries earn "excess profits." The same study notes, however, that defense industry costs—including levels of compensation, payment for lobbying, and inefficiencies in production—tend to be higher than for civil industry. See David E. Kaun, *Where Have All the Profits Gone? An Analysis of the Major U.S. Defense Contractors, 1950–1985,* Research Paper no. 4 (La Jolla: University of California Institute on Global Conflict and Cooperation, 1988). For an insightful comparative examination of the links between technological advances and the superpower arms race, see Matthew Evange-

lista, *Innovation and the Arms Race: How the United States and the Soviet Union Develop New Military Technologies* (Ithaca: Cornell University Press, 1988).

2. In a thoughtful historical study of the impact of atomic weapons on strategic concepts and practice, Lawrence Freedman rightly points out that the introduction of the atomic bomb did not immediately make previous conceptions of warfare obsolete. At first, most strategists were inclined to think of the new device as one that would extend and increase the importance of strategic bombing, which had already come to play a critical role in World War II. Only gradually, as the Soviet Union also became a nuclear power, as ICBMs entered the arsenals of two blocs, and as it became more and more obvious that nuclear war could not easily be kept limited, did the concept of stable deterrence become a commonly accepted framework for strategic planning. Within this framework there is still room for disagreement over counterforce targeting or assured destruction, levels of sufficiency, the role of first-strike and second-strike weapons, and a host of other similar issues. The basic framework is generally accepted and represents a fundamentally new way of thinking about warfare, allowing for a corresponding consensus on the value of arms control as a means of preserving parity and stability at the lowest possible levels of armament. Freedman is nevertheless right to warn that "an international order that rests upon a stability created by nuclear weapons will be the most terrible legacy with which each succeeding generation will endow the next. To believe that this can go on indefinitely without major disaster requires an optimism unjustified by an historical or political perspective. . . . The major task for the future must be to address the problems of nuclear arsenals in a world of political change." Lawrence Freedman, *The Evolution of Nuclear Strategy* (New York: St. Martin's, 1981), p. 399.

3. For a fuller account of President Truman's decision to develop a thermonuclear bomb, see Herbert F. York, *The Advisors: Oppenheimer, Teller, and the Superbomb* (San Francisco: W. H. Freeman, 1976).

4. "A powerful flow of people and money moves between the defense contractors, the Executive branch (DOD and NASA), and Congress, creating an 'iron triangle' on defense policy and procurement that excludes outsiders and alternative perspectives." Gordon Adams, *The Politics of Defense Contracting: The Iron Triangle* (New Brunswick, N.J.: Transaction, 1981), p. 3.

5. The Thor-Jupiter conflict is a classic instance of interservice rivalry in weapons innovation. For a useful critical account, see Michael H. Armacost, *The Politics of Weapons Innovation: The Thor-Jupiter Controversy* (New York: Columbia University Press, 1969). The army's promotion of Jupiter is also "a textbook example of how personal determination and zeal, combined with interservice rivalry, can fuel the arms race and result in the production and deployment of needless weapons and in the needless expenditure of billions of dollars." Herbert F. York, *Race to Oblivion: A Participant's View of the Arms Race* (New York: Simon and Schuster, 1970), p. 98.

6. Reagan had help in resuscitating the B-1, however, not only from the prime contractor, Rockwell, and the others organized by Rockwell to lobby for the plane, but also from two influential Democratic politicians, Sen. Alan Cranston (D., Calif.) and Sen. John Glenn (D., Ohio). In 1980 they sponsored a

successful amendment to a bill calling for development of a "strategic weapons launcher," guaranteeing that the next president would have $350 million to spend and an early deadline for producing plans for a new aircraft. Bipartisan congressional support kept the program alive and enabled Reagan to fulfill his campaign pledge to reverse Carter's decision. See Nick Kotz, *Wild Blue Yonder: Money, Politics, and the B-1 Bomber* (New York: Pantheon, 1988), p. 194.

7. Lt. Gen. Harley Hughes, U.S. Air Force deputy chief of staff for plans and operations (Address to an Air Force Association symposium), quoted in *Military Space*, June 8, 1987, p. 8.

8. Louis Harris and Associates, October 22, 1984.

9. CBS News / *New York Times*, October 25, 1984.

10. CBS News / *New York Times*, January 2–4, 1985.

11. ABC News / *Washington Post*, October 14, 1986.

12. CBS News / *New York Times*, October 24–28, 1986.

13. Roper Organization, October 15–16, 1986.

14. NBC News / *Wall Street Journal*, October 14, 1986.

15. ABC News / *Washington Post*, November 10–13, 1985.

16. ABC News / *Washington Post*, October 24–28, 1985.

17. Gallup Organization, October 14, 1985.

18. Gallup Organization, November 13–14, 1985.

19. CBS News / *New York Times*, November 6–10, 1985.

20. Yankelovich, Clancy, Shulman, September 8–10, 1986.

21. CBS News / *New York Times*, January 4, 1985.

22. ABC News / *Washington Post*, October 24–28, 1985.

23. *Los Angeles Times*, November 1–7, 1985.

24. CBS News / *New York Times*, January 18–21, 1987.

25. William Schneider, a public-opinion analyst, has interpreted the poll data as indicating that the public "simply does not see any inconsistency between support for SDI and arms control." The Democrats in Congress opposed to SDI, he noted, were trying to "educate" the public to appreciate the difficulties SDI was posing for arms control. See William Schneider, "Congress Openly Defies Public Opinion on SDI," *National Journal* 19 (May 23, 1987): 1366. Although Schneider's analysis of the data is plausible, there is enough inconsistency in responses to questions that do and do not link SDI to arms control to suggest significant confusion and ambivalence.

26. Louis Marquet's comments on the costs of early deployment are quoted in *Arms Control Reporter* (January 19, 1987) 575.B.185.

27. Lloyd Dumas, *The Overburdened Economy: Uncovering the Causes of Chronic Unemployment, Inflation, and National Decline* (Berkeley and Los Angeles: University of California Press, 1986), p. 211.

28. The document appeared to be typed on the stationery of the Heritage Foundation and was identified as "NSR [National Security Report?] #46: High Frontier: A New Option in Space." Excerpts were published in John Bosma, "A Proposed Plan for Project on BMD and Arms Control," in *Harper's* (June 1985), p. 22. In a letter to the British newspaper, *The Observer*, July 27, 1985, an official of the foundation disclaimed responsibility and attributed the report to High Frontier. See E. P. Thompson, "Folly's Comet," in *Star Wars: Science-*

Fiction Fantasy or Serious Probability?, ed. E. P. Thompson (Harmondsworth, England: Penguin, 1985), n. 4, p. 157. Thompson gives great weight to this document to support his blanket indictment of SDI as a deceptive conspiracy on the part of the munitions makers: "The cynicism of this well-funded salesmanship is such as to bring into question the integrity of all appearances. . . . In the marketing of bad faith, the proponents of arguments about human destiny wear masks, and the zealous advocates of 'defence against missiles' (not only in the USA but in Europe) may have a secret retainer from the U.S. aerospace industry," ibid., p. 96. That a professional historian should attach so much significance to a document of such doubtful provenance and bearing is a striking illustration of the degree to which political passions often influence judgments on SDI.

29. Ashton B. Carter, *Directed Energy Missile Defense in Space* (Background paper prepared under contract for the Office of Technology Assessment [Washington, D.C.: U.S. Congress, Office of Technology Assessment, April 1984]).

30. See Richard L. Garwin, Kurt Gottfried, and Henry W. Kendall, *The Fallacy of Star Wars* (New York: Random House, 1984), and John Tirman, ed., Union of Concerned Scientists, *Empty Promise: The Growing Case Against Star Wars* (Boston: Beacon, 1986).

31. Robert Jastrow, "Reagan vs. the Scientists: Why the President Is Right About Missile Defense," *Commentary* 77 (January 1984): 23–32 (an exchange of letters followed in the same magazine's June issue), and "The War Against 'Star Wars,'" *Commentary* 78 (December 1984): 19–25.

32. Harvey Brooks, "The Strategic Defense Initiative as Science Policy," *International Security* 11 (Fall 1986): 177–84.

33. John P. Holdren and F. Bailey Green, "Military Spending, the SDI, and Government Support of Research and Development: Effects on the Economy and the Health of American Science," *F.A.S. Public Opinion Report* 39 (September 1986): 1–17.

34. See Lisbeth Gronlund et al., "A Status Report on the Boycott of Star Wars Research by Academic Scientists and Engineers," May 13, 1986, typescript, and John Kogut and Michael Weissman, "Taking the Pledge Against Star Wars," *Bulletin of the Atomic Scientists* 42 (January 1986): 27–30.

35. Report on the NAS poll prepared by Peter Stein, professor of physics, Cornell University, December 17, 1986. See also *Science* 234 (November 14, 1986): 816.

36. Report by Michael Heylin, *Chemical & Engineering News* (July 21, 1986), p. 18.

37. Ibid.

38. Ibid.

39. Roy D. Woodruff, quoted in Robert Scheer, "The Man Who Blew the Whistle on Star Wars," *Los Angeles Times Magazine,* July 17, 1988. See also William J. Broad, *New York Times,* July 15, July 24, 1988.

40. Harvey Brooks, "The Military Innovation System and the Qualitative Arms Race," in *Arms, Defense Policy, and Arms Control,* ed. Franklin A. Long and George W. Rathjens (New York: W. W. Norton, 1976), p. 91.

41. David Lorge Parnas, "Software Aspects of Strategic Defense Systems,"

American Scientist 73 (September–October 1985): 432–40, and "SDI: A Violation of Professional Responsibility," *Abacus* 4 (Winter 1987): 46–52, rpt. in David Lorge Parnas and Danny Cohen, *SDI: Two Views of Professional Responsibility,* Policy Paper no. 5 (La Jolla: University of California Institute on Global Conflict and Cooperation, 1987).

42. "Joint Opening Statement of Drs. Lowell Wood and Gregory Canavan before the House Republican Research Committee, May 12, 1987" typescript. See also Gregory H. Canavan, Nicolaas Bloembergen, and C. Kumar Patel, "Debate on APS Directed-Energy Weapons Study," *Physics Today* 40 (November 1987): 48–53.

43. Edward Teller, "An Open Letter to Hans Bethe," *Policy Review* 39 (Winter 1987): 20, 23.

44. Erik Pratt, John Pike, and Daniel Lindley, "SDI Contracting: Building a Star Wars Constituency," in *Lost in Space: The Domestic Politics of the Strategic Defense Initiative,* ed. Gerald M. Steinberg (Lexington, Mass.: Lexington Books, 1988), p. 111.

45. Nathan Rosenberg, "Civilian Spillovers from Military R & D Spending: The U.S. Experience Since World War II," in *Strategic Defense and the Western Alliance,* ed. Sanford Lakoff and Randy Willoughby (Lexington, Mass.: Lexington Books, 1987), pp. 174–75.

46. Pratt, Pike, and Lindley, "SDI Contracting," p. 114.

47. Ibid., pp. 115–17.

48. Ibid.

49. Ibid., p. 120.

50. William D. Hartung et al., with Jeb Brugman, in *The Strategic Defense Initiative: Costs, Contractors & Consequences,* ed. Alice Tepper Marlin and Paula Lippin (New York: Council on Economic Priorities, 1985), table 3.5, p. 33.

51. Holdren and Green, "Military Spending," p. 12.

52. R. Jeffrey Smith, "Pentagon's R & D Chief Roils the Waters," *Science,* April 25, 1986, pp. 443–45.

53. John E. Pike, "Corporate Interest in the SDI," *F.A.S. Public Interest Report* 40 (April 1987): 6.

54. Pratt, Pike, and Lindley, "SDI Contracting," p. 114.

55. Ibid., p. 138.

56. Gerold Yonas, quoted in David E. Sanger, *New York Times,* February 11, 1987.

57. President Ford made this remark during a question-and-answer session following a lecture delivered at the Faculty Seminar on International Security, the University of California, San Diego, February 4, 1986.

58. Jack Kemp, "The Politics of SDI," *National Review* 38 (December 31, 1986): 28–31.

59. Douglas Waller, James T. Bruce, and Douglas Cook, "SDI: Progress and Challenges" (U.S. Congress, staff report submitted to senators William Proxmire, J. Bennett Johnston, and Lawton Chiles, Washington, D.C., March 17, 1986, typescript).

60. Douglas Waller, James T. Bruce, and Douglas Cook, "SDI: Progress and

Challenges, Part II" (U.S. Congress, staff report submitted to senators William Proxmire, J. Bennett Johnston, and Lawton Chiles, Washington, D.C., March 19, 1987, typescript).

61. James T. Bruce, Bruce W. MacDonald, and Ronald Tammen, "Star Wars at the Crossroads: The Strategic Defense Initiative After Five Years" (U.S. Congress, staff report to senators J. Bennett Johnston, Dale Bumpers, William Proxmire, Washington, D.C., June 12, 1988, typescript), p. 97.

62. Ibid., p. 98.

63. Ibid.

64. Ibid., p. 99.

65. Ibid.

66. Ibid., p. 38.

67. Ibid., pp. 69–71.

68. Ibid., p. 33.

69. *Defense News,* March 23, 1987.

70. For Senator Nunn's analysis, see "Interpretation of the ABM Treaty, Part One: The Senate Ratification Proceedings," *Congressional Record* 133 (March 11, 1987).

71. Edward Weisband, *Foreign Policy by Congress* (New York: Oxford University Press, 1978), p. 77.

72. Graham Allison and Peter Szanton, *Remaking Foreign Policy* (New York: Basic, 1976), p. 99.

73. See Samuel Kernell, *Going Public: New Strategies of Presidential Leadership* (Washington, D.C.: Congressional Quarterly Press, 1986).

8. CALCULATING THE COSTS AND BENEFITS

1. James T. Bruce, Bruce W. MacDonald, and Ronald L. Tammen, "Star Wars at the Crossroads: The Strategic Defense Initiative After Five Years" (U.S. Congress, staff report to senators J. Bennett Johnston, Dale Bumpers, and William Proxmire, June 12, 1988, typescript), p. 66.

2. John P. Holdren and F. Bailey Green, "Military Spending, the SDI, and Government Support of Research and Development: Effects on the Economy and the Health of American Science," *F.A.S. Public Interest Report* 39 (September 1986): 10.

3. Bruce, MacDonald, and Tammen, "Star Wars at the Crossroads," p. 67.

4. John Pike, "Corporate Interests in the SDI," *F.A.S. Public Interest Report* 40 (April 1987): 3.

5. Strategic Defense Initiative Organization, *Report to the Congress on the Strategic Defense Initiative* (Washington, D.C.: SDIO, April 1987), chap. 2, p. 14.

6. Ibid., table 7.2.

7. Ibid., chap. 4, p. 2.

8. Ibid., chap. 4, p. 3.

9. Ibid.

10. U.S. Congress, Office of Technology Assessment, *Ballistic Missile De-*

fense Technologies, OTA-ISC-254 (Washington, D.C.: U.S. Government Printing Office, September 1985), p. 217.

11. U.S. Congress, Office of Technology Assessment, *SDI: Technology, Survivability and Software,* OTA-ISC-353 (Washington, D.C.: U.S. Government Printing Office, May 1988), p. 24.

12. Ashton B. Carter, "Ballistic Missile Defense Applications: Performance and Limitations," in *Ballistic Missile Defense,* ed. Ashton B. Carter and David N. Schwartz (Washington, D.C.: Brookings Institution, 1984), p. 119.

13. William D. Hartung et al., with Jeb Brugman, *The Strategic Defense Initiative: Costs, Contractors & Consequences,* ed. Alice Tepper Marlin and Paula Lippin (New York: Council on Economic Priorities, 1985), p. 121.

14. Office of the Secretary of Defense, SDIO, "Directed Energy Missile Defense in Space: With Comments," table 13, cited ibid., p. 127.

15. Ashton B. Carter, *Directed Energy Missile Defense in Space* (background paper prepared under contract for the Office of Technology Assessment [Washington, D.C.: U.S. Congress, Office of Technology Assessment, April 1984]), p. 130.

16. Hartung et al., *Contractors & Consequences,* pp. 70–72.

17. Ibid., p. 75.

18. Ibid., pp. 78–80.

19. Ibid., p. 79.

20. Bruce, MacDonald, and Tammen, "Star Wars at the Crossroads," p. 69.

21. Ibid., pp. 69–71.

22. Barry M. Blechman and Victor A. Utgoff, *Fiscal and Economic Implications of Strategic Defenses,* SAIS Papers in International Affairs no. 12 (Boulder, Colo.: Westview / Foreign Policy Institute [School of Advanced International Studies, Johns Hopkins University], 1986).

23. Ibid., pp. 145–46.

24. William Loomis, quoted in *SDI Monitor* 2 (April 6, 1987): 94.

25. George C. Marshall Institute, *Report of the Technical Panel on Missile Defense in the 1990s* (Washington, D.C.: Marshall Institute, February 1987), p. 3.

26. Ibid., p. 6.

27. Ibid.

28. Ibid., pp. 7–8.

29. Ibid., pp. 8–11.

30. Ibid., pp. 10–11.

31. Harold Brown, "Too Much, Too Soon," *Arms Control Today* 17 (May 1987): 3.

32. Blechman and Utgoff, *Implications of Strategic Defenses,* p. 60.

33. Ibid., pp. 66–72.

34. R. G. Finke et al., *Continuing Issues (FY 1985) Concerning Military Use of the Space Transportation System,* IDA Paper P-1889 (Alexandria, Va.: Institute for Defense Analyses, December 1985).

35. Hartung et al., *Contractors & Consequences,* p. 111.

36. SDIO, *Report to Congress,* chap. 8, pp. 1–4.

37. Hartung et al., *Contractors & Consequences,* pp. 93–99. See also Coun-

cil on Economic Priorities (CEP), *Star Wars: The Economic Fallout* (Cambridge, Mass.: Ballinger, 1988), esp. chap. 8, pp. 119–44.

38. CEP, *Star Wars,* p. 106.

39. Ibid. See also Stewart Nozette and Robert Lawrence Kuhn, eds., *Commercializing SDI Technologies* (New York: Praeger, 1987), esp. pt. IV, "SDI Technologies and Spin-Offs," pp. 95–170.

9. SECURITY THROUGH TECHNOLOGY: AN ILLUSORY FAITH

1. Gerard C. Smith, letter to the editor, *Issues in Science and Technology* 1 (Winter 1985): 4, in reply to an article by George A. Keyworth II in the previous issue.

2. For a review of earlier examples of the same folly—attempting to achieve security by unilateral reliance on technology—see Herbert F. York, *Race to Oblivion: A Participant's View of the Arms Race* (New York: Simon and Schuster, 1970).

3. See Robert Scheer, *With Enough Shovels: Reagan, Bush & Nuclear War* (New York: Random House, 1982).

4. In a television address reporting on the meeting at Reykjavík in 1986, Soviet leader Mikhail Gorbachev recounted his response to the United States' offer to share SDI technology: "Mr. President, I cannot take this idea of yours seriously, the idea that you will share the results with us. You do not want to share with us even equipment for dairy plants at this point, and now you're promising us that you're going to share results on S.D.I. development? This would be a second American Revolution if something like this happened, but revolutions don't happen that often," excerpted in *New York Times,* October 15, 1986.

5. General Rogers was interviewed by Robert Hutchinson, *Jane's Defence Weekly,* April 27, 1985, p. 724.

6. Adm. William J. Crowe, Jr., quoted in *Arms Control Reporter,* January 21, 1987.

7. Gen. John Chain, quoted in *Military Space,* June 8, 1987, p. 8.

8. Harold Brown, *Thinking About National Security* (Boulder, Colo.: Westview, 1983), p. 56.

9. For a discussion of the difficulties in moving beyond the proposed initial reduction, see Sanford Lakoff, ed., *Beyond Start? A Soviet Report with Commentaries,* IGCC Policy Paper no. 7 (La Jolla, Calif.: 1988).

10. M. Stanton Evans, "SDI Facing 'Death by Research,'" *Human Events* 46 (August 9, 1986): 7.

11. Commenting on Reagan's proposal of SDI, Jonathan Schell wrote: "Only the order of events in his proposal was wrong. If we seek first to defend ourselves, and not to abolish nuclear weapons until after we have made that effort, we will never abolish them, because of the underlying, technically irreversible superiority of the offensive in the nuclear world. But if we abolish nuclear weapons first, and then build the defenses, as a hedge against cheating, we can succeed." Jonathan Schell, *The Abolition* (New York: Knopf, 1984), p. 115.

12. In a public opinion poll, Americans were asked "What is the most im-

portant element in the U.S. defense against an attack by Soviet nuclear missiles?" Forty-four percent of those polled said they "did not know," 13 percent said "our weapons," 12 percent said "early detection," and 5 percent said "Star Wars." Among the remaining responses, only 5 percent said that it was "Soviet fear of U.S. retaliation." Associated Press / Media General poll, June 20–28, 1986.

Select Bibliography

Adelman, Kenneth. "SDI: Setting the Record Straight." Current Policy no. 370. Washington, D.C.: U.S. Department of State, Bureau of Public Affairs, August 7, 1985.

American Physical Society, Committee on the Study of Directed Energy Weapons. *Science and Technology of Directed Energy Weapons. Report of the American Physical Society Study Group*. New York: American Physical Society, April 1987.

Anderson, Martin. *Revolution*. San Diego: Harcourt Brace Jovanovich, 1988.

Arms Control Association. *Star Wars Quotes: An Anthology of Quotes by the Administration, Congress and Outside Experts,* comp. Jonathan Thompson and Julie Strawn. Washington, D.C.: Arms Control Association, 1986.

Aspen Strategy Group. *The Strategic Defense Initiative and American Security.* Lanham, Md.: University Press of America, 1987.

Bethe, Hans A., Richard L. Garwin, Kurt Gottfried, and Henry W. Kendall. "Space-Based Ballistic-Missile Defense." *Scientific American* 251, no. 4 (October 1984): 29–49.

Blacker, Coit D. "Defending Missiles, Not People: Hard-Site Defense." *Issues in Science and Technology* 2, no. 1 (Fall 1985): 30–44.

Blechman, Barry M., and Victor A. Utgoff. *Fiscal and Economic Implications of Strategic Defenses,* SAIS Papers in International Affairs no. 12. Boulder, Colo.: Westview / Foreign Policy Institute (School of Advanced International Studies, Johns Hopkins University), 1986.

Bluth, Christoph. "SDI: The Challenge to West Germany." *International Affairs* 62, no. 2 (Spring 1986): 247–64.

Boffey, Philip M., William J. Broad, Leslie H. Gelb, Charles Mohr, and Holcombe B. Noble, *Claiming the Heavens:* The New York Times *Complete Guide to the Star Wars Debate*. New York: Times Books, 1988.

Bowman, Robert. *Star Wars: A Defense Insider's Case Against the Strategic Defense Initiative.* New York: St. Martin's, 1986.
Brauch, Hans Günter, ed. *Star Wars and European Defence: Implications for Europe: Perceptions and Assessments.* New York: St. Martin's, 1987.
Broad, William, J. "The Secrets of Soviet Star Wars." *New York Times Magazine,* June 28, 1987.
————. *Star Warriors: A Penetrating Look into the Lives of the Young Scientists Behind Our Space Age Weaponry.* New York: Simon and Schuster, 1985.
Brody, Richard I. *Strategic Defences in NATO Strategy.* London: International Institute for Strategic Studies, 1987.
Brooks, Harvey. "The Strategic Defense Initiative as Science Policy." *International Security* 11, no. 2 (Fall 1986): 177–84.
Brown, Harold. "Is SDI Technically Feasible?" *Foreign Affairs,* America and the World, 64, no. 3 (1986): 435–54.
————. "The SDI: Defensive Systems and the Strategic Debate." *Survival* 27, no. 2 (March–April 1985): 55–64.
————. "Strategic Defense Initiative: ABM Revisited." Address before the California Seminar on International Security and Foreign Policy, California Institute of Technology, November 7, 1984.
————. *Thinking About National Security.* Boulder, Colo.: Westview, 1983.
————, ed. *The Strategic Defense Initiative: Shield or Snare?* Boulder, Colo.: Westview, 1987.
Bruce, James T., Bruce W. MacDonald, and Ronald L. Tammen. "Star Wars at the Crossroads: The Strategic Defense Initiative After Five Years." U.S. Congress, staff report to senators J. Bennett Johnston, Dale Bumpers, William Proxmire. Washington, D.C., June 12, 1988. Typescript.
Brzezinski, Zbigniew, Robert Jastrow, and Max M. Kampelman. "Defense in Space Is Not Star Wars." *New York Times Magazine,* January 27, 1985.
Brzezinski, Zbigniew, ed., with Richard Sincere, Marin Strmecki and Peter Wehner, *Promise or Peril, the Strategic Defense Initiative: Thirty-Five Essays by Statesmen, Scholars, and Strategic Analysts.* Washington, D.C.: Ethics and Public Policy Center, 1986.
Buchheim, Robert W., and Philip J. Farley. "The U.S.-Soviet Standing Consultative Commission." In *U.S.-Soviet Security Cooperation: Achievements, Failures, Lessons,* ed. Alexander L. George, Philip J. Farley, and Alexander Dallin, pp. 254–69. New York: Oxford University Press, 1988.
Bundy, McGeorge, George F. Kennan, Robert S. McNamara, and Gerard Smith. "The President's Choice: Star Wars or Arms Control." *Foreign Affairs* 63, no. 2 (Winter 1984–85): 264–78.
Byers, R. B., John Hamre, G. R. Lindsey. *Aerospace Defence: Canada's Future Role?* Toronto: Canadian Institute of International Affairs, 1985.
Canavan, Gregory. "Simple Discussion of the Stability of Strategic Defense." Los Alamos National Laboratory, April 12, 1985.
————. "Theater Applications of Strategic Defense Concepts." Los Alamos National Laboratory, June 20–21, 1985.
Canavan, G., H. Flicker, L. Hantel, O. Judd, D. Roeder, K. Taggart, and J. Tay-

lor. "Alternative Concepts Evaluation for Strategic Defense." Los Alamos National Laboratory, July 1, 1985.

Canavan, G., H. Flicker, O. Judd, and K. Taggart. "Comparison of Analyses of Strategic Defense." Los Alamos National Laboratory, February 1, 1985.

Carter, Ashton B. *Directed Energy Missile Defense in Space—A Background Paper.* OTA-BP-ISC-26. Washington, D.C.: U.S. Congress, Office of Technology Assessment, April 1984.

Carter, Ashton B., and David N. Schwartz, eds. *Ballistic Missile Defense.* Washington, D.C.: Brookings Institution, 1984.

Chalfont, Alun. *Star Wars: Suicide or Survival?* Boston: Little, Brown, 1986.

Charlton, Michael. *From Deterrence to Defense: The Inside Story of Strategic Policy.* Cambridge: Harvard University Press, 1987.

Chayes, Abram, and Antonia Handler Chayes. "Testing and Development of 'Exotic' Systems Under the ABM Treaty: The Great Reinterpretation Caper." *Harvard Law Review* 99, no. 8 (June 1986): 1956–1971.

Chayes, Abram, Antonia Handler Chayes, and Jerome Wiesner, eds. *ABM: An Evaluation of the Decision to Deploy an Antiballistic Missile System.* New York: New American Library, 1969.

Cimbala, Stephen J., ed. *The Technology, Strategy, and Politics of SDI.* Boulder, Colo.: Westview, 1987.

Codevilla, Angelo M. "How SDI Is Being Undone from Within," *Commentary* 81, no. 5 (May 1986): 21–29.

———. *While Others Build: The Commonsense Approach to the Strategic Defense Initiative.* New York: Free Press, 1988.

Cordesman, Andrew H. "SDI and Europe: Where Does Theatre Defense Fit In?" *International Defense Review* 20, no. 4 (April 1987): 109–14.

Council on Economic Priorities. *Star Wars: The Economic Fallout.* Cambridge: Ballinger, 1988.

Cowen, Regina H. F., Peter Rajcsanyi, and Vladimir Bilandzic. *SDI and European Security.* Boulder, Colo.: Westview / Institute for East-West Security Studies, 1987.

Daalder, Ivo H. *The SDI Challenge to Europe.* Cambridge: Ballinger, 1987.

———. "A Tactical Defense Initiative for Europe?" *Bulletin of the Atomic Scientists* 43, no. 4 (May 1987): 34–39.

"Weapons in Space." *Daedalus* 114, no. 2 (Spring 1985), and no. 3 (Summer 1985).

Dallmeyer, Dorinda G., ed., with Daniel S. Papp. *The Strategic Defense Initiative: New Perspectives on Deterrence.* Boulder, Colo.: Westview, 1986.

Davis, Jacquelyn K., and Robert L. Pfaltzgraff, Jr. *Strategic Defense and Extended Deterrence: A New Transatlantic Debate.* Cambridge: Institute for Foreign Policy Analysis, 1986.

Davis, William A. *Asymmetries in U.S. and Soviet Strategic Defense Programs: Implications for Near-Term American Deployment Options.* Washington, D.C.: Pergamon / Brassey's International Defense, 1986.

De Santis, Hugh. "A Theatre Missile Defense for Europe." *SAIS Review* 6, no. 2 (Summer–Fall 1986): 99–116.

Deschamps, Louis. *The SDI and European Security Interests*. London: Croom Helm / Atlantic Institute for International Affairs, 1987.

Domenici, Pete V. "Towards a Decision on Ballistic Missile Defense." *Strategic Review* 10, no. 1 (Winter 1982): 22–27.

Drell, Sidney D., and Thomas Johnson. *Strategic Missile Defense: Necessities, Prospects, and Dangers in the Near Term*. Report of a workshop at the Center for International Security and Arms Control. Stanford, Calif.: Stanford University, March 13, 1985.

Drell, Sidney D., and Wolfgang K. H. Panofsky. "The Case Against Strategic Defense: Technical and Strategic Realities." *Issues in Science and Technology* 1, no. 1 (Fall 1984): 45–65.

Drell, Sidney D., Philip J. Farley, and David Holloway. *The Reagan Strategic Defense Initiative: A Technical, Political, and Arms Control Assessment*. Stanford, Calif.: Center for International Security and Arms Control (Stanford University), July 1984.

Durch, William J., ed. *National Interests and the Military Uses of Space*. Cambridge: Ballinger, 1984.

Dyson, Freeman. *Weapons and Hope*. New York: Harper and Row, 1984.

Enders, Thomas. *Missile Defense as Part of an Extended NATO Air Defense*. St. Augustin, Federal Republic of Germany: Sozialwissenschaftliches Forschungsinstitut der Konrad-Adenauer-Stiftung, May 1986.

Evangelista, Matthew. *Innovation and the Arms Race: How the U.S. and the Soviet Union Develop New Military Technologies*. Ithaca: Cornell University Press, 1988.

Fenske, John. "France and the Strategic Defense Initiative: speeding up or putting on the brakes?" *International Affairs* 62, no. 2 (Spring 1986): 231–46.

Fletcher, James C. "The Technologies for Ballistic Missile Defense." *Issues in Science and Technology* 1, no. 1 (Fall 1984): 15–26.

Freedman, Lawrence. *The Evolution of Nuclear Strategy*. New York: St. Martin's, 1981.

Garfinkle, Adam M. "The Politics of Space Defense." *Orbis* 28, no. 2 (Summer 1984): 240–55.

Garthoff, Raymond L. *Policy Versus the Law: The Reinterpretation of the ABM Treaty*. Washington, D.C.: Brookings Institution, 1987.

Garwin, Richard L. "How Many Orbiting Lasers for Boost Phase Intercept?" *Nature* 315 (May 23, 1985): 286–90.

George C. Marshall Institute. *Report of the Technical Panel on Missile Defense in the 1990s*. Washington, D.C.: Marshall Institute, February, 1987.

Glaser, Charles L. "Do We Want the Missile Defenses We Can Build?" *International Security* 10, no. 1 (Summer 1985): 25–27.

Gormley, Dennis M. "A New Dimension to Soviet Theater Strategy." *Orbis* 29, no. 3 (Fall 1985): 537–70.

Graham, Daniel O. *High Frontier: A New National Strategy*. Washington, D.C.: High Frontier, 1983.

Gray, Colin S. *American Military Space Policy*. Cambridge: Abt, 1982.

———. "Deterrence, Arms Control, and the Defense Transition." *Orbis* 28, no. 2 (Summer 1984): 227–40.

————. "The Transition from Offense to Defense." *Washington Quarterly* 9, no. 3 (1986): 59–72.

Greb, G. Allen. *Science Advice to Presidents: From Test Bans to the Strategic Defense Initiative.* Research Paper no. 3. La Jolla: University of California Institute on Global Conflict and Cooperation, 1987.

Gromoll, Robert H. "SDI and the Dynamics of Strategic Uncertainty." *Political Science Quarterly* 102, no. 3 (Fall 1987): 481–500.

Guerrier, Steven W., and Wayne C. Thompson, eds. *Perspectives on Strategic Defense.* Boulder, Colo.: Westview, 1987.

Guertner, Gary L., and Donald M. Snow. *The Last Frontier: An Analysis of the Strategic Defense Initiative.* Lexington, Mass.: Lexington Books, 1986.

Haley, P. Edward, and Jack Merritt, eds. *Strategic Defense Initiative: Folly or Future?* Boulder, Colo.: Westview, 1986.

Hanrieder, Wolfram F. "SDI: Strategic Disengagement and Independence." In *Arms Control, the FRG, and the Future of East-West Relations,* ed. Wolfram F. Hanrieder, pp. 119–34. Boulder, Colo.: Westview, 1987.

Hartung, William D., Robert W. De Grasse, Jr., Rosy Nimroody, and Stephen Daggett with Jeb Brugman. In *The Strategic Defense Initiative: Costs, Contractors, and Consequences,* ed. Alice Tepper Marlin and Paula Lippin. New York: Council on Economic Priorities, 1985.

Herken, Gregg. "The Earthly Origins of 'Star Wars.'" *Bulletin of the Atomic Scientists* 43 (October 1987): 20–28.

Hoffman, Fred S. "The SDI in U.S. Nuclear Strategy." *International Security* 10, no. 1 (Summer 1985): 13–24.

————, study director. "Ballistic Missile Defenses and U.S. National Security." Summary report prepared for the Future Security Strategy Group [Hoffman Report]. October 1983.

Hoffman, Fred S., Albert Wohlstetter, and David S. Yost, eds. *Swords and Shields: NATO, the U.S.S.R. and New Choices for Long-Range Offense and Defense.* Lexington, Mass.: Lexington Books, 1987.

Holdren, John P. and F. Bailey Green. "Military Spending, the SDI, and Government Support of Research and Development: Effects on the Economy and the Health of American Science." *F.A.S. Public Interest Report* 39, no. 7 (September 1986): 1–17.

Holdren, John P., and Joseph Rotblat, eds. *Strategic Defenses and the Future of the Arms Race: A Pugwash Symposium.* Houndmills, Basingstoke, Hampshire: MacMillan, 1987.

Jasani, Bhupendra M., ed. *Outer Space—A New Dimension of the Arms Race.* London: Taylor and Francis, 1982.

————, ed. *Space Weapons—The Arms Control Dilemma.* London: Taylor and Francis, 1984.

————, ed. *Space Weapons and International Security.* Oxford: Oxford University Press, 1987.

Jastrow, Robert. *How to Make Nuclear Weapons Obsolete.* Boston: Little, Brown, 1985.

————. "Reagan vs. the Scientists: Why the President Is Right About Missile Defense." *Commentary* 77, no. 1 (January 1984): 23–32.

———. "The War Against 'Star Wars.'" *Commentary* 78, no. 6 (December 1984): 19–25.

Jastrow, Robert, and critics. "'Star Wars'—An Exchange." *Commentary* 77, no. 6 (June 1984): 2–12.

Karas, Thomas. *The New High Ground: Strategies and Weapons of Space-Age War.* New York: Simon and Schuster, 1983.

Kavka, Gregory S. "Space War Ethics." *Ethics* 95, no. 3 (April 1985): 673–91.

Kemp, Jack. "The Politics of SDI." *National Review* 38, no. 25 (December 31, 1986): 28–31.

Kent, Glenn A. *A Suggested Policy Framework for Strategic Defenses.* Santa Monica, Calif.: Rand, 1986.

Kent, Glenn A., and Randall J. De Valle. *Strategic Defenses and the Transition to Assured Survival.* Santa Monica, Calif.: Rand, 1986.

Keyworth, George A., II. "The Case for Strategic Defense: An Option for a World Disarmed." *Issues in Science and Technology* 1, no. 1 (Fall 1984): 30–44.

———. *Security and Stability: The Role for Strategic Defense.* La Jolla: University of California Institute on Global Conflict and Cooperation, 1985.

Kogut, John, and Michael Weissman. "Taking the Pledge Against Star Wars." *Bulletin of the Atomic Scientists* 42, no. 1 (January 1986): 27–30.

Lakoff, Sanford. "Implications of SDI for NATO and Possibilities of Agreement." In *Space Weapons and International Security,* ed. Bhupendra Jasani, pp. 229–43. Oxford: Oxford University Press, 1987.

———. "Scientists, Technologists and Political Power." In *Science, Technology and Society: A Cross-Disciplinary Perspective,* ed. Ina Spiegel-Rosing and Derek J. de Solla Price, pp. 355–92. Beverly Hills: Sage, 1977.

———. "The SDI or Star Wars? An Owlish Perspective." In *Global Peace and Security: Trends and Challenges,* ed. Wolfram F. Hanrieder, pp. 171–89. Boulder, Colo.: Westview, 1987.

———. "Strategic Defense and the Future of NATO." In *Arms Control, the FRG, and the Future of East-West Relations,* ed. Wolfram F. Hanrieder, pp. 103–118. Boulder, Colo.: Westview, 1987.

———. "Toward a Broader Framework for U.S.-Soviet Agreement." In *Strategic Defenses and Arms Control,* ed. Alvin Weinberg and Jack Barkenbus, pp. 66–88. New York: Paragon House, 1987.

Lakoff, Sanford, and Randy Willoughby, eds. *Strategic Defense and the Western Alliance.* Lexington, Mass.: Lexington Books, 1987.

Lambeth, Benjamin S., and Kevin N. Lewis. *The Soviet Union and the Strategic Defense Initiative: Preliminary Findings and Impressions.* Santa Monica, Calif.: Rand, 1986.

Lawrence, Robert M. *Strategic Defense Initiative: Bibliography and Research Guide.* Boulder, Colo.: Westview, 1987.

Lewis, Kevin N. *Possible Soviet Responses to the Strategic Defense Initiative: A Functionally Organized Taxonomy.* Santa Monica, Calif.: Rand, 1986.

———. *U.S. Strategic Force Modernization and SDI: Four Key Issues.* Santa Monica, Calif.: Rand, 1986.

Long, Franklin A., Donald Hafner, and Jeffrey Boutwell, eds. *Weapons in Space.* New York: W. W. Norton, 1986.

Longstreth, Thomas K., John E. Pike, and John B. Rhinelander. *The Impact of U.S. and Soviet Ballistic Missile Defense Programs on the ABM Treaty.* Washington, D.C.: National Campaign to Save the ABM Treaty, March 1985.

Lucas, Michael. "SDI and Europe." *World Policy Journal* 3, no. 2 (Spring 1986): 219–49.

———. "The United States and Post-INF Europe." *World Policy Journal* 5, no. 2 (Spring 1988): 183–233.

Maust, R. L., G. W. Goodman, Jr., C. E. McLain. *History of Strategic Defense.* Report prepared for Defense Science Board. Arlington, Va.: System Planning Corp., September 1981.

May, Michael M. "Safeguarding Our Military Space Systems." *Science* 232 (May 2, 1986): 336–40.

———. "War or Peace in Space." Discussion Paper no. 93. California Seminar on International Security and Foreign Policy. Santa Monica, Calif.: March 1981.

MccGwire, Michael. *Military Objectives in Soviet Foreign Policy.* Washington, D.C.: Brookings Institution, 1987.

McNamara, Robert S. *Blundering Into Disaster: Surviving the First Century of the Nuclear Age.* New York: Pantheon, 1986.

Miller, Steven E., and Stephen Van Evera, eds. *The Star Wars Controversy: An International Security Reader.* Princeton, N.J.: Princeton University Press, 1986.

Mische, Patricia M. *Star Wars and the State of Our Souls: Deciding the Future of Planet Earth.* Minneapolis: Winston, 1985.

Morel, Benoit. "ATBM—A Solution in Search of a Problem," *Bulletin of the Atomic Scientists* 43, no. 4 (May 1987): 39–41.

Nitze, Paul H. "The Impact of SDI on U.S.-Soviet Relations." Current Policy no. 830. Washington, D.C.: U.S. Department of State, Bureau of Public Affairs, April 29, 1986.

———. "On the Road to a More Stable Peace." Current Policy no. 657. Washington, D.C.: U.S. Department of State, Bureau of Public Affairs, August 20, 1985.

———. "SDI: Its Nature and Rationale." Current Policy no. 751. Washington, D.C.: U.S. Department of State, Bureau of Public Affairs, October 15, 1985, pp. 1–3.

———. "SDI: The Soviet Program." Current Policy no. 717. Washington, D.C.: U.S. Department of State, Bureau of Public Affairs, June 28, 1985, pp. 1–4.

Nozette, Stewart, and Robert Lawrence Kuhn, eds. *Commercializing SDI Technologies.* New York: Praeger, 1987.

Ochmanek, David A. *SDI and/or Arms Control.* Santa Monica, Calif.: Rand, 1987.

Paine, Christopher. "The ABM Treaty: Looking for Loopholes." *Bulletin of the Atomic Scientists* 39, no. 7 (August–September 1983): 13–16.

Panofsky, Wolfgang K. H. "The Strategic Defense Initiative: Perception vs. Reality." *Physics Today* 38, no. 6 (June 1985): 34–45.

Parnas, David Lorge. "Software Aspects of Strategic Defense System." *American Scientist* 73 (September–October 1985): 432–40.

Parnas, David Lorge, and Danny Cohen. *SDI: Two Views of Professional Responsibility*. Policy Paper no. 5. La Jolla: University of California Institute on Global Conflict and Cooperation, 1987.

Payne, Keith B. "Strategic Defense and Stability." *Orbis* 28, no. 2 (Summer 1984): 215–227.

———. "The Soviet Union and Strategic Defense: The Failure and Future of Arms Control." *Orbis* 29, no. 4 (Winter 1986): 673–89.

———. *Strategic Defense: "Star Wars" in Perspective*. Lanham, Md.: Hamilton, 1986.

———, ed. *Laser Weapons in Space*. Boulder, Colo.: Westview, 1983.

Payne, Keith B., and Colin S. Gray. "Nuclear Policy and the Defensive Transition." *Foreign Affairs* 62, no. 4 (Spring 1984): 820–42.

Pressler, Larry. *Star Wars: the Strategic Defense Initiative Debates in Congress*. New York: Praeger, 1986.

Quayle, Dan, Robert E. Hunter, and C. Elliott Farmer, eds. *Strategic Defense and the Western Alliance*. Washington, D.C.: Center for Strategic and International Studies, Georgetown University, 1986.

Reed, Fred. "The Star Wars Swindle: Hawking Nuclear Snake Oil." *Harper's* 272, no. 1632 (May 1986): 39–48.

Rhinelander, John B. "Reagan's 'Exotic' Interpretation of the ABM Treaty." *Arms Control Today* 15, no. 8 (October 1985): 3–6.

Richelson, Jeffrey. "Ballistic Missile Defense and Soviet Strategy." In *The Soviet Calculus of Nuclear War*, ed. Roman Kolkowicz and Ellen Propper Mickiewicz, pp. 69–84. Lexington, Mass.: Lexington Books, 1986.

Robinson, David Z. *The Strategic Defense Initiative: Its Effect on the Economy and Arms Control*. New York: New York University Press, 1987.

Scheer, Robert. "The Man Who Blew the Whistle on Star Wars." *Los Angeles Times Magazine*, July 17, 1988.

Schlesinger, James R. "Rhetoric and Realities in the Star Wars Debate." *International Security* 10, no. 1 (Summer 1985): 3–12.

Schneider, William. "Public Prefers Arms Negotiations to Star Wars." *National Journal* 17, no. 36 (September 1985): 2008–2009.

Schroeer, Dietrich. *Directed-Energy Weapons and Strategic Defence: A Primer*. London: International Institute for Strategic Studies, 1987.

Sherr, Alan B. *Legal Issues of the "Star Wars" Defense Program*. Issue Brief no. 3. Boston: Lawyers Alliance for Nuclear Arms Control, June 1986.

Sloss, Leon. "The Return of Strategic Defense." *Strategic Review* 12, no. 3 (Summer 1984): 37–44.

Smith, Hedrick. *The Power Game: How Washington Works*. New York: Random House, 1988.

Snyder, Craig, ed. *The Strategic Defense Debate: Can "Star Wars" Make Us Safe?* Philadelphia: University of Pennsylvania Press, 1986.

Sofaer, Abraham D. "The ABM Treaty and the Strategic Defense Initiative." *Harvard Law Review* 99, no. 8 (June 1986): 1972–1985.

Sokolsky, Joel J. "Changing Strategies, Technologies and Organization: The Continuing Debate on NORAD and the Strategic Defense Initiative." *Canadian Journal of Political Science* 19, no. 4 (December 1986): 751–74.

Stares, Paul B. *The Militarization of Space: U.S. Policy, 1945–84*. Ithaca: Cornell University Press, 1985.

———. *Space and National Security*. Washington, D.C.: Brookings Institution, 1987.

Stein, Jonathan B. *From H-Bombs to Star Wars: The Politics of Strategic Decision Making*. Lexington, Mass.: D.C. Heath, 1984.

Steinberg, Gerald M., ed. *Lost in Space: The Domestic Politics of the Strategic Defense Initiative*. Lexington, Mass.: Lexington Books, 1988.

Stevens, Sayre. "The Soviet Factor in SDI." *Orbis* 29, no. 4 (Winter 1986): 689–700.

Talbott, Strobe. *Deadly Gambits: The Reagan Administration and the Stalemate in Nuclear Arms Control*. New York: Knopf, 1984.

Taylor, Trevor. "Britain's Response to the Strategic Defense Initiative." *International Affairs* 62, no. 2 (Spring 1986): 217–30.

Teller, Edward. *Better a Shield Than a Sword: Perspectives on Defense and Technology*. New York: Free Press, 1987.

———. "An Open Letter to Hans Bethe." *Policy Review* no. 39 (Winter 1987): 18–23.

Committee on International Arms Control and Security Affairs, Association of the Bar of the City of New York, *The Anti-Ballistic Missile Treaty Interpretation Dispute*. New York: Association of the Bar of the City of New York: 1987.

"The Strategic Defense Initiative: A Survey of the National Academy of Sciences." Ithaca: Floyd R. Newman Laboratory of Nuclear Studies, Cornell University, 1986. Typescript.

Thompson, E. P., ed. *Star Wars: Science-Fiction Fantasy or Serious Probability?* Harmondsworth, England: Penguin Books, 1985.

U.S. Congress, House Committee on Armed Services. *Strategic Defense Initiative (SDI) Program: Hearings*. June 6, 1985. Washington, D.C.: U.S. Government Printing Office, 1986.

U.S. Congress, House Committee on Armed Services, Defense Policy Panel. *The MX Missile and the Strategic Defense Initiative—Their Implications on Arms Control Negotiations: Hearings*. Washington, D.C.: U.S. Government Printing Office, 1985.

U.S. Congress, House Committee on Banking, Finance, and Urban Affairs, Subcommittee on Economic Stabilization. *Impact of Strategic Defense Initiative (SDI) on the U.S. Industrial Base: Hearing*. Washington, D.C.: U.S. Government Printing Office, 1986.

U.S. Congress, House Committee on Foreign Affairs, Subcommittee on Arms Control, International Security, and Science. *Review of ABM Treaty Interpretation Dispute and SDI: Hearing*. Washington, D.C.: U.S. Government Printing Office, 1987.

U.S. Congress, House Committee on International Security and Science, Subcommittee on Arms Control. *ABM Treaty Interpretation Dispute: Hearing.* 99th Cong., 1st sess., Washington, D.C.: U.S. Government Printing Office, October 22, 1985.

U.S. Congress, Office of Technology Assessment, *Ballistic Missile Defense Technologies.* OTA-ISC-254. Washington, D.C.: U.S. Government Printing Office, September 1985; also published as *Strategic Defenses.* Princeton, N.J.: Princeton University Press, 1986.

———. *SDI, Technology, Survivability, and Software.* OTA-ISC-353. Washington, D.C.: U.S. Government Printing Office, May 1988.

U.S. Congress, Senate Committee on Armed Services, Subcommittee on Strategic and Theater Nuclear Forces. *Strategic Defense Initiative: Hearings.* Washington, D.C.: U.S. Government Printing Office, 1986.

U.S. Department of Defense. *The SDI—Defensive Technologies Study* [Fletcher Report]. Washington, D.C.: U.S. Government Printing Office, April 1984.

———. *Soviet Military Power 1986.* Washington, D.C.: Department of Defense, 1986.

Union of Concerned Scientists (John Tirman, ed.). *Empty Promise: The Growing Case Against Star Wars.* Boston: Beacon, 1986.

———. *The Fallacy of Star Wars.* Co-chaired by Richard L. Garwin, Kurt Gottfried, and Henry W. Kendall. New York: Vintage Books, 1984.

Van Cleave, William R. *Fortress U.S.S.R.: The Soviet Strategic Defense Initiative and the U.S. Strategic Defense Response.* Stanford, Calif.: Hoover Institution Press, 1986.

Velikhov, Yevgeny, Roald Sagdeyev, and Andrei Kokoshin, eds. *Weaponry in Space: The Dilemma of Security.* Moscow: Mir Publishers, 1986.

Vlahos, Michael. *Strategic Defense and the American Ethos: Can the Nuclear World Be Changed?* Boulder, Colo.: Westview, 1986.

Waller, Douglas C., James T. Bruce, and Douglas Cook. "SDI: Progress and Challenges." U.S. Congress, staff report submitted to senators William Proxmire, J. Bennett Johnston, and Lawton Chiles. Washington, D.C.: March 17, 1986. Typescript.

———. "SDI: Progress and Challenges, Part II." U.S. Congress, staff report submitted to senators William Proxmire, J. Bennett Johnston, and Lawton Chiles. Washington, D.C.: March 19, 1987.

———. *The Strategic Defense Initiative, Progress and Challenges: A Guide to Issues and References.* Claremont, Calif.: Regina Books, 1987.

Warner, Edward L. *Soviet Interests, Concerns, and Activities with Regard to Ballistic Missile Defense.* Santa Monica, Calif.: Rand, 1987.

Weinberg, Alvin M., and Jack N. Barkenbus. "Stabilizing Star Wars." *Foreign Policy* no. 54 (Spring 1984): 164–70.

———, eds. *Strategic Defenses and Arms Control.* New York: Paragon House, 1988.

Weinrod, W. Bruce. "Strategic Defense and the ABM Treaty." *Washington Quarterly* 9, no. 3 (Summer 1986): 73–87.

Wells, Samuel F., Jr., and Robert S. Litwak, eds. *Strategic Defenses and Soviet-American Relations.* Cambridge: Ballinger, 1987.

Worden, Simon P. "What Can We Do? When Can We Do It?" *National Review* 38, no. 25 (December 31, 1986): 36–40.

Wörner, Manfred. "A Missile Defense for NATO Europe." *Strategic Review* 14, no. 1 (Winter 1986): 13–20.

Yonas, Gerold. "Research and the Strategic Defense Initiative." *International Security* 11, no. 2 (Fall 1986): 185–89.

———. "Strategic Defense Initiative: The Politics and Science of Weapons in Space." *Physics Today* 38, no. 6 (June 1985): 24–32.

York, Herbert F. *The Advisors: Oppenheimer, Teller, and the Superbomb.* San Francisco: W. H. Freeman, 1976.

———. *Does Strategic Defense Breed Offense?* Lanham, Md.: University Press of America / Center for Science and International Affairs, Harvard University, 1987.

———. *Making Weapons, Talking Peace: A Physicist's Odyssey from Hiroshima to Geneva.* New York: Basic Books, 1987.

———. *Race to Oblivion: A Participant's View of the Arms Race.* New York: Simon and Schuster, 1970.

Yost, David S. "Ballistic Missile Defense and the Atlantic Alliance." *International Security* 7, no. 2 (Fall 1982): 143–74.

Zimmerman, Peter D. "Pork Bellies and SDI." *Foreign Policy* no. 63 (Summer 1986): 76–87.

Zuckerman, Solly. "The Politics of Outer Space." *New Republic,* June 3, 1985, pp. 25–32.

———. *Star Wars in a Nuclear World.* London: William Kimber, 1986.

———. "The Wonders of Star Wars." *New York Review of Books* 33, no. 1 (January 30, 1986): 32–40.

INDEX

Compositor: G&S Typesetters, Inc.
Text: 10/13 Sabon
Display: Sabon
Printer: Maple-Vail Book Mfg. Group
Binder: Maple-Vail Book Mfg. Group